Belinda by Maria Edgeworth

Maria Edgeworth was born at Black Bourton, Oxfordshire on January 1st 1768. Her early years were with her mother's family in England. Sadly, her mother died when Maria was five.

Maria was educated at Mrs Lattafière's school in Derby in 1775. There she studied dancing, French and other subjects. Maria transferred to Mrs Devis's school in Upper Wimpole Street, London. Her father began to focus more attention on Maria in 1781 when she nearly lost her sight to an eye infection.

She returned home to Ireland at 14 and took charge of her younger siblings. She herself was home-tutored by her father in Irish economics and politics, science, literature and law. Despite her youth literature was in her blood. Maria also became her father's assistant in managing the family's large Edgeworthstown estate.

Maria first published 1795 with 'Letters for Literary Ladies'. That same year 'An Essay on the Noble Science of Self-Justification', written for a female audience, advised women on how to obtain better rights in general and specifically from their husbands.

'Practical Education' (1798) is a progressive work on education. Maria's ambition was to create an independent thinker who understands the consequences of his or her actions.

Her first novel, 'Castle Rackrent' was published anonymously in 1800 without her father's knowledge. It was an immediate success and firmly established Maria's appeal to the public.

Her father married four times and the last of these to Frances, a year younger and a confidante of Maria, who pushed them to travel more widely: London, Britain and Europe were all now visited.

The second series of 'Tales of Fashionable Life' (1812) did so well that she was now the most commercially successful novelist of her age.

She particularly worked hard to improve the living standards of the poor in Edgeworthstown and to provide schools for the local children of all and any denomination.

After a visit to see her relations Maria had severe chest pains and died suddenly of a heart attack in Edgeworthstown on 22nd May 1849. She was 81.

Index of Contents

BELINDA

CHAPTER I — CHARACTERS

Mrs. Stanhope, a well-bred woman, accomplished in that branch of knowledge which is called the art of rising in the world, had, with but a small fortune, contrived to live in the highest company. She prided herself upon having established half a dozen nieces most happily, that is to say, upon having married them to men of fortunes far superior to their own. One niece still remained unmarried—Belinda Portman, of whom she was determined to get rid with all convenient expedition. Belinda was handsome, graceful, sprightly, and highly accomplished; her aunt had endeavoured to teach her that a young lady's chief business is to please in society, that all her charms and accomplishments should be invariably subservient to one grand object—the establishing herself in the world:

"For this, hands, lips, and eyes were put to school,
And each instructed feature had its rule."

Mrs. Stanhope did not find Belinda such a docile pupil as her other nieces, for she had been educated chiefly in the country; she had early been inspired with a taste for domestic pleasures; she was fond of reading, and disposed to conduct herself with prudence and integrity. Her character, however, was yet to be developed by circumstances.

Mrs. Stanhope lived at Bath, where she had opportunities of showing her niece off, as she thought, to advantage; but as her health began to decline, she could not go out with her as much as she wished. After manoeuvring with more than her usual art, she succeeded in fastening Belinda upon the fashionable Lady Delacour for the season. Her ladyship was so much pleased by Miss Portman's accomplishments and vivacity, as to invite her to spend the winter with her in London. Soon after her arrival in town, Belinda received the following letter from her aunt Stanhope.

"Crescent, Bath.

"After searching every place I could think of, Anne found your bracelet in your dressing-table, amongst a heap of odd things, which you left behind you to be thrown away: I have sent it to you by a young gentleman, who came to Bath (unluckily) the very day you left me—Mr. Clarence Hervey—an acquaintance, and great admirer of my Lady Delacour. He is really an uncommonly pleasant young man, is highly connected, and has a fine independent fortune. Besides, he is a man of wit and gallantry, quite a connoisseur in female grace and beauty—just the man to bring a new face into fashion: so, my dear Belinda, I make it a point—look well when he is introduced to you, and remember, what I have so often told you, that nobody can look well without taking some pains to please.

"I see—or at least when I went out more than my health will at present permit—I used to see multitudes of silly girls, seemingly all cut out upon the same pattern, who frequented public places day after day, and year after year, without any idea farther than that of diverting themselves, or of obtaining transient admiration. How I have pitied and despised the giddy creatures, whilst I have observed them playing off their unmeaning airs, vying with one another in the most obvious, and consequently the most ridiculous manner, so as to expose themselves before the very men they would attract: chattering, tittering, and flirting; full of the present moment, never reflecting upon the future; quite satisfied if they got a partner at a ball, without ever thinking of a partner for life! I have often asked myself, what is to become of such girls when they grow old or ugly, or when the public eye grows tired of them? If they have large fortunes, it is all very well; they can afford to divert themselves for a season or two, without doubt; they are sure to be sought after and followed, not by mere danglers, but by men of suitable views and pretensions: but nothing to my mind can be more miserable than the situation of a poor girl, who, after spending not only the interest, but the solid capital of her small fortune in dress, and frivolous extravagance, fails in her matrimonial expectations (as many do merely from not beginning to speculate in time). She finds herself at five or six-and-thirty a burden to her friends, destitute of the means of rendering herself independent (for the girls I speak of never think of learning to play cards), de trop in society, yet obliged to hang upon all her acquaintance, who wish her in heaven, because she is unqualified to make the expected return for civilities, having no home, I mean no establishment, no house, &c. fit for the reception of company of a certain rank.—My dearest Belinda, may this never be your case!—You have every possible advantage, my love: no pains have been spared in your education, and (which is the essential point) I have taken care that this should be known—so that you have the name of being perfectly accomplished. You will also have the name of being very fashionable, if you go much into public, as doubtless you will with Lady Delacour.—Your own good sense must make you aware, my dear, that from her ladyship's situation and knowledge of the world, it will always be proper, upon all subjects of conversation, for her to lead and you to follow: it would be very unfit for a young girl like you to suffer yourself to stand in competition with Lady Delacour, whose high pretensions to wit and beauty are indisputable. I need say no more to you upon this subject, my dear. Even with your limited experience, you must have observed how foolish young people offend those who are the most necessary to their interests, by an imprudent indulgence of their vanity.

"Lady Delacour has an incomparable taste in dress: consult her, my dear, and do not, by an ill-judged economy, counteract my views—apropos, I have no objection to your being presented at court. You will, of course, have credit with all her ladyship's tradespeople, if you manage properly. To know how and when to lay out money is highly commendable, for in some situations, people judge of what one can afford by what one actually spends.—I know of no law which compels a young lady to tell what her age or her fortune may be. You have no occasion for caution yet on one of these points.

"I have covered my old carpet with a handsome green baize, and every stranger who comes to see me, I observe, takes it for granted that I have a rich carpet under it. Say every thing that is proper, in your best manner, for me to Lady Delacour.

"Adieu, my dear Belinda,

"Yours, very sincerely,

"SELINA STANHOPE."

It is sometimes fortunate, that the means which are taken to produce certain effects upon the mind have a tendency directly opposite to what is expected. Mrs. Stanhope's perpetual anxiety about her niece's appearance, manners, and establishment, had completely worn out Belinda's patience; she had become more insensible to the praises of her personal charms and accomplishments than young women of her age usually are, because she had been so much flattered and shown off, as it is called, by her match-making aunt.—Yet Belinda was fond of amusement, and had imbibed some of Mrs. Stanhope's prejudices in favour of rank and fashion. Her taste for literature declined in proportion to her intercourse with the fashionable world, as she did not in this society perceive the least use in the knowledge that she had acquired. Her mind had never been roused to much reflection; she had in general acted but as a puppet in the hands of others. To her aunt Stanhope she had hitherto paid unlimited, habitual, blind obedience; but she was more undesigning, and more free from affectation and coquetry, than could have been expected, after the course of documenting which she had gone through. She was charmed with the idea of a visit to Lady Delacour, whom she thought the most agreeable—no, that is too feeble an expression—the most fascinating person she had ever beheld. Such was the light in which her ladyship appeared, not only to Belinda, but to all the world—that is to say, all the world of fashion, and she knew of no other.—The newspapers were full of Lady Delacour's parties, and Lady Delacour's dresses, and Lady Delacour's bon mots: every thing that her ladyship said was repeated as witty; every thing that her ladyship wore was imitated as fashionable. Female wit sometimes depends on the beauty of its possessor for its reputation; and the reign of beauty is proverbially short, and fashion often capriciously deserts her favourites, even before nature withers their charms. Lady Delacour seemed to be a fortunate exception to these general rules: long after she had lost the bloom of youth, she continued to be admired as a fashionable bel esprit; and long after she had ceased to be a novelty in society, her company was courted by all the gay, the witty, and the gallant. To be seen in public with Lady Delacour, to be a visitor at her house, were privileges of which numbers were vehemently ambitious; and Belinda Portman was congratulated and envied by all her acquaintance, for being admitted as an inmate. How could she avoid thinking herself singularly fortunate?

A short time after her arrival at Lady Delacour's, Belinda began to see through the thin veil with which politeness covers domestic misery.—Abroad, and at home, Lady Delacour was two different persons. Abroad she appeared all life, spirit, and good humour—at home, listless, fretful, and melancholy; she seemed like a spoiled actress off the stage, over-stimulated by applause, and exhausted by the exertions of supporting a fictitious character.—When her house was filled with well-dressed crowds, when it blazed with lights, and resounded with music and dancing, Lady Delacour, in the character of Mistress of the Revels, shone the soul and spirit of pleasure and frolic: but the moment the company retired, when the music ceased, and the lights were extinguishing, the spell was dissolved.

She would sometimes walk up and down the empty magnificent saloon, absorbed in thoughts seemingly of the most painful nature.

For some days after Belinda's arrival in town she heard nothing of Lord Delacour; his lady never mentioned his name, except once accidentally, as she was showing Miss Portman the house, she said, "Don't open that door—those are only Lord Delacour's apartments."—The first time Belinda ever saw his lordship, he was dead drunk in the arms of two footmen, who were carrying him up stairs to his bedchamber: his lady, who was just returned from Ranelagh, passed by him on the landing-place with a look of sovereign contempt.

"What is the matter?—Who is this?" said Belinda.

"Only the body of my Lord Delacour," said her ladyship: "his bearers have brought it up the wrong staircase. Take it down again, my good friends: let his lordship go his own way. Don't look so shocked and amazed, Belinda—don't look so new, child: this funeral of my lord's intellects is to me a nightly, or," added her ladyship, looking at her watch and yawning, "I believe I should say a daily ceremony—six o'clock, I protest!"

The next morning, as her ladyship and Miss Portman were sitting at the breakfast-table, after a very late breakfast, Lord Delacour entered the room.

"Lord Delacour, sober, my dear,"—said her ladyship to Miss Portman, by way of introducing him. Prejudiced by her ladyship, Belinda was inclined to think that Lord Delacour sober would not be more agreeable or more rational than Lord Delacour drunk. "How old do you take my lord to be?" whispered her ladyship, as she saw Belinda's eye fixed upon the trembling hand which carried his teacup to his lips: "I'll lay you a wager," continued she aloud—"I'll lay your birth-night dress, gold fringe, and laurel wreaths into the bargain, that you don't guess right."

"I hope you don't think of going to this birth-night, lady Delacour?" said his lordship.

"I'll give you six guesses, and I'll bet you don't come within sixteen years," pursued her ladyship, still looking at Belinda.

"You cannot have the new carriage you have bespoken," said his lordship. "Will you do me the honour to attend to me, Lady Delacour?"

"Then you won't venture to guess, Belinda," said her ladyship (without honouring her lord with the smallest portion of her attention)—"Well, I believe you are right—for certainly you would guess him to be six-and-sixty, instead of six-and-thirty; but then he can drink more than any two-legged animal in his majesty's dominions, and you know that is an advantage which is well worth twenty or thirty years of a man's life—especially to persons who have no other chance of distinguishing themselves."

"If some people had distinguished themselves a little less in the world," retorted his lordship, "it would have been as well!"

"As well!—how flat!"

"Flatly then I have to inform you, Lady Delacour, that I will neither be contradicted nor laughed at—you understand me,—it would be as well, flat or not flat, my Lady Delacour, if your ladyship would attend more to your own conduct, and less to others!"

"To that of others—his lordship means, if he means any thing. Apropos, Belinda, did not you tell me Clarence Hervey is coming to town?—You have never seen him.—Well, I'll describe him to you by negatives. He is not a man who ever says any thing flat—he is not a man who must be wound up with half a dozen bottles of champaign before he can go—he is not a man who, when he does go, goes wrong, and won't be set right—he is not a man, whose whole consequence, if he were married, would depend on his wife—he is not a man, who, if he were married, would be so desperately afraid of being governed by his wife, that he would turn gambler, jockey, or sot, merely to show that he could govern himself."

"Go on, Lady Delacour," said his lordship, who had been in vain attempting to balance a spoon on the edge of his teacup during the whole of this speech, which was delivered with the most animated desire to provoke—"Go on, Lady Delacour—all I desire is, that you should go on; Clarence Hervey will be much obliged to you, and I am sure so shall I. Go on, my Lady Delacour—go on, and you'll oblige me."

"I never will oblige you, my lord, that you may depend upon," cried her ladyship, with a look of indignant contempt.

His lordship whistled, rang for his horses, and looked at his nails with a smile. Belinda, shocked and in a great confusion, rose to leave the room, dreading the gross continuance of this matrimonial dialogue.

"Mr. Hervey, my lady," said a footman, opening the door; and he was scarcely announced, when her ladyship went forward to receive him with an air of easy familiarity.—"Where have you buried yourself, Hervey, this age past?" cried she, shaking hands with him: "there's absolutely no living in this most stupid of all worlds without you.—Mr. Hervey—Miss Portman—but don't look as if you were half asleep, man—What are you dreaming of, Clarence? Why looks your grace so heavily to-day?"

"Oh! I have passed a miserable night," replied Clarence, throwing himself into an actor's attitude, and speaking in a fine tone of stage declamation.

"What was your dream, my lord? I pray you, tell me," said her ladyship in a similar tone.—Clarence went on—

"O Lord, methought what pain it was to dance!
What dreadful noise of fiddles in my ears!
What sights of ugly belles within my eyes!

—Then came wandering by,
A shadow like a devil, with red hair,
'Dizen'd with flowers; and she bawl'd out aloud,
Clarence is come; false, fleeting, perjured Clarence!"

"O, Mrs. Luttridge to the life!" cried Lady Delacour: "I know where you have been now, and I pity you—but sit down," said she, making room for him between Belinda and herself upon the sofa, "sit down here, and tell me what could take you to that odious Mrs. Luttridge's."

Mr. Hervey threw himself on the sofa; Lord Delacour whistled as before, and left the room without uttering a syllable.

"But my dream has made me forget myself strangely," said Mr. Hervey, turning to Belinda, and producing her bracelet: "Mrs. Stanhope promised me that if I delivered it safely, I should be rewarded with the honour of putting it on the owner's fair arm." A conversation now took place on the nature of ladies' promises—on fashionable bracelets—on the size of the arm of the Venus de Medici—on Lady Delacour's and Miss Portman's—on the thick legs of ancient statues—and on the various defects and absurdities of Mrs. Luttridge and her wig. On all these topics Mr. Hervey displayed much wit, gallantry, and satire, with so happy an effect, that Belinda, when he took leave, was precisely of her aunt's opinion, that he was a most uncommonly pleasant young man.

Clarence Hervey might have been more than a pleasant young man, if he had not been smitten with the desire of being thought superior in every thing, and of being the most admired person in all companies. He had been early flattered with the idea that he was a man of genius; and he imagined that, as such, he was entitled to be imprudent, wild, and eccentric. He affected singularity, in order to establish his claims to genius. He had considerable literary talents, by which he was distinguished at Oxford; but he was so dreadfully afraid of passing for a pedant, that when he came into the company of the idle and the ignorant, he pretended to disdain every species of knowledge. His chameleon character seemed to vary in different lights, and according to the different situations in which he happened to be placed. He could be all things to all men—and to all women. He was supposed to be a favourite with the fair sex; and of all his various excellencies and defects, there was none on which he valued himself so much as on his gallantry. He was not profligate; he had a strong sense of honour, and quick feelings of humanity; but he was so easily led, or rather so easily excited by his companions, and his companions were now of such a sort, that it was probable he would soon become vicious. As to his connexion with Lady Delacour, he would have started with horror at the idea of disturbing the peace of a family; but in her family, he said, there was no peace to disturb; he was vain of having it seen by the world that he was distinguished by a lady of her wit and fashion, and he did not think it incumbent on him to be more scrupulous or more attentive to appearances than her ladyship. By Lord Delacour's jealousy he was sometimes provoked, sometimes amused, and sometimes flattered. He was constantly of all her ladyship's parties in public and private; consequently he saw Belinda almost every day, and every day he saw her with increasing admiration of her beauty, and with increasing dread of being taken in to marry a niece of "the catch-match-maker," the name by which Mrs. Stanhope was known amongst the men of his acquaintance. Young ladies who have the misfortune to be conducted by these artful dames, are always supposed to be partners in all the speculations, though their names may not appear in the firm. If he had not been prejudiced by the character of her aunt, Mr. Hervey would have thought Belinda an undesigning, unaffected girl; but now he suspected her of artifice in every word, look, and motion; and even when he felt himself most charmed by her powers of pleasing, he was most inclined to despise her, for what he thought such premature proficiency in scientific coquetry. He had not sufficient resolution to keep beyond the sphere of her attraction; but, frequently, when he found himself within it, he cursed his folly, and drew back with sudden terror. His manner towards her was so variable and inconsistent, that she knew not how to interpret its language. Sometimes she fancied, that with all the eloquence of eyes he said, "I adore you, Belinda;" at other times she imagined that his guarded silence meant to warn her that he was so entangled by Lady Delacour, that he could not extricate himself from her snares. Whenever this last idea struck her, it excited, in the most edifying manner, her indignation against coquetry in general, and against her ladyship's in particular: she became wonderfully clear-sighted to all the improprieties of her ladyship's conduct. Belinda's newly acquired moral sense was so much shocked, that she actually wrote a full statement of her observations and her scruples to her aunt Stanhope; concluding by a request, that she might not remain under the protection of a lady, of whose character she could not approve, and whose intimacy might perhaps be injurious to her reputation, if not to her principles.

Mrs. Stanhope answered Belinda's letter in a very guarded style; she rebuked her niece severely for her imprudence in mentioning names in such a manner, in a letter sent by the common post; assured her that her reputation was in no danger; that she hoped no niece of hers would set up for a prude—a character more suspected by men of the world than even that of a coquette; that the person alluded to was a perfectly fit chaperon for any young lady to appear with in public, as long as she was visited by the first people in town; that as to any thing in the private conduct of that person, and as to any private brouillieries between her and her lord, Belinda should observe on these dangerous topics a profound silence, both in her letters and her conversation; that as long as the lady continued under the protection of her husband, the world might whisper, but would not speak out; that as to Belinda's own principles, she would be utterly inexcusable if, after the education she had received, they could be hurt by any bad examples; that she could not be too cautious in her management of a man of —'s character; that she could have no serious cause for jealousy in the quarter she apprehended, as marriage there could not be the object; and there was such a difference of age, that no permanent influence could probably be obtained by the lady; that the most certain method for Miss Portman to expose herself to the ridicule of one of the parties, and to the total neglect of the other, would be to betray anxiety or jealousy; that, in short, if she were fool enough to lose her own heart, there would be little chance of her being wise enough to win that of—, who was evidently a man of gallantry rather than of sentiment, and who was known to play his cards well, and to have good luck whenever hearts were trumps.

Belinda's fears of Lady Delacour, as a dangerous rival, were much quieted by the artful insinuations of Mrs. Stanhope, with respect to her age, &c.; and in proportion as her fears subsided, she blamed herself for having written too harshly of her ladyship's conduct. The idea that whilst she appeared as Lady Delacour's friend she ought not to propagate any stories to her disadvantage, operated powerfully upon Belinda's mind, and she reproached herself for having told even her aunt what she had seen in private. She thought that she had been guilty of treachery, and she wrote again immediately to Mrs. Stanhope, to conjure her to burn her last letter; to forget, if possible, its contents; and to believe that not a syllable of a similar nature should ever more be heard from her: she was just concluding with the words—"I hope my dear aunt will consider all this as an error of my judgment, and not of my heart," when Lady Delacour burst into the room, exclaiming, in a tone of gaiety, "Tragedy or comedy, Belinda? The masquerade dresses are come. But how's this?" added she, looking full in Belinda's face—"tears in the eyes! blushes in the cheeks! tremors in the joints! and letters shuffling away! But, you novice of novices, how awkwardly shuffled!—A niece of Mrs. Stanhope's, and so unpractised a shuffler!—And is it credible she should tremble in this ridiculous way about a love-letter or two?"

"No love-letters, indeed, Lady Delacour," said Belinda, holding the paper fast, as her ladyship, half in play, half in earnest, attempted to snatch it from her.

"No love-letters! then it must be treason; and see it I must, by all that's good, or by all that's bad—I see the name of Delacour!"—and her ladyship absolutely seized the letters by force, in spite of all Belinda's struggles and entreaties.

"I beg, I request, I conjure you not to read it!" cried Miss Portman, clasping her hands. "Read mine, read mine, if you must, but don't read my aunt Stanhope's—Oh! I beg, I entreat, I conjure you!" and she threw herself upon her knees.

"You beg! you entreat! you conjure! Why, this is like the Duchess de Brinvilliers, who wrote on her paper of poisons, 'Whoever finds this, I entreat, I conjure them, in the name of more saints than I can remember, not to open the paper any farther.'—What a simpleton, to know so little of the nature of curiosity!"

As she spoke, Lady Delacour opened Mrs. Stanhope's letter, read it from beginning to end, folded it up cooly when she had finished it, and simply said, "The person alluded to is almost as bad as her name at full length: does Mrs. Stanhope think no one can make out an inuendo in a libel, or fill up a blank, but an attorney-general?" pointing to a blank in Mrs. Stanhope's letter, left for the name of Clarence Hervey.

Belinda was in too much confusion either to speak or think.

"You were right to swear they were not love-letters," pursued her ladyship, laying down the papers. "I protest I snatched them by way of frolic—I beg pardon. All I can do now is not to read the rest."

"Nay—I beg—I wish—I insist upon your reading mine," said Belinda.

When Lady Delacour had read it, her countenance suddenly changed—"Worth a hundred of your aunt's, I declare," said she, patting Belinda's cheek. "What a treasure to meet with any thing like a new heart!—all hearts, now-a-days, are second-hand, at best."

Lady Delacour spoke with a tone of feeling which Belinda had never heard from her before, and which at this moment touched her so much, that she took her ladyship's hand and kissed it.

CHAPTER II — MASKS

"Where were we when all this began?" cried Lady Delacour, forcing herself to resume an air of gaiety— "O, masquerade was the order of the day—tragedy or comedy? which suits your genius best, my dear?"

"Whichever suits your ladyship's taste least."

"Why, my woman, Marriott, says I ought to be tragedy; and, upon the notion that people always succeed best when they take characters diametrically opposite to their own—Clarence Hervey's principle—perhaps you don't think that he has any principles; but there you are wrong; I do assure you, he has sound principles—of taste."

"Of that," said Belinda, with a constrained smile, "he gives the most convincing proof, by his admiring your ladyship so much."

"And by his admiring Miss Portman so much more. But whilst we are making speeches to one another, poor Marriott is standing in distress, like Garrick, between tragedy and comedy."

Lady Delacour opened her dressing-room door, and pointed to her as she stood with the dress of the comic muse on one arm, and the tragic muse on the other.

"I am afraid I have not spirits enough to undertake the comic muse," said Miss Portman.

Marriott, who was a personage of prodigious consequence, and the judge in the last resort at her mistress's toilette, looked extremely out of humour at having been kept waiting so long; and yet more so at the idea that her appellant jurisdiction could be disputed.

"Your ladyship's taller than Miss Portman by half ahead," said Marriott, "and to be sure will best become tragedy with this long train; besides, I had settled all the rest of your ladyship's dress. Tragedy, they say, is always tall; and, no offence, your ladyship's taller than Miss Portman by half a head."

"For head read inch," said Lady Delacour, "if you please."

"When things are settled, one can't bear to have them unsettled—but your ladyship must have your own way, to be sure—I'll say no more," cried she, throwing down the dresses.

"Stay, Marriott," said Lady Delacour, and she placed herself between the angry waiting-maid and the door.

"Why will you, who are the best creature in the world, put yourself into these furies about nothing? Have patience with us, and you shall be satisfied."

"That's another affair," said Marriott.

"Miss Portman," continued her ladyship, "don't talk of not having spirits, you that are all life!—What say you, Belinda?—O yes, you must be the comic muse; and I, it seems, must be tragedy, because Marriott has a passion for seeing me 'come sweeping by.' And because Marriott must have her own way in every thing—she rules me with a rod of iron, my dear, so tragedy I needs must be.—Marriott knows her power."

There was an air of extreme vexation in Lady Delacour's countenance as she pronounced these last words, in which evidently more was meant than met the ear. Upon many occasions Miss Portman had observed, that Marriott exercised despotic authority over her mistress; and she had seen, with surprise, that a lady, who would not yield an iota of power to her husband, submitted herself to every caprice of the most insolent of waiting-women. For some time, Belinda imagined that this submission was merely an air, as she had seen some other fine ladies proud of appearing to be governed by a favourite maid; but she was soon convinced that Marriott was no favourite with Lady Delacour; that her ladyship's was not proud humility, but fear. It seemed certain that a woman, extravagantly fond of her own will, would never have given it up without some very substantial reason. It seemed as if Marriott was in possession of some secret, which should for ever remain unknown. This idea had occurred to Miss Portman more than once, but never so forcibly as upon the present occasion. There had always been some mystery about her ladyship's toilette: at certain hours doors were bolted, and it was impossible for any body but Marriott to obtain admission. Miss Portman at first imagined that Lady Delacour dreaded the discovery of her cosmetic secrets, but her ladyship's rouge was so glaring, and her pearl powder was so obvious, that Belinda was convinced there must be some other cause for this toilette secrecy. There was a little cabinet beyond her bedchamber, which Lady Delacour called her boudoir, to which there was an entrance by a back staircase; but no one ever entered there but Marriott. One night, Lady Delacour, after dancing with great spirit at a ball, at her own house, fainted suddenly: Miss Portman attended her to her bedchamber, but Marriott begged that her lady might be left alone with her, and she would by no means suffer Belinda to follow her into the boudoir. All these things Belinda recollected in the space of a few seconds, as she stood contemplating Marriott and the dresses. The hurry of getting ready for the masquerade, however, dispelled these thoughts, and by the time she was dressed, the idea of what Clarence Hervey would think of her appearance was uppermost in her mind. She was anxious to know whether he would discover her in the character of the comic muse. Lady Delacour was discontented with her tragic attire, and she grew still more out of humour with herself, when she saw Belinda.

"I protest Marriott has made a perfect fright of me," said her ladyship, as she got into her carriage, "and I'm positive my dress would become you a million of times better than your own."

Miss Portman regretted that it was too late to change.

"Not at all too late, my dear," said Lady Delacour; "never too late for women to change their minds, their dress, or their lovers. Seriously, you know, we are to call at my friend Lady Singleton's—she sees masks to-night: I'm quite intimate there; I'll make her let me step up to her own room, where no soul can interrupt us, and there we can change our dresses, and Marriott will know nothing of the matter. Marriott's a faithful creature, and very fond of me; fond of power too—but who is not?—we must all have our faults: one would not quarrel with such a good creature as Marriott for a trifle." Then suddenly changing her tone, she said, "Not a human being will find us out at the masquerade; for no one but Mrs. Freke knows that we are the two muses. Clarence Hervey swears he should know me in any disguise— but I defy him—I shall take special delight in puzzling him. Harriot Freke has told him, in confidence, that I'm to be the widow Brady, in man's clothes: now that's to be Harriot's own character; so Hervey will make fine confusion."

As soon as they got to Lady Singleton's, Lady Delacour and Miss Portman immediately went up stairs to exchange dresses. Poor Belinda, now that she felt herself in spirits to undertake the comic muse, was rather vexed to be obliged to give up her becoming character; but there was no resisting the polite energy of Lady Delacour's vanity. Her ladyship ran as quick as lightning into a closet within the dressing-room, saying to Lady Singleton's woman, who attempted to follow with—"Can I do any thing for your ladyship?"—"No, no, no—nothing, nothing—thank ye, thank ye,—I want no assistance—I never let any body do any thing for me but Marriott;" and she bolted herself in the closet. In a few minutes she half opened the door, threw out her tragic robes, and cried, "Here, Miss Portman, give me yours—quick— and let's see whether comedy or tragedy will be ready first."

"Lord bless and forgive me," said Lady Singleton's woman, when Lady Delacour at last threw open the door, when she was completely dressed—"but if your la'ship has not been dressing all this time in that den, without any thing in the shape of a looking-glass, and not to let me help! I that should have been so proud."

Lady Delacour put half a guinea into the waiting-maid's hand, laughed affectedly at her own whimsicalities, and declared that she could always dress herself better without a glass than with one. All this went off admirably well with every body but Miss Portman; she could not help thinking it extraordinary that a person who was obviously fond of being waited upon would never suffer any person to assist her at her toilet except Marriott, a woman of whom she was evidently afraid. Lady Delacour's quick eye saw curiosity painted in Belinda's countenance, and for a moment she was embarrassed; but she soon recovered herself, and endeavoured to turn the course of Miss Portman's thoughts by whispering to her some nonsense about Clarence Hervey—a cabalistical name, which she knew had the power, when pronounced in a certain tone, of throwing Belinda into confusion.

The first person they saw, when they went into the drawing-room at Lady Singleton's, was this very Clarence Hervey, who was not in a masquerade dress. He had laid a wager with one of his acquaintance, that he could perform the part of the serpent, such as he is seen in Fuseli's well-known picture. For this purpose he had exerted much ingenuity in the invention and execution of a length of coiled skin, which he manoeuvred with great dexterity, by means of internal wires; his grand difficulty had been to manufacture the rays that were to come from his eyes. He had contrived a set of phosphoric rays, which he was certain would charm all the fair daughters of Eve. He forgot, it seems, that phosphorus could not well be seen by candlelight. When he was just equipped as a serpent, his rays set fire to part of his envelope, and it was with the greatest difficulty that he was extricated. He escaped unhurt, but his serpent's skin was utterly consumed; nothing remained but the melancholy spectacle of its skeleton. He was obliged to give up the hopes of shining at the masquerade, but he resolved to be at Lady Singleton's that he might meet Lady Delacour and Miss Portman. The moment that the tragic and comic muse appeared, he invoked them with much humour and mock pathos, declaring that he knew not which of them could best sing his adventure. After a recital of his misfortune had entertained the company, and after the muses had performed their parts to the satisfaction of the audience and their own, the conversation ceased to be supported in masquerade character; muses and harlequins, gipsies and Cleopatras, began to talk of their private affairs, and of the news and the scandal of the day.

A group of gentlemen, amongst whom was Clarence Hervey, gathered round the tragic muse; as Mr. Hervey had hinted that he knew she was a person of distinction, though he would not tell her name. After he had exercised his wit for some time, without obtaining from the tragic muse one single syllable, he whispered, "Lady Delacour, why this unnatural reserve? Do you imagine that, through this tragical disguise, I have not found you out?"

The tragic muse, apparently absorbed in meditation, vouchsafed no reply.

"The devil a word can you get for your pains, Hervey," said a gentleman of his acquaintance, who joined the party at this instant. "Why didn't you stick to t'other muse, who, to do her justice, is as arrant a flirt as your heart could wish for?"

"There's danger in flirting," said Clarence, "with an arrant flirt of Mrs. Stanhope's training. There's a kind of electricity about that girl. I have a sort of cobweb feeling, an imaginary net coming all over me."

"Fore-warned is fore-armed," replied his companion: "a man must be a novice indeed that could be taken in at this time of day by a niece of Mrs. Stanhope's."

"That Mrs. Stanhope must be a good clever dame, faith," said a third gentleman: "there's no less than six of her nieces whom she has got off within these four winters—not one of 'em now that has not made a catch-match.—There's the eldest of the set, Mrs. Tollemache, what had she, in the devil's name, to set up with in the world but a pair of good eyes?—her aunt, to be sure, taught her the use of them early enough: they might have rolled to all eternity before they would have rolled me out of my senses; but you see they did Tollemache's business. However, they are going to part now, I hear: Tollemache was tired of her before the honey-moon was over, as I foretold. Then there's the musical girl, Joddrell, who has no more ear than a post, went and married her, because he had a mind to set up for a connoisseur in music; and Mrs. Stanhope flattered him that he was one."

The gentlemen joined in the general laugh: the tragic muse sighed.

"Even were she at the School for Scandal, the tragic muse dare not laugh, except behind her mask," said Clarence Hervey.

"Far be it from her to laugh at those follies which she must for ever deplore!" said Belinda, in a feigned voice.—"What miseries spring from these ill-suited marriages! The victims are sacrificed before they have sense enough to avoid their fate."

Clarence Hervey imagined that this speech alluded to Lady Delacour's own marriage.

"Damn me if I know any woman, young or old, that would avoid being married, if she could, though," cried Sir Philip Baddely, a gentleman who always supplied "each vacuity of sense" with an oath: "but, Rochfort, didn't Valleton marry one of these nieces?"

"Yes: she was a mighty fine dancer, and had good legs enough: Mrs. Stanhope got poor Valleton to fight a duel about her place in a country dance, and then he was so pleased with himself for his prowess, that he married the girl."

Belinda made an effort to change her seat, but she was encompassed so that she could not retreat.

"As to Jenny Mason, the fifth of the nieces," continued the witty gentleman, "she was as brown as mahogany, and had neither eyes, nose, mouth, nor legs: what Mrs. Stanhope could do with her I often wondered; but she took courage, rouged her up, set her a going as a dasher, and she dashed herself into Tom Levit's curricle, and Tom couldn't get her out again till she was the honourable Mrs. Levit: she then took the reins into her own hands, and I hear she's driving him and herself the road to ruin as fast as they can gallop. As for this Belinda Portman, 'twas a good hit to send her to Lady Delacour's; but, I take it she hangs upon hand; for last winter, when I was at Bath, she was hawked about every where, and the aunt was puffing her with might and main. You heard of nothing, wherever you went, but of Belinda Portman, and Belinda Portman's accomplishments: Belinda Portman, and her accomplishments, I'll swear, were as well advertised as Packwood's razor strops."

"Mrs. Stanhope overdid the business, I think," resumed the gentleman who began the conversation: "girls brought to the hammer this way don't go off well. It's true, Christie himself is no match for dame Stanhope. Many of my acquaintance were tempted to go and look at the premises, but not one, you may be sure, had a thought of becoming a tenant for life."

"That's an honour reserved for you, Clarence Hervey," said another, tapping him upon the shoulder.—"Give ye joy, Hervey; give ye joy!"

"Me!" said Clarence, starting.

"I'll be hanged if he didn't change colour," said his facetious companion; and all the young men again joined in a laugh.

"Laugh on, my merry men all!" cried Clarence; "but the devil's in it if I don't know my own mind better than any of you. You don't imagine I go to Lady Delacour's to look for a wife?—Belinda Portman's a good pretty girl, but what then? Do you think I'm an idiot?—do you think I could be taken in by one of the Stanhope school? Do you think I don't see as plainly as any of you that Belinda Portman's a composition of art and affectation?"

"Hush—not so loud, Clarence; here she comes," said his companion. "The comic muse, is not she—?"

Lady Delacour, at this moment, came lightly tripping towards them, and addressing herself, in the character of the comic muse, to Hervey, exclaimed,

"Hervey! my Hervey! most favoured of my votaries, why do you forsake me?

'Why mourns my friend, why weeps his downcast eye?
That eye where mirth and fancy used to shine.'
Though you have lost your serpent's form, yet you may please any of the fair daughters of Eve in your own."

Mr. Hervey bowed; all the gentlemen who stood near him smiled; the tragic muse gave an involuntary sigh.

"Could I borrow a sigh, or a tear, from my tragic sister," pursued Lady Delacour, "however unbecoming to my character, I would, if only sighs or tears can win the heart of Clarence Hervey:—let me practise"—and her ladyship practised sighing with much comic effect.

"Persuasive words and more persuasive sighs,"

said Clarence Hervey.

"A good bold Stanhope cast of the net, faith," whispered one of his companions. "Melpomene, hast thou forgot thyself to marble?" pursued Lady Delacour. "I am not very well," whispered Miss Portman to her ladyship: "could we get away?"

"Get away from Clarence Hervey, do you mean?" replied her ladyship, in a whisper: "'tis not easy, but we'll try what can be done, if it is necessary."

Belinda had no power to reply to this raillery; indeed, she scarcely heard the words that were said to her; but she put her arm within Lady Delacour's, who, to her great relief, had the good nature to leave the room with her immediately. Her ladyship, though she would sacrifice the feelings of others, without compunction, to her vanity, whenever the power of her wit was disputed, yet towards those by whom it was acknowledged she showed some mercy.

"What is the matter with the child?" said she, as she went down the staircase.

"Nothing, if I could have air," said Belinda. There was a crowd of servants in the hall.

"Why does Lady Delacour avoid me so pertinaciously? What crime have I committed, that I was not favoured with one word?" said Clarence Hervey, who had followed them down stairs, and overtook them in the hall.

"Do see if you can find any of my people," cried Lady Delacour.

"Lady Delacour, the comic muse!" exclaimed Mr. Hervey. "I thought—"

"No matter what you thought," interrupted her ladyship. "Let my carriage draw up, for here's a young friend of yours trembling so about nothing, that I am half afraid she will faint; and you know it would not be so pleasant to faint here amongst footmen. Stay! this room is empty. O, I did not mean to tell you to stay," said she to Hervey, who involuntarily followed her in the utmost consternation.

"I'm perfectly well, now—perfectly well," said Belinda.

"Perfectly a simpleton, I think," said Lady Delacour. "Nay, my dear, you must be ruled; your mask must come off: didn't you tell me you wanted air?—What now! This is not the first time Clarence Hervey has ever seen your face without a mask, is it? It's the first time indeed he, or anybody else, ever saw it of such a colour, I believe."

When Lady Delacour pulled off Belinda's mask, her face was, during the first instant, pale; the next moment, crimsoned over with a burning blush.

"What is the matter with ye both? How he stands!" said Lady Delacour, turning to Mr. Hervey. "Did you never see a woman blush before?—or did you never say or do any thing to make a woman blush before? Will you give Miss Portman a glass of water?—there's some behind you on that sideboard, man!—but he has neither eyes, ears, nor understanding.—Do go about your business," said her ladyship, pushing him towards the door—"Do go about your business, for I haven't common patience with you: on my conscience I believe the man's in love—and not with me! That's sal-volatile for you, child, I perceive," continued she to Belinda. "O, you can walk now—but remember you are on slippery ground: remember Clarence Hervey is not a marrying man, and you are not a married woman."

"It is perfectly indifferent to me, madam," Belinda said, with a voice and look of proud indignation.

"Lady Delacour, your carriage has drawn up," said Clarence Hervey, returning to the door, but without entering.

"Then put this 'perfectly well' and 'perfectly indifferent' lady into it," said Lady Delacour.

He obeyed without uttering a syllable.

"Dumb! absolutely dumb! I protest," said her ladyship, as he handed her in afterwards. "Why, Clarence, the casting of your serpent's skin seems to have quite changed your nature—nothing but the simplicity of the dove left; and I expect to hear, you cooing presently—don't you, Miss Portman?" She ordered the coachman to drive to the Pantheon.

"To the Pantheon! I was in hopes your ladyship would have the goodness to set me down at home; for indeed I shall be a burden to you and everybody else at the masquerade."

"If you have made any appointment for the rest of the evening in Berkley-square, I'll set you down, certainly, if you insist upon it, my dear—for punctuality is a virtue; but prudence is a virtue too, in a young lady; who, as your aunt Stanhope would say, has to establish herself in the world. Why these tears, Belinda?—or are they tears? for by the light of the lamps I can scarcely tell; though I'll swear I saw the handkerchief at the eyes. What is the meaning of all this? You'd best trust me—for I know as much of men and manners as your aunt Stanhope at least; and in one word, you have nothing to fear from me, and every thing to hope from yourself, if you will only dry up your tears, keep on your mask, and take my advice; you'll find it as good as your aunt Stanhope's."

"My aunt Stanhope's! O," cried Belinda, "never, never more will I take such advice; never more will I expose myself to be insulted as a female adventurer.—Little did I know in what a light I appeared; little did I know what gentlemen thought of my aunt Stanhope, of my cousins, of myself!"

"Gentlemen! I presume Clarence Hervey stands at this instant, in your imagination, as the representative of all the gentlemen in England; and he, instead of Anacharsis Cloots, is now, to be sure, l'orateur du genre humain. Pray let me have a specimen of the eloquence, which, to judge by its effects, must be powerful indeed."

Miss Portman, not without some reluctance, repeated the conversation which she had heard.—"And is this all?" cried Lady Delacour. "Lord, my dear, you must either give up living in the world, or expect to hear yourself, and your aunts, and your cousins, and your friends, from generation to generation, abused every hour in the day by their friends and your friends; 'tis the common course of things. Now you know what a multitude of obedient humble servants, dear creatures, and very sincere and most affectionate friends, I have in my writing-desk, and on my mantel-piece, not to mention the cards which crowd the common rack from intimate acquaintance, who cannot live without the honour, or favour, or pleasure of seeing Lady Delacour twice a week;—do you think I'm fool enough to imagine that they would care the hundredth part of a straw if I were this minute thrown into the Red or the Black Sea?— No, I have not one real friend in the world except Harriot Freke; yet, you see I am the comic muse, and mean to keep it up—keep it up to the last—on purpose to provoke those who would give their eyes to be able to pity me;—I humbly thank them, no pity for Lady Delacour. Follow my example, Belinda; elbow your way through the crowd: if you stop to be civil and beg pardon, and 'hope I didn't hurt ye,' you will be trod under foot. Now you'll meet those young men continually who took the liberty of laughing at your aunt, and your cousins, and yourself; they are men of fashion. Show them you've no feeling, and they'll acknowledge you for a woman of fashion. You'll marry better than any of your cousins,—Clarence Hervey if you can; and then it will be your turn to laugh about nets and cages. As to love and all that—"

The carriage stopped at the Pantheon just as her ladyship came to the words "love and all that." Her thoughts took a different turn, and during the remainder of the night she exhibited, in such a manner as to attract universal admiration, all the ease, and grace, and gaiety, of Euphrosyne.

To Belinda the night appeared long and dull: the commonplace wit of chimney-sweepers and gipsies, the antics of harlequins, the graces of flower-girls and Cleopatras, had not power to amuse her; for her thoughts still recurred to that conversation which had given her so much pain—a pain which Lady Delacour's raillery had failed to obliterate.

"How happy you are, Lady Delacour," said she, when they got into the carriage to go home; "how happy you are to have such an amazing flow of spirits!"

"Amazing you might well say, if you knew all," said Lady Delacour; and she heaved a deep sigh, threw herself back in the carriage, let fall her mask, and was silent. It was broad daylight, and Belinda had a full view of her countenance, which was the picture of despair. She uttered not one syllable more, nor had Miss Portman the courage to interrupt her meditations till they came within sight, of Lady Singleton's, when Belinda ventured to remind her that she had resolved to stop there and change dresses before Marriott saw them.

"No, it's no matter," said Lady Delacour; "Marriott will leave me at the last, like all the rest—'tis no matter." Her ladyship sunk back into her former attitude; but after she had remained silent for some minutes, she started up and exclaimed—

"If I had served myself with half the zeal that I have served the world, I should not now be thus forsaken! I have sacrificed reputation, happiness, every thing to the love of frolic:—all frolic will soon be at an end with me—I am dying—and I shall die unlamented by any human being. If I were to live my life over again, what a different life it should be!—What a different person I would be!—But it is all over now—I am dying."

Belinda's astonishment at these words, and at the solemn manner in which they were pronounced, was inexpressible; she gazed at Lady Delacour, and then repeated the word,—'dying!'—"Yes, dying!" said Lady Delacour.

"But you seem to me, and to all the world, in perfect health; and but half an hour ago in perfect spirits," said Belinda.

"I seem to you and to all the world, what I am not—I tell you I am dying," said her ladyship in an emphatic tone.

Not a word more passed till they got home. Lady Delacour hurried up stairs, bidding Belinda follow her to her dressing-room. Marriott was lighting the six wax candles on the dressing-table.—"As I live, they have changed dresses after all," said Marriott to herself, as she fixed her eyes upon Lady Delacour and Miss Portman. "I'll be burnt, if I don't make my lady remember this."

"Marriott, you need not wait; I'll ring when I want you," said Lady Delacour; and taking one of the candles from the table, she passed on hastily with Miss Portman through her dressing-room, through her bedchamber, and to the door of the mysterious cabinet.

"Marriott, the key of this door," cried she impatiently, after she had in vain attempted to open it.

"Heavenly graciousness!" cried Marriott; "is my lady out of her senses?"

"The key—the key—quick, the key," repeated Lady Delacour, in a peremptory tone. She seized it as soon as Marriott drew it from her pocket, and unlocked the door.

"Had not I best put the things to rights, my lady?" said Marriott, catching fast hold of the opening door.

"I'll ring when you are wanted, Marriott," said Lady Delacour; and pushing open the door with violence she rushed forward to the middle of the room, and turning back, she beckoned to Belinda to follow her—"Come in; what is it you are afraid of?" said she. Belinda went on, and the moment she was in the room, Lady Delacour shut and locked the door. The room was rather dark, as there was no light in it except what came from the candle which Lady Delacour held in her hand, and which burned but dimly. Belinda, as she looked round, saw nothing but a confusion of linen rags; vials, some empty, some full, and she perceived that there was a strong smell of medicines.

Lady Delacour, whose motions were all precipitate, like those of a person whose mind is in great agitation, looked from side to side of the room, without seeming to know what she was in search of. She then, with a species of fury, wiped the paint from her face, and returning to Belinda, held the candle so as to throw the light full upon her livid features. Her eyes were sunk, her cheeks hollow; no trace of youth or beauty remained on her death-like countenance, which formed a horrid contrast with her gay fantastic dress.

"You are shocked, Belinda," said she; "but as yet you have seen nothing—look here,"—and baring one half of her bosom, she revealed a hideous spectacle.

Belinda sunk back into a chair; Lady Delacour flung herself on her knees before her.

"Am I humbled, am I wretched enough?" cried she, her voice trembling with agony. "Yes, pity me for what you have seen, and a thousand times more for that which you cannot see:—my mind is eaten away like my body by incurable disease—inveterate remorse—remorse for a life of folly—of folly which has brought on me all the punishments of guilt."

"My husband," continued she, and her voice suddenly altered from the tone of grief to that of anger—"my husband hates me—no matter—I despise him. His relations hate me—no matter—I despise them. My own relations hate me—no matter, I never wish to see them more—never shall they see my sorrow—never shall they hear a complaint, a sigh from me. There is no torture which I could not more easily endure than their insulting pity. I will die, as I have lived, the envy and admiration of the world. When I am gone, let them find out their mistake; and moralize, if they will, over my grave." She paused. Belinda had no power to speak.

"Promise, swear to me," resumed Lady Delacour vehemently, seizing Belinda's hand, "that you will never reveal to any mortal what you have seen and heard this night. No living creature suspects that Lady Delacour is dying by inches, except Marriott and that woman whom but a few hours ago I thought my real friend, to whom I trusted every secret of my life, every thought of my heart. Fool! idiot! dupe that I was to trust to the friendship of a woman whom I knew to be without principle: but I thought she had honour; I thought she could never betray me,—O Harriot! Harriot! you to desert me!—Any thing else I could have borne—but you, who I thought would have supported me in the tortures of mind and body which I am to go through—you that I thought would receive my last breath—you to desert me!—Now I am alone in the world—left to the mercy of an insolent waiting-woman."

Lady Delacour hid her face in Belinda's lap, and almost stifled by the violence of contending emotions, she at last gave vent to them, and sobbed aloud.

"Trust to one," said Belinda, pressing her hand, with all the tenderness which humanity could dictate, "who will never leave you at the mercy of an insolent waiting-woman—trust to me."

"Trust to you!" said Lady Delacour, looking up eagerly in Belinda's face; "yes—I think—I may trust to you; for though a niece of Mrs. Stanhope's, I have seen this day, and have seen with surprise, symptoms of artless feeling about you. This was what tempted me to open my mind to you when I found that I had lost the only friend—but I will think no more of that—if you have a heart, you must feel for me.—Leave me now—tomorrow you shall hear my whole history—now I am quite exhausted—ring for Marriott." Marriott appeared with a face of constrained civility and latent rage. "Put me to bed, Marriott," said Lady Delacour, with a subdued voice; "but first light Miss Portman to her room—she need not—yet— see the horrid business of my toilette."

Belinda, when she was left alone, immediately opened her shutters, and threw up the sash, to refresh herself with the morning air. She felt excessively fatigued, and in the hurry of her mind she could not think of any thing distinctly. She took off her masquerade dress, and went to bed in hopes of forgetting, for a few hours, what she felt indelibly impressed upon her imagination. But it was in vain that she endeavoured to compose herself to sleep; her ideas were in too great and painful confusion. For some time, whenever she closed her eyes, the face and form of Lady Delacour, such as she had just beheld them, seemed to haunt her; afterwards, the idea of Clarence Hervey, and the painful recollection of the conversation she had overheard, recurred to her: the words, "Do you think I don't know that Belinda Portman is a composition of art and affectation?" fixed in her memory. She recollected with the utmost minuteness every look of contempt which she had seen in the faces of the young men whilst they spoke of Mrs. Stanhope, the match-maker. Belinda's mind, however, was not yet sufficiently calm to reflect; she seemed only to live over again the preceding night. At last, the strange motley figures which she had seen at the masquerade flitted before her eyes, and she sunk into an uneasy slumber.

CHAPTER III — LADY DELACOUR'S HISTORY

Miss Portman was awakened by the ringing of Lady Delacour's bedchamber bell. She opened her eyes with the confused idea that something disagreeable had happened; and before she had distinctly recollected herself, Marriott came to her bedside, with a note from Lady Delacour: it was written with a pencil.

"DELACOUR—my lord!!!! is to have to-day what Garrick used to call a gander feast—will you dine with me tête-à-tête, and I'll write an excuse, alias a lie, to Lady Singleton, in the form of a charming note—I pique myself sur l'éloquence du billet—then we shall have the evening to ourselves. I have much to say, as people usually have when they begin to talk of themselves.

"I have taken a double dose of opium, and am not so horribly out of spirits as I was last night; so you need not be afraid of another scene.

"Let me see you in my dressing-room, dear Belinda, as soon as you have adored

'With head uncover'd the cosmetic powers.'

"But you don't paint—no matter—you will—you must—every body must, sooner or later. In the mean time, whenever you want to send a note that shall not be opened by the bearer, put your trust neither in wafer nor wax, but twist it as I twist mine. You see I wish to put you in possession of some valuable secrets before I leave this world—this, by-the-bye, I don't, upon second thoughts, which are always best, mean to do yet. There certainly were such people as Amazons—I hope you admire them—for who could live without the admiration of Belinda Portman?—not Clarence Hervey assuredly—nor yet

"T. C. H. DELACOUR."

Belinda obeyed the summons to her ladyship's dressing-room: she found Lady Delacour with her face completely repaired with paint, and her spirits with opium. She was in high consultation with Marriott and Mrs. Franks, the milliner, about the crape petticoat of her birthnight dress, which was extended over a large hoop in full state. Mrs. Franks descanted long and learnedly upon festoons and loops, knots and fringes, submitting all the time every thing to her ladyship's better judgment.

Marriott was sulky and silent. She opened her lips but once upon the question of laburnum or no laburnum flowers.

Against them she quoted the memoirs and authority of the celebrated Mrs. Bellamy, who has a case in point to prove that "straw colour must ever look like dirty white by candlelight." Mrs. Franks, to compromise the matter, proposed gold laburnums, "because nothing can look better by candlelight, or any light, than gold;" and Lady Delacour, who was afraid that the milliner's imagination, now that it had once touched upon gold, might be led to the vulgar idea of ready money, suddenly broke up the conference, by exclaiming,

"We shall be late at Phillips's exhibition of French china. Mrs. Franks must let us see her again to-morrow, to take into consideration your court dress, my dear Belinda—'Miss Portman presented by Lady Delacour'—Mrs. Franks, let her dress, for heaven's sake, be something that will make a fine paragraph:—I give you four-and-twenty hours to think of it. I have done a horrid act this day," continued she, after Mrs. Franks had left the room—"absolutely written a twisted note to Clarence Hervey, my dear—but why did I tell you that? Now your head will run upon the twisted note all day, instead of upon 'The Life and Opinions of a Lady of Quality, related by herself.'"

After dinner Lady Delacour having made Belinda protest and blush, and blush and protest, that her head was not running upon the twisted note, began the history of her life and opinions in the following manner:—

"I do nothing by halves, my dear. I shall not tell you my adventures as Gil Blas told his to the Count d'Olivarez—skipping over the useful passages. I am no hypocrite, and have nothing worse than folly to conceal: that's bad enough—for a woman who is known to play the fool is always suspected of playing the devil. But I begin where I ought to end—with my moral, which I dare say you are not impatient to anticipate. I never read or listened to a moral at the end of a story in my life:—manners for me, and morals for those that like them. My dear, you will be woefully disappointed if in my story you expect any thing like a novel. I once heard a general say, that nothing was less like a review than a battle; and I can tell you that nothing is more unlike a novel than real life. Of all lives, mine has been the least romantic. No love in it, but a great deal of hate. I was a rich heiress—I had, I believe, a hundred thousand pounds, or more, and twice as many caprices: I was handsome and witty—or, to speak with that kind of circumlocution which is called humility, the world, the partial world, thought me a beauty and a bel-esprit. Having told you my fortune, need I add, that I, or it, had lovers in abundance—of all sorts and degrees—not to reckon those, it may be presumed, who died of concealed passions for me? I had sixteen declarations and proposals in form; then what in the name of wonder, or of common sense—which by-the-bye is the greatest of wonders—what, in the name of common sense, made me marry Lord Delacour? Why, my dear, you—no, not you, but any girl who is not used to have a parcel of admirers, would think it the easiest thing in the world to make her choice; but let her judge by what she feels when a dexterous mercer or linen-draper produces pretty thing after pretty thing—and this is so becoming, and this will wear for ever, as he swears; but then that's so fashionable;—the novice stands in a charming perplexity, and after examining, and doubting, and tossing over half the goods in the shop, it's ten to one, when it begins to get late, the young lady, in a hurry, pitches upon the very ugliest and worst thing that she has seen. Just so it was with me and my lovers, and just so—

'Sad was the hour, and luckless was the day,'

I pitched upon Viscount Delacour for my lord and judge. He had just at that time lost at Newmarket more than he was worth in every sense of the word; and my fortune was the most convenient thing in the world to a man in his condition. Lozenges are of sovereign use in some complaints. The heiress lozenge is a specific in some consumptions. You are surprised that I can laugh and jest about such a melancholy thing as my marriage with Lord Delacour; and so am I, especially when I recollect all the circumstances; for though I bragged of there being no love in my history, there was when I was a goose or a gosling of about eighteen—just your age, Belinda, I think—something very like love playing about my heart, or my head. There was a certain Henry Percival, a Clarence Hervey of a man—no, he had ten times the sense, begging your pardon, of Clarence Hervey—his misfortune, or mine, was, that he had too much sense—he was in love with me, but not with my faults; now I, wisely considering that my faults were the greatest part of me, insisted upon his being in love with my faults. He wouldn't, or couldn't—I said wouldn't, he said couldn't. I had been used to see the men about me lick the dust at my feet, for it was gold dust. Percival made wry faces—Lord Delacour made none. I pointed him out to Percival as an example—it was an example he would not follow. I was provoked, and I married in hopes of provoking the man I loved. The worst of it was, I did not provoke him as much as I expected. Six months afterwards I heard of his marriage with a very amiable woman. I hate those very amiable women. Poor Percival! I should have been a very happy woman, I fancy, if I had married you—for I believe you were the only man who ever really loved me; but all that is over now!—Where were we? O, I married my Lord Delacour, knowing him to be a fool, and believing that, for this reason, I should find no trouble in governing him. But what a fatal mistake!-a fool, of all animals in the creation, is the most difficult to govern. We set out in the fashionable world with a mutual desire to be as extravagant as possible. Strange, that with this similarity of taste we could never agree!—strange, that this similarity of taste was the cause of our perpetual quarrels! During the first year of our marriage, I had always the upper hand in these disputes, and the last word; and I was content. Stubborn as the brute was, I thought I should in time break him in. From the specimens you have seen, you may guess that I was even then a tolerable proficient in the dear art of tormenting. I had almost gained my point, just broken my lord's heart, when one fair morning I unluckily told his man Champfort that he knew no more how to cut hair than a sheep-shearer. Champfort, who is conceit personified, took mortal offence at this; and the devil, who is always at hand to turn anger into malice, put it into Champfort's head to put it into my lord's head, that the world thought—'My lady governed him.' My lord took fire. They say the torpedo, the coldest of cold creatures, sometimes gives out a spark—I suppose when electrified with anger. The next time that innocent I insisted upon my Lord Delacour's doing or not doing—I forget which—the most reasonable thing in the world, my lord turns short round, and answers—'My Lady Delacour, I am not a man to be governed by a wife.'—And from that time to this the words, 'I am not a man to be governed by a wife,' have been written in his obstinate face, as all the world who can read the human countenance may see. My dear, I laugh; but even in the midst of laughter there is sadness. But you don't know what it is—I hope you never may—to have an obstinate fool for a bosom friend.

"I at first flattered myself that my lord's was not an inveterate, incurable malady: but from his obvious weakness, I might have seen that there was no hope; for cases of obstinacy are always dangerous in proportion to the weakness of the patient. My lord's case was desperate. Kill or cure was my humane or prudent maxim. I determined to try the poison of jealousy, by way of an alterative. I had long kept it in petto as my ultimate remedy. I fixed upon a proper subject—a man with whom I thought that I could coquette to all eternity, without any danger to myself—a certain Colonel Lawless, as empty a coxcomb as you would wish to see. The world, said I to myself, can never be so absurd as to suspect Lady Delacour with such a man as this, though her lord may, and will; for nothing is too absurd for him to believe. Half my theory proved just; that is saying a great deal for any theory. My lord swallowed the remedy that I had prepared for him with an avidity and a bonhommie which it did me good to behold; my remedy operated beyond my most sanguine expectations. The poor man was cured of his obstinacy, and became stark mad with jealousy. Then indeed I had some hopes of him; for a madman can be managed, a fool cannot. In a month's time I made him quite docile. With a face longer than the weeping philosopher's, he came to me one morning, and assured me, 'he would do every thing I pleased, provided I would consult my own honour and his, and give up Colonel Lawless.'

"'Give up!'—I could hardly forbear laughing at the expression. I replied, 'that as long as my lord treated me with becoming respect, I had never in thought or deed given him just cause of complaint; but that I was not a woman to be insulted, or to be kept, as I had hitherto been, in leading-strings by a husband.' My lord, flattered as I meant he should be with the idea that it was possible he should be suspected of keeping a wife in leading-strings, fell to making protestations—'He hoped his future conduct would prove,' &c. Upon this hint, I gave the reins to my imagination, and full drive I went into a fresh career of extravagance: if I were checked, it was an insult, and I began directly to talk of leading-strings. This ridiculous game I played successfully enough for some time, till at length, though naturally rather slow at calculation, he actually discovered, that if we lived at the rate of twenty thousand a-year, and had only ten thousand a-year to spend, we should in due time have nothing left. This notable discovery he communicated to me one morning, after a long preamble. When he had finished prosing, I agreed that it was demonstrably just that he should retrench his expenses; but that it was equally unjust and impossible that I could make any reformation in my civil list: that economy was a word which I had never heard of in my life till I married his lordship; that, upon second recollection, it was true I had heard of such a thing as national economy, and that it would be a very pretty, though rather hackneyed topic of declamation for a maiden speech in the House of Lords. I therefore advised him to reserve all he had to say upon the subject for the noble lord upon the woolsack; nay, I very graciously added, that upon this condition I would go to the house myself to give his arguments and eloquence a fair hearing, and that I would do my best to keep myself awake. This was all mighty playful and witty; but it happened that my Lord Delacour, who never had any great taste for wit, could not this unlucky morning at all relish it. Of course I grew angry, and reminded him, with an indelicacy which his want of generosity justified, that an heiress, who had brought a hundred thousand pounds into his family, had some right to amuse herself, and that it was not my fault if elegant amusements were more expensive than others.

"Then came a long criminating and recriminating chapter. It was, 'My lord, your Newmarket blunders'—'My lady, your cursed theatricals'—'My lord, I have surely a right'—and, 'My lady, I have surely as good a right.'

"But, my dear Belinda, however we might pay one another, we could not pay all the world with words. In short, after running through thousands and tens of thousands, we were actually in distress for money. Then came selling of lands, and I don't know what devices for raising money, according to the modes of lawyers and attorneys. It was quite indifferent to me how they got money, provided they did get it. By what art these gentlemen raised money, I never troubled myself to inquire; it might have been the black art, for any thing I know to the contrary. I know nothing of business. So I signed all the papers they brought to me; and I was mighty well pleased to find, that by so easy an expedient as writing 'T. C. H. Delacour,' I could command money at will. I signed, and signed, till at last I was with all due civility informed that my signature was no longer worth a farthing; and when I came to inquire into the cause of this phenomenon, I could nowise understand what my Lord Delacour's lawyer said to me: he was a prig, and I had not patience either to listen to him or to look at him. I sent for an old uncle of mine, who used to manage all my money matters before I was married: I put the uncle and the lawyer into a room, together with their parchments, to fight the matter out, or to come to a right understanding if they could. The last, it seems, was quite impossible. In the course of half an hour, out comes my uncle in such a rage! I never shall forget his face—all the bile in his body had gotten into it; he had literally no whites to his eyes. 'My dear uncle,' said I, 'what is the matter? Why, you are absolutely gold stick in waiting.'

"'No matter what I am, child,' said the uncle; 'I'll tell you what you are, with all your wit—a dupe: 'tis a shame for a woman of your sense to be such a fool, and to know nothing of business; and if you knew nothing yourself, could not you send for me?'

"'I was too ignorant to know that I know nothing,' said I. But I will not trouble you with all the said I's and said he's. I was made to understand, that if Lord Delacour were to die the next day, I should live a beggar. Upon this I grew serious, as you may imagine. My uncle assured me that I had been grossly imposed upon by my lord and his lawyer; and that I had been swindled out of my senses, and out of my dower. I repeated all that my uncle said, very faithfully, to Lord Delacour; and all that either he or his lawyer could furnish out by way of answer was, that 'Necessity had no law.' Necessity, it must be allowed, though it might be the mother of law, was never with my lord the mother of invention. Having now found out that I had a good right to complain, I indulged myself in it most gloriously; in short, my dear, we had a comfortable family quarrel. Love quarrels are easily made up, but of money quarrels there is no end. From the moment these money quarrels commenced, I began to hate Lord Delacour; before, I had only despised him. You can have no notion to what meanness extravagance reduces men. I have known Lord Delacour shirk, and look so shabby, and tell so many lies to people about a hundred guineas—a hundred guineas!—what do I say?—about twenty, ten, five! O, my dear, I cannot bear the thoughts of it!

"But I was going on to tell you, that my good uncle and all my relations quarrelled with me for having ruined myself, as they said; but I said they quarrelled with me for fear I should ask them for some of their 'vile trash.' Accordingly, I abused and ridiculed them, one and all; and for my pains, all my acquaintance said, that 'Lady Delacour was a woman of a vast deal of spirit.'

"We were relieved from our money embarrassments by the timely death of a rich nobleman, to whose large estate my Lord Delacour was heir-at-law. I was intoxicated with the idle compliments of all my acquaintance, and I endeavoured to console myself for misery at home by gaiety abroad. Ambitious of pleasing universally, I became the worst of slaves—a slave to the world. Not a moment of my time was at my own disposal—not one of my actions; I may say, not one of my thoughts was my own; I was obliged to find things 'charming' every hour, which tired me to death; and every day it was the same dull round of hypocrisy and dissipation. You wonder to hear me speak in this manner, Belinda—but one must speak the truth sometimes; and this is what I have been saying to Harriot Freke continually, for these ten years past. Then why persist in the same kind of life? you say. Why, my dear, because I could not stop: I was fit for this kind of life and for no other: I could not be happy at home; for what sort of a companion could I have made of Lord Delacour? By this time he was tired of his horse Potatoe, and his horse Highflyer, and his horse Eclipse, and Goliah, and Jenny Grey, &c.; and he had taken to hard drinking, which soon turned him, as you see, quite into a beast.

"I forgot to tell you that I had three children during the first five years of my marriage. The first was a boy: he was born dead; and my lord, and all his odious relations, laid the blame upon me, because I would not be kept prisoner half a year by an old mother of his, a vile Cassandra, who was always prophesying that my child would not be born alive. My second child was a girl; but a poor diminutive, sickly thing. It was the fashion at this time for fine mothers to suckle their own children: so much the worse for the poor brats. Fine nurses never made fine children. There was a prodigious rout made about the matter; a vast deal of sentiment and sympathy, and compliments and inquiries; but after the novelty was over, I became heartily sick of the business; and at the end of about three months my poor child was sick too—I don't much like to think of it—it died. If I had put it out to nurse, I should have been thought by my friends an unnatural mother; but I should have saved its life. I should have bewailed the loss of the infant more, if Lord Delacour's relations and my own had not made such lamentations upon the occasion that I was stunned. I couldn't or wouldn't shed a tear; and I left it to the old dowager to perform in public, as she wished, the part of chief mourner, and to comfort herself in private by lifting up her hands and eyes, and railing at me as the most insensible of mothers. All this time I suffered more than she did; but that is what she shall never have the satisfaction of knowing. I determined, that if ever I had another child, I would not have the barbarity to nurse it myself. Accordingly when my third child, a girl, was born, I sent it off immediately to the country, to a stout, healthy, broad-faced nurse, under whose care it grew and flourished; so that at three years old, when it was brought back to me, I could scarcely believe the chubby little thing was my own child. The same reasons which convinced me I ought not to nurse my own child, determined me, à plus forte raison, not to undertake its education. Lord Delacour could not bear the child, because it was not a boy. The girl was put under the care of a governess, who plagued my heart out with her airs and tracasseries for three or four years; at the end of which time, as she turned out to be Lord Delacour's mistress in form, I was obliged—in form—to beg she would leave my house: and I put her pupil into better hands, I hope, at a celebrated academy for young ladies. There she will, at any rate, be better instructed than she could be at home. I beg your pardon, my dear, for this digression on nursing and schooling; but I wanted only to explain to you why it was that, when I was weary of the business, I still went on in a course of dissipation. You see I had nothing at home, either in the shape of husband or children, to engage my affections. I believe it was this 'aching void' in my heart which made me, after looking abroad some time for a bosom friend, take such a prodigious fancy to Mrs. Freke. She was just then coming into fashion; she struck me, the first time I met her, as being downright ugly; but there was a wild oddity in her countenance which made one stare at her, and she was delighted to be stared at, especially by me; so we were mutually agreeable to each other—I as starer, and she as staree. Harriot Freke had, without comparison, more assurance than any man or woman I ever saw; she was downright brass, but of the finest kind—Corinthian brass. She was one of the first who brought what I call harum scarum manners into fashion. I told you that she had assurance—impudence I should have called it, for no other word is strong enough. Such things as I have heard Harriot Freke say!—You will not believe it—but her conversation at first absolutely made me, like an old-fashioned fool, wish I had a fan to play with. But, to my astonishment, all this took surprisingly with a set of fashionable young men. I found it necessary to reform my manners. If I had not taken heart of grace, and publicly abjured the heresies of false delicacy, I should have been excommunicated. Lady Delacour's sprightly elegance—allow me to speak of myself in the style in which the newspaper writers talk of me—Lady Delacour's sprightly elegance was but pale, not to say faded pink, compared with the scarlet of Mrs. Freke's dashing audacity. As my rival, she would on certain ground have beat me hollow; it was therefore good policy to make her my friend: we joined forces, and nothing could stand against us. But I have no right to give myself credit for good policy in forming this intimacy; I really followed the dictates of my heart or my imagination. There was a frankness in Harriot's manner which I mistook for artlessness of character: she spoke with such unbounded freedom on certain subjects, that I gave her credit for unbounded sincerity on all subjects: she had the talent of making the world believe that virtue to be invulnerable by nature which disdained the common outworks of art for its defence. I, amongst others, took it for granted, that the woman who could make it her sport to 'touch the brink of all we hate,' must have a stronger head than other people. I have since been convinced, however, of my mistake. I am persuaded that few can touch the brink without tumbling headlong down the precipice. Don't apply this, my dear, literally, to the person of whom we were speaking; I am not base enough to betray her secrets, however I may have been provoked by her treachery. Of her character and history you shall hear nothing but what is necessary for my own justification. The league of amity between us was scarcely ratified before my Lord Delacour came, with his wise remonstrating face, to beg me 'to consider what was due to my own honour and his.' Like the cosmogony-man in the Vicar of Wakefield, he came out over and over with this cant phrase, which had once stood him in stead. 'Do you think, my lord,' said I, 'that because I gave up poor Lawless to oblige you, I shall give up all common sense to suit myself to your taste? Harriot Freke is visited by every body but old dowagers and old maids: I am neither an old dowager nor an old maid—the consequence is obvious, my lord.' Pertness in dialogue, my dear, often succeeds better with my lord than wit: I therefore saved the sterling gold, and bestowed upon him nothing but counters. I tell you this to save the credit of my taste and judgment.

"But to return to my friendship for Harriot Freke. I, of course, repeated to her every word which had passed between my husband and me. She out-heroded Herod upon the occasion; and laughed so much at what she called my folly in pleading guilty in the Lawless cause, that I was downright ashamed of myself, and, purely to prove my innocence, I determined, upon the first convenient opportunity, to renew my intimacy with the colonel. The opportunity which I so ardently desired of redeeming my independence was not long wanting. Lawless, as my stars (which you know are always more in fault than ourselves) would have it, returned just at this time from the continent, where he had been with his regiment; he returned with a wound across his forehead and a black fillet, which made him look something more like a hero, and ten times more like a coxcomb, than ever. He was in fashion, at all events; and amongst other ladies, Mrs. Luttridge, odious Mrs. Luttridge! smiled upon him. The colonel, however, had taste enough to know the difference between smile and smile: he laid himself and his laurels at my feet, and I carried him and them about in triumph. Wherever I went, especially to Mrs. Luttridge's, envy and scandal joined hands to attack me, and I heard wondering and whispering wherever I went. I had no object in view but to provoke my husband; therefore, conscious of the purity of my intentions, it was my delight to brave the opinion of the wondering world. I gave myself no concern about the effect my coquetry might have upon the object of this flirtation. Poor Lawless! Heart, I took it for granted, he had none; how should a coxcomb come by a heart? Vanity I knew he had in abundance, but this gave me no alarm, as I thought that if it should ever make him forget him self, I mean forget what was due to me, I could, by one flash of my wit, strike him to the earth, or blast him for ever. One night we had been together at Mrs. Luttridge's;—she, amongst other good things, kept a faro bank, and, I am convinced, cheated. Be that as it may, I lost an immensity of money, and it was my pride to lose with as much gaiety as any body else could win; so I was, or appeared to be, in uncommonly high spirits, and Lawless had his share of my good humour. We left Mrs. Luttridge's together early, about half-past one. As the colonel was going to hand me to my carriage, a smart-looking young man, as I thought, came up close to the coach door, and stared me full in the face: I was not a woman to be disconcerted at such a thing as this, but I really was startled when the young fellow jumped into the carriage after me: I thought he was mad: I had only courage enough to scream. Lawless seized hold of the intruder to drag him out, and out he dragged the youth, exclaiming, in a high tone, 'What is the meaning of all this, sir? Who the devil are you? My name's Lawless: who the devil are you?' The answer to this was a convulsion of laughter. By the laugh I knew it to be Harriot Freke. 'Who am I? only a Freke!' cried she: 'shake hands.' I gave her my hand, into the carriage she sprang, and desired the colonel to follow her: Lawless laughed, we all laughed, and drove away. 'Where do you think I've been?' said Harriot; 'in the gallery of the House of Commons; almost squeezed to death these four hours; but I swore I'd hear Sheridan's speech to-night, and I did; betted fifty guineas I would with Mrs. Luttridge, and have won. Fun and Freke for ever, huzza!' Harriot was mad with spirits, and so noisy and unmanageable, that, as I told her, I was sure she was drunk. Lawless, in his silly way, laughed incessantly, and I was so taken up with her oddities, that, for some time, I did not perceive we were going the Lord knows where; till, at last, when the 'larum of Harriot's voice ceased for an instant, I was struck with the strange sound of the carriage. 'Where are we? not upon the stones, I'm sure,' said I; and putting my head out of the window, I saw we were beyond the turnpike. 'The coachman's drunk as well as you, Harriot,' said I; and I was going to pull the string to stop him, but Harriot had hold of it. 'The man is going very right,' said she; 'I've told him where to go. Now don't fancy that Lawless and I are going to run away with you. All this is unnecessary now-a-days, thank God!' To this I agreed, and laughed for fear of being ridiculous. 'Guess where you are going,' said Harriot, I guessed and guessed, but could not guess right; and my merry companions were infinitely diverted with my perplexity and impatience, more especially as, I believe, in spite of all my efforts, I grew rather graver than usual. We went on to the end of Sloane-street, and quite out of town; at last we stopped. It was dark; the footman's flambeau was out; I could only just see by the lamps that we were at the door of a lone, odd-looking house. The house door opened, and an old woman appeared with a lantern in her hand.

"'Where is this farce, or freak, or whatever you call it, to end?' said I, as Harriot pulled me into the dark passage along with her.

"Alas! my dear Belinda," said Lady Delacour, pausing, "I little foresaw where or how it was to end. But I am not come yet to the tragical part of my story, and as long as I can laugh I will. As the old woman and her miserable light went on before us, I could almost have thought of Sir Bertrand, or of some German horrifications; but I heard Lawless, who never could help laughing at the wrong time, bursting behind me, with a sense of his own superiority.

"'Now you will learn your destiny, Lady Delacour!' said Harriot, in a solemn tone.

"'Yes! from the celebrated Mrs. W—, the modern dealer in art magic,' said I, laughing, 'for, now I guess whereabouts I am. Colonel Lawless's laugh broke the spell. Harriot Freke, never whilst you live expect to succeed in the sublime.' Harriot swore at the colonel for the veriest spoil-sport she had ever seen, and she whispered to me—'The reason he laughs is because he is afraid of our suspecting the truth of him, that he believes tout de bon in conjuration, and the devil, and all that.' The old woman, whose cue I found was to be dumb, opened a door at the top of a narrow staircase, and pointing to a tall figure, completely enveloped in fur, left us to our fate. I will not trouble you with a pompous description of all the mummery of the scene, my dear, as I despair of being able to frighten you out of your wits. I should have been downright angry with Harriot Freke for bringing me to such a place, but that I knew women of the first fashion had been with Mrs. W— before us—some in sober sadness, some by way of frolic. So as there was no fear of being ridiculous, there was no shame, you know, and my conscience was quite at ease. Harriot had no conscience, so she was always at ease; and never more so than in male attire, which she had been told became her particularly. She supported the character of a young rake with such spirit and truth, that I am sure no common conjuror could have discovered any thing feminine about her. She rattled on with a set of nonsensical questions; and among other things she asked, 'How soon will Lady Delacour marry again after her lord's death?'

"'She will never marry after her lord's death,' answered the oracle. 'Then she will marry during his lifetime,' said Harriot. 'True,' answered the oracle. Colonel Lawless laughed; I was angry; and the colonel would have been quiet, for he was a gentleman, but there was no such thing as managing Mrs. Freke, who, though she had laid aside the modesty of her own sex, had not acquired the decency of the other. 'Who is to be Lady Delacour's second husband?' cried she; 'you'll not offend any of the present company by naming the man.' 'Her second husband I cannot name,' replied the oracle, 'but let her beware of a Lawless lover.' Mrs. Freke and Colonel Lawless, encouraged by her, triumphed over me without mercy—I may say, without shame! Well, my dear, I am in a hurry to have done with all this: though I 'doted upon folly,' yet I was terrified at the thoughts of any thing worse. The idea of a divorce, the public brand of a shameful life, shocked me in spite of all my real and all my assumed levity. O that I had, at this instant, dared to be myself! But my fear of ridicule was greater than my fear of vice. 'Bless me, my dear Lady Delacour,' whispered Harriot, as we left this house, 'what can make you in such a desperate hurry to get home? You gape and fidget: one would think you had never sat up a night before in your life. I verily believe you are afraid to trust yourself with us. Which of us are you afraid of, Lawless, or me, or yourself?' There was a tone of contempt in the last words which piqued me to the quick; and however strange it may seem, I was now anxious only to convince Harriot that I was not afraid of myself. False shame made me act as if I had no shame. You would not suspect me of knowing any thing of false shame, but depend upon it, my dear, many, who appear to have as much assurance as I have, are secretly its slaves. I moralize, because I am come to a part of my story which I should almost be glad to omit; but I promised you that there should be no sins of omission. It was light, but not broad daylight, when we got to Knightsbridge. Lawless, encouraged (for I cannot deny it) by the levity of my manner, as well as of Harriot's, was in higher and more familiar spirits than I ever saw him. Mrs. Freke desired me to set her down at her sister's, who lived in Grosvenor-place: I did so, and I beg you to believe that I was in an agony, to get rid of my colonel at the same time; but you know I could not, before Harriot Freke, absolutely say to him, 'Get out!' Indeed, to tell things as they were, it was scarcely possible to guess by my manner that I was under any anxiety, I acted my part so well, or so ill. As Harriot Freke jumped out of the coach, a cock crowed in the area of her sister's house: 'There!' cried Harriot, 'do you hear the cock crow, Lady Delacour? Now it's to be hoped your fear of goblins is over, else I would not be so cruel as to leave the pretty dear all alone.' 'All alone!' answered I: 'your friend the colonel is much obliged to you for making nobody of him.' 'My friend the colonel,' whispered Harriot, leaning with her bold masculine arms on the coach door—'my friend the colonel is much obliged to me, I'm sure, for remembering what the cunning or the knowing woman told us just now: so when I said I left you alone, I was not guilty of a bull, was I?' I had the grace to be heartily ashamed of this speech, and called out, in utter confusion, 'To Berkley-square. But where shall I set you down, colonel? Harriot, good morning: don't forget you are in man's clothes.' I did not dare to repeat the question of 'where shall I set you down, colonel?' at this instant, because Harriot gave me such an arch, sneering look, as much as to say, 'Still afraid of yourself!' We drove on: I'm persuaded that the confusion which, in spite of all my efforts, broke through my affected levity, encouraged Lawless, who was naturally a coxcomb and a fool, to believe that I was actually his, else he never could have been so insolent. In short, my dear, before we had got through the turnpike gate, I was downright obliged to say to him, 'Get out!' which I did with a degree of indignation that quite astonished him. He muttered something about ladies knowing their minds; and I own, though I went off with flying colours, I secretly blamed myself as much as I did him, and I blamed Harriot more than I did either. I sent for her the next day, as soon as I could, to consult her. She expressed such astonishment, and so much concern at this catastrophe of our night's frolic, and blamed herself with so many oaths, and execrated Lawless for a coxcomb, so much to the ease and satisfaction of my conscience, that I was confirmed in my good opinion of her, and indeed felt for her the most lively affection and esteem; for observe, with me esteem ever followed affection, instead of affection following esteem. Woe be to all who in morals preposterously put the cart before the horse! But to proceed with my history: all fashionable historians stop to make reflections, supposing that no one else can have the sense to make any. My esteemed friend agreed with me that it would be best for all parties concerned to hush up this business; that as Lawless was going out of town in a few days, to be elected for a borough, we should get rid of him in the best way possible, without 'more last words;' that he had been punished sufficiently on the spot, and that to punish twice for the same offence, once in private and once in public, would be contrary to the laws of Englishmen and Englishwomen, and in my case would be contrary to the evident dictates of prudence, because I could not complain without calling upon Lord Delacour to call Lawless out; this I could not do without acknowledging that his lordship had been in the right, in warning me about his honour and my own, which old phrase I dreaded to hear for the ninety-ninth time: besides, Lord Delacour was the last man in the world I should have chosen for my knight, though unluckily he was my lord; besides, all things considered, I thought the whole story might not tell so well in the world for me, tell it which way I would: we therefore agreed that it would be most expedient to hold our tongues. We took it for granted that Lawless would hold his, and as for my people, they knew nothing, I thought, or if they did, I was sure of them. How the thing got abroad I could not at the time conceive, though now I am well acquainted with the baseness and treachery of the woman I called my friend. The affair was known and talked of every where the next day, and the story was told especially at odious Mrs. Luttridge's, with such exaggerations as drove me almost mad. I was enraged, inconceivably enraged with Lawless, from whom I imagined the reports originated.

"I was venting my indignation against him in a room full of company, where I had just made my story good, when a gentleman, to whom I was a stranger, came in breathless, with the news that Colonel Lawless was killed in a duel by Lord Delacour; that they were carrying him home to his mother's, and that the body was just going by the door. The company all crowded to the windows immediately, and I was left standing alone till I could stand no longer. What was said or done after this I do not remember; I only know that when I came to myself, the most dreadful sensation I ever experienced was the certainty that I had the blood of a fellow-creature to answer for.—I wonder," said Lady Delacour, breaking off at this part of her history, and rising suddenly, "I wonder what is become of Marriott!—surely it is time for me to have my drops. Miss Portman, have the goodness to ring, for I must have something immediately." Belinda was terrified at the wildness of her manner. Lady Delacour became more composed, or put more constraint upon herself, at the sight of Marriott. Marriott brought from the closet in her lady's room the drops, which Lady Delacour swallowed with precipitation. Then she ordered coffee, and afterward chasse-café, and at last, turning to Belinda, with a forced smile, she said—

"Now shall the Princess Scheherazade go on with her story?"

CHAPTER IV — LADY DELACOUR'S HISTORY CONTINUED

"I left off with the true skill of a good story-teller, at the most interesting part—a duel; and yet duels are so common now that they are really vulgar incidents.

"But we think that a duel concerning ourselves must be more extraordinary than any other. We hear of men being shot in duels about nothing every day, so it is really a weakness in me to think so much about poor Lawless's death, as Harriot Freke said to me at the time. She expected to see me show sorrow in public; but very fortunately for me, she roused my pride, which was always stronger than my reason; and I behaved myself upon the occasion as became a fine lady. There were some things, however, I could hardly stand. You must know that Lawless, fool and coxcomb as he was, had some magnanimity, and showed it—as some people do from whom it is least expected—on his death-bed. The last words he said were, 'Lady Delacour is innocent—I charge you, don't prosecute Lord Delacour.' This he said to his mother, who, to complete my misery, is one of the most respectable women in England, and was most desperately fond of Lawless, who was an only son. She never has recovered his loss. Do you remember asking me who a tall elderly lady in mourning was, that you saw getting into her carriage one day, at South Audley-street chapel, as we passed by in our way to the park? That was Lady Lawless: I believe I didn't answer you at the time. I meet her every now and then—to me a spectre of dismay. But, as Harriot Freke said, certainly such a man as poor Lawless was a useless being in society, however he may be regretted by a doting mother. We should see things in a philosophical light, if we can. I should not have suffered half as much as I did if he had been a man of a stronger understanding; but he was a poor, vain, weak creature, that I actually drew on and duped with my own coquetry, whilst all the time I was endeavouring only to plague Lord Delacour. I was punished enough by the airs his lordship doubly gave himself, upon the strength of his valour and his judgment—they roused me completely; and I blamed him with all my might, and got an enormous party of my friends, I mean my acquaintance, to run him down full cry, for having fought for me. It was absurd—it was rash—it was want of proper confidence in his wife; thus we said. Lord Delacour had his partisans, it is true; amongst whom the loudest was odious Mrs. Luttridge. I embraced the first opportunity I met with of retaliation. You must know that Mrs. Luttridge, besides being a great faro-player, was a great dabbler in politics; for she was almost as fond of power as of money: she talked loud and fluently, and had, somehow or other, partly by intriguing, partly by relationship, connected herself with some of the leading men in parliament. There was to be a contested election in our country: Mr. Luttridge had a good estate there next to Lord Delacour's, and being of an ancient family, and keeping a good table, the Luttridges were popular enough. At the first news of an election, out comes a flaming advertisement from Mr. Luttridge; away posted Mrs. Luttridge to begin her canvass, and away posted Lady Delacour after her, to canvass for a cousin of Harriot Freke. This was a new scene for me; but I piqued myself on the versatility of my talents, and I laid myself out in please all the squires, and, what was more difficult, all the squires' ladies, in —shire. I was ambitious to have it said of me, 'that I was the finest figure that ever appeared upon a canvass.' O, ye —shireians, how hard did I work to obtain your praise! All that the combined force of vanity and hatred could inspire I performed, and with success. You have but little curiosity, I presume, to know how many hogsheads of port went down the throat of John Bull, or how many hecatombs were offered up to the genius of English liberty. My hatred to Mrs. Luttridge was, of course, called love of my country. Lady Delacour was deified by all true patriots; and, luckily, a handsome legacy left me for my spirit, by an uncle who died six weeks before the election, enabled us to sustain the expense of my apotheosis. The day of election came; Harriot Freke and I made our appearance on the hustings, dressed in splendid party uniforms; and before us our knights and squires held two enormous panniers full of ribands and cockades, which we distributed with a grace that won all hearts, if not all votes. Mrs. Luttridge thought the panniers would carry the election; and forthwith she sent off an express for a pair of panniers twice as large as ours. I took out my pencil, and drew a caricature of the ass and her panniers; wrote an epigram at the bottom of it; and the epigram and the caricature were soon in the hands of half —shire. The verses were as bad as impromptus usually are, and the drawing was not much better than the writing; but the good-will of the critics supplied all my deficiencies; and never was more praise bestowed upon the pen of Burke, or the pencil of Reynolds, than was lavished upon me by my honest friends. My dear Belinda, if you will not quarrel with the quality, you may have what quantity of praise you please. Mrs. Luttridge, as I hoped and expected, was beyond measure enraged at the sight of the caricature and epigram. She was, besides being a gamester and a politician—what do you think?—an excellent shot! She wished, she said, to be a man, that she might be qualified to take proper notice of my conduct. The same kind friends who showed her my epigram repeated to me her observation upon it. Harriot Freke was at my elbow, and offered to take any message I might think proper to Mrs. Luttridge. I scarcely thought her in earnest till she added, that the only way left now-a-days for a woman to distinguish herself was by spirit; as every thing else was grown 'cheap and vulgar in the eyes of men;' that she knew one of the cleverest young men in England, and a man of fashion into the bargain, who was just going to publish a treatise 'upon the Propriety and Necessity of Female Duelling;' and that he had demonstrated, beyond a possibility of doubt, that civilized society could not exist half a century longer without this necessary improvement. I had prodigious deference for the masculine superiority, as I thought it, of Harriot's understanding. She was a philosopher, and a fine lady—I was only a fine lady; I had never fired a pistol in my life, and I was a little inclined to cowardice; but Harriot offered to bet any wager upon the steadiness of my hand, and assured me that I should charm all beholders in male attire. In short, as my second, if I would furnish her with proper credentials, she swore she would undertake to furnish me with clothes, and pistols, and courage, and every thing I wanted. I sat down to pen my challenge. When I was writing it, my hand did not tremble much—not more than my Lord Delacour's always does. The challenge was very prettily worded: I believe I can repeat it.

"'Lady Delacour presents her compliments to Mrs. Luttridge—she is informed that Mrs. L— wishes she were a man, that she might be qualified to take proper notice of Lady D—'s conduct. Lady Delacour begs leave to assure Mrs. Luttridge, that though she has the misfortune to be a woman, she is willing to account for her conduct in any manner Mrs. L— may think proper, and at any hour and place she may appoint. Lady D— leaves the choice of the weapons to Mrs. L—. Mrs. H. Freke, who has the honour of presenting this note, is Lady Delacour's friend upon this occasion.'

"I cannot repeat Mrs. Luttridge's answer; all I know is, it was not half as neatly worded as my note; but the essential part of it was, that she accepted my challenge with pleasure, and should do herself the honour of meeting me at six o'clock the next morning; that Miss Honour O'Grady would be her friend upon the occasion; and that pistols were the weapons she preferred. The place of appointment was behind an old barn, about two miles from the town of —. The hour was fixed to be early in the morning, to prevent all probability of interruption. In the evening, Harriot and I rode to the ground. There were several bullets sticking in the posts of the barn: this was the place where Mrs. Luttridge had been accustomed to exercise herself in firing at a mark. I own my courage 'oozed out' a little at this sight. The Duke de la Rochefoucault, I believe, said truly, that 'many would be cowards if they dared.' There seemed to me to be no physical and less moral necessity for my fighting this duel; but I did not venture to reason on a point of honour with my spirited second. I bravadoed to Harriot most magnanimously; but at night, when Marriott was undressing me, I could not forbear giving her a hint, which I thought might tend to preserve the king's peace, and the peace of the county. I went to the ground in the morning in good spirits, and with a safe conscience. Harriot was in admiration of my 'lion-port;' and, to do her justice, she conducted herself with great coolness upon the occasion; but then it may be observed, that it was I who was to stand fire, and not she. I thought of poor Lawless a billion of times, at least, as we were going to the ground; and I had my presentiments, and my confused notions of poetic justice: but poetic justice, and all other sorts of justice, went clear out of my head, when I saw my antagonist and her friend, actually pistol in hand, waiting for us; they were both in men's clothes. I secretly called upon the name of Marriott with fervency, and I looked round with more anxiety than ever Bluebeard's wife, or 'Anne, sister Anne!' looked to see if any body was coming: nothing was to be seen but the grass blown by the wind—no Marriott to throw herself toute éplorée between the combatants—no peace-officers to bind us over to our good behaviour—no deliverance at hand; and Mrs. Luttridge, by all the laws of honour, as challenged, was to have the first shot. Oh, those laws of honour! I was upon the point of making an apology, in spite of them all, when, to my inexpressible joy, I was relieved from the dreadful alternative of being shot through the head, or of becoming a laughing-stock for life, by an incident, less heroic, I'll grant you, than opportune. But you shall have the whole scene, as well as I can recollect it; as well—for those who for the first time go into a field of battle do not, as I am credibly informed and internally persuaded, always find the clearness of their memories improved by the novelty of their situation. Mrs. Luttridge, when we came up, was leaning, with a truly martial negligence, against the wall of the barn, with her pistol, as I told you, in her hand. She spoke not a word; but her second, Miss Honour O'Grady, advanced towards us immediately, and, taking off her hat very manfully, addressed herself to my second—'Mistress Harriot Freke, I presume, if I mistake not.' Harriot bowed slightly, and answered, 'Miss Honour O'Grady, I presume, if I mistake not.' 'The same, at your service,' replied Miss Honour. 'I have a few words to suggest that may save a great deal of noise, and bloodshed, and ill-will.' 'As to noise,' said Harriot, 'it is a thing in which I delight, therefore I beg that mayn't be spared on my account; as to bloodshed, I beg that may not be spared on Lady Delacour's account, for her honour, I am sure, is dearer to her than her blood; and, as to ill-will, I should be concerned to have that saved on Mrs. Luttridge's account, as we all know it is a thing in which she delights, even more than I do in noise, or Lady Delacour in blood: but pray proceed, Miss Honour O'Grady; you have a few words to suggest.' 'Yes, I would willingly observe, as it is my duty to my principal,' said Honour, 'that one who is compelled to fire her pistol with her left hand, though ever so good a shot naturally, is by no means on a footing with one who has the advantage of her right hand.' Harriot rubbed my pistol with the sleeve of her coat, and I, recovering my wit with my hopes of being witty with impunity, answered, 'Unquestionably, left-handed wisdom and left-handed courage are neither of them the very best of their kinds; but we must content ourselves with them if we can have no other.' 'That if,' cried Honour O'Grady, 'is not, like most of the family of the ifs, a peace-maker. My Lady Delacour, I was going to observe that my principal has met with an unfortunate accident, in the shape of a whitlow on the fore-finger of her right hand, which incapacitates her from drawing a trigger; but I am at your service, ladies, either of you, that can't put up with a disappointment with good humour.' I never, during the whole course of my existence, was more disposed to bear a disappointment with good humour, to prove that I was incapable of bearing malice; and to oblige the seconds, for form's sake, I agreed that we should take our ground, and fire our pistols into the air. Mrs. Luttridge, with her left-handed wisdom, fired first; and I, with great magnanimity, followed her example. I must do my adversary's second, Miss Honour O'Grady, the justice to observe, that in this whole affair she conducted herself not only with the spirit, but with the good-nature and generosity characteristic of her nation. We met enemies, and parted friends.

"Life is a tragicomedy! Though the critics will allow of no such thing in their books, it is a true representation of what passes in the world; and of all lives mine has been the most grotesque mixture, or alternation, I should say, of tragedy and comedy. All this is apropos to something I have not told you yet. This comic duel ended tragically for me. 'How?' you say. Why, 'tis clear that I was not shot through the head; but it would have been better, a hundred times better for me, if I had; I should have been spared, in this life at least, the torments of the damned. I was not used to priming and loading: my pistol was overcharged: when I fired, it recoiled, and I received a blow on my breast, the consequences of which you have seen.

"The pain was nothing at the moment compared with what I have since experienced: but I will not complain till I cannot avoid it. I had not, at the time I received the blow, much leisure for lamentation; for I had scarcely discharged my pistol when we heard a loud shout on the other side of the barn, and a crowd of town's people, country people, and haymakers, came pouring down the lane towards us, with rakes and pitchforks in their hands. An English mob is really a formidable thing. Marriott had mismanaged her business most strangely: she had, indeed, spread a report of a duel—a female duel; but the untutored sense of propriety amongst these rustics was so shocked at the idea of a duel fought by women in men's clothes, that I verily believe they would have thrown us into the river with all their hearts. Stupid blockheads! I am convinced that they would not have been half so much scandalized if we had boxed in petticoats. The want of these petticoats had nearly proved our destruction, or at least our disgrace: a peeress after being ducked, could never have held her head above water again with any grace. The mob had just closed round us, crying, 'Shame! shame! shame!—duck 'em—duck 'em—gentle or simple—duck 'em—duck 'em'—when their attention was suddenly turned towards a person who was driving up the lane a large herd of squeaking, grunting pigs. The person was clad in splendid regimentals, and he was armed with a long pole, to the end of which hung a bladder, and his pigs were frightened, and they ran squeaking from one side of the road to the other; and the pig-driver in regimentals, in the midst of the noise, could not without difficulty make his voice heard; but at last he was understood to say, that a bet of a hundred guineas depended upon his being able to keep these pigs ahead of a flock of turkeys that were following them; and he begged the mob to give him and his pigs fair play. At the news of this wager, and at the sight of the gentleman turned pig-driver, the mob were in raptures; and at the sound of his voice, Harriot Freke immediately exclaimed, 'Clarence Hervey! by all that's lucky!'"

"Clarence Hervey!" interrupted Belinda. "Clarence Hervey, my dear," said Lady Delacour, coolly: "he can do every thing, you know, even drive pigs, better than any body else!—but let me go on.

"Harriot Freke shouted in a stentorian voice, which actually made your pig-driver start: she explained to him in French our distress, and the cause of it, Clarence was, as I suppose you have discovered long ago, 'that cleverest young man in England who had written on the propriety and necessity of female duelling.' He answered Harriot in French—'To attempt your rescue by force would be vain; but I will do better, I will make a diversion in your favour.' Immediately our hero, addressing himself to the sturdy fellow who held me in custody, exclaimed, 'Huzza, my boys! Old England for ever! Yonder comes a Frenchman with a flock of turkeys. My pigs will beat them, for a hundred guineas. Old England for ever, huzza!'

"As he spoke, the French officer, with whom Clarence Hervey had laid the wager, appeared at the turn of the lane—his turkeys half flying—half hobbling up the road before him. The Frenchman waved a red streamer over the heads of his flock—Clarence shook a pole, from the top of which hung a bladder full of beans. The pigs grunted, the turkeys gobbled, and the mob shouted: eager for the fame of Old England, the crowd followed Clarence with loud acclamations. The French officer was followed with groans and hisses. So great was the confusion, and so great the zeal of the patriots, that even the pleasure of ducking the female duellists was forgotten in the general enthusiasm. All eyes and all hearts were intent upon the race; and now the turkeys got foremost, and now the pigs. But when we came within sight of the horsepond, I heard one man cry, 'Don't forget the ducking.' How I trembled! but our knight shouted to his followers—'For the love of Old England, my brave boys, keep between my pigs and the pond:—if our pigs see the water, they'll run to it, and England's undone.'

"The whole fury of the mob was by this speech conducted away from us. 'On, on, my boys, into town, to the market-place: whoever gains the market-place first wins the day.' Our general shook the rattling bladder in triumph over the heads of 'the swinish multitude,' and we followed in perfect security in his train into the town.

"Men, women, and children, crowded to the windows and doors. 'Retreat into the first place you can,' whispered Clarence to us: we were close to him. Harriot Freke pushed her way into a milliner's shop: I could not get in after her, for a frightened pig turned back suddenly, and almost threw me down. Clarence Hervey caught me, and favoured my retreat into the shop. But poor Clarence lost his bet by his gallantry. Whilst he was manoeuvring in my favour, the turkeys got several yards ahead of the pigs, and reaching the market-place first, won the race.

"The French officer found great difficulty in getting safe out of the town; but Clarence represented to the mob that he was a prisoner on his parole, and that it would be unlike Englishmen to insult a prisoner. So he got off without being pelted, and they both returned in safety to the house of General Y—, where they were to dine, and where they entertained a large party of officers with the account of this adventure.

"Mrs. Freke and I rejoiced in our escape, and we thought that the whole business was now over; but in this we were mistaken. The news of our duel, which had spread in the town, raised such an uproar as had never been heard, even at the noisiest election. Would you believe it?—The fate of the election turned upon this duel. The common people, one and all, declared that they would not vote either for Mr. Luttridge or Mr. Freke, because as how—but I need not repeat all the platitudes that they said. In short, neither ribands nor brandy could bring them to reason. With true English pig-headedness, they went every man of them and polled for an independent candidate of their own choosing, whose wife, forsooth, was a proper behaved woman.

"The only thing I had to console me for all this was Clarence Hervey's opinion that I looked better in man's clothes than my friend Harriot Freke. Clarence was charmed with my spirit and grace; but he had not leisure at that time to attach himself seriously to me, or to any thing. He was then about nineteen or twenty: he was all vivacity, presumption, and paradox; he was enthusiastic in support of his opinions; but he was at the same time the most candid man in the world, for there was no set of tenets which could be called exclusively his: he adopted in liberal rotation every possible absurdity; and, to do him justice, defended each in its turn with the most ingenious arguments that could be devised, and with a flow of words which charmed the ear, if not the sense. His essay on female duelling was a most extraordinary performance; it was handed about in manuscript till it was worn out; he talked of publishing it, and dedicating it to me. However, this scheme, amongst a million of others, he talked of, but never put into execution. Luckily for him, many of his follies evaporated in words. I saw but little either of him or his follies at this time. All I know about him is, that after he had lost his bet of a hundred guineas, as a pig-driver, by his knight-errantry in rescuing the female duellists from a mob, he wrote a very charming copy of verses upon the occasion; and that he was so much provoked by the stupidity of some of his brother officers who could not understand the verses, that he took a disgust to the army, and sold his commission. He set out upon a tour to the continent, and I returned with Harriot Freke to London, and forgot the existence of such a person as Clarence Hervey for three or four years. Unless people can be of some use, or unless they are actually present, let them be ever so agreeable or meritorious, we are very apt to forget them. One grows strangely selfish by living in the world: 'tis a perfect cure for romantic notions of gratitude, and love, and so forth. If I had lived in the country in an old manor-house, Clarence Hervey would have doubtless reigned paramount in my imagination as the deliverer of my life, &c. But in London one has no time for thinking of deliverers. And yet what I did with my time I cannot tell you: 'tis gone, and no trace left. One day after another went I know not how. Had I wept for every day I lost, I'm sure I should have cried my eyes out before this time. If I had enjoyed any amusement in the midst of this dissipation, it would all have been very well; but I declare to you in confidence I have been tired to death. Nothing can be more monotonous than the life of a hackneyed fine lady;—I question whether a dray-horse, or—a horse in a mill, would willingly exchange places with one, if they could know as much of the matter as I do. You are surprised at hearing all this from me. My dear Belinda, how I envy you! You are not yet tired of every thing. The world has still the gloss of novelty for you; but don't expect that can last above a season. My first winter was certainly entertaining enough. One begins with being charmed with the bustle and glare, and what the French call spectacle; this is over, I think, in six months. I can but just recollect having been amused at the Theatres, and the Opera, and the Pantheon, and Ranelagh, and all those places, for their own sakes. Soon, very soon, we go out to see people, not things: then we grow tired of seeing people; then we grow tired of being seen by people; and then we go out merely because we can't stay at home. A dismal story, and a true one. Excuse me for showing you the simple truth; well-dressed falsehood is a personage much more presentable. I am now come to an epoch in my history in which there is a dearth of extraordinary events. What shall I do? Shall I invent? I would if I could; but I cannot. Then I must confess to you that during these last four years I should have died of ennui if I had not been kept alive by my hatred of Mrs. Luttridge and of my husband. I don't know which I hate most—O, yes, I do—I certainly hate Mrs. Luttridge the most; for a woman can always hate a woman more than she can hate a man, unless she has been in love with him, which I never was with poor Lord Delacour. Yes! I certainly hate Mrs. Luttridge the most; I cannot count the number of extravagant things I have done on purpose to eclipse her. We have had rival routs, rival concerts, rival galas, rival theatres: she has cost me more than she's worth; but then I certainly have mortified her once a month at least. My hatred to Mrs. Luttridge, my dear, is the remote cause of my love for you; for it was the cause of my intimacy with your aunt Stanhope.—Mrs. Stanhope is really a clever woman—she knows how to turn the hatred of all her friends and acquaintance to her own advantage.—To serve lovers is a thankless office compared with that of serving haters—polite haters I mean. It may be dangerous, for aught I know, to interpose in the quarrels of those who hate their neighbours, not only with all their souls, but with all their strength—the barbarians fight it out, kiss, and are friends. The quarrels which never come to blows are safer for a go-between; but even these are not to be compared to such as never come to words: your true silent hatred is that which lasts for ever. The moment it was known that Mrs. Luttridge and I had come to the resolution never to speak to one another, your aunt Stanhope began to minister to my hatred so, that she made herself quite agreeable. She one winter gave me notice that my adversary had set her heart upon having a magnificent entertainment on a particular day. On that day I determined, of course, to have a rival gala. Mrs. Stanhope's maid had a lover, a gardener, who lived at Chelsea; and the gardener had an aloe, which was expected soon to blow. Now a plant that blows but once in a hundred years is worth having. The gardener intended to make a public exhibition of it, by which he expected to gain about a hundred guineas. Your aunt Stanhope's maid got it from him for me for fifty; and I had it whispered about that an aloe in full blow would stand in the middle of one of Lady Delacour's supper tables. The difficulty was to make Mrs. Luttridge fix upon the very day we wanted; for you know we could not possibly put off the blowing of our aloe. Your aunt Stanhope managed the thing admirably by means of a common friend, who was not a suspected person with the Luttridges; in short, my dear, I gained my point—every body came from Mrs. Luttridge's to me, or to my aloe. She had a prodigiously fine supper, but scarcely a soul stayed with her; they all came to see what could be seen but once in a hundred years. Now the aloe, you know, is of a cumbersome height for a supper ornament. My saloon luckily has a dome, and under the dome we placed it. Round the huge china vase in which it was planted we placed the most beautiful, or rather the most expensive hothouse plants we could procure. After all, the aloe was an ugly thing; but it answered my purpose—it made Mrs. Luttridge, as I am credibly informed, absolutely weep with vexation. I was excessively obliged to your aunt Stanhope; and I assured her that if ever it were in my power, she might depend upon my gratitude. Pray, when you write, repeat the same thing to her, and tell her that since she has introduced Belinda Portman to me, I am a hundred times more obliged to her than ever I was before.

"But to proceed with my important history.—I will not tire you with fighting over again all my battles in my seven years' war with Mrs. Luttridge. I believe love is more to your taste than hatred; therefore I will go on as fast as possible to Clarence Hervey's return from his travels. He was much improved by them, or at least I thought so; for he was heard to declare, that after all he had seen in France and Italy, Lady Delacour appeared to him the most charming woman, of her age, in Europe. The words, of her age, piqued me; and I spared no pains to make him forget them. A stupid man cannot readily be persuaded out of his senses—what he sees he sees, and neither more nor less; but 'tis the easiest thing in the world to catch hold of a man of genius: you have nothing to do but to appeal from his senses to his imagination, and then he sees with the eyes of his imagination, and hears with the ears of his imagination; and then no matter what the age, beauty, or wit of the charmer may be—no matter whether it be Lady Delacour or Belinda Portman. I think I know Clarence Hervey's character au fin fond, and I could lead him where I pleased: but don't be alarmed, my dear; you know I can't lead him into matrimony. You look at me, and from me, and you don't well know which way to look. You are surprised, perhaps, after all that passed, all that I felt, and all that I still feel about poor Lawless, I should not be cured of coquetry. So am I surprised; but habit, fashion, the devil, I believe, lead us on: and then, Lord Delacour is so obstinate and jealous—you can't have forgotten the polite conversation that passed one morning at breakfast between his lordship and me about Clarence Hervey; but neither does his lordship know, nor does Clarence Hervey suspect, that my object with him is to conceal from the world what I cannot conceal from myself—that I am a dying woman. I am, and I see you think me, a strange, weak, inconsistent creature. I was intended for something better, but now it is too late; a coquette I have lived, and a coquette I shall die: I speak frankly to you. Let me have the glory of leading Clarence Hervey about with me in public for a few months longer, then I must quit the stage. As to love, you know with me that is out of the question; all I ask or wish for is admiration."

Lady Delacour paused, and leaned back on the sofa; she appeared in great pain.

"Oh!—I am sometimes," resumed she, "as you see, in terrible pain. For two years after I gave myself that blow with the pistol, I neglected the warning twinges that I felt from time to time; at last I was terrified. Marriott was the only person to whom I mentioned my fears, and she was profoundly ignorant: she flattered me with false hopes, till, alas! it was in vain to doubt of the nature of my complaint: then she urged me to consult a physician; that I would not do—I could not—I never will consult a physician,— I would not for the universe have my situation known. You stare—you cannot enter into my feelings. Why, my dear, if I lose admiration, what have I left? Would you have me live upon pity? Consider what a dreadful thing it must be to me, who have no friends, no family, to be confined to a sick room—a sick bed; 'tis what I must come to at last, but not yet—not yet. I have fortitude; I should despise myself if I had no species of merit: besides, it is still some occupation to me to act my part in public; and bustle, noise, nonsense, if they do not amuse or interest me, yet they stifle reflection. May you never know what it is to feel remorse! The idea of that poor wretch, Lawless, whom I actually murdered as much as if I had shot him, haunts me whenever I am alone. It is now between eight and nine years since he died, and I have lived ever since in a constant course of dissipation; but it won't do—conscience, conscience will be heard! Since my health has been weakened, I believe I have acquired more conscience. I really think that my stupid lord, who has neither ideas nor sensations, except when he is intoxicated, is a hundred times happier than I am. But I will spare you, Belinda; I promised that you should not have a scene, and I will keep my word. It is, however, a great relief to open my mind to one who has some feeling: Harriot Freke has none; I am convinced that she has no more feeling than this table. I have not yet told you how she has used me. You know that it was she who led or rather dragged me into that scrape with Lawless; for that I never reproached her. You know it was she who frightened me into fighting that duel with Mrs. Luttridge; for this I never reproached her. She has cost me my peace of mind, my health, my life; she knows it, and she forsakes, betrays, insults, and leaves me to die. I cannot command my temper sufficiently to be coherent when I speak of her; I cannot express in words what I feel. How could that most treacherous of beings, for ten years, make me believe that she was my friend? Whilst I thought she really loved me, I pardoned her all her faults—all—what a comprehensive word!— All, all I forgave; and continually said—'but she has a good heart.' A good heart!—she has no heart!— she has no feeling for any living creature but herself. I always thought that she cared for no one but for me; but now I find she can throw me off as easily as she would her glove. And this, too, I suppose she calls a frolic; or, in her own vulgar language, fun. Can you believe it?—What do you think she has done, my dear? She has gone over at last to odious Mrs. Luttridge-actually she has gone down with the Luttridges to—shire. The independent member having taken the Chiltern Hundreds, vacates his seat: a new election comes on directly: the Luttridges are to bring in Freke—not Harriot's cousin—they have cut him,—but her husband, who is now to commence senator: he is to come in for the county, upon condition that Luttridge shall have Freke's borough. Lord Delacour, without saying one syllable, has promised his interest to this precious junto, and Lady Delacour is left a miserable cipher. My lord's motives I can clearly understand: he lost a thousand guineas to Mrs. Luttridge this winter, and this is a convenient way of paying her. Why Harriot should be so anxious to serve a husband whom she hates, bitterly hates, might surprise any body who did not know les dessous des cartes as well as I do. You are but just come into the world, Belinda—the world of wickedness, I mean, my dear, or you would have heard what a piece of work there was a few years ago about Harriot Freke and this cousin of hers. Without betraying her confidence, I may just tell you what is known to every body, that she went so far, that if it had not been for me, not a soul would have visited her: she swam in the sea of folly out of her depth—the tide of fashion ebbed, and there was she left sticking knee deep in the mud—a ridiculous, scandalous figure. I had the courage and foolish good-nature to hazard myself for her, and actually dragged her to terra firma:—how she has gone on since I cannot tell you precisely, because I am in the secret; but the catastrophe is public: to make her peace with her husband, she gives up her friend. Well, that I could have pardoned, if she had not been so base as to go over to Mrs. Luttridge. Mrs. Luttridge offered (I've seen the letter, and Harriot's answer) to bring in Freke, the husband, and to make both a county and a family peace, on condition that Harriot should give up all connexion with Lady Delacour. Mrs. Luttridge knew this would provoke me beyond measure, and there is nothing she would not do to gratify her mean, malevolent passions. She has succeeded for once in her life. The blame of the duel, of course, is all thrown upon me. And (would you believe it?) Harriot Freke, I am credibly informed, throws all the blame of Lawless's business on me; nay, hints that Lawless's deathbed declaration of my innocence was very generous. Oh, the treachery, the baseness of this woman! And it was my fate to hear all this last night at the masquerade. I waited, and waited, and looked every where for Harriot—she was to be the widow Brady, I knew: at last the widow Brady made her appearance, and I accosted her with all my usual familiarity. The widow was dumb. I insisted upon knowing the cause of this sudden loss of speech. The widow took me into another apartment, unmasked, and there I beheld Mr. Freke, the husband. I was astonished—had no idea of the truth. 'Where is Harriot?' I believe, were the first words I said. 'Gone to the country.' 'To the country!' 'Yes; to—shire, with Mrs. Luttridge.'—Mrs. Luttridge— odious Mrs. Luttridge! I could scarcely believe my senses. But Freke, who always hated me, believing that I led his wife, instead of her leading me into mischief, would have enjoyed my astonishment and my rage; so I concealed both, with all possible presence of mind. He went on over-whelming me with explanations and copies of letters; and declared it was at Mrs. Freke's request he did and said all this, and that he was to follow her early the next morning to —shire. I broke from him, simply wishing him a good journey, and as much family peace as his patience merited. He knows that I know his wife's history, and though she has no shame, he has some. I had the satisfaction to leave him blushing with anger, and I supported the character of the comic muse a full hour afterwards, to convince him that all their combined malice would fail to break my spirit in public: what I suffer in private is known only to my own heart."

As she finished these words, Lady Delacour rose abruptly, and hummed a new opera air. Then she retired to her boudoir, saying, with an air of levity, to Belinda as she left the room,

"Good bye, my dear Belinda; I leave you to ruminate sweet and bitter thoughts; to think of the last speech and confession of Lady Delacour, or what will interest you much more, the first speech and confession of—Clarence Hervey."

CHAPTER V — BIRTHDAY DRESSES

Lady Delacour's history, and the manner in which it was related, excited in Belinda's mind astonishment, pity, admiration, and contempt: astonishment at her inconsistency, pity for her misfortunes, admiration of her talents, and contempt for her conduct. To these emotions succeeded the recollection of the promise which she had made, not to leave her in her last illness at the mercy of an insolent attendant. This promise Belinda thought of with terror: she dreaded the sight of sufferings which she knew must end in death: she dreaded the sight of that affected gaiety and of that real levity which so ill became the condition of a dying woman. She trembled at the idea of being under the guidance of one who was so little able to conduct herself: and she could not help blaming her aunt Stanhope severely for placing her in such a perilous situation. It was obvious that some of Lady Delacour's history must have been known to Mrs. Stanhope; and Belinda, the more she reflected, was the more surprised at her aunt's having chosen such a chaperon for a young woman just entering into the world. When the understanding is suddenly roused and forced to exert itself, what a multitude of deductions it makes in a short time! Belinda saw things in a new light; and for the first time in her life she reasoned for herself upon what she saw and felt. It is sometimes safer for young people to see than to hear of certain characters. At a distance, Lady Delacour had appeared to Miss Portman the happiest person in the world; upon a nearer view, she discovered that her ladyship was one of the most miserable of human beings. To have married her niece to such a man as Lord Delacour, Mrs. Stanhope would have thought the most fortunate thing imaginable; but it was now obvious to Belinda, that neither the title of viscountess, nor the pleasure of spending three fortunes, could ensure felicity. Lady Delacour confessed, that in the midst of the utmost luxury and dissipation she had been a constant prey to ennui; that the want of domestic happiness could never be supplied by that public admiration of which she was so ambitious; and that the immoderate indulgence of her vanity had led her, by inevitable steps, into follies and imprudences which had ruined her health, and destroyed her peace of mind. "If Lady Delacour, with all the advantages of wealth, rank, wit, and beauty, has not been able to make herself happy in this life of fashionable dissipation," said Belinda to herself, "why should I follow the same course, and expect to be more fortunate?"

It is singular, that the very means which Mrs. Stanhope had taken to make a fine lady of her niece tended to produce an effect diametrically opposite to what might have been expected. The result of

Belinda's reflections upon Lady Delacour's history was a resolution to benefit by her bad example; but this resolution it was more easy to form than to keep. Her ladyship, where she wished to please or to govern, had fascinating manners, and could alternately use the sarcastic powers of wit, and the fond tone of persuasion, to accomplish her purposes. It was Belinda's intention, in pursuance of her new plans of life, to spend, whilst she remained in London, as little money as possible upon superfluities and dress. She had, at her own disposal, only 100l. per annum, the interest of her fortune; but besides this, her aunt, who was desirous that she should go to court, and make a splendid figure there, had sent her a draught on her banker for two hundred guineas. "You will, I trust," said her aunt, at the conclusion of the letter, "repay me when you are established in the world; as I hope and believe, from what I hear from Lady Delacour of the power of your charms, you will soon be, to the entire satisfaction of all your friends. Pray do not neglect to mention my friend Clarence Hervey particularly when you write next. I understand from one who is well acquainted with him, and who has actually seen his rent-roll, that he has a clear 10,000l. a year."

Belinda resolved neither to go to court, nor to touch her aunt's two hundred guineas; and she wrote a long letter to her, in which she explained her feelings and views at large. In this letter she meant to have returned Mrs. Stanhope's draught, but her feelings and views changed between the writing of this epistle and the going out of the post. Mrs. Franks, the milliner, came in the interim, and brought home Lady Delacour's beautiful dress: it was not the sight of this, however, which changed Belinda's mind; but she could not resist Lady Delacour's raillery.

"Why, my dear," said her ladyship, after having listened to all Miss Portman could say about her love of independence, and the necessity of economy to preserve that independence, "all this is prodigiously fine—but shall I translate it into plain English? You were mortally wounded the other night by some random reflections of a set of foolish young men—Clarence Hervey amongst the number; and instead of punishing them, you sagely and generously determined to punish yourself. Then, to convince this youth that you have not a thought of those odious nets and cages, that you have no design whatever upon his heart, and that he has no manner of influence on yours, you very judiciously determine, at the first hint from him, to change your dress, your manners, and your character, and thus to say to him, in as plain terms as possible—'You see, sir, a word to the wise is enough; I understand you disapprove of showy dress and coquetry, and therefore, as I dressed and coquetted only to please you, now I shall lay aside dress and coquetry, since I find that they are not to your taste—and I hope, sir, you like my simplicity!' Depend upon it, my dear, Clarence Hervey understands simplicity as well as you or I do. All this would be vastly well, if he did not know that you overheard that conversation; but as he does know it, trust me, he will attribute any sudden change in your manners and appearance, right or wrong, to the motives I have mentioned. So don't, novice as you are! set about to manoeuvre for yourself. Leave all that to your aunt Stanhope, or to me, and then you know your conscience will be all the time as white as your hands,—which, by-the-bye, Clarence Hervey, the other day, said were the whitest hands he had ever seen. Perhaps all this time you have taken it into your head that full dress will not become you; but I assure you that it will—you look well in any thing—

'But from the hoop's bewitching round,
The very shoe has power to wound.'

So come down to Mrs. Franks, and order your birthnight dress like a reasonable creature."

Like a reasonable creature, Miss Portman followed Lady Delacour, and bespoke, or rather let her ladyship bespeak for her, fifty guineas' worth of elegance and fashion. "You must go to the drawing-room with me next week, and be presented," said Lady Delacour, "and then, as it is the first time, you must be elegantly dressed, and you must not wear the same dress on the birthnight. So, Mrs. Franks, let this be finished first, as fast as you can, and by that time, perhaps, we shall think of something superlatively charming for the night of nights."

Mrs. Franks departed, and Belinda sighed. "A silver penny for your thoughts!" cried Lady Delacour. "You are thinking that you are like Camilla, and I like Mrs. Mitten. Novel reading.—as I dare say you have been told by your governess, as I was told by mine, and she by hers, I suppose—novel reading for young ladies is the most dangerous—

"Oh, Clarence Hervey, I protest!" cried Lady Delacour, as he at this instant entered the room. "Do, pray, Clarence, help me out, for the sake of this young lady, with a moral sentence against novel reading: but that might go against your conscience, or your interest; so we'll spare you. How I regret that we had not the charming serpent at the masquerade the other night!"

The moment her ladyship mentioned the masquerade, the conversation which had passed at Lady Singleton's came full into Clarence Hervey's recollection, and his embarrassment was evident—not indeed to Belinda, who had turned away to look over some new music that lay upon a stand at the farthest end of the room; and she found this such a wonderfully interesting occupation, that she did not for some minutes hear, or appear to hear, one word of the conversation which was going on between Mr. Hervey and Lady Delacour. At last, her ladyship tapped her upon the shoulder, saying, in a playful tone, "Miss Portman, I arrest your attention at the suit of Clarence Hervey: this gentleman is passionately fond of music—to my curse—for he never sees my harp but he worries me with reproaches for having left off playing upon it. Now he has just given me his word that he will not reproach me again for a month to come if you will favour us with one air. I assure you, Clarence, that Belinda touches a harp divinely—she would absolutely charm—" "Your ladyship should not waste such valuable praise," interrupted Belinda. "Do you forget that Belinda Portman and her accomplishments have already been as well advertised as Packwood's razor-strops?"

The manner in which these words were pronounced made a great impression upon Clarence Hervey, and he began to believe it was possible that a niece of the match-making Mrs. Stanhope might not be "a compound of art and affectation." "Though her aunt has advertised her," said he to himself, "she seems to have too much dignity to advertise herself, and it would be very unjust to blame her for the faults of another person. I will see more of her."

Some morning visitors were announced, who for the time suspended Clarence Hervey's reflections: the effect of them, however, immediately appeared; for as his good opinion of Belinda increased, his ambition to please her was strongly excited. He displayed all his powers of wit and humour; and not only Lady Delacour but every body present observed, "that Mr. Hervey, who was always the most entertaining man in the world, this morning surpassed himself, and was absolutely the most entertaining man in the universe." He was mortified, notwithstanding; for he distinctly perceived, that whilst Belinda joined with ease and dignity in the general conversation, her manner towards him was grave and reserved. The next morning he called earlier than usual; but though Lady Delacour was always at home to him, she was then unluckily dressing to go to court: he inquired whether Miss Portman would accompany her ladyship, and he learnt from his friend Marriott that she was not to be presented this day, because Mrs. Franks had not brought home her dress. Mr. Hervey called again two hours afterwards.—Lady Delacour was gone to court. He asked for Miss Portman. "Not at home," was the mortifying answer; though, as he had passed by the windows, he had heard the delightful sound of her harp. He walked up and down in the square impatiently, till he saw Lady Delacour's carriage appear.

"The drawing-room has lasted an unconscionable time this morning," said he, as he handed her ladyship out of her coach, "Am not I the most virtuous of virtuous women," said Lady Delacour, "to go to court such a day as this? But," whispered she, as she went up stairs, "like all other amazingly good people, I have amazingly good reasons for being good. The queen is soon to give a charming breakfast at Frogmore, and I am paying my court with all my might, in hopes of being asked; for Belinda must see one of their galas before we leave town, that I'm determined upon.—But where is she?" "Not at home," said Clarence, smiling. "Oh, not at home is nonsense, you know. Shine out, appear, be found, my lovely Zara!" cried Lady Delacour, opening the library door. "Here she is—what doing I know not—studying Hervey's Meditations on the Tombs, I should guess, by the sanctification of her looks. If you be not totally above all sublunary considerations, admire my lilies of the valley, and let me give you a lecture, not upon heads, or upon hearts, but on what is of much more consequence, upon hoops. Every body wears hoops, but how few—'tis a melancholy consideration—how very few can manage them! There's my friend Lady C—; in an elegant undress she passes for very genteel, but put her into a hoop and she looks as pitiable a figure, as much a prisoner, and as little able to walk, as a child in a go-cart. She gets on, I grant you, and so does the poor child; but, getting on, you know, is not walking. Oh, Clarence, I wish you had seen the two Lady R.'s sticking close to one another, their father pushing them on together, like two decanters in a bottle-coaster, with such magnificent diamond labels round their necks!"

Encouraged by Clarence Hervey's laughter, Lady Delacour went on to mimic what she called the hoop awkwardness of all her acquaintance; and if these could have failed to divert Belinda, it was impossible for her to be serious when she heard Clarence Hervey declare that he was convinced he could manage a hoop as well as any woman in England, except Lady Delacour.

"Now here," said he, "is the purblind dowager, Lady Boucher, just at the door, Lady Delacour; she would not know my face, she would not see my beard, and I will bet fifty guineas that I come into a room in a hoop, and that she does not find me out by my air—that I do not betray myself, in short, by my masculine awkwardness."

"I hold you to your word, Clarence," cried Lady Delacour. "They have let the purblind dowager in; I hear her on the stairs. Here—through this way you can go: as you do every thing quicker than any body else in the world, you will certainly be full dressed in a quarter of an hour; I'll engage to keep the dowager in scandal for that time. Go! Marriott has old hoops and old finery of mine, and you have all-powerful influence, I know, with Marriott: so go and use it, and let us see you in all your glory—though I vow I tremble for my fifty guineas."

Lady Delacour kept the dowager in scandal, according to her engagement, for a good quarter of an hour; then the dresses at the drawing-room took up another quarter; and, at last, the dowager began to give an account of sundry wonderful cures that had been performed, to her certain knowledge, by her favourite concentrated extract or anima of quassia. She entered into the history of the negro slave named Quassi, who discovered this medical wood, which he kept a close secret till Mr. Daghlberg, a magistrate of Surinam, wormed it out of him, brought a branch of the tree to Europe, and communicated it to the great Linnaeus—when Clarence Hervey was announced by the title of "The Countess de Pomenars."

"An émigrée—a charming woman!" whispered Lady Delacour "she was to have been at the drawing-room to-day but for a blunder of mine: ready dressed she was, and I didn't call for her! Ah, Mad. de Pomenars, I am actually ashamed to see you," continued her ladyship; and she went forward to meet Clarence Hervey, who really made his entrée with very composed assurance and grace. He managed his hoop with such skill and dexterity, that he well deserved the praise of being a universal genius. The Countess de Pomenars spoke French and broken English incomparably well, and she made out that she was descended from the Pomenars of the time of Mad. de Sevigné: she said that she had in her possession several original letters of Mad. de Sevigné, and a lock of Mad. de Grignan's fine hair.

"I have sometimes fancied, but I believe it is only my fancy," said Lady Delacour, "that this young lady," turning to Belinda, "is not unlike your Mad. de Grignan. I have seen a picture of her at Strawberry-hill."

Mad. de Pomenars acknowledged that there was a resemblance, but added, that it was flattery in the extreme to Mad. de Grignan to say so.

"It would be a sin, undoubtedly, to waste flattery upon the dead, my dear countess," said Lady Delacour; "but here, without flattery to the living, as you have a lock of Mad. de Grignan's hair, you can tell us whether la belle chevelure, of which Mad. de Sevigné talked so much, was any thing to be compared to my Belinda's." As she spoke, Lady Delacour, before Belinda was aware of her intentions, dexterously let down her beautiful tresses; and the Countess de Pomenars was so much struck at the sight, that she was incapable of paying the necessary compliments. "Nay, touch it," said Lady Delacour—"it is so fine and so soft."

At this dangerous moment her ladyship artfully let drop the comb. Clarence Hervey suddenly stooped to pick it up, totally forgetting his hoop and his character. He threw down the music-stand with his hoop. Lady Delacour exclaimed "Bravissima!" and burst out a-laughing. Lady Boucher, in amazement, looked from one to another for an explanation, and was a considerable time before, as she said, she could believe her own eyes. Clarence Hervey acknowledged he had lost his bet, joined in the laugh, and declared that fifty guineas was too little to pay for the sight of the finest hair that he had ever beheld. "I declare he deserves a lock of la belle chevelure for that speech, Miss Portman," cried Lady Delacour; "I'll appeal to all the world—Mad. de Pomenars must have a lock to measure with Mad. de Grignan's? Come, a second rape of the lock, Belinda."

Fortunately for Belinda, "the glittering forfex" was not immediately produced, as fine ladies do not now, as in former times, carry any such useless implements about with them.

Such was the modest, graceful dignity of Miss Portman's manners, that she escaped without even the charge of prudery. She retired to her own apartment as soon as she could.

"She passes on in unblenched majesty," said Lady Delacour.

"She is really a charming woman," said Clarence Hervey, in a low voice, to Lady Delacour, drawing her into a recessed window: he in the same low voice continued, "Could I obtain a private audience of a few minutes when your ladyship is at leisure?—I have—" "I am never at leisure," interrupted Lady Delacour; "but if you have any thing particular to say to me—as I guess you have, by my skill in human nature—come here to my concert to-night, before the rest of the world. Wait patiently in the music-room, and perhaps I may grant you a private audience, as you had the grace not to call it a tête-à-tête. In the mean time, my dear Countess de Pomenars, had we not better take off our hoops?" In the evening, Clarence

Hervey was in the music-room a considerable time before Lady Delacour appeared: how patiently he waited is not known to any one but himself.

"Have not I given you time to compose a charming speech?" said Lady Delacour as she entered the room; "but make it as short as you can, unless you wish that Miss Portman should hear it, for she will be down stairs in three minutes."

"In one word, then, my dear Lady Delacour, can you, and will you, make my peace with Miss Portman?— I am much concerned about that foolish razor-strop dialogue which she overheard at Lady Singleton's."

"You are concerned that she overheard it, no doubt."

"No," said Clarence Hervey, "I am rejoiced that she overheard it, since it has been the means of convincing me of my mistake; but I am concerned that I had the presumption and injustice to judge of Miss Portman so hastily. I am convinced that, though she is a niece of Mrs. Stanhope's, she has dignity of mind and simplicity of character. Will you, my dear Lady Delacour, tell her so?"

"Stay," interrupted Lady Delacour; "let me get it by heart. I should have made a terrible bad messenger of the gods and goddesses, for I never in my life could, like Iris, repeat a message in the same words in which it was delivered to me. Let me see—'Dignity of mind and simplicity of character,' was not it? May not I say at once, 'My dear Belinda, Clarence Hervey desires me to tell you that he is convinced you are an angel?' That single word angel is so expressive, so comprehensive, so comprehensible, it contains, believe me, all that can be said or imagined on these occasions, de part et d'autre."

"But," said Mr. Hervey, "perhaps Miss Portman has heard the song of—

'What know we of angels?—' I spake it in jest.'"

"Then you are not in jest, but in downright sober earnest?—Ha!" said Lady Delacour, with an arch look, "I did not know it was already come to this with you."

And her ladyship, turning to her piano-forte, played—

"There was a young man in Ballinacrasy,
Who wanted a wife to make him unasy,
And thus in gentle strains he spoke her,
Arrah, will you marry me, my dear Ally Croker?"

"No, no," exclaimed Clarence, laughing, "it is not come to that with me yet, Lady Delacour, I promise you; but is not it possible to say that a young lady has dignity of mind and simplicity of character without having or suggesting any thoughts of marriage?"

"You make a most proper, but not sufficiently emphatic difference between having or suggesting such thoughts," said Lady Delacour. "A gentleman sometimes finds it for his interest, his honour, or his pleasure, to suggest what he would not for the world promise,—I mean perform."

"A scoundrel," cried Clarence Hervey, "not a gentleman, may find it for his honour, or his interest, or his pleasure, to promise what he would not perform; but I am not a scoundrel. I never made any promise to man or woman that I did not keep faithfully. I am not a swindler in love."

"And yet," said Lady Delacour, "you would have no scruple to trifle or flatter a woman out of her heart."

"Cela est selon!" said Clarence smiling; "a fair exchange, you know, is no robbery. When a fine woman robs me of my heart, surely Lady Delacour could not expect that I should make no attempt upon hers."—"Is this part of my message to Miss Portman?" said Lady Delacour. "As your ladyship pleases," said Clarence; "I trust entirely to your discretion."

"Why I really have a great deal of discretion," said Lady Delacour; "but you trust too much to it when you expect that I should execute, both with propriety and success, the delicate commission of telling a young lady, who is under my protection, that a young gentleman, who is a professed admirer of mine, is in love with her, but has no thoughts, and wishes to suggest no thoughts, of marriage."

"In love!" exclaimed Clarence Hervey; "but when did I ever use the expression? In speaking of Miss Portman, I simply expressed esteem and ad—"

"No additions," said Lady Delacour; "content yourself with esteem—simply,—and Miss Portman is safe, and you too, I presume. Apropos; pray, Clarence, how do your esteem and admiration (I may go as far as that, may not I?) of Miss Portman agree with your admiration of Lady Delacour?"

"Perfectly well," replied Clarence; "for all the world must be sensible that Clarence Hervey is a man of too much taste to compare a country novice in wit and accomplishments to Lady Delacour. He might, as men of genius sometimes do, look forward to the idea of forming a country novice for a wife. A man must marry some time or other—but my hour, thank Heaven, is not come yet."

"Thank Heaven!" said Lady Delacour; "for you know a married man is lost to the world of fashion and gallantry."

"Not more so, I should hope, than a married woman," said Clarence Harvey. Here a loud knocking at the door announced the arrival of company to the concert. "You will make my peace, you promise me, with Miss Portman," cried Clarence eagerly.

"Yes, I will make your peace, and you shall see Belinda smile upon you once more, upon condition," continued Lady Delacour, speaking very quickly, as if she was hurried by the sound of people coming up stairs—"but we'll talk of that another time."

"Nay, nay, my dear Lady Delacour, now, now," said Clarence, seizing her hand.—"Upon condition! upon what condition?"

"Upon condition that you do a little job for me—indeed for Belinda. She is to go with me to the birthnight, and she has often hinted to me that our horses are shockingly shabby for people of our condition. I know she wishes that upon such an occasion—her first appearance at court, you know—we should go in style. Now my dear positive lord has said he will not let us have a pair of the handsomest horses I ever saw, which are at Tattersal's, and on which Belinda, I know, has secretly set her heart, as I have openly, in vain."

"Your ladyship and Miss Portman cannot possibly set your hearts on any thing in vain—especially on any thing that it is in the power of Clarence Hervey to procure. Then," added he, gallantly kissing her hand, "may I thus seal my treaty of peace?"

"What audacity!—don't you see these people coming in?" cried Lady Delacour; and she withdrew her hand, but with no great precipitation. She was evidently, "at this moment, as in all the past," neither afraid nor ashamed that Mr. Hervey's devotions to her should be paid in public. With much address she had satisfied herself as to his views with respect to Belinda. She was convinced that he had no immediate thoughts of matrimony; but that if he were condemned to marry, Miss Portman would be his wife. As this did not interfere with her plans, Lady Delacour was content.

CHAPTER VI — WAYS AND MEANS

When Lady Delacour repeated to Miss Portman the message about "simplicity of mind and dignity of character," she frankly said—

"Belinda, notwithstanding all this, observe, I'm determined to retain Clarence Hervey among the number of my public worshippers during my life—which you know cannot last long. After I am gone, my dear, he'll be all your own, and of that I give you joy. Posthumous fame is a silly thing, but posthumous jealousy detestable."

There was one part of the conversation between Mr. Hervey and her ladyship which she, in her great discretion, did not immediately repeat to Miss Portman—that part which related to the horses. In this transaction Belinda had no farther share than having once, when her ladyship had the handsome horses brought for her to look at, assented to the opinion that they were the handsomest horses she ever beheld. Mr. Hervey, however gallantly he replied to her ladyship, was secretly vexed to find that Belinda had so little delicacy as to permit her name to be employed in such a manner. He repented having used the improper expression of dignity of mind, and he relapsed into his former opinion of Mrs. Stanhope's niece. A relapse is always more dangerous than the first disease. He sent home the horses to Lady Delacour the next day, and addressed Belinda, when he met her, with the air of a man of gallantry, who thought that his peace had been cheaply made. But in proportion as his manners became more familiar, hers grew more reserved. Lady Delacour rallied her upon her prudery, but in vain. Clarence Hervey seemed to think that her ladyship had not fulfilled her part of the bargain.—"Is not smiling," said he, "the epithet always applied to peace? yet I have not been able to obtain one smile from Miss Portman since I have been promised peace." Embarrassed by Mr. Hervey's reproaches, and provoked to find that Belinda was proof against all her raillery, Lady Delacour grew quite ill-humoured towards her. Belinda, unconscious of having given any just cause of offence, was unmoved; and her ladyship's embarrassment increased. At last, resuming all her former appearance of friendship and confidence, she suddenly exclaimed one night after she had flattered Belinda into high spirits—

"Do you know, my dear, that I have been so ashamed of myself for this week past, that I have hardly dared to look you in the face. I am sensible I was downright rude and cross to you one day, and ever since I have been penitent; and, as all penitents are, very stupid and disagreeable, I am sure: but tell me you forgive my caprice, and Lady Delacour will be herself again."

It was not difficult to obtain Belinda's forgiveness.

"Indeed," continued Lady Delacour, "you are too good; but then in my own justification I must say, that I have more things to make me ill-humoured than most people have. Now, my dear, that most obstinate of human beings, Lord Delacour, has reduced me to the most terrible situation—I have made Clarence Hervey buy a pair of horses for me, and I cannot make my Lord Delacour pay for them; but I forgot to tell you that I took your name—not in vain indeed—in this business. I told Clarence, that upon condition he would do this job for me, you would forgive him for all his sins, and—nay, my dear, why do you look as if I had stabbed you to the heart?—after all, I only drew upon your pretty mouth for a few smiles. Pray let me see whether it has actually forgotten how to smile."

Belinda was too much vexed at this instant to understand raillery. She was inspired by anger with unwonted courage, and, losing all fear of Lady Delacour's wit, she very seriously expostulated with her ladyship upon having thus used her name without her consent or knowledge. Belinda felt she was now in danger of being led into a situation which might be fatal to her reputation and her happiness; and she was the more surprised at her ladyship, when she recollected the history she had so lately heard of Harriot Freke and Colonel Lawless.

"You cannot but be sensible, Lady Delacour," said Belinda, "that after the contempt I have heard Mr. Hervey express for match-making with Mrs. Stanhope's nieces, I should degrade myself by any attempts to attract his attention. No wit, no eloquence, can change my opinion upon this subject—I cannot endure contempt."

"Very likely—no doubt"—interrupted Lady Delacour; "but if you would only open your eyes, which heroines make it a principle never to do—or else there would be an end of the novel—if you would only open your eyes, you would see that this man is in love with you; and whilst you are afraid of his contempt, he is a hundred times more afraid of yours; and as long as you are each of you in such fear of you know not what, you must excuse me if I indulge myself in a little wholesome raillery."—Belinda smiled.—"There now; one such smile as that for Clarence Hervey, and I'm out of debt and danger," said Lady Delacour.

"O Lady Delacour, why, why will you try your power over me in this manner?" said Belinda. "You know that I ought not to be persuaded to do what I am conscious is wrong. But a few days ago you told me yourself that Mr. Hervey is—is not a marrying man; and a woman of your penetration must see that—that he only means to flirt with me. I am not a match for Mr. Hervey in any respect. He is a man of wit and gallantry—I am unpractised in the ways of the world. I was not educated by my aunt Stanhope—I have only been with her a few years—I wish I had never been with her in my life."

"I'll take care Mr. Hervey shall know that," said Lady Delacour; "but in the mean time I do think any fair appraiser of delicate distresses would decide that I am, all the circumstances considered, more to be pitied at this present moment than you are: for the catastrophe of the business evidently is, that I must pay two hundred guineas for the horses somehow or other."

"I can pay for them," exclaimed Belinda, "and will with the greatest pleasure. I will not go to the birthnight—my dress is not bespoke. Will two hundred guineas pay for the horses? Oh, take the money—pay Mr. Hervey, dear Lady Delacour, and it will all be right."

"You are a charming girl," said Lady Delacour, embracing her; "but how can I answer for it to my conscience, or to your aunt Stanhope, if you don't appear on the birthnight? That cannot be, my dear; besides, you know Mrs. Franks will send home your drawing-room dress to-day, and it would be so foolish to be presented for nothing—not to go to the birthnight afterwards. If you say a you must say b."

"Then," said Belinda, "I will not go to the drawing-room."—"Not go, my dear! What! throw away fifty guineas for nothing! Really I never saw any one so lavish of her money, and so economic of her smiles."

"Surely," said Miss Portman, "it is better for me to throw away fifty guineas, poor as I am, than to hazard the happiness of my life. Your ladyship knows that if I say a to Mr. Hervey, I must say b. No, no, my dear Lady Delacour; here is the draught for two hundred guineas: pay Mr. Hervey, for Heaven's sake, and there is an end of the business."

"What a positive child it is! Well, then, it shall not be forced to say the a, b, c, of Cupid's alphabet, to that terrible pedagogue, Clarence Hervey, till it pleases: but seriously, Miss Portman, I am concerned that you will make me take this draught: it is absolutely robbing you. But Lord Delacour's the person you must blame—it is all his obstinacy: having once said he would not pay for the horses, he would see them and me and the whole human race expire before he would change his silly mind.—Next month I shall have it in my power, my dear, to repay you with a thousand thanks; and in a few months more we shall have another birthday, and a new star shall appear in the firmament of fashion, and it shall be called Belinda. In the mean time, my dear, upon second thoughts, perhaps we can get Mrs. Franks to dispose of your drawing-room dress to some person of taste, and you may keep your fifty guineas for the next occasion. I'll see what can be done.—Adieu! a thousand thanks, silly child as you are."

Mrs. Franks at first declared that it would be an impossibility to dispose of Miss Portman's dress, though she would do any thing upon earth to oblige Lady Delacour; however, ten guineas made every thing possible. Belinda rejoiced at having, as she thought, extricated herself at so cheap a rate; and well pleased with her own conduct, she wrote to her aunt Stanhope, to inform her of as much of the transaction as she could disclose, without betraying Lady Delacour. "Her ladyship," she said, "had immediate occasion for two hundred guineas, and to accommodate her with this sum she had given up the idea of going to court."

The tenor of Miss Portman's letter will be sufficiently apparent from Mrs. Stanhope's answer.

MRS. STANHOPE TO MISS PORTMAN.

"Bath, June 2nd.

"I cannot but feel some astonishment, Belinda, at your very extraordinary conduct, and more extraordinary letter. What you can mean by principles and delicacy I own I don't pretend to understand, when I see you not only forget the respect that is due to the opinions and advice of the aunt to whom you owe every thing; but you take upon yourself to lavish her money, without common honesty. I send you two hundred guineas, and desire you to go to court—you lend my two hundred guineas to Lady Delacour, and inform me that as you think yourself bound in honour to her ladyship, you cannot explain all the particulars to me, otherwise you are sure I should approve of the reasons which have influenced you. Mighty satisfactory, truly! And then, to mend the matter, you tell me that you do not think that in your situation in life it is necessary that you should go to court. Your opinions and mine, you add, differ in many points. Then I must say that you are as ungrateful as you are presumptuous; for I am not such a novice in the affairs of the world as to be ignorant that when a young lady professes to be of a different opinion from her friends, it is only a prelude to something worse. She begins by saying that she is determined to think for herself, and she is determined to act for herself—and then it is all over with her: and all the money, &c. that has been spent upon her education is so much dead loss to her friends.

"Now I look upon it that a young girl who has been brought up, and brought forward in the world as you have been by connexions, is bound to be guided implicitly by them in all her conduct. What should you think of a man who, after he had been brought into parliament by a friend, would go and vote against that friend's opinions? You do not want sense, Belinda—you perfectly understand me; and consequently your errors I must impute to the defect of your heart, and not of your judgment. I see that, on account of the illness of the princess, the king's birthday is put off for a fortnight. If you manage properly, and if (unknown to Lady —, who certainly has not used you well in this business, and to whom therefore you owe no peculiar delicacy) you make Lord — sensible how much your aunt Stanhope is disappointed and displeased (as I most truly am) at your intention of missing this opportunity of appearing at court; it is ten to one but his lordship—who has not made it a point to refuse your request, I suppose—will pay you your two hundred guineas. You of course will make proper acknowledgments; but at the same time entreat that his lordship will not commit you with his lady, as she might be offended at your application to him. I understand from an intimate acquaintance of his, that you are a great favourite of his lordship; and though an obstinate, he is a good-natured man, and can have no fear of being governed by you; consequently he will do just as you would have him.

"Then you have an opportunity of representing the thing in the prettiest manner imaginable to Lady —, as an instance of her lord's consideration for her: so you will oblige all parties (a very desirable thing) without costing yourself one penny, and go to the birthnight after all: and this only by using a little address, without which nothing is to be done in this world.

"Yours affectionately (if you follow my advice),

"SELINA STANHOPE."

Belinda, though she could not, consistently with what she thought right, follow the advice so artfully given to her in this epistle, was yet extremely concerned to find that she had incurred the displeasure of an aunt to whom she thought herself under obligations. She resolved to lay by as much as she possibly could, from the interest of her fortune, and to repay the two hundred guineas to Mrs. Stanhope. She was conscious that she had no right to lend this money to Lady Delacour, if her aunt had expressly desired that she should spend it only on her court-dress; but this had not distinctly been expressed when Mrs. Stanhope sent her niece the draft. That lady was in the habit of speaking and writing ambiguously, so that even those who knew her best were frequently in doubt how to interpret her words. Yet she was extremely displeased when her hints and her half-expressed wishes were not understood. Beside the concern she felt from the thoughts of having displeased her aunt, Belinda was both vexed and mortified to perceive that in Clarence Hervey's manner towards her there was not the change which she had expected that her conduct would naturally produce.

One day she was surprised at his reproaching her for caprice in having given up her intentions of going to court. Lady Delacour's embarrassment whilst Mr. Hervey spoke, Belinda attributed to her ladyship's desire that Clarence should not know that she had been obliged to borrow the money to pay him for the horses. Belinda thought that this was a species of mean pride; but she made it a point to keep her ladyship's secret—she therefore slightly answered Mr. Hervey, "that she wondered that a man who was so well acquainted with the female sex should be surprised at any instance of caprice from a woman." The conversation then took another turn, and whilst they were talking of indifferent subjects, in came Lord Delacour's man, Champfort, with Mrs. Stanhope's draft for two hundred guineas, which the coachmaker's man had just brought back because Miss Portman had forgotten to endorse it. Belinda's astonishment was almost as great at this instant as Lady Delacour's confusion.

"Come this way, my dear, and we'll find you a pen and ink. You need not wait, Champfort; but tell the man to wait for the draft—Miss Portman will endorse it immediately."—And she took Belinda into another room.

"Good Heavens! Has not this money been paid to Mr. Hervey?" exclaimed Belinda.

"No, my dear; but I will take all the blame upon myself, or, which will do just as well for you, throw it all upon my better half. My Lord Delacour would not pay for my new carriage. The coachmaker, insolent animal, would not let it out of his yard without two hundred guineas in ready money. Now you know I had the horses, and what could I do with the horses without the carriage? Clarence Hervey, I knew, could wait for his money better than a poor devil of a coachmaker; so I paid the coachmaker, and a few months sooner or later can make no difference to Clarence, who rolls in gold, my dear—if that will be any comfort to you, as I hope it will."

"Oh, what will he think of me!" said Belinda.

"Nay, what will he think of me, child!"

"Lady Delacour," said Belinda, in a firmer tone than she had ever before spoken, "I must insist upon this draft being given to Mr. Hervey."

"Absolutely impossible, my dear.—I cannot take it from the coachmaker; he has sent home the carriage: the thing's done, and cannot be undone. But come, since I know nothing else will make you easy, I will take this mighty favour from Mr. Hervey entirely upon my own conscience: you cannot object to that, for you are not the keeper of my conscience. I will tell Clarence the whole business, and do you honour due, my dear: so endorse the check, whilst I go and sound both the praises of your dignity of mind, and simplicity of character, &c. &c. &c. &c."

Her ladyship broke away from Belinda, returned to Clarence Hervey, and told the whole affair with that peculiar grace with which she knew how to make a good story of a bad one. Clarence was as favourable an auditor at this time as she could possibly have found; for no human being could value money less than he did, and all sense of her ladyship's meanness was lost in his joy at discovering that Belinda was worthy of his esteem. Now he felt in its fullest extent all the power she had over his heart, and he was upon the point of declaring his attachment to her, when malheureusement Sir Philip Baddely and Mr. Rochfort announced themselves by the noise they made on the staircase. These were the young men who had spoken in such a contemptuous manner at Lady Singleton's of the match-making Mrs. Stanhope and her nieces. Mr. Hervey was anxious that they should not penetrate into the state of his heart, and he concealed his emotion by instantly assuming that kind of rattling gaiety which always delighted his companions, who were ever in want of some one to set their stagnant ideas in motion. At last they insisted upon carrying Clarence away with them to taste some wines for Sir Philip Baddely.

In his way to St. James's street, where the wine-merchant lived, Sir Philip Baddely picked up several young men of his acquaintance, who were all eager to witness a trial of taste, of epicurean taste, between the baronet and Clarence Hervey. Amongst his other accomplishments our hero piqued himself upon the exquisite accuracy of his organs of taste. He neither loved wine, nor was he fond of eating; but at fine dinners, with young men who were real epicures, Hervey gave himself the airs of a connoisseur, and asserted superiority even in judging of wine and sauces. Having gained immortal honour at an entertainment by gravely protesting that some turtle would have been excellent if it had not been done a bubble too much, he presumed, elate as he was with the applauses of the company, to assert, that no man in England had a more correct taste than himself.—Sir Philip Baddely could not passively submit to this arrogance; he loudly proclaimed, that though he would not dispute Mr. Hervey's judgment as far as eating was concerned, yet he would defy him as a connoisseur in wines, and he offered to submit the competition to any eminent wine-merchant in London, and to some common friend of acknowledged taste and experience.—Mr. Rochfort was chosen as the common friend of acknowledged taste and experience; and a fashionable wine-merchant was pitched upon to decide with him the merits of these candidates for bacchanalian fame. Sir Philip, who was just going to furnish his cellars, was a person of importance to the wine-merchant, who produced accordingly his choicest treasures. Sir Philip and Clarence tasted of all in their turns; Sir Philip with real, and Clarence with affected gravity; and they delivered their opinions of the positive and comparative merits of each. The wine-merchant evidently, as Mr. Hervey thought, leaned towards Sir Philip. "Upon my word, Sir Philip, you are right—that wine is the best I have—you certainly have a most discriminating taste," said the complaisant wine-merchant.

"I'll tell you what," cried Sir Philip, "the thing is this: by Jove! now, there's no possibility now—no possibility now, by Jove! of imposing upon me."

"Then," said Clarence Hervey, "would you engage to tell the differences between these two wines ten times running, blind-fold?"

"Ten times! that's nothing," replied Sir Philip: "yes, fifty times, I would, by Jove!"

But when it came to the trial, Sir Philip had nothing left but oaths in his own favour. Clarence Hervey was victorious; and his sense of the importance of this victory was much increased by the fumes of the wine, which began to operate upon his brain. His triumph was, as he said it ought to be, bacchanalian: he laughed and sang with anacreontic spirit, and finished by declaring that he deserved to be crowned with vine-leaves.

"Dine with me, Clarence," said Rochfort, "and we'll crown you with three times three; and," whispered he to Sir Philip, "we'll have another trial after dinner."

"But as it's not near dinner-time yet—what shall we do with ourselves till dinner-time?" said Sir Philip, yawning pathetically.

Clarence not being used to drink in a morning, though all his companions were, was much affected by the wine, and Rochfort proposed that they should take a turn in the park to cool Hervey's head. To Hyde-park they repaired; Sir Philip boasting, all the way they walked, of the superior strength of his head.

Clarence protested that his own was stronger than any man's in England, and observed, that at this instant he walked better than any person in company, Sir Philip Baddely not excepted. Now Sir Philip Baddely was a noted pedestrian, and he immediately challenged our hero to walk with him for any money he pleased. "Done," said Clarence, "for ten guineas—for any money you please:" and instantly they set out to walk, as Rochfort cried "one, two, three, and away; keep the path, and whichever reaches that elm tree first has it."

They were exactly even for some yards, then Clarence got ahead of Sir Philip, and he reached the elm tree first; but as he waved his hat, exclaiming, "Clarence has won the day," Sir Philip came up with his companions, and coolly informed him that he had lost his wager—"Lost! lost! lost! Clarence—fairly lost."

"Didn't I reach the tree first?" said Clarence.

"Yes," answered his companions; "but you didn't keep the path. You turned out of the way when you met that crowd of children yonder."

"Now I," said Sir Philip, "dashed fairly through them—kept the path, and won my bet."

"But," said Hervey, "would you have had me run over that little child, who was stooping down just in my way?"

"I!' not I," said Sir Philip; "but I would have you go through with your civility: if a man will be polite, he must pay for his politeness sometimes.—You said you'd lay me any money I pleased, recollect—now I'm very moderate—and as you are a particular friend, Clarence, I'll only take your ten guineas."

A loud laugh from his companions provoked Clarence; they were glad "to have a laugh against him," because he excited universal envy by the real superiority of his talents, and by his perpetually taking the lead in those trifles which were beneath his ambition, and exactly suited to engage the attention of his associates.

"Be it so, and welcome; I'll pay ten guineas for having better manners than any of you," cried Hervey, laughing; "but remember, though I've lost this bet, I don't give up my pedestrian fame.—Sir Philip, there are no women to throw golden apples in my way now, and no children for me to stumble over: I dare you to another trial—double or quit."

"I'm off, by Jove!" said Sir Philip. "I'm too hot, damme, to walk with you any more—but I'm your man if you've a mind for a swim—here's the Serpentine river, Clarence—hey? damn it!—hey?"

Sir Philip and all his companions knew that Clarence had never learned to swim.

"You may wink at one another, as wisely as you please," said Clarence, "but come on, my boys—I am your man for a swim—hundred guineas upon it!

—'Darest thou, Rochfort, now
Leap in with me into this weedy flood,
And swim to yonder point?'"

and instantly Hervey, who had in his confused head some recollection of an essay of Dr. Franklin on swimming, by which he fancied that he could ensure at once his safety and his fame, threw off his coat and jumped into the river—luckily he was not in boots. Rochfort, and all the other young men stood laughing by the river side.

"Who the devil are these two that seem to be making up to us?" said Sir Philip, looking at two gentlemen who were coming towards them; "St. George, hey? you know every body."

"The foremost is Percival, of Oakly-park, I think, 'pon my honour," replied Mr. St. George, and he then began to settle how many thousands a year Mr. Percival was worth. This point was not decided when the gentlemen came up to the spot where Sir Philip was standing.

The child for whose sake Clarence Hervey had lost his bet was Mr. Percival's, and he came to thank him for his civility.—The gentleman who accompanied Mr. Percival was an old friend of Clarence Hervey's; he had met him abroad, but had not seen him for some years.

"Pray, gentlemen," said he to Sir Philip and his party, "is Mr. Clarence Hervey amongst you? I think I saw him pass by me just now."

"Damn it, yes—where is Clary, though?" exclaimed Sir Philip, suddenly recollecting himself.—Clarence Hervey at this instant was drowning: he had got out of his depth, and had struggled in vain to recover himself.

"Curse me, if it's not all over with Clary," continued Sir Philip. "Do any of you see his head any where? Damn you, Rochfort, yonder it is."

"Damme, so it is," said Rochfort; "but he's so heavy in his clothes, he'd pull me down along with him to Davy's locker:—damme, if I'll go after him."

"Damn it, though, can't some of ye swim? Can't some of ye jump in?" cried Sir Philip, turning to his companions: "damn it, Clarence will go to the bottom."

And so he inevitably would have done, had not Mr. Percival at this instant leaped into the river, and seized hold of the drowning Clarence. It was with great difficulty that he dragged him to the shore.—Sir Philip's party, as soon as the danger was over, officiously offered their assistance. Clarence Hervey was absolutely senseless. "Damn it, what shall we do with him now?" said Sir Philip: "Damn it, we must call some of the people from the boat-house—he's as heavy as lead: damn me, if I know what to do with him."

Whilst Sir Philip was damning himself, Mr. Percival ran to the boat-house for assistance, and they carried the body into the house. The elderly gentleman who had accompanied Mr. Percival now made his way through the midst of the noisy crowd, and directed what should be done to restore Mr. Hervey's suspended animation. Whilst he was employed in this benevolent manner, Clarence's worthy friends were sneering at him, and whispering to one another; "Ecod, he talks as if he was a doctor," said Rochfort.

"'Pon honour, I do believe," said St. George, "he is the famous Dr. X—; I met him at a circulating library t'other day."

"Dr. X— the writer, do you mean?" said Sir Philip; "then, damn me, we'd better get out of his way as fast as we can, or he'll have some of us down in black and white; and curse me, if I should choose to meet with myself in a book."

"No danger of that," said Rochfort; "for how can one meet with oneself in a book, Sir Philip, if one never opens one?—By Jove, that's the true way."

"But, 'pon my honour," said St. George, "I should like of all things to see myself in print; 'twould make one famously famous."

"Damn me, if I don't flatter myself, though, one can make oneself famous enough to all intents and purposes without having any thing to say to these author geniuses. You're a famous fellow, faith! to want to see yourself in print—I'll publish this in Bond-street: damn it, in point of famousness, I'd sport my Random against all the books that ever were read or written, damn me! But what are we doing here?"

"Hervey's in good hands," said Rochfort, "and this here's a cursed stupid lounge for us—besides, it's getting towards dinner-time; so my voice is, let's be off, and we can leave St. George (who has such a famous mind to be in the doctor's book) to bring Clary after us, when he's ready for dinner and good company again, you know—ha! ha! ha!"

Away the faithful friends went to the important business of their day.

When Clarence Hervey came to his senses he started up, rubbed his eyes, and looked about, exclaiming—"What's all this?—Where am I?—Where's Baddely?—Where's Rochfort?—Where are they all?"

"Gone home to dinner," answered Mr. St. George, who was a hanger-on of Sir Philip's; "but they left me to bring you after them. Faith, Clary, you've had a squeak for your life! 'Pon my honour, we thought at one time it was all over with you—but you're a rough one: we shan't have to 'pour over your grave a full bottle of red' as yet, my boy—you'll do as well as ever. So I'll step and call a coach for you, Clary, and we shall be at dinner as soon as the best of 'em after all, by jingo! I leave you in good hands with the doctor here, that brought you to life, and the gentleman that dragged you out of the water. Here's a note for you," whispered Mr. St. George, as he leaned over Clarence Hervey—"here's a note for you from Sir Philip and Rochfort: read it, do you mind, to yourself."

"If I can," said Clarence; "but Sir Philip writes a bloody bad hand."

"Oh, he's a baronet," said St. George, "ha! ha! ha!" and, charmed with his own wit, he left the boat-house.

Clarence with some difficulty deciphered the note, which contained these words:

"Quiz the doctor, Clary, as soon as you are up to it—he's an author—so fair game—quiz the doctor, and we'll drink your health with three times three in Rochfort's burgundy.

"Yours, &c.

"PHIL. BADDELY.

"P.S. Burn this when read."

With the request contained in the postscript Clarence immediately complied; he threw the note into the fire with indignation the moment that he had read it, and turning towards the gentleman to whom it alluded, he began to express, in the strongest terms, his gratitude for their benevolence. But he stopped short in the midst of his acknowledgments, when he discovered to whom he was speaking.

"Dr. X—!" cried he. "Is it possible? How rejoiced I am to see you, and how rejoiced I am to be obliged to you! There is not a man in England to whom I would rather be obliged."

"You are not acquainted with Mr. Percival, I believe," said Dr. X—: "give me leave, Mr. Percival, to introduce to you the young gentleman whose life you have saved, and whose life—though, by the company in which you found him, you might not think so—is worth saving. This, sir, is no less a man than Mr. Clarence Hervey, of whose universal genius you have just had a specimen; for which he was crowned with sedges, as he well deserved, by the god of the Serpentine river. Do not be so unjust as to imagine that he has any of the presumption which is sometimes the chief characteristic of a man of universal genius. Mr. Clarence Hervey is, without exception, the most humble man of my acquaintance; for whilst all good judges would think him fit company for Mr. Percival, he has the humility to think himself upon a level with Mr. Rochfort and Sir Philip Baddely."

"You have lost as little of your satirical wit, Dr. X—, as of your active benevolence, I perceive," said Clarence Hervey, "since I met you abroad. But as I cannot submit to your unjust charge of humility, will you tell me where you are to be found in town, and to-morrow—"

"To-morrow, and to-morrow, and to-morrow," said Dr. X—: "why not to-day?"

"I am engaged," said Clarence, hesitating and laughing—"I am unfortunately engaged to-day to dine with Mr. Rochfort and Sir Philip Baddely, and in the evening I am to be at Lady Delacour's."

"Lady Delacour! Not the same Lady Delacour whom four years ago, when we met at Florence, you compared to the Venus de Medici—no, no, it cannot be the same—a goddess of four years' standing!—Incredible!"

"Incredible as it seems," said Clarence, "it is true: I admire her ladyship more than ever I did."

"Like a true connoisseur," said Dr. X—, "you admire a fine picture the older it grows: I hear that her ladyship's face is really one of the finest pieces of painting extant, with the advantage of

'Ev'ry grace which time alone can grant.'"

"Come, come, Dr. X—," cried Mr. Percival, "no more wit at Lady Delacour's expense: I have a fellow-feeling for Mr. Hervey."

"Why, you are not in love with her ladyship, are you?" said Dr. X—. "I am not in love with Lady Delacour's picture of herself," replied Mr. Percival, "but I was once in love with the original."

"How?—When?—Where?" cried Clarence Hervey, in a tone totally different from that in which he had first addressed Mr. Percival.

"To-morrow you shall know the how, the when, and the where," said Mr. Percival: "here's your friend, Mr. St. George, and his coach."

"The deuce take him!" said Clarence: "but tell me, is it possible that you are not in love with her still?—and why?"

"Why?" said Mr. Percival—"why? Come to-morrow, as you have promised, to Upper Grosvenor-street, and let me introduce you to Lady Anne Percival; she can answer your question better than I can—if not entirely to your satisfaction, at least entirely to mine, which is more surprising, as the lady is my wife."

By this time Clarence Hervey was equipped in a dry suit of clothes; and by the strength of an excellent constitution, which he had never injured, even amongst his dissipated associates, he had recovered from the effects of his late imprudence.—"Clary, let's away, here's the coach," said Mr. St. George. "Why, my boy—that's a famous fellow, faith!—why, you look the better for being drowned. 'Pon honour, if I were you, I would jump into the Serpentine river once a day."

"If I could always be sure of such good friends to pull me out," said Hervey.—"Pray, St. George, by-the-bye, what were you, and Rochfort, and Sir Philip, and all the rest of my friends doing, whilst I was drowning?"

"I can't say particularly, upon my soul," replied Mr. St. George; "for my own part, I was in boots, so you know I was out of the question. But what signifies all that now? Come, come, we had best think of looking after our dinners."

Clarence Hervey, who had very quick feelings, was extremely hurt by the indifference which his dear friends had shown when his life was in danger: he was apt to believe that he was really an object of affection and admiration amongst his companions; and that though they were neither very wise, nor very witty, they were certainly very good-natured. When they had forfeited, by their late conduct, these claims to his regard, his partiality for them was changed into contempt.

"You had better come home and dine with me, Mr. Hervey," said Mr. Percival, "if you be not absolutely engaged; for here is your physician, who tells me that temperance is necessary for a man just recovered from drowning, and Mr. Rochfort keeps too good a table, I am told, for one in your condition."

Clarence accepted of this invitation with a degree of pleasure which perfectly astonished Mr. St. George.

"Every man knows his own affairs best," said he to Clarence, as he stepped into his hackney coach; "but for my share, I will do my friend Rochfort the justice to say that no one lives as well as he does."

"If to live well mean nothing but to eat," said Clarence.

"Now," said Dr. X—, looking at his watch, "it will be eight o'clock by the time we get to Upper Grosvenor-street, and Lady Anne will probably have waited dinner for us about two hours, which I apprehend is sufficient to try the patience of any woman but Griselda. Do not," continued he, turning to

Clarence Hervey, "expect to see an old-fashioned, spiritless, patient Griselda, in Lady Anne Percival: I can assure you that she is—but I will neither tell you what she is, nor what she is not. Every man who has any abilities, likes to have the pleasure and honour of finding out a character by his own penetration, instead of having it forced upon him at full length in capital letters of gold, finely emblazoned and illuminated by the hand of some injudicious friend: every child thinks the violet of his own finding the sweetest. I spare you any farther allusion and illustrations," concluded Dr. X—, "for here we are, thank God, in Upper Grosvenor-street."

CHAPTER VIII — A FAMILY PARTY

They found Lady Anne Percival in the midst of her children, who all turned their healthy, rosy, intelligent faces towards the door, the moment that they heard their father's voice. Clarence Hervey was so much struck with the expression of happiness in Lady Anne's countenance, that he absolutely forgot to compare her beauty with Lady Delacour's. Whether her eyes were large or small, blue or hazel, he could not tell; nay, he might have been puzzled if he had been asked the colour of her hair. Whether she were handsome by the rules of art, he knew not; but he felt that she had the essential charm of beauty, the power of prepossessing the heart immediately in her favour. The effect of her manners, like that of her beauty, was rather to be felt than described. Every body was at ease in her company, and none thought themselves called upon to admire her. To Clarence Hervey, who had been used to the brilliant and exigeante Lady Delacour, this respite from the fatigue of admiration was peculiarly agreeable. The unconstrained cheerfulness of Lady Anne Percival spoke a mind at ease, and immediately imparted happiness by exacting sympathy; but in Lady Delacour's wit and gaiety there was an appearance of art and effort, which often destroyed the pleasure that she wished to communicate. Mr. Hervey was, perhaps unusually, disposed to reflection, by having just escaped from drowning; for he had made all these comparisons, and came to this conclusion, with the accuracy of a metaphysician, who has been accustomed to study cause and effect—indeed there was no species of knowledge for which he had not taste and talents, though, to please fools, he too often affected "the bliss of ignorance."

The children at Lady Anne Percival's happened to be looking at some gold fish, which were in a glass globe, and Dr. X—, who was a general favourite with the younger as well as with the elder part of the family, was seized upon the moment he entered the room: a pretty little girl of five years old took him prisoner by the flap of the coat, whilst two of her brothers assailed him with questions about the ears, eyes, and fins of fishes. One of the little boys filliped the glass globe, and observed, that the fish immediately came to the surface of the water, and seemed to hear the noise very quickly; but his brother doubted whether the fish heard the noise, and remarked, that they might be disturbed by seeing or feeling the motion of the water, when the glass was struck.

Dr. X— observed, that this was a very learned dispute, and that the question had been discussed by no less a person than the Abbé Nollet; and he related some of the ingenious experiments tried by that gentleman, to decide whether fishes can or cannot hear. Whilst the doctor was speaking, Clarence Hervey was struck with the intelligent countenance of one of the little auditors, a girl of about ten or twelve years old; he was surprised to discover in her features, though not in their expression, a singular resemblance to Lady Delacour. He remarked this to Mr. Percival, and the child, who overheard him, blushed as red as scarlet. Dinner was announced at this instant, and Clarence Hervey thought no more of the circumstance, attributing the girl's blush to confusion at being looked at so earnestly. One of the little boys whispered as they were going down to dinner, "Helena, I do believe that this is the good-natured gentleman who went out of the path to make room for us, instead of running over us as the other man did." The children agreed that Clarence Hervey certainly was the good-natured gentleman, and upon the strength of this observation, one of the boys posted himself next to Clarence at dinner, and by all the little playful manoeuvres in his power endeavoured to show his gratitude, and to cultivate a friendship which had been thus auspiciously commenced. Mr. Hervey, who piqued himself upon being able always to suit his conversation to his companions, distinguished himself at dinner by an account of the Chinese fishing-bird, from which he passed to the various ingenious methods of fishing practised by the Russian Cossacks. From modern he went to ancient fish, and he talked of that which was so much admired by the Roman epicures for exhibiting a succession of beautiful colours whilst it is dying; and which was, upon that account, always suffered to die in the presence of the guests, as part of the entertainment.—Clarence was led on by the questions of the children from fishes to birds; he spoke of the Roman aviaries, which were so constructed as to keep from the sight of the prisoners that they contained, "the fields, woods, and every object which might remind them of their former liberty."—From birds he was going on to beasts, when he was nearly struck dumb by the forbidding severity with which an elderly lady, who sat opposite to him, fixed her eyes upon him. He had not, till this instant, paid the smallest attention to her; but her stern countenance was now so strongly contrasted with the approving looks of the children who sat next to her, that he could not help remarking it. He asked her to do him the honour to drink a glass of wine with him. She declined doing him that honour; observing that she never drank more than one glass of wine at dinner, and that she had just taken one with Mr. Percival. Her manner was well-bred, but haughty in the extreme; and she was so passionate, that her anger sometimes conquered even her politeness. Her dislike to Clarence Hervey was apparent, even in her silence. "If the old gentlewoman has taken an antipathy to me at first sight, I cannot help it," thought he, and he went on to the beasts. The boy, who sat next him, had asked some questions about the proboscis of the elephant, and Mr. Hervey mentioned Ives's account of the elephants in India, who have been set to watch young children, and who draw them back gently with their trunks, when they go out of bounds. He talked next of the unicorn; and addressing himself to Dr. X— and Mr. Percival, he declared that in his opinion Herodotus did not deserve to be called the father of lies; he cited the mammoth to prove that the apocryphal chapter in the history of beasts should not be contemned—that it would in all probability be soon established as true history. The dessert was on the table before Clarence had done with the mammoth.

As the butler put a fine dish of cherries upon the table, he said,

"My lady, these cherries are a present from the old gardener to Miss Delacour."

"Set them before Miss Delacour then," said Lady Anne. "Helena, my dear, distribute your own cherries."

At the name of Delacour, Clarence Hervey, though his head was still half full of the mammoth, looked round in astonishment; and when he saw the cherries placed before the young lady, whose resemblance to Lady Delacour he had before observed, he could not help exclaiming,

"That young lady then is not a daughter of your ladyship's?"

"No; but I love her as well as if she were," replied Lady Anne.—"What were you saying about the mammoth?"

"That the mammoth is supposed to be—" but interrupting himself, Clarence said in an inquiring tone—"A niece of Lady Delacour's?"

"Her ladyship's daughter, sir," said the severe old lady, in a voice more terrific than her looks.

"Shall I give you some strawberries, Mr. Hervey," said lady Anne, "or will you let Helena help you to some cherries?"

"Her ladyship's daughter!" exclaimed Clarence Hervey in a tone of surprise.

"Some cherries, sir?" said Helena; but her voice faltered so much, that she could hardly utter the words.

Clarence perceived that he had been the cause of her agitation, though he knew not precisely by what means; and he now applied himself in silence to the picking of his strawberries with great diligence.

The ladies soon afterwards withdrew, and as Mr. Percival did not touch upon the subject again, Clarence forbore to ask any further questions, though he was considerably surprised by this sudden discovery. When he went into the drawing-room to tea, he found his friend, the stern old lady, speaking in a high declamatory tone. The words which he heard as he came into the room were—

"If there were no Clarence Herveys, there would be no Lady Delacours."—Clarence bowed as if he had received a high compliment—the old lady walked away to an antechamber, fanning herself with great energy.

"Mrs. Margaret Delacour," said Lady Anne, in a low voice to Hervey, "is an aunt of Lord Delacour's. A woman whose heart is warmer than her temper."

"And that is never cool," said a young lady, who sat next to Lady Anne. "I call Mrs. Margaret Delacour the volcano; I'm sure I am never in her company without dreading an eruption. Every now and then out comes with a tremendous noise, fire, smoke, and rubbish."

"And precious minerals," said Lady Anne, "amongst the rubbish."

"But the best of it is," continued the young lady, "that she is seldom in a passion without making a hundred mistakes, for which she is usually obliged afterwards to ask a thousand pardons."

"By that account," said Lady Anne, "which I believe to be just, her contrition is always ten times as great as her offence."

"Now you talk of contrition, Lady Anne," said Mr. Hervey, "I should think of my own offences: I am very sorry that my indiscreet questions gave Miss Delacour any pain—my head was so full of the mammoth, that I blundered on without seeing what I was about till it was too late."

"Pray, sir," said Mrs. Margaret Delacour, who now returned, and took her seat upon a sofa, with the solemnity of a person who was going to sit in judgment upon a criminal, "pray, sir, may I ask how long you have been acquainted with my Lady Delacour?"

Clarence Hervey took up a book, and with great gravity kissed it, as if he had been upon his oath in a court of justice, and answered,

"To the best of my recollection, madam, it is now four years since I had first the pleasure and honour of seeing Lady Delacour."

"And in that time, intimately as you have had the pleasure of being acquainted with her ladyship, you have never discovered that she had a daughter?"

"Never," said Mr. Hervey.

"There, Lady Anne!—There!" cried Mrs. Delacour, "will you tell me after this, that Lady Delacour is not a monster?"

"Every body says that she's a prodigy," said Lady Anne; "and prodigies and monsters are sometimes thought synonymous terms."

"Such a mother was never heard of," continued Mrs. Delacour, "since the days of Savage and Lady Macclesfield. I am convinced that she hates her daughter. Why she never speaks of her—she never sees her—she never thinks of her!"

"Some mothers speak more than they think of their children, and others think more than they speak of them," said Lady Anne.

"I always thought," said Mr. Hervey, "that Lady Delacour was a woman of great sensibility."

"Sensibility!" exclaimed the indignant old lady, "she has no sensibility, sir—none—none. She who lives in a constant round of dissipation, who performs no one duty, who exists only for herself; how does she show her sensibility?—Has she sensibility for her husband—for her daughter—for any one useful purpose upon earth?—Oh, how I hate the cambric handkerchief sensibility that is brought out only to weep at a tragedy!—Yes; Lady Delacour has sensibility enough, I grant ye, when sensibility is the fashion. I remember well her performing the part of a nurse with vast applause; and I remember, too, the sensibility she showed, when the child that she nursed fell a sacrifice to her dissipation. The second of her children, that she killed—"

"Killed!—Oh! surely, my dear Mrs. Delacour, that is too strong a word," said Lady Anne: "you would not make a Medea of Lady Delacour!"

"It would have been better if I had," cried Mrs. Delacour, "I can understand that there may be such a thing in nature as a jealous wife, but an unfeeling mother I cannot comprehend—that passes my powers of imagination."

"And mine, so much," said Lady Anne, "that I cannot believe such a being to exist in the world—notwithstanding all the descriptions I have heard of it: as you say, my dear Mrs. Delacour, it passes my powers of imagination. Let us leave it in Mr. Hervey's apocryphal chapter of animals, and he will excuse us if I never admit it into true history, at least without some better evidence than I have yet heard."

"Why, my dear, dear Lady Anne," cried Mrs. Delacour—"I've made this coffee so sweet, there's no drinking it—what evidence would you have?"

"None," said Lady Anne, smiling, "I would have none." "That is to say, you will take none," said Mrs. Delacour: "but can any thing be stronger evidence than her ladyship's conduct to my poor Helen—to your Helen, I should say—for you have educated, you have protected her, you have been a mother to her. I am an infirm, weak, ignorant, passionate old woman—I could not have been what you have been to that child—God bless you!—God will bless you!"

She rose as she spoke, to set down her coffee-cup on the table. Clarence Hervey took it from her with a look which said much, and which she was perfectly capable of understanding.

"Young man," said she, "it is very unfashionable to treat age and infirmity with politeness. I wish that your friend, Lady Delacour, may at my time of life meet with as much respect, as she has met with admiration and gallantry in her youth. Poor woman, her head has absolutely been turned with admiration—and if fame say true, Mr. Hervey has had his share in turning that head by his flattery."

"I am sure her ladyship has turned mine by her charms," said Clarence; "and I certainly am not to be blamed for admiring what all the world admires."

"I wish," said the old lady, "for her own sake, for the sake of her family, and for the sake of her reputation, that my Lady Delacour had fewer admirers, and more friends."

"Women who have met with so many admirers, seldom meet with many friends," said Lady Anne.

"No," said Mrs. Delacour, "for they seldom are wise enough to know their value."

"We learn the value of all things, but especially of friends, by experience," said Lady Anne; "and it is no wonder, therefore, that those who have little experience of the pleasures of friendship should not be wise enough to know their value."

"This is very good-natured sophistry; but Lady Delacour is too vain ever to have a friend," said Mrs. Delacour. "My dear Lady Anne, you don't know her as well as I do—she has more vanity than ever woman had."

"That is certainly saying a great deal," said Lady Anne; "but then we must consider, that Lady Delacour, as an heiress, a beauty, and a wit, has a right to a triple share at least."

"Both her fortune and her beauty are gone; and if she had any wit left, it is time it should teach her how to conduct herself, I think," said Mrs. Delacour: "but I give her up—I give her up."

"Oh, no," said Lady Anne, "you must not give her up yet, I have been informed, and upon the best authority, that Lady Delacour was not always the unfeeling, dissipated fine lady that she now appears to be. This is only one of the transformations of fashion—the period of her enchantment will soon be at an end, and she will return to her natural character. I should not be at all surprised, if Lady Delacour were to appear at once la femme comme il y en a pen."

"Or la bonne mère?" said Mrs. Delacour, sarcastically, "after thus leaving her daughter—"

"Pour bonne bouche," interrupted Lady Anne, "when she is tired of the insipid taste of other pleasures, she will have a higher relish for those of domestic life, which will be new and fresh to her."

"And so you really think, my dear Lady Anne, that my Lady Delacour will end by being a domestic woman. Well," said Mrs. Margaret, after taking two pinches of snuff, "some people believe in the millennium; but I confess I am not one of them—are you, Mr. Hervey?"

"If it were foretold to me by a good angel," said Clarence, smiling, as his eye glanced at Lady Anne; "if it were foretold to me by a good angel, how could I doubt it?"

Here the conversation was interrupted by the entrance of one of Lady Anne's little boys, who came running eagerly up to his mother, to ask whether he might have "the sulphurs to show to Helena Delacour. I want to show her Vertumnus and Pomona, mamma," said he. "Were not the cherries that the old gardener sent very good?"

"What is this about the cherries and the old gardener, Charles?" said the young lady who sat beside Lady Anne: "come here and tell me the whole story."

"I will, but I should tell it you a great deal better another time," said the boy, "because now Helena's waiting for Vertumnus and Pomona."

"Go then to Helena," said Lady Anne, "and I will tell the story for you."

Then turning to the young lady she began—"Once upon a time there lived an old gardener at Kensington; and this old gardener had an aloe, which was older than himself; for it was very near a hundred years of age, and it was just going to blossom, and the old gardener calculated how much he might make by showing his aloe, when it should be in full blow, to the generous public—and he calculated that he might make a 100l.; and with this 100l. he determined to do more than was ever done with a 100l. before: but, unluckily, as he was thus reckoning his blossoms before they were blown, he chanced to meet with a fair damsel, who ruined all his calculations."

"Ay, Mrs. Stanhope's maid, was not it?" interrupted Mrs. Margaret Delacour. "A pretty damsel she was, and almost as good a politician as her mistress. Think of that jilt's tricking this poor old fellow out of his aloe, and—oh, the meanness of Lady Delacour, to accept of that aloe for one of her extravagant entertainments!"

"But I always understood that she paid fifty guineas for it," said Lady Anne.

"Whether she did or not," said Mrs. Delacour, "her ladyship and Mrs. Stanhope between them were the ruin of this poor old man. He was taken in to marry that jade of a waiting-maid; she turned out just as you might expect from a pupil of Mrs. Stanhope's—the match-making Mrs. Stanhope—you know, sir." (Clarence Hervey changed colour.) "She turned out," continued Mrs. Delacour, "every thing that was bad—ruined her husband—ran away from him—and left him a beggar."

"Poor man!" said Clarence Hervey.

"But now," said Lady Anne, "let's come to the best part of the story—mark how good comes out of evil. If this poor man had not lost his aloe and his wife, I probably should never have been acquainted with Mrs. Delacour, or with my little Helena. About the time that the old gardener was left a beggar, as I happened to be walking one fine evening in Sloane-street, I met a procession of school-girls—an old man begged from them in a most moving voice; and as they passed, several of the young ladies threw halfpence to him. One little girl, who observed that the old man could not stoop without great difficulty, stayed behind the rest of her companions, and collected the halfpence which they had thrown to him, and put them into his hat. He began to tell his story over again to her, and she stayed so long listening to it, that her companions had turned the corner of the street, and were out of sight. She looked about in great distress; and I never shall forget the pathetic voice with which she said, 'Oh! what will become of me? every body will be angry with me.' I assured her that nobody should be angry with her, and she gave me her little hand with the utmost innocent confidence. I took her home to her schoolmistress, and I was so pleased with the beginning of this acquaintance, that I was determined to cultivate it. One good acquaintance I have heard always leads to another. Helena introduced me to her aunt Delacour as her best friend. Mrs. Margaret Delacour has had the goodness to let her little niece spend the holidays and all her leisure time with me, so that our acquaintance has grown into friendship. Helena has become quite one of my family."

"And I am sure she has become quite a different creature since she has been so much with you," cried Mrs. Delacour; "her spirits were quite broken by her mother's neglect of her: young as she is, she has a great deal of real sensibility; but as to her mother's sensibility—"

At the recollection of Lady Delacour's neglect of her child, Mrs. Delacour was going again to launch forth into indignant invective, but Lady Anne stopped her, by whispering—

"Take care what you say of the mother, for here is the daughter coming, and she has, indeed, a great deal of real sensibility."

Helena and her young companions now came into the room, bringing with them the sulphurs at which they had been looking.

"Mamma," said little Charles Percival, "we have brought the sulphurs to you, because there are some of them that I don't know."

"Wonderful!" said Lady Anne; "and what is not quite so wonderful, there are some of them that I don't know."

The children spread the sulphurs upon a little table, and all the company gathered round it.

"Here are all the nine muses for you," said the least of the boys, who had taken his seat by Clarence Hervey at dinner; "here are all the muses for you, Mr. Hervey: which do you like best?—Oh, that's the tragic muse that you have chosen!—You don't like the tragic better than the comic muse, do you?"

Clarence Hervey made no answer, for he was at that instant recollecting how Belinda looked in the character of the tragic muse.

"Has your ladyship ever happened to meet with the young lady who has spent this winter with Lady Delacour?" said Clarence to Lady Anne.

"I sat near her one night at the opera," said Lady Anne: "she has a charming countenance."

"Who?—Belinda Portman, do you mean?" said Mrs. Delacour. "I am sure if I were a young man, I would not trust to the charming countenance of a young lady who is a pupil of Mrs. Stanhope's, and a friend of—Helena, my dear, shut the door—the most dissipated woman in London."

"Indeed," said Lady Anne, "Miss Portman is in a dangerous situation; but some young people learn prudence by being placed in dangerous situations, as some young horses, I have heard Mr. Percival say, learn to be sure-footed, by being left to pick their own way on bad roads."

Here Mr. Percival, Dr. X—, and some other gentlemen, came up stairs to tea, and the conversation took another turn. Clarence Hervey endeavoured to take his share in it with his usual vivacity, but he was thinking of Belinda Portman, dangerous situations, stumbling horses, &c; and he made several blunders, which showed his absence of mind.

"What have you there, Mr. Hervey?" said Dr. X—, looking over his shoulder—"the tragic muse? This tragic muse seems to rival Lady Delacour in your admiration."

"Oh," said Clarence, smiling, "you know I was always a votary of the muses."

"And a favoured votary," said Dr. X—. "I wish for the interests of literature, that poets may always be lovers, though I cannot say that I desire lovers should always be poets. But, Mr. Hervey, you must never marry, remember," continued Dr. X—, "never—for your true poet must always be miserable. You know Petrarch tells us, he would not have been happy if he could; he would not have married his mistress if it had been in his power; because then there would have been an end of his beautiful sonnets."

"Every one to his taste," said Clarence; "for my part I have even less ambition to imitate the heroism than hope of being inspired with the poetic genius of Petrarch. I have no wish to pass whole nights composing sonnets. I would (am I not right, Mr. Percival?) infinitely rather be a slave of the ring than a slave of the lamp."

Here the conversation ended; Clarence took his leave, and Mrs. Margaret Delacour said, the moment he had left the room, "Quite a different sort of young man from what I had expected to see!"

CHAPTER IX — ADVICE

The next morning Mr. Hervey called on Dr. X—, and begged that he would accompany him to Lady Delacour's.

"To be introduced to your tragic muse?" said the doctor.

"Yes," said Mr. Hervey: "I must have your opinion of her before I devote myself."

"My opinion! but of whom?—Of Lady Delacour?"

"No; but of a young lady whom you will see with her."

"Is she handsome?"

"Beautiful!"

"And young?"

"And young."

"And graceful?"

"The most graceful person you ever beheld."

"Young, beautiful, graceful; then the deuce take me," said Dr. X—, "if I give you my opinion of her: for the odds are, that she has a thousand faults, at least, to balance these perfections."

"A thousand faults! a charitable allowance," said Clarence, smiling.

"There now," said Dr. X—

'Touch him, and no minister's so sore.'
To punish you for wincing at my first setting out, I promise you, that if the lady have a million of faults, each of them high as huge Olympus, I will see them as with the eye of a flatterer—not of a friend."

"I defy you to be so good or so bad as your word, doctor," said Hervey. "You have too much wit to make a good flatterer."

"And perhaps you think too much to make a good friend," said Dr. X—.

"Not so," said Clarence: "I would at any time rather be cut by a sharp knife than by a blunt one. But, my dear doctor, I hope you will not be prejudiced against Belinda, merely because she is with Lady Delacour; for to my certain knowledge, she in not under her ladyship's influence. She judges and acts for herself, of which I have had an instance."

"Very possibly!" interrupted Dr. X—. "But before we go any farther, will you please to tell me of what Belinda you are talking?"

"Belinda Portman. I forgot that I had not told you."

"Miss Portman, a niece of Mrs. Stanhope's?"

"Yes, but do not be prejudiced against her on that account," said Clarence, eagerly, "though I was at first myself."

"Then you will excuse my following your example instead of your precepts."

"No," said Clarence, "for my precepts are far better than my example."

Lady Delacour received Dr. X— most courteously, and thanked Mr. Hervey for introducing to her a gentleman with whom she had long desired to converse. Dr. X— had a great literary reputation, and she saw that he was a perfectly well-bred man; consequently she was ambitious of winning his admiration. She perceived also that he had considerable influence with Clarence Hervey, and this was a sufficient reason to make her wish for his good opinion. Belinda was particularly pleased with his manners and conversation; she saw that he paid her much attention, and she was desirous that he should think favourably of her; but she had the good sense and good taste to avoid a display of her abilities and accomplishments. A sensible man, who has any knowledge of the world and talents for conversation, can easily draw out the knowledge of those with whom he converses. Dr. X— possessed this power in a superior degree.

"Well," cried Clarence, when their visit was over, "what is your opinion of Lady Delacour?"

"I am 'blasted with excess of light,'" said the doctor.

"Her ladyship is certainly very brilliant," said Clarence, "but I hope that Miss Portman did not overpower you."

"No—I turned my eyes from Lady Delacour upon Miss Portman, as a painter turns his eyes upon mild green, to rest them, when they have been dazzled by glaring colours.

'She yields her charms of mind with sweet delay.'"

"I was afraid," said Hervey, "that you might think her manners too reserved and cold: they are certainly become more so than they used to be. But so much the better; by and by we shall find beautiful flowers spring up from beneath the snow.'"

"A very poetical hope," said Dr. X—; "but in judging of the human character, we must not entirely trust to analogies and allusions taken from the vegetable creation."

"What!" cried Clarence Hervey, looking eagerly in the doctor's eyes, "what do you mean? I am afraid you do not approve of Belinda."

"Your fears are almost as precipitate as your hopes, my good sir: but to put you out of pain, I will tell you, that I approve of all I have seen of this young lady, but that it is absolutely out of my power to form a decisive judgment of a woman's temper and character in the course of a single morning visit. Women, you know, as well as men, often speak with one species of enthusiasm, and act with another. I must see your Belinda act, I must study her, before I can give you my final judgment. Lady Delacour has honoured me with her commands to go to her as often as possible. For your sake, my dear Hervey, I shall obey her ladyship most punctually, that I may have frequent opportunities of seeing your Miss Portman."

Clarence expressed his gratitude with much energy, for this instance of the doctor's friendship. Belinda, who had been entertained by Dr. X—'s conversation during this first visit, was more and more delighted with his company as she became more acquainted with his understanding and character. She felt that he unfolded her powers, and that with the greatest politeness and address he raised her confidence in herself, without ever descending to flattery. By degrees she learned to look upon him as a friend; she imparted to him with great ingenuousness her opinions on various subjects, and she was both amused and instructed by his observations on the characters and manners of the company who frequented Lady Delacour's assemblies. She did not judge of the doctor's sincerity merely by the kindness he showed her, but by his conduct towards others.

One night, at a select party at Lady Delacour's, a Spanish gentleman was amusing the company with some anecdotes, to prove the extraordinary passion which some of his countrymen formerly showed for the game of chess. He mentioned families, in which unfinished games, bequeathed by will, had descended from father to son, and where victory was doubtful for upwards of a century.

Mr. Hervey observed, that gaining a battle was, at that time, so common to the court of Spain, that a victory at chess seemed to confer more éclat; for that an abbé, by losing adroitly a game at chess to the Spanish minister, obtained a cardinal's hat.

The foreigner was flattered by the manner in which Hervey introduced this slight circumstance, and he directed to him his conversation, speaking in French and Italian successively; he was sufficiently skilled in both languages, but Clarence spoke them better. Till he appeared, the foreigner was the principal object of attention, but he was soon eclipsed by Mr. Hervey. Nothing amusing or instructive that could be said upon the game of chess escaped him, and the literary ground, which the slow Don would have taken some hours to go regularly over, our hero traversed in a few minutes. From Twiss to Vida, from Irwin to Sir William Jones, from Spain to India, he passed with admirable celerity, and seized all that could adorn his course from Indian Antiquities or Asiatic Researches.

By this display of knowledge he surprised even his friend Dr. X—. The ladies admired his taste as a poet, the gentlemen his accuracy as a critic; Lady Delacour loudly applauded, and Belinda silently approved. Clarence was elated. The Spanish gentleman, to whom he had just quoted a case in point from Vida's Scacchia, asked him if he were as perfect in the practice as in the theory of the game. Clarence was too proud of excelling in every thing to decline the Spaniard's challenge. They sat down to chess. Lady Delacour, as they ranged the pieces on the board, cried, "Whoever wins shall be my knight; and a silver chess-man shall be his prize. Was it not Queen Elizabeth who gave a silver chess-man to one of her courtiers as a mark of her royal favour? I am ashamed to imitate such a pedantic coquet—but since I have said it, how can I retract?"

"Impossible! impossible!" cried Clarence Hervey: "a silver chess-man be our prize; and if I win it, like the gallant Raleigh, I will wear it in my cap; and what proud Essex shall dare to challenge it?"

The combat now began—the spectators were silent. Clarence made an error in his first move, for his attention was distracted by seeing Belinda behind his adversary's chair. The Spaniard was deceived by this mistake into a contemptuous opinion of his opponent—Belinda changed her place—Clarence recovered his presence of mind, and convinced him that he was not a man to be despised. The combat was long doubtful, but at length to the surprise of all present, Clarence Hervey was victorious.

Exulting in his success, he looked round for Lady Delacour, from whom he expected the honours of his triumph. She had left the room, but soon she returned, dressed in the character of Queen Elizabeth, in which she had once appeared at a masquerade, with a large ruff, and all the costume of the times.

Clarence Hervey, throwing himself at her feet, addressed her in that high-flown style which her majesty was wont to hear from the gallant Raleigh, or the accomplished Essex.

Soon the coquetry of the queen entirely conquered her prudery; and the favoured courtier, evidently elated by his situation, was as enthusiastic as her majesty's most insatiable vanity could desire. The characters were well supported; both the actor and actress were highly animated, and seemed so fully possessed by their parts as to be insensible to the comments that were made upon the scene. Clarence Hervey was first recalled to himself by the deep blush which he saw on Belinda's cheek, when Queen Elizabeth addressed her as one of her maids of honour, of whom she affected to be jealous. He was conscious that he had been hurried by the enthusiasm of the moment farther than he either wished or intended. It was difficult to recede, when her majesty seemed disposed to advance; but Sir Walter Raleigh, with much presence of mind, turned to the foreigner, whom he accosted as the Spanish ambassador.

"Your excellency sees," said he, "how this great queen turns the heads of her faithful subjects, and afterwards has the art of paying them with nothing but words. Has the new world afforded you any coin half so valuable?"

The Spanish gentleman's grave replies to this playful question gave a new turn to the conversation, and relieved Clarence Hervey from his embarrassment. Lady Delacour, though still in high spirits, was easily diverted to other objects. She took the Spaniard with her to the next room, to show him a picture of Mary, Queen of Scots. The company followed her—Clarence Hervey remained with Dr. X— and Belinda, who had just asked the doctor, to teach her the moves at chess.

"Lady Delacour has charming spirits," said Clarence Hervey; "they inspire every body with gaiety."

"Every body! they incline me more to melancholy than mirth," said Dr. X—. "These high spirits do not seem quite natural. The vivacity of youth and of health, Miss Portman, always charms me; but this gaiety of Lady Delacour's does not appear to me that of a sound mind in a sound body."

The doctor's penetration went so near the truth, that Belinda, afraid of betraying her friend's secrets, never raised her eyes from the chess-board whilst he spoke, but went on setting up the fallen castles, and bishops, and kings, with expeditious diligence.

"You are putting the bishop into the place of the knight," said Clarence.

"Lady Delacour," continued the doctor, "seems to be in a perpetual fever, either of mind or body—I cannot tell which—and as a professional man, I really have some curiosity to determine the question. If I could feel her pulse, I could instantly decide; but I have heard her say that she has a horror against having her pulse felt, and a lady's horror is invincible, by reason—"

"But not by address," said Clarence. "I can tell you a method of counting her pulse, without her knowing it, without her seeing you, without your seeing her."

"Indeed!" said Dr. X—, smiling; "that may be a useful secret in my profession; pray impart it to me—you who excel in every thing."

"Are you in earnest, Mr. Hervey?" said Belinda.

"Perfectly in earnest—my secret is quite simple. Look through the door at the shadow of Queen Elizabeth's ruff—observe how it vibrates; the motion as well as the figure is magnified in the shadow. Cannot you count every pulsation distinctly?"

"I can," said Dr. X—, "and I give you credit for making an ingenious use of a trifling observation." The doctor paused and looked round. "Those people cannot hear what we are saying, I believe?"

"Oh, no," said Belinda, "they are intent upon themselves." Doctor X—fixed his eyes mildly upon Clarence Hervey, and exclaimed in an earnest friendly tone—"What a pity, Mr. Hervey, that a young man of your talents and acquirements, a man who might be any thing, should—pardon the expression—choose to be—nothing; should waste upon petty objects powers suited to the greatest; should lend his soul to every contest for frivolous superiority, when the same energy concentrated might ensure honourable pre-eminence among the first men in his country. Shall he who might not only distinguish himself in any science or situation, who might not only acquire personal fame, but, oh, far more noble motive! who might be permanently useful to his fellow-creatures, content himself with being the evanescent amusement of a drawing-room?—Shall one, who might be great in public, or happy in private life, waste in this deplorable manner the best years of his existence—time that can never be recalled?—This is declamation!—No: it is truth put into the strongest language that I have power to use, in the hope of making some impression: I speak from my heart, for I have a sincere regard for you, Mr. Hervey, and if I have been impertinent, you must forgive me."

"Forgive you!" cried Clarence Hervey, taking Dr. X— by the hand, "I think you a real friend; you shall have the best thanks not in words, but in actions: you have roused my ambition, and I will pursue noble ends by noble means. A few years have been sacrificed; but the lessons that they have taught me remain. I cannot, presumptuous as I am, flatter myself that my exertions can be of any material utility to my fellow-creatures, but what I can do I will, my excellent friend! If I be hereafter either successful in public, or happy in private life, it is to you I shall owe it."

Belinda was touched by the candour and good sense with which Clarence Hervey spoke. His character appeared in a new light: she was proud of her own judgment, in having discerned his merit, and for a moment she permitted herself to feel "unreproved pleasure in his company."

The next morning, Sir Philip Baddely and Mr. Rochfort called at Lady Delacour's—Mr. Hervey was present—her ladyship was summoned to Mrs. Franks, and Belinda was left with these gentlemen.

"Why, damme, Clary! you have been a lost man," cried Sir Philip, "ever since you were drowned. Damme, why did not you come to dine with us that day, now I recollect it? We were all famously merry; but for your comfort, Clarence, we missed you cursedly, and were damned sorry you ever took that unlucky jump into the Serpentine river—damned sorry, were not we, Rochfort?"

"Oh," said Clarence, in an ironical tone, "you need no vouchers to convince me of the reality of your sorrow. You know I can never forget your jumping so courageously into the river, to save the life of your friend."

"Oh, pooh! damn it," said Sir Philip, "what signifies who pulled you out, now you are safe and sound? By-the-bye, Clary, did you ever quiz that doctor, as I desired you? No, that I'm sure you didn't; but I think he has made a quiz of you: for, damme, I believe you have taken such a fancy to the old quizzical fellow, that you can't live without him. Miss Portman, don't you admire Hervey's taste?"

"In this instance I certainly do admire Mr. Hervey's taste," said Belinda, "for the best of all possible reasons, because it entirely agrees with my own."

"Very extraordinary, faith," said Sir Philip.

"And what the devil can you find to like in him, Clary?" continued Mr. Rochfort, "for one wouldn't be so rude to put that question to a lady. Ladies, you know, are never to be questioned about their likings and dislikings. Some have pet dogs, some have pet cats: then why not a pet quiz?"

"Ha! ha! ha! that's a good one, Rochfort—a pet quiz!—Ha! ha! ha! Dr. X— shall be Miss Portman's pet quiz. Put it about, put it about, Rochfort," continued the witty baronet, and he and his facetious companion continued to laugh as long as they possibly could at this happy hit.

Belinda, without being in the least discomposed by their insolent folly, as soon as they had finished laughing, very coolly observed, that she could have no objection to give her reasons for preferring Dr. X—'s company but for fear they might give offence to Sir Philip and his friends. She then defended the doctor with so much firmness, and yet with so much propriety, that Clarence Hervey was absolutely enchanted with her, and with his own penetration in having discovered her real character, notwithstanding her being Mrs. Stanhope's niece.

"I never argue, for my part," cried Mr. Rochfort: "'pon honour, 'tis a deal too much trouble. A lady, a handsome lady, I mean, is always in the right with me."

"But as to you, Hervey," said Sir Philip, "damme, do you know, my boy, that our club has come to a determination to black-ball you, if you keep company with this famous doctor?"

"Your club, Sir Philip, will do me honour by such an ostracism."

"Ostracism!" repeated Sir Philip.—"In plain English, does that mean that you choose to be black-balled by us? Why, damn it, Clary, you'll be nobody. But follow your own genius—damn me, if I take it upon me to understand your men of genius—they are in the Serpentine river one day, and in the clouds the next: so fare ye well, Clary. I expect to see you a doctor of physic, or a methodist parson, soon, damn me if I don't: so fare ye well, Clary. Is black-ball your last word? or will you think better on't, and give up the doctor?"

"I can never give up Dr. X—'s friendship—I would sooner be black-balled by every club in London. The good lesson you gave me, Sir Philip, the day I was fool enough to jump into the Serpentine river, has made me wiser for life. I know, for I have felt, the difference between real friends and fashionable acquaintance. Give up Dr. X—! Never! never!"

"Then fare you well, Clary," said Sir Philip, "you're no longer one of us."

"Then fare ye well, Clary, you're no longer the man for me," said Rochfort.

"Tant pis, and tant mieux" said Clarence, and so they parted.

As they left the room, Clarence Hervey involuntarily turned to Belinda, and he thought that he read in her ingenuous, animated countenance, full approbation of his conduct.

"Hist! are they gone? quite gone?" said Lady Delacour, entering the room from an adjoining apartment; "they have stayed an unconscionable time. How much I am obliged to Mrs. Franks for detaining me! I have escaped their vapid impertinence; and in truth, this morning I have such a multiplicity of business, that I have scarcely a moment even for wit and Clarence Hervey. Belinda, my dear, will you have the charity to look over some of these letters for me, which, as Marriott tells me, have been lying in my writing-table this week—expecting, most unreasonably, that I should have the grace to open them? We are always punished for our indolence, as your friend Dr. X— said the other day: if we suffer business to accumulate, it drifts with every ill wind like snow, till at last an avalanche of it comes down at once, and quite overwhelms us. Excuse me, Clarence," continued her ladyship, as she opened her letters, "this is very rude: but I know I have secured my pardon from you by remembering your friend's wit—wisdom, I should say: how seldom are wit and wisdom joined! They might have been joined in Lady Delacour, perhaps—there's vanity!—if she had early met with such a friend as Dr. X—; but it's too late now," said she, with a deep sigh.

Clarence Hervey heard it, and it made a great impression upon his benevolent imagination. "Why too late?" said he to himself. "Mrs. Margaret Delacour is mistaken, if she thinks this woman wants sensibility."

"What have you got there, Miss Portman?" said Lady Delacour, taking from Belinda's hand one of the letters which she had begged her to look over: "something wondrous pathetic, I should guess, by your countenance. 'Helena Delacour.' Oh! read it to yourself, my dear—a school-girl's letter is a thing I abominate—I make it a rule never to read Helena's epistles."

"Let me prevail upon your ladyship to make an exception to the general rule then," said Belinda; "I can assure you this is not a common school-girl's letter: Miss Delacour seems to inherit her mother's 'eloquence de billet.'"

"Miss Portman seems to possess, by inheritance, by instinct, by magic, or otherwise, powers of persuasion, which no one can resist. There's compliment for compliment, my dear. Is there any thing half so well turned in Helena's letter? Really, 'tis vastly well," continued her ladyship, as she read the letter: "where did the little gipsy learn to write so charmingly? I protest I should like of all things to have her at home with me this summer—the 21st of June—well, after the birthday, I shall have time to think about it. But then, we shall be going out of town, and at Harrowgate I should not know what to do with her; she had better, much better, go to her humdrum Aunt Margaret's, as she always does—she is a fixture in Grosvenor-square. These stationary good people, these zoophite friends, are sometimes very convenient; and Mrs. Margaret Delacour is the most unexceptionable zoophite in the creation. She has, it is true, an antipathy to me, because I'm of such a different nature from herself; but then her antipathy does not extend to my offspring: she is kind beyond measure to Helena, on purpose, I believe, to provoke me. Now I provoke her in my turn, by never being provoked, and she saves me a vast deal of trouble, for which she is overpaid by the pleasure of abusing me. This is the way of the world, Clarence. Don't look so serious—you are not come yet to daughters and sons, and schools and holidays, and all the evils of domestic life."

"Evils!" repeated Clarence Hervey, in a tone which surprised her ladyship. She looked immediately with a significant smile at Belinda. "Why do not you echo evils, Miss Portman?"

"Pray, Lady Delacour," interrupted Clarence Hervey, "when do you go to Harrowgate?"

"What a sudden transition!" said Lady Delacour. "What association of ideas could just at that instant take you to Harrowgate? When do I go to Harrowgate? Immediately after the birthday, I believe we shall—I advise you to be of the party."

"Your ladyship does me a great deal of honour," said Hervey: "I shall, if it be possible, do myself the honour of attending you."

And soon after this arrangement was made, Mr. Hervey took his leave.

"Well, my dear, are you still poring over that letter of Helena's?" said Lady Delacour to Miss Portman.

"I fancy your ladyship did not quite finish it," said Belinda.

"No; I saw something about the Leverian Museum, and a swallow's nest in a pair of garden-shears; and I was afraid I was to have a catalogue of curiosities, for which I have little taste and less time."

"You did not see, then, what Miss Delacour says of the lady who took her to that Museum?"

"Not I. What lady? her Aunt Margaret?"

"No; Mrs. Margaret Delacour, she says, has been so ill for some time past, that she goes no where but to Lady Anne Percival's."

"Poor woman," said Lady Delacour, "she will die soon, and then I shall have Helena upon my hands, unless some other kind friend takes a fancy to her. Who is this lady that has carried her to the Leverian Museum?"

"Lady Anne Percival; of whom she speaks with so much gratitude and affection, that I quite long—"

"Lord bless me!" interrupted Lady Delacour, "Lady Anne Percival! Helena has mentioned this Lady Anne Percival to me before, I recollect, in some of her letters."

"Then you did read some of her letters?"

"Half!—I never read more than half, upon my word," said Lady Delacour, laughing.

"Why will you delight in making yourself appear less good than you are, my dear Lady Delacour?" said Belinda, taking her hand.

"Because I hate to be like other people," said her ladyship, "who delight in making themselves appear better than they are. But I was going to tell you, that I do believe I did provoke Percival by marrying Lord Delacour: I cannot tell you how much this Mea delights me—I am sure that the man has a lively remembrance of me, or else he would never make his wife take so much notice of my daughter."

"Surely, your ladyship does not think," said Belinda, "that a wife is a being whose actions are necessarily governed by a husband."

"Not necessarily—but accidentally. When a lady accidentally sets up for being a good wife, she must of course love, honour, and obey. Now, you understand, I am not in the least obliged to Lady Anne for her kindness to Helena, because it all goes under the head of obedience, in my imagination; and her ladyship is paid for it by an accession of character: she has the reward of having it said, 'Oh, Lady Anne Percival is the best wife in the world!'—'Oh, Lady Anne Percival is quite a pattern woman!' I hate pattern women. I hope I may never see Lady Anne; for I'm sure I should detest her beyond all things living—Mrs. Luttridge not excepted."

Belinda was surprised and shocked at the malignant vehemence with which her ladyship uttered these words; it was in vain, however, that she remonstrated on the injustice of predetermining to detest Lady Anne, merely because she had shown kindness to Helena, and because she bore a high character. Lady Delacour was a woman who never listened to reason, or who listened to it only that she might parry it by wit. Upon this occasion, her wit had not its usual effect upon Miss Portman; instead of entertaining, it disgusted her.

"You have called me your friend, Lady Delacour," said she; "I should but ill deserve that name, if I had not the courage to speak the truth to you—if I had not the courage to tell you when I think you are wrong."

"But I have not the courage to hear you, my dear," said Lady Delacour, stopping her ears. "So your conscience may be at ease; you may suppose that you have said every thing that is wise, and good, and proper, and sublime, and that you deserve to be called the best of friends; you shall enjoy the office of censor to Lady Delacour, and welcome; but remember, it is a sinecure place, though I will pay you with my love and esteem to any extent you please. You sigh—for my folly. Alas! my dear, 'tis hardly worth while—my follies will soon be at an end. Of what use could even the wisdom of Solomon be to me now? If you have any humanity, you will not force me to reflect: whilst I yet live, I must keep it up with incessant dissipation—the teetotum keeps upright only while it spins: so let us talk of the birthnight, or the new play that we are to see to-night, or the ridiculous figure Lady H— made at the concert; or let us talk of Harrowgate, or what you will."

Pity succeeded to disgust and displeasure in Belinda's mind, and she could hardly refrain from tears, whilst she saw this unhappy creature, with forced smiles, endeavour to hide the real anguish of her soul: she could only say, "But, my dear Lady Delacour, do not you think that your little Helena, who seems to have a most affectionate disposition, would add to your happiness at home?"

"Her affectionate disposition can be nothing to me," said Lady Delacour.

Belinda felt a hot tear drop upon her hand, which lay upon Lady Delacour's lap.

"Can you wonder," continued her ladyship, hastily wiping away the tear which she had let fall; "can you wonder that I should talk of detesting Lady Anne Percival? You see she has robbed me of the affections of my child. Helena asks to come home: yes, but how does she ask it? Coldly, formally,—as a duty. But look at the end of her letter; I have read it all—every bitter word of it I have tasted. How differently she writes—look even at the flowing hand—the moment she begins to speak of Lady Anne Percival; then her soul breaks out: 'Lady Anne has offered to take her to Oakly-park—she should be extremely happy to go, if I please.' Yes, let her go; let her go as far from me as possible; let her never, never see her wretched mother more!—Write," said Lady Delacour, turning hastily to Belinda, "write in my name, and tell her to go to Oakly-park, and to be happy."

"But why should you take it for granted that she cannot be happy with you?" said Belinda. "Let us see her—let us try the experiment."

"No," said Lady Delacour; "no—it is too late: I will never condescend in my last moments to beg for that affection to which it may be thought I have forfeited my natural claim."

Pride, anger, and sorrow, struggled in her countenance as she spoke. She turned her face from Belinda, and walked out of the room with dignity.

Nothing remains for me to do, thought Belinda, but to sooth this haughty spirit: all other hope, I see, is vain.

At this moment Clarence Hervey, who had no suspicion that the gay, brilliant Lady Delacour was sinking into the grave, had formed a design worthy of his ardent and benevolent character. The manner in which her ladyship had spoken of his friend Dr. X—, the sigh which she gave at the reflection that she might have been a very different character if she had early had a sensible friend, made a great impression upon Mr. Hervey. Till then, he had merely considered her ladyship as an object of amusement, and an introduction to high life; but he now felt so much interested for her, that he determined to exert all his influence to promote her happiness. He knew that influence to be considerable: not that he was either coxcomb or dupe enough to imagine that Lady Delacour was in love with him; he was perfectly sensible that her only wish was to obtain his admiration, and he resolved to show her that it could no longer be secured without deserving his esteem. Clarence Hervey was a thoroughly generous young man: capable of making the greatest sacrifices, when encouraged by the hope of doing good, he determined to postpone the declaration of his attachment to Belinda, that he might devote himself entirely to his new project. His plan was to wean Lady Delacour by degrees from dissipation, by attaching her to her daughter, and to Lady Anne Percival. He was sanguine in all his hopes, and rapid, but not unthinking, in all his decisions. From Lady Delacour he went immediately to Dr. X—, to whom he communicated his designs.

"I applaud your benevolent intentions," said the doctor: "but have you really the presumption to hope, that an ingenuous young man of four-and-twenty can reform a veteran coquet of four-and-thirty?"

"Lady Delacour is not yet thirty," said Clarence; "but the older she is, the better the chance of her giving up a losing game. She has an admirable understanding, and she will soon—I mean as soon as she is acquainted with Lady Anne Percival—discover that she has mistaken the road to happiness. All the difficulty will be to make them fairly acquainted with each other; for this, my dear doctor, I must trust to you. Do you prepare Lady Anne to tolerate Lady Delacour's faults, and I will prepare Lady Delacour to tolerate Lady Anne's virtues."

"You have generously taken the more difficult task of the two," replied Dr. X—. "Well, we shall see what can be done. After the birthday, Lady Delacour talks of going to Harrowgate: you know, Oakly-park is not far from Harrowgate, so they will have frequent opportunities of meeting. But, take my word for it, nothing can be done till after the birthday; for Lady Delacour's head is at present full of crape petticoats, and horses, and carriages, and a certain Mrs. Luttridge, whom she hates with a hatred passing that of women."

CHAPTER X — THE MYSTERIOUS BOUDOIR

Accustomed to study human nature, Dr. X— had acquired peculiar sagacity in judging of character. Notwithstanding the address with which Lady Delacour concealed the real motives for her apparently thoughtless conduct, he quickly discovered that the hatred of Mrs. Luttridge was her ruling passion. Above nine years of continual warfare had exasperated the tempers of both parties, and no opportunities of manifesting their mutual antipathy were ever neglected. Extravagantly as Lady Delacour loved admiration, the highest possible degree of positive praise was insipid to her taste, if it did not imply some superiority over the woman whom she considered as a perpetual rival.

Now it had been said by the coachmaker, that Mrs. Luttridge would sport a most elegant new vis-à-vis on the king's birthday. Lady Delacour was immediately ambitious to outshine her in equipage; and it was this paltry ambition that made her condescend to all the meanness of the transaction by which she obtained Miss Portman's draft, and Clarence Hervey's two hundred guineas. The great, the important day, at length arrived—her ladyship's triumph in the morning at the drawing-room was complete. Mrs. Luttridge's dress, Mrs. Luttridge's vis-à-vis, Mrs. Luttridge's horses were nothing, absolutely nothing, in comparison with Lady Delacour's: her ladyship enjoyed the full exultation of vanity; and at night she went in high spirits to the ball.

"Oh, my dearest Belinda," said she, as she left her dressing-room, "how terrible a thing it is that you cannot go with me!—None of the joys of this life are without alloy!—'Twould be too much to see in one night Mrs. Luttridge's mortification, and my Belinda's triumph. Adieu! my love: we shall live to see another birthday, it is to be hoped. Marriott, my drops. Oh, I have taken them."

Belinda, after her ladyship's departure, retired to the library. Her time passed so agreeably during Lady Delacour's absence, that she was surprised when she heard the clock strike twelve.

"Is it possible," thought she, "that I have spent two hours by myself in a library without being tired of my existence?—How different are my feelings now from what they would have been in the same circumstances six months ago!—I should then have thought the loss of a birthnight ball a mighty trial of temper. It is singular, that my having spent a winter with one of the most dissipated women in England should have sobered my mind so completely. If I had never seen the utmost extent of the pleasures of the world, as they are called, my imagination might have misled me to the end of my life; but now I can judge from my own experience, and I am convinced that the life of a fine lady would never make me happy. Dr. X— told me, the other day, that he thinks me formed for something better, and he is incapable of flattery."

The idea of Clarence Hervey was so intimately connected with that of his friend, that Miss Portman could seldom separate them in her imagination; and she was just beginning to reflect upon the manner in which Clarence looked, whilst he declared to Sir Philip Baddely, that he would never give up Dr. X—, when she was startled by the entrance of Marriott.

"Oh, Miss Portman, what shall we do? what shall we do?-My lady! my poor lady!" cried she.

"What is the matter?" said Belinda.

"The horses—the young horses!—Oh, I wish my lady had never seen them. Oh, my lady, my poor lady, what will become of her?"

It was some minutes before Belinda could obtain from Marriott any intelligible account of what had happened.

"All I know, ma'am, is what James has just told me," said Marriott. "My lady gave the coachman orders upon no account to let Mrs. Luttridge's carriage get before hers. Mrs. Luttridge's coachman would not give up the point either. My lady's horses were young and ill broke, they tell me, and there was no managing of them no ways. The carriages got somehow across one another, and my lady was overturned, and all smashed to atoms. Oh, ma'am," continued Marriott, "if it had not been for Mr. Hervey, they say, my lady would never have been got out of the crowd alive. He's bringing her home in his own carriage, God bless him!"

"But is Lady Delacour hurt?" cried Belinda.

"She must,—to be sure, she must, ma'am," cried Marriott, putting her hand upon her bosom. "But let her be ever so much hurt, my lady will keep it to herself: the footmen swear she did not give a scream, not a single scream; so it's their opinion she was no ways hurt—but that, I know, can't be—and, indeed, they are thinking so much about the carriage, that they can't give one any rational account of any thing; and, as for myself, I'm sure I'm in such a flutter. Lord knows, I advised my lady not to go with the young horses, no later than—"

"Hark!" cried Belinda, "here they are." She ran down stairs instantly. The first object that she saw was Lady Delacour in convulsions—the street-door was open—the hall was crowded with servants. Belinda made her way through them, and, in a calm voice, requested that Lady Delacour might immediately be brought to her own dressing-room, and that she should there be left to Marriott's care and hers. Mr. Hervey assisted in carrying Lady Delacour—she came to her senses as they were taking her up stairs. "Set me down, set me down," she exclaimed: "I am not hurt—I am quite well,—Where's Marriott? Where's Miss Portman?"

"Here we are—you shall be carried quite safely—trust to me," said Belinda, in a firm tone, "and do not struggle."

Lady Delacour submitted: she was in agonizing pain, but her fortitude was so great that she never uttered a groan. It was the constraint which she had put upon herself, by endeavouring not to scream, which threw her into convulsions. "She is hurt—I am sure she is hurt, though she will not acknowledge it," cried Clarence Hervey. "My ankle is sprained, that's all," said Lady Delacour—"lay me on this sofa, and leave me to Belinda."

"What's all this?" cried Lord Delacour, staggering into the room: he was much intoxicated, and in this condition had just come home, as they were carrying Lady Delacour up stairs: he could not be made to understand the truth, but as soon as he heard Clarence Hervey's voice, he insisted upon going up to his wife's dressing-room. It was a very unusual thing, but neither Champfort nor any one else could restrain him, the moment that he had formed this idea; he forced his way into the room.

"What's all this?—Colonel Lawless!" said he, addressing himself to Clarence Hervey, whom, in the confusion of his mind, he mistook for the colonel, the first object of his jealousy. "Colonel Lawless," cried his lordship, "you are a villain. I always knew it."

"Softly!—she's in great pain, my lord," said Belinda, catching Lord Delacour's arm, just as he was going to strike Clarence Hervey. She led him to the sofa where Lady Delacour lay, and uncovering her ankle, which was much swelled, showed it to him. His lordship, who was a humane man, was somewhat moved by this appeal to his remaining senses, and he began roaring as loud as he possibly could for arquebusade.

Lady Delacour rested her head upon the back of the sofa, her hands moved with convulsive twitches—she was perfectly silent. Marriott was in a great bustle, running backwards and forwards for she knew not what, and continually repeating, "I wish nobody would come in here but Miss Portman and me. My lady says nobody must come in. Lord bless me! my lord here too!"

"Have you any arquebusade, Marriott? Arquebusade, for your lady, directly!" cried his lordship, following her to the door of the boudoir, where she was going for some drops.

"Oh, my lord, you can't come in, I assure you, my lord, there's nothing here, my lord, nothing of the sort," said Marriott, setting her back against the door. Her terror and embarrassment instantly recalled all the jealous suspicions of Lord Delacour. "Woman!" cried he, "I will see whom you have in this room!—You have some one concealed there, and I will go in." Then with brutal oaths he dragged Marriott from the door, and snatched the key from her struggling hand.

Lady Delacour started up, and gave a scream of agony. "My lord!—Lord Delacour," cried Belinda, springing forward, "hear me."

Lord Delacour stopped short. "Tell me, then," cried Lord Delacour, "is not a lover of Lady Delacour's concealed there?" "No!—No!—No!" answered Belinda. "Then a lover of Miss Portman?" said Lord Delacour. "Gad! we have hit it now, I believe."

"Believe whatever you please, my lord," said Belinda, hastily, "but give me the key."

Clarence Hervey drew the key from Lord Delacour's hand, gave it to Miss Portman without looking at her, and immediately withdrew. Lord Delacour followed him with a sort of drunken laugh; and no one remained in the room but Marriott, Belinda, and Lady Delacour. Marriott was so much fluttered, as she said, that she could do nothing. Miss Portman locked the room door, and began to undress Lady Delacour, who lay motionless. "Are we by ourselves?" said Lady Delacour, opening her eyes.

"Yes—are you much hurt?" said Belinda. "Oh, you are a charming girl!" said Lady Delacour. "Who would have thought you had so much presence of mind and courage—have you the key safe?" "Here it is," said Belinda, producing it; and she repeated her question, "Are you much hurt?" "I am not in pain now," said Lady Delacour, "but I have suffered terribly. If I could get rid of all this finery, if you could put me to bed, I could sleep perhaps."

Whilst Belinda was undressing Lady Delacour, she shrieked several times; but between every interval of pain she repeated, "I shall be better to-morrow." As soon as she was in bed, she desired Marriott to give her double her usual quantity of laudanum; for that all the inclination which she had felt to sleep was gone, and that she could not endure the shooting pains that she felt in her breast.

"Leave me alone with your lady, Marriott," said Miss Portman, taking the bottle of laudanum from her trembling hand, "and go to bed; for I am sure you are not able to sit up any longer."

As she spoke, she took Marriott into the adjoining dressing-room. "Oh, dear Miss Portman," said Marriott, who was sincerely attached to her lady, and who at this instant forgot all her jealousies, and all her love of power, "I'll do any thing you ask me; but pray let me stay in the room, though I know I'm quite helpless. It will be too much for you to be here all night by yourself. The convulsions may take my lady. What shrieks she gives every now and then!—and nobody knows what's the matter but ourselves; and every body in the house is asking me why a surgeon is not sent for, if my lady is so much hurt. Oh, I can't answer for it to my conscience, to have kept the matter secret so long; for to be sure a physician, if had in time, might have saved my lady—but now nothing can save her!" And here Marriott burst into tears.

"Why don't you give me the laudanum?" cried Lady Delacour, in a loud peremptory voice; "Give it to me instantly."—"No," said Miss Portman, firmly.—"Hear me, Lady Delacour—you must allow me to judge, for you know that you are not in a condition to judge for yourself, or rather you must allow me to send for a physician, who may judge for us both."

"A physician!" cried Lady Delacour, "Never—never. I charge you let no physician be sent for. Remember your promise: you cannot betray me—you will not betray me."

"No," said Belinda, "of that I have given sufficient proof—but you will betray yourself: it is already known by your servants that you have been hurt by the overturn of your carriage; if you do not let either a surgeon or physician see you it will excite surprise and suspicion. It is not in your power, when violent pain seizes you, to refrain from—"

"It is," interrupted Lady Delacour; "not another scream shall you hear—only do not, do not, my dear Belinda, send for a physician."

"You will throw yourself again into convulsions," said Belinda. "Marriott, you see, has lost all command of herself—I shall not have strength to manage you—perhaps I may lose my presence of mind—I cannot answer for myself—your husband may desire to see you."

"No danger of that," said Lady Delacour: "tell him my ankle is sprained—tell him I am bruised all over—tell him any thing you will—he will not trouble himself any more about me—he will forget all that passed to-night by the time he is sober. Oh! give me the laudanum, dearest Belinda, and say no more about physicians."

It was in vain to reason with Lady Delacour. Belinda attempted to persuade her: "For my sake, dear Lady Delacour," said she, "let me send for Dr. X—; he is a man of honour, your secret will be perfectly safe with him."

"He will tell it to Clarence Hervey," said Lady Delacour: "of all men living, I would not send for Dr. X—; I will not see him if he comes."

"Then," said Belinda, calmly, but with a fixed determination of countenance, "I must leave you to-morrow morning—I must return to Bath."

"Leave me! remember your promise."

"Circumstances have occurred, about which I have made no promise," said Belinda; "I must leave you, unless you will now give me your permission to send for Dr. X—."

Lady Delacour hesitated. "You see," continued Belinda, "that I am in earnest: when I am gone, you will have no friend left; when I am gone, your secret will inevitably be discovered; for without me, Marriott will not have sufficient strength of mind to keep it."

"Do you think we might trust Dr. X—?" said Lady Delacour.

"I am sure you may trust him," said Belinda, with energy; "I will pledge my life upon his honour."

"Then send for him, since it must be so," said Lady Delacour.

No sooner had the words passed Lady Delacour's lips than Belinda flew to execute her orders. Marriott recovered her senses when she heard that her ladyship had consented to send for a physician; but she declared that she could not conceive how any thing less than the power of magic could have brought her lady to such a determination.

Belinda had scarcely despatched a servant for Dr. X—, when Lady Delacour repented of the permission she had given, and all that could be said to pacify only irritated her temper. She became delirious; Belinda's presence of mind never forsook her, she remained quietly beside the bed waiting for the arrival of Dr. X—, and she absolutely refused admittance to the servants, who, drawn by their lady's outrageous cries, continually came to her door with offers of assistance.

About four o'clock the doctor arrived, and Miss Portman was relieved from some of her anxiety. He assured her that there was no immediate danger, and he promised that the secret which she had entrusted to him should be faithfully kept. He remained with her some hours, till Lady Delacour became more quiet and fell asleep, exhausted with delirious exertions.—"I think I may now leave you," said Dr. X—; but as he was going through the dressing-room, Belinda stopped him.—"Now that I have time to think of myself," said she, "let me consult you as my friend: I am not used to act entirely for myself, and I shall be most grateful if you will assist me with your advice. I hate all mysteries, but I feel myself bound in honour to keep the secret with which Lady Delacour has entrusted me. Last night I was so circumstanced, that I could not extricate her ladyship without exposing myself to—to suspicion."

Miss Portman then related all that had passed about the mysterious door, which Lord Delacour, in his fit of drunken jealousy, had insisted upon breaking open.

"Mr. Hervey," continued Belinda, "was present when all this happened—he seemed much surprised: I should be sorry that he should remain in an error which might be fatal to my reputation—you know a woman ought not even to be suspected; yet how to remove this suspicion I know not, because I cannot enter into any explanation, without betraying Lady Delacour—she has, I know, a peculiar dread of Mr. Hervey's discovering the truth."

"And is it possible," cried Dr. X—, "that any woman should be so meanly selfish, as thus to expose the reputation of her friend merely to preserve her own vanity from mortification?"

"Hush—don't speak so loud," said Belinda, "you will awaken her; and at present she is certainly more an object of pity than of indignation.—If you will have the goodness to come with me, I will take you by a back staircase up to the mysterious boudoir. I am not too proud to give positive proofs of my speaking truth; the key of that room now lies on Lady Delacour's bed—it was that which she grasped in her hand during her delirium—she has now let it fall—it opens both the doors of the boudoir—you shall see," added Miss Portman, with a smile, "that I am not afraid to let you unlock either of them."

"As a polite man," said Dr. X—, "I believe that I should absolutely refuse to take any external evidence of a lady's truth; but demonstration is unanswerable even by enemies, and I will not sacrifice your interests to the foppery of my politeness—so I am ready to follow you. The curiosity of the servants may have been excited by last night's disturbance, and I see no method so certain as that which you propose of preventing busy rumour. That goddess (let Ovid say what he pleases) was born and bred in a kitchen, or a servants' hall.—But," continued Dr. X—, "my dear Miss Portman, you will put a stop to a number of charming stories by this prudence of yours—a romance called the Mysterious Boudoir, of nine volumes at least, might be written on this subject, if you would only condescend to act like almost all other heroines, that is to say, without common sense."

The doctor now followed Belinda, and satisfied himself by ocular demonstration, that this cabinet was the retirement of disease, and not of pleasure.

It was about eight o'clock in the morning when Dr. X— got home; he found Clarence Hervey waiting for him. Clarence seemed to be in great agitation, though he endeavoured, with all the power which he possessed over himself, to suppress his emotion.

"You have been to see Lady Delacour," said he, calmly: "is she much hurt?—It was a terrible accident."

"She has been much hurt," said Dr. X—, "and she has been for some hours delirious; but ask me no more questions now, for I am asleep, and must go to bed, unless you have any thing to say that can waken me: you look as if some great misfortune had befallen you; what is the matter?"

"Oh, my dear friend," said Hervey, taking his hand, "do not jest with me; I am not able to bear your raillery in my present temper—in one word, I fear that Belinda is unworthy of my esteem: I can tell you no more, except that I am more miserable than I thought any woman could make me."

"You are in a prodigious hurry to be miserable," said Dr. X—. "Upon my word I think you would make a mighty pretty hero in a novel; you take things very properly for granted, and, stretched out upon that sofa, you act the distracted lover vastly well—and to complete the matter, you cannot tell me why you are more miserable than ever man or hero was before. I must tell you, then, that you have still more cause for jealousy than you suspect. Ay, start—every jealous man starts at the sound of the word jealousy—a certain symptom this of the disease."

"You mistake me," cried Clarence Hervey; "no man is less disposed to jealousy than I am—but—"

"But your mistress—no, not your mistress, for you have never yet declared to her your attachment—but the lady you admire will not let a drunken man unlock a door, and you immediately suppose—"

"She has mentioned the circumstance to you!" exclaimed Hervey, in a joyful tone: "then she must be innocent."

"Admirable reasoning!—I was going to have told you just now, if you would have suffered me to speak connectedly, that you have more reason for jealousy than you suspect, for Miss Portman has actually unlocked for me—for me! look at me—the door, the mysterious door—and whilst I live, and whilst she lives, we can neither of us ever tell you the cause of the mystery. All I can tell you is, that no lover is in the case, upon my honour—and now, if you should ever mistake curiosity in your own mind for jealousy, expect no pity from me."

"I should deserve none," said Clarence Hervey; "you have made me the happiest of men."

"The happiest of men!—No, no; keep that superlative exclamation for a future occasion. But now you behave like a reasonable creature, you deserve to hear the praises of your Belinda—I am so much charmed with her, that I wish—"

"When can I see her?" interrupted Hervey; "I'll go to her this instant."

"Gently," said Dr. X—, "you forget what time of the day it is—you forget that Miss Portman has been up all night—that Lady Delacour is extremely ill—and that this would be the most unseasonable opportunity you could possibly choose for your visit."

To this observation Clarence Hervey assented; but he immediately seized a pen from the doctor's writing table, and began a letter to Belinda. The doctor threw himself upon the sofa, saying, "Waken me when you want me," and in a few minutes he was fast asleep.

"Doctor, upon second thoughts," said Clarence, rising suddenly, and tearing his letter down the middle, "I cannot write to her yet—I forgot the reformation of Lady Delacour: how soon do you think she will be well? Besides, I have another reason for not writing to Belinda at present—you must know, my dear doctor, that I have, or had, another mistress."

"Another mistress, indeed!" cried Dr. X—, trying to waken himself.

"Good Heavens! I do believe you've been asleep."

"I do believe I have."

"But is it possible that you could fall sound asleep in that time?"

"Very possible," said the doctor: "what is there so extraordinary in a man's falling asleep? Men are apt to sleep sometime within the four-and-twenty hours, unless they have half-a-dozen mistresses to keep them awake, as you seem to have, my good friend."

A servant now came into the room with a letter, that had just arrived express from the country for Dr. X—.

"This is another affair," cried he, rousing himself.

The letter required the doctor's immediate attendance. He shook hands with Clarence Hervey: "My dear friend, I am really concerned that I cannot stay to hear the history of your six mistresses; but you see that this is an affair of life and death."

"Farewell," said Clarence: "I have not six, I have only three goddesses; even if you count Lady Delacour for one. But I really wanted your advice in good earnest."

"If your case be desperate, you can write, cannot you? Direct to me at Horton-hall, Cambridge. In the mean time, as far as general rules go, I can give you my advice gratis, in the formula of an old Scotch song—

"'Tis good to be merry and wise,
'Tis good to be honest and true,
'Tis good to be off with the old love
Before you be on with the new.'"

CHAPTER XI — DIFFICULTIES

Before he left town, Dr. X— called in Berkeley-square, to see Lady Delacour; he found that she was out of all immediate danger. Miss Portman was sorry that he was obliged to quit her at this time, but she felt the necessity for his going; he was sent for to attend Mr. Horton, an intimate friend of his, a gentleman of great talents, and of the most active benevolence, who had just been seized with a violent fever, in consequence of his exertions in saving the poor inhabitants of a village in his neighbourhood from the effects of a dreadful fire, which broke out in the middle of the night.

Lady Delacour, who heard Dr. X— giving this account to Belinda, drew back her curtain, and said, "Go this instant, doctor—I am out of all immediate danger, you say; but if I were not—I must die in the course of a few months, you know—and what is my life, compared with the chance of saving your excellent friend! He is of some use in the world—I am of none—go this instant, doctor."

"What a pity," said Dr. X—, as he left the room, "that a woman who is capable of so much magnanimity should have wasted her life on petty objects!"

"Her life is not yet at an end—oh, sir, if you could save her!" cried Belinda.

Doctor X— shook his head; but returning to Belinda, after going half way down stairs, he added, "when you read this paper, you will know all that I can tell you upon the subject."

Belinda, the moment the doctor was gone, shut herself up in her own room to read the paper which he had given to her. Dr. X— first stated that he was by no means certain that Lady Delacour really had the complaint which she so much dreaded; but it was impossible for him to decide without farther examination, to which her ladyship could not be prevailed upon to submit. Then he mentioned all that he thought would be most efficacious in mitigating the pain that Lady Delacour might feel, and all that could be done, with the greatest probability of prolonging her life. And he concluded with the following words: "These are all temporizing expedients: according to the usual progress of the disease, Lady Delacour may live a year, or perhaps two.

"It is possible that her life might be saved by a skilful surgeon. By a few words that dropped from her ladyship last night, I apprehend that she has some thoughts of submitting to an operation, which will be attended with much pain and danger, even if she employ the most experienced surgeon in London; but if she put herself, from a vain hope of secrecy, into ignorant hands, she will inevitably destroy herself."

After reading this paper, Belinda had some faint hopes that Lady Delacour's life might be saved; but she determined to wait till Dr. X—should return to town, before she mentioned his opinion to his patient; and she earnestly hoped that no idea of putting herself into ignorant hands would recur to her ladyship.

Lord Delacour, in the morning, when he was sober, retained but a confused idea of the events of the preceding night; but he made an awkwardly good-natured apology to Miss Portman for his intrusion, and for the disturbance he had occasioned, which, he said, must be laid to the blame of Lord Studley's admirable burgundy. He expressed much concern for Lady Delacour's terrible accident; but he could not help observing, that if his advice had been taken, the thing could not have happened—that it was the consequence of her ladyship's self-willedness about the young horses.

"How she got the horses without paying for them, or how she got money to pay for them, I know not," said his lordship; "for I said I would have nothing to do with the business, and I have kept to my resolution."

His lordship finished his morning visit to Miss Portman, by observing that "the house would now be very dull for her: that the office of a nurse was ill-suited to so young and beautiful a lady, but that her undertaking it with so much cheerfulness was a proof of a degree of good-nature that was not always to be met with in the young and handsome."

The manner in which Lord Delacour spoke convinced Belinda that he was in reality attached to his wife, however the fear of being, or of appearing to be, governed by her ladyship might have estranged him from her, and from home. She now saw in him much more good sense, and symptoms of a more amiable character, than his lady had described, or than she ever would allow that he possessed.

The reflections, however, which Miss Portman made upon the miserable life this ill-matched couple led together, did not incline her in favour of marriage in general; great talents on one side, and good-nature on the other, had, in this instance, tended only to make each party unhappy. Matches of interest, convenience, and vanity, she was convinced, diminished instead of increasing happiness. Of domestic felicity she had never, except during her childhood, seen examples—she had, indeed, heard from Dr. X— descriptions of the happy family of Lady Anne Percival, but she feared to indulge the romantic hope of ever being loved by a man of superior genius and virtue, with a temper and manners suited to her taste. The only person she had seen, who at all answered this description, was Mr. Hervey; and it was firmly fixed in her mind, that he was not a marrying man, and consequently not a man of whom any prudent woman would suffer herself to think with partiality. She could not doubt that he liked her society and conversation; his manner had sometimes expressed more than cold esteem. Lady Delacour had assured her that it expressed love; but Lady Delacour was an imprudent woman in her own conduct, and not scrupulous as to that of others. Belinda was not guided by her opinions of propriety; and now that her ladyship was confined to her bed, and not in a condition to give her either advice or protection, she felt that it was peculiarly incumbent on her to guard, not only her conduct from reproach, but her heart from the hopeless misery of an ill-placed attachment. She examined herself with firm impartiality; she recollected the excessive pain that she had endured, when she first heard Clarence Hervey say, that Belinda Portman was a compound of art and affectation; but this she thought was only the pain of offended pride—of proper pride. She recollected the extreme anxiety she had felt, even within the last four-and-twenty hours, concerning the opinion which he might form of the transaction about the key of the boudoir—but this anxiety she justified to herself; it was due, she thought, to her reputation; it would have been inconsistent with female delicacy to have been indifferent about the suspicions that necessarily arose from the circumstances in which she was placed. Before Belinda had completed her self-examination, Clarence Hervey called to inquire after Lady Delacour. Whilst he spoke of her ladyship, and of his concern for the dreadful accident of which he believed himself to be in a great measure the cause, his manner and language were animated and unaffected; but the moment that this subject was exhausted, he became embarrassed; though he distinctly expressed perfect confidence and esteem for her, he seemed to wish, and yet to be unable, to support the character of a friend, contradistinguished to an admirer. He seemed conscious that he could not, with propriety, advert to the suspicions and jealousy which he had felt the preceding night; for a man who has never declared love would be absurd and impertinent, were he to betray jealousy. Clarence was destitute neither of address nor presence of mind; but an accident happened, when he was just taking leave of Miss Portman, which threw him into utter confusion. It surprised, if it did not confound, Belinda. She had forgotten to ask Dr. X— for his direction; and as she thought it might be necessary to write to him concerning Lady Delacour's health, she begged of Mr. Hervey to give it to her. He took a letter out of his pocket, and wrote the direction with a pencil; but as he opened the paper, to tear off the outside, on which he had been writing, a lock of hair dropped out of the letter; he hastily stooped for it, and as he took it up from the ground the lock unfolded. Belinda, though she cast but one involuntary, hasty glance at it, was struck with the beauty of its colour, and its uncommon length. The confusion of Clarence Hervey convinced her that he was extremely interested about the person to whom the hair belonged, and the species of alarm which she had felt at this discovery opened her eyes effectually to the state of her own heart. She was sensible that the sight of a lock of hair, however long, or however beautiful, in the hands of any man but Clarence Hervey, could not possibly have excited any emotion in her mind. "Fortunately," thought she, "I have discovered that he is attached to another, whilst it is yet in my power to command my affections; and he shall see that I am not so weak as to form any false expectations from what I must now consider as mere common-place flattery." Belinda was glad that Lady Delacour was not present at the discovery of the lock of hair, as she was aware that she would have rallied her unmercifully upon the occasion; and she rejoiced that she had not been prevailed upon to give Madame la Comtesse de Pomenars a lock of her belle chevelure. She could not help thinking, from the recollection of several minute circumstances, that Clarence Hervey had endeavoured to gain an interest in her affections, and she felt that there would be great impropriety in receiving his ambiguous visits during Lady Delacour's confinement to her room. She therefore gave orders that Mr. Hervey should not in future be admitted, till her ladyship should again see company. This precaution proved totally superfluous, for Mr. Hervey never called again, during the whole course of Lady Delacour's confinement, though his servant regularly came every morning with inquiries after her ladyship's health. She kept her room for about ten days; a confinement to which she submitted with extreme impatience: bodily pain she bore with fortitude, but constraint and ennui she could not endure.

One morning as she was sitting up in bed, looking over a large collection of notes, and cards of inquiry after her health, she exclaimed—

"These people will soon be tired of bidding their footman put it into their heads to inquire whether I am alive or dead—I must appear amongst them again, if it be only for a few minutes, or they will forget me.

When I am fatigued, I will retire, and you, my dear Belinda, shall represent me; so tell them to open my doors, and unmuffle the knocker: let me hear the sound of music and dancing, and let the house be filled again, for Heaven's sake. Dr. Zimmermann should never have been my physician, for he would have prescribed solitude. Now solitude and silence are worse for me than poppy and mandragora. It is impossible to tell how much silence tires the ears of those who have not been used to it. For mercy's sake, Marriott," continued her ladyship, turning to Marriott, who just then came softly into the room, "for mercy's sake, don't walk to all eternity on tiptoes: to see people gliding about like ghosts makes me absolutely fancy myself amongst the shades below. I would rather be stunned by the loudest peal that ever thundering footman gave at my door, than hear Marriott lock that boudoir, as if my life depended on my not hearing the key turned."

"Dear me! I never knew any lady that was ill, except my lady, complain of one's not making a noise to disturb her," said Marriott.

"Then to please you, Marriott, I will complain of the only noise that does, or ever did disturb me—the screaming of your odious macaw."

Now Marriott had a prodigious affection for this macaw, and she defended it with as much eagerness as if it had been her child.

"Odious! O dear, my lady! to call my poor macaw odious!—I didn't expect it would ever have come to this—I am sure I don't deserve it—I'm sure I don't deserve that my lady should have taken such a dislike to me."

And here Marriott actually burst into tears. "But, my dear Marriott," said Lady Delacour, "I only object to your macaw—may not I dislike your macaw without disliking you?—I have heard of 'love me, love my dog;' but I never heard of 'love me, love my bird'—did you, Miss Portman?"

Marriott turned sharply round upon Miss Portman, and darted a fiery look at her through the midst of her tears. "Then 'tis plain," said she, "who I'm to thank for this;" and as she left the room her lady could not complain of her shutting the door after her too gently.

"Give her three minutes' grace and she will come to her senses," said Lady Delacour, "for she is not a bankrupt in sense. Oh, three minutes won't do; I must allow her three days' grace, I perceive," said Lady Delacour when Marriott half an hour afterward reappeared, with a face which might have sat for the picture of ill-humour. Her ill-humour, however, did not prevent her from attending her lady as usual; she performed all her customary offices with the most officious zeal but in profound silence, except every now and then she would utter a sigh, which seemed to say, "See how much I'm attached to my lady, and yet my lady hates my macaw!" Her lady, who perfectly understood the language of sighs, and felt the force of Marriott's, forbore to touch again on the tender subject of the macaw, hoping that when her house was once more filled with company, she should be relieved by more agreeable noises from continually hearing this pertinacious tormentor.

As soon as it was known that Lady Delacour was sufficiently recovered to receive company, her door was crowded with carriages; and as soon as it was understood that balls and concerts were to go on as usual at her house, her "troops of friends" appeared to congratulate her, and to amuse themselves.

"How stupid it is," said Lady Delacour to Belinda, "to hear congratulatory speeches from people, who would not care if I were in the black hole at Calcutta this minute; but we must take the world as it goes—dirt and precious stones mixed together. Clarence Hervey, however, n'a pas une ame de boue; he, I am sure, has been really concerned for me: he thinks that his young horses were the sole cause of the whole evil, and he blames himself so sincerely, and so unjustly, that I really was half tempted to undeceive him; but that would have been doing him an injury, for you know great philosophers tell us that there is no pleasure in the world equal to that of being well deceived, especially by the fair sex. Seriously, Belinda, is it my fancy, or is not Clarence wonderfully changed? Is not he grown pale, and thin, and serious, not to say melancholy? What have you done to him since I have been ill?"

"Nothing—I have never seen him."

"No! then the thing is accounted for very naturally—he is in despair because he has been banished from your divine presence."

"More likely because he has been in anxiety about your ladyship," said Belinda.

"I will find out the cause, let it be what it may," said Lady Delacour: "luckily my address is equal to my curiosity, and that is saying a great deal."

Notwithstanding all her ladyship's address, her curiosity was baffled; she could not discover Clarence Hervey's secret, and she began to believe that the change which she had noticed in his looks and manner was imaginary or accidental. Had she seen more of him at this time, she would not have so easily given up her suspicions; but she saw him only for a few minutes every day, and during that time he talked to her with all his former gaiety; besides, Lady Delacour had herself a daily part to perform, which occupied almost her whole attention. Notwithstanding the vivacity which she affected, Belinda perceived that she was now more seriously alarmed than she had ever been about her health. It was all that her utmost exertions could accomplish, to appear for a short time in the day—some evenings she came into company only for half an hour, on other days only for a few minutes, just walked through the rooms, paid her compliments to every body, complained of a nervous head-ache, left Belinda to do the honours for her, and retired.

Miss Portman was now really placed in a difficult and dangerous situation, and she had ample opportunities of learning and practising prudence. All the fashionable dissipated young men in London frequented Lady Delacour's house, and it was said that they were drawn thither by the attractions of her fair representative. The gentlemen considered a niece of Mrs. Stanhope as their lawful prize. The ladies wondered that the men could think Belinda Portman a beauty; but whilst they affected to scorn, they sincerely feared her charms. Thus left entirely to her own discretion, she was exposed at once to the malignant eye of envy, and the insidious voice of flattery—she had no friend, no guide, and scarcely a protector: her aunt Stanhope's letters, indeed, continually supplied her with advice, but with advice which she could not follow consistently with her own feelings and principles. Lady Delacour, even if she had been well, was not a person on whose counsels she could rely; our heroine was not one of those daring spirits, who are ambitious of acting for themselves; she felt the utmost diffidence of her own powers, yet at the same time a firm resolution not to be led even by timidity into follies which the example of Lady Delacour had taught her to despise. Belinda's prudence seemed to increase with the necessity for its exertion. It was not the mercenary wily prudence of a young lady, who has been taught to think it virtue to sacrifice the affections of her heart to the interests of her fortune—it was not the prudence of a cold and selfish, but of a modest and generous woman. She found it most difficult to satisfy herself in her conduct towards Clarence Hervey: he seemed mortified and miserable if she treated him merely as a common acquaintance, yet she felt the danger of admitting him to the familiarity of friendship. Had she been thoroughly convinced that he was attached to some other woman, she hoped that she could freely converse with him, and look upon him as a married man; but notwithstanding the lock of beautiful hair, she could not entirely divest herself of the idea that she was beloved, when she observed the extreme eagerness with which Clarence Hervey watched all her motions, and followed her with his eye as if his fate depended upon her. She remarked that he endeavoured as much as possible to prevent this species of attention from being noticed, either by the public or by herself; his manner towards her every day became more distant and respectful, more constrained and embarrassed; but now and then a different look and expression escaped. She had often heard of Mr. Hervey's great address in affairs of gallantry, and she was sometimes inclined to believe that he was trifling with her, merely for the glory of a conquest over her heart; at other times she suspected him of deeper designs upon her, such as would deserve contempt and detestation; but upon the whole she was disposed to believe that he was entangled by some former attachment from which he could not extricate himself with honour; and upon this supposition she thought him worthy of her esteem, and of her pity.

About this time Sir Philip Baddely began to pay a sort of lounging attention to Belinda: he knew that Clarence Hervey liked her, and this was the principal cause of his desire to attract her attention. "Belinda Portman" became his favourite toast, and amongst his companions he gave himself the air of talking of her with rapture.

"Rochfort," said he, one day, to his friend, "damme, if I was to think of Belinda Portman in any way—you take me—Clary would look damned blue—hey?—damned blue, and devilish small, and cursed silly too—hey?"

"'Pon honour, I should like to see him," said Rochfort: "'pon honour, he deserves it from us, Sir Phil, and I'll stand your friend with the girl, and it will do no harm to give her a hint of Clary's Windsor flame, as a dead secret—'pon honour, he deserves it from us."

Now it seems that Sir Philip Baddely and Mr. Rochfort, during the time of Clarence Hervey's intimacy with them, observed that he paid frequent visits at Windsor, and they took it into their heads that he kept a mistress there. They were very curious to see her: and, unknown to Clarence, they made several attempts for this purpose: at last one evening, when they were certain that he was not at Windsor, they scaled the high garden wall of the house which he frequented, and actually obtained a sight of a beautiful young girl and an elderly lady, whom they took for her gouvernante. This adventure they kept a profound secret from Clarence, because they knew that he would have quarrelled with them immediately, and would have called them to account for their intrusion. They now determined to avail themselves of their knowledge, and of his ignorance of this circumstance: but they were sensible that it was necessary to go warily to work, lest they should betray themselves. Accordingly they began by dropping distant mysterious hints about Clarence Hervey to Lady Delacour and Miss Portman. Such for instance as—"Damme, we all know Clary's a perfect connoisseur in beauty—hey, Rochfort?—one beauty at a time is not enough for him—hey, damme? And it is not fashion, nor wit, nor elegance, and all that, that he looks for always."

These observations were accompanied with the most significant looks. Belinda heard and saw all this in painful silence, but Lady Delacour often used her address to draw some farther explanation from Sir

Philip: his regular answer was, "No, no, your ladyship must excuse me there; I can't peach, damme—hey, Rochfort?"

He was in hopes, from the reserve with which Miss Portman began to treat Clarence, that he should, without making any distinct charge, succeed in disgusting her with his rival. Mr. Hervey was about this time less assiduous than formerly in his visits at Lady Delacour's; Sir Philip was there every day, and often for Miss Portman's entertainment exerted himself so far as to tell the news of the town. One morning, when Clarence Hervey happened to be present, the baronet thought it incumbent upon him to eclipse his rival in conversation, and he began to talk of the last fête champêtre at Frogmore.

"What a cursed unlucky overturn that was of yours, Lady Delacour, with those famous young horses! Why, what with this sprain, and this nervous business, you've not been able to stir out since the birthday, and you've missed the breakfast, and all that, at Frogmore—why, all the world stayed broiling in town on purpose for it, and you that had a card too—how damned provoking!"

"I regret extremely that my illness prevented me from being at this charming fête; I regret it more on Miss Portman's account than on my own," said her ladyship. Belinda assured her that she felt no mortification from the disappointment.

"O, damme! but I would have driven you in my curricle," said Sir Philip: "it was the finest sight and best conducted I ever saw, and only wanted Miss Portman to make it complete. We had gipsies, and Mrs. Mills the actress for the queen of the gipsies; and she gave us a famous good song, Rochfort, you know—and then there was two children upon an ass—damme, I don't know how they came there, for they're things one sees every day—and belonged only to two of the soldiers' wives—for we had the whole band of the Staffordshire playing at dinner, and we had some famous glees—and Fawcett gave us his laughing song, and then we had the launching of the ship, and only it was a boat, it would have been well enough—but damme, the song of Polly Oliver was worth the whole—except the Flemish Hercules, Ducrow, you know, dressed in light blue and silver, and—Miss Portman, I wish you had seen this—three great coach-wheels on his chin, and a ladder and two chairs and two children on them—and after that, he sported a musquet and bayonet with the point of the bayonet on his chin—faith! that was really famous! But I forgot the Pyrrhic dance, Miss Portman, which was damned fine too—danced in boots and spurs by those Hungarian fellows—they jump and turn about, and clap their knees with their hands, and put themselves in all sorts of ways—and then we had that song of Polly Oliver, as I told you before, and Mrs. Mills gave us—no, no—it was a drummer of the Staffordshire dressed as a gipsy girl, gave us the cottage on the moor, the most charming thing, and would suit your voice, Miss Portman—damme, you'd sing it like an angel—But where was I?—Oh, then they had tea—and fireplaces built of brick, out in the air—and then the entrance to the ball-room was all a colonnade done with lamps and flowers, and that sort of thing—and there was some bon-mot (but that was in the morning) amongst the gipsies about an orange and the stadtholder—and then there was a Turkish dance, and a Polonese dance, all very fine, but nothing to come up to the Pyrrhic touch, which was a great deal the most knowing, in boots and spurs—damme, now, I can't describe the thing to you, 'tis a cursed pity you weren't there, damme."

Lady Delacour assured Sir Philip that she had been more entertained by the description than she could have been by the reality.—"Clarence, was not it the best description you ever heard? But pray favour us with a touch of the Pyrrhic dance, Sir Philip."

Lady Delacour spoke with such polite earnestness, and the baronet had so little penetration and so much conceit, that he did not suspect her of irony: he eagerly began to exhibit the Pyrrhic dance, but in such a manner that it was impossible for human gravity to withstand the sight—Rochfort laughed first, Lady Delacour followed him, and Clarence Hervey and Belinda could no longer restrain themselves.

"Damme, now I believe you've all been quizzing me," cried the baronet, and he fell into a sulky silence, eyeing Clarence Hervey and Miss Portman from time to time with what he meant for a knowing look. His silence and sulkiness lasted till Clarence took his leave. Soon afterward Belinda retired to the music-room. Sir Philip then begged to speak a few words to Lady Delacour, with a face of much importance: and after a preamble of nonsensical expletives, he said that his regard for her ladyship and Miss Portman made him wish to explain hints which had been dropped from him at times, and which he could not explain to her satisfaction, without a promise of inviolable secresy. "As Hervey is or was a sort of a friend, I can't mention this sort of thing without such a preliminary."—Lady Delacour gave the preliminary promise, and Sir Philip informed her, that people began to take notice that Hervey was an admirer of Miss Portman, and that it might be a disadvantage to the young lady, as Mr. Hervey could have no serious intentions, because he had an attachment, to his certain knowledge, elsewhere.

"A matrimonial attachment?" said Lady Delacour.

"Why, damme, as to matrimony, I can't say; but the girl's so famously beautiful, and Clary has been constant to her so many years—"

"Many years! then she is not young?"

"Oh, damme, yes, she is not more than seventeen,—and, let her be what else she will, she's a famous fine girl. I had a sight of her once at Windsor, by stealth."

And then the baronet described her after his manner.—"Where Clary keeps her now, I can't make out; but he has taken her away from Windsor. She was then with a gouvernante, and is as proud as the devil, which smells like matrimony for Clary."

"And do you know this peerless damsel's name?"

"I think the old Jezebel called her Miss St. Pierre—ay, damme, it was Virginia too—Virginia St. Pierre."

"Virginia St. Pierre, a pretty romantic name," said Lady Delacour: "Miss Portman and I are extremely obliged by your attention to the preservation of our hearts, and I promise you we shall keep your counsel and our own."

Sir Philip then, with more than his usual complement of oaths, pronounced Miss Portman to be the finest girl he had ever seen, and took his leave.

When Lady Delacour repeated this story to Belinda, she concluded by saying, "Now, my dear, you know Sir Philip Baddely has his own views in telling us all this—in telling you, all this; for evidently he admires you, and consequently hates Clarence. So I believe only half the man says; and the other half, though it has made you turn so horribly pale, my love, I consider as a thing of no manner of consequence to you."

"Of no manner of consequence to me, I assure your ladyship," said Belinda; "I have always considered Mr. Hervey as—"

"Oh, as a common acquaintance, no doubt—but we'll pass over all those pretty speeches: I was going to say that this 'mistress in the wood' can be of no consequence to your happiness, because, whatever that fool Sir Philip may think, Clarence Hervey is not a man to go and marry a girl who has been his mistress for half a dozen years. Do not look so shocked, my dear—I really cannot help laughing. I congratulate you, however, that the thing is no worse—it is all in rule and in course—when a man marries, he sets up new equipages, and casts off old mistresses; or if you like to see the thing as a woman of sentiment rather than as a woman of the world, here is the prettiest opportunity for your lover's making a sacrifice. I am sorry I cannot make you smile, my dear; but consider, as nobody knows this naughty thing but ourselves, we are not called upon to bristle up our morality, and the most moral ladies in the world do not expect men to be as moral as themselves: so we may suit the measure of our external indignation to our real feelings. Sir Philip cannot stir in the business, for he knows Clarence would call him out if his secret visit to Virginia were to come to light. I advise you d'aller votre train with Clarence, without seeming to suspect him in the least; there is nothing like innocence in these cases, my dear: but I know by the Spanish haughtiness of your air at this instant, that you would sooner die the death of the sentimental—than follow my advice."

Belinda, without any haughtiness, but with firm gentleness, replied, that she had no designs whatever upon Mr. Hervey, and that therefore there could be no necessity for any manoeuvring on her part;—that the ambiguity of his conduct towards her had determined her long since to guard her affections, and that she had the satisfaction to feel that they were entirely under her command.

"That is a great satisfaction, indeed, my dear," said Lady Delacour. "It is a pity that your countenance, which is usually expressive enough, should not at this instant obey your wishes and express perfect felicity. But though you feel no pain from disappointed affection, doubtless the concern that you show arises from the necessity you are under of withdrawing a portion of your esteem from Mr. Hervey—this is the style for you, is it not? After all, my dear, the whole maybe a quizzification of Sir Philip's—and yet he gave me such a minute description of her person! I am sure the man has not invention or taste enough to produce such a fancy piece."

"Did he mention," said Belinda, in a low voice, "the colour of her hair?"

"Yes, light brown; but the colour of this hair seems to affect you more than all the rest."

Here, to Belinda's great relief, the conversation was interrupted by the entrance of Marriott. From all she had heard, but especially from the agreement between the colour of the hair which dropped from Hervey's letter with Sir Philip's description of Virginia's, Miss Portman was convinced that Clarence had some secret attachment; and she could not help blaming him in her own mind for having, as she thought, endeavoured to gain her affections, whilst he knew that his heart was engaged to another. Mr. Hervey, however, gave her no farther reason to suspect him of any design to win her love; for about this time his manner towards her changed,—he obviously endeavoured to avoid her; his visits were short, and his attention was principally directed to Lady Delacour; when she retired, he took his leave, and Sir Philip Baddely had the field to himself. The baronet, who thought that he had succeeded in producing a coldness between Belinda and his rival, was surprised to find that he could not gain any advantage for himself; for some time he had not the slightest thoughts of any serious connexion with the lady, but at last he was piqued by her indifference, and by the raillery of his friend Rochfort.

"'Pon honour," said Rochfort, "the girl must be in love with Clary, for she minds you no more than if you were nobody."

"I could make her sing to another tune, if I pleased," said Sir Philip; "but, damme, it would cost me too much—a wife's too expensive a thing, now-a-days. Why, a man could have twenty curricles, and a fine stud, and a pack of hounds, and as many mistresses as he chooses into the bargain, for what it would cost him to take a wife. Oh, damme, Belinda Portman's a fine girl, but not worth so much as that comes to; and yet, confound me, if I should not like to see how blue Clary would look, if I were to propose for her in good earnest—hey, Rochfort?—I should like to pay him for the way he served us about that quiz of a doctor, hey?"

"Ay," said Rochfort, "you know he told us there was a tant pis and a tant mieux in every thing—he's not come to the tant pis yet. 'Pon honour, Sir Philip, the thing rests with you."

The baronet vibrated for some time between the fear of being taken in by one of Mrs. Stanhope's nieces, and the hope of triumphing over Clarence Hervey. At last, what he called love prevailed over prudence, and he was resolved, cost him what it would, to have Belinda Portman. He had not the least doubt of being accepted, if he made a proposal of marriage; consequently, the moment that he came to this determination, he could not help assuming d'avance the tone of a favoured lover.

"Damme," cried Sir Philip, one night, at Lady Delacour's concert, "I think that Mr. Hervey has taken out a patent for talking to Miss Portman; but damme if I give up this place, now I have got it," cried the baronet, seating himself beside Belinda.

Mr. Hervey did not contest his seat, and Sir Philip kept his post during the remainder of the concert; but, though he had the field entirely to himself, he could not think of any thing more interesting, more amusing, to whisper in Belinda's ear, than, "Don't you think the candles want snuffing famously?"

CHAPTER XII — THE MACAW

The baronet determined the next day upon the grand attack. He waited upon Miss Portman with the certainty of being favourably received; but he was, nevertheless, somewhat embarrassed to know how to begin the conversation, when he found himself alone with the lady.

He twirled and twisted a short stick that he held in his hand, and put it into and out of his boot twenty times, and at last he began with—"Lady Delacour's not gone to Harrowgate yet?"

"No: her ladyship has not yet felt herself well enough to undertake the journey."

"That was a cursed unlucky overturn! She may thank Clarence Hervey for that: it's like him,—he thinks he's a better judge of horses, and wine, and every thing else, than any body in the world. Damme, now if I don't believe he thinks nobody else but himself has eyes enough to see that a fine woman's a fine woman; but I'd have him to know, that Miss Belinda Portman has been Sir Philip Baddely's toast these two months."

As this intelligence did not seem to make the expected impression upon Miss Belinda Portman, Sir Philip had recourse again to his little stick, with which he went through the sword exercise. After a silence of some minutes, and after walking to the window, and back again, as if to look for sense, he exclaimed, "How is Mrs. Stanhope now, pray, Miss Portman? and your sister, Mrs. Tollemache? she was the finest woman, I thought, the first winter she came out, that ever I saw, damme. Have you ever been told that you're like her?"

"Never, sir."

"Oh, damn it then, but you are; only ten times handsomer."

"Ten times handsomer than the finest woman you ever saw, Sir Philip?" said Belinda, smiling.

"Than the finest woman I had ever seen then," said Sir Philip; "for, damme, I did not know what it was to be in love then" (here the baronet heaved an audible sigh): "I always laughed at love, and all that, then, and marriage particularly. I'll trouble you for Mrs. Stanhope's direction, Miss Portman; I believe, to do the thing in style, I ought to write to her before I speak to you."

Belinda looked at him with astonishment; and laying down the pencil with which she had just begun to write a direction to Mrs. Stanhope, she said, "Perhaps, Sir Philip, to do the thing in style, I ought to pretend at this instant not to understand you; but such false delicacy might mislead you: permit me, therefore, to say, that if I have any concern in the letter which you, are going to write to my aunt Stanhope—"

"Well guessed!" interrupted Sir Philip: "to be sure you have, and you're a charming girl—damn me if you aren't—for meeting my ideas in this way, which will save a cursed deal of trouble," added the polite lover, seating himself on the sofa, beside Belinda.

"To prevent your giving yourself any further trouble then, sir, on my account," said Miss Portman—

"Nay, damme, don't catch at that unlucky word, trouble, nor look so cursed angry; though it becomes you, too, uncommonly, and I like pride in a handsome woman, if it was only for variety's sake, for it's not what one meets with often, now-a-days. As to trouble, all I meant was, the trouble of writing to Mrs. Stanhope, which of course I thank you for saving me; for to be sure, I'd rather (and you can't blame me for that) have my answer from your own charming lips, if it was only for the pleasure of seeing you blush in this heavenly sort of style."

"To put an end to this heavenly sort of style, sir," said Belinda, withdrawing her hand, which the baronet took as if he was confident of its being his willing prize, "I must explicitly assure you, that it is not in my power to encourage your addresses. I am fully sensible," added Miss Portman, "of the honour Sir Philip Baddely has done me, and I hope he will not be offended by the frankness of my answer."

"You can't be in earnest, Miss Portman!" exclaimed the astonished baronet.

"Perfectly in earnest, Sir Philip."

"Confusion seize me," cried he, starting up, "if this isn't the most extraordinary thing I ever heard! Will you do me the honour, madam, to let me know your particular objections to Sir Philip Baddely?"

"My objections," said Belinda, "cannot be obviated, and therefore it would be useless to state them."

"Nay, pray, ma'am, do me the favour—I only ask for information sake—is it to Sir Philip Baddely's fortune, 15,000l. a year, you object, or to his family, or to his person?—Oh, curse it!" said he, changing his tone, "you're only quizzing me to see how I should look—damn me, you did it too well, you little coquet!"

Belinda again assured him that she was entirely in earnest, and that she was incapable of the sort of coquetry which he ascribed to her.

"Oh, damme, ma'am, then I've no more to say—a coquet is a thing I understand as well as another, and if we had been only talking in the air, it would have been another thing; but when I come at once to a proposal in form, and a woman seriously tells me she has objections that cannot be obviated, damme, what must I, or what must the world conclude, but that she's very unaccountable, or that she's engaged—which last I presume to be the case, and it would have been a satisfaction to me to have known it sooner—at any rate, it is a satisfaction to me to know it now."

"I am sorry to deprive you of so much satisfaction," said Miss Portman, "by assuring you, that I am not engaged to any one."

Here the conversation was interrupted by the entrance of Lord Delacour, who came to inquire of Miss Portman how his lady did. The baronet, after twisting his little black stick into all manner of shapes, finished by breaking it, and then having no other resource, suddenly wished Miss Portman a good morning, and decamped with a look of silly ill-humour. He was determined to write to Mrs. Stanhope, whose influence over her niece he had no doubt would be decisive in his favour. "Sir Philip seems to be a little out of sorts this morning," said Lord Delacour: "I am afraid he's angry with me for interrupting his conversation; but really I did not know he was here, and I wanted to catch you a moment alone, that I might, in the first place, thank you for all your goodness to Lady Delacour. She has had a tedious sprain of it; these nervous fevers and convulsions—I don't understand them, but I think Dr. X—'s prescriptions seem to have done her good, for she is certainly better of late, and I am glad to hear music and people again in the house, because I know all this is what my Lady Delacour likes, and there is no reasonable indulgence that I would not willingly allow a wife; but I think there is a medium in all things. I am not a man to be governed by a wife, and when I have once said a thing, I like to be steady and always shall. And I am sure Miss Portman has too much good sense to think me wrong: for now, Miss Portman, in that quarrel about the coach and horses, which you heard part of one morning at breakfast—I must tell you the beginning of that quarrel."

"Excuse me, my lord, but I would rather hear of the end than of the beginning of quarrels."

"That shows your good sense as well as your good nature. I wish you could make my Lady Delacour of your taste—she does not want sense—but then (I speak to you freely of all that lies upon my mind, Miss Portman, for I know—I know you have no delight in making mischief in a house,) between you and me, her sense is not of the right kind. A woman may have too much wit—now too much is as bad as too little, and in a woman, worse; and when two people come to quarrel, then wit on either side, but more especially on the wife's, you know is very provoking—'tis like concealed weapons, which are wisely forbidden by law. If a person kill another in a fray, with a concealed weapon, ma'am, by a sword in a cane, for instance, 'tis murder by the law. Now even if it were not contrary to law, I would never have such a thing in my cane to carry about with me; for when a man's in a passion he forgets every thing, and would as soon lay about him with a sword as with a cane: so it is better such a thing should not be in his power. And it is the same with wit, which would be safest and best out of the power of some people."

"But is it fair, my lord, to make use of wit yourself to abuse wit in others?" said Belinda with a smile, which put his lordship into perfect good-humour with both himself and his lady.

"Why, really," said he, "there would be no living with Lady Delacour, if I did not come out with a little sly bit of wit now and then; but it is what I am not in the habit of doing, I assure you, except when very hard pushed. But, Miss Portman, as you like so much to hear the end of quarrels, here's the end of one which you have a particular right to hear something of," continued his lordship, taking out his pocket-book and producing some bank-notes: "you should have received this before, madam, if I had known of the transaction sooner—of your part of it, I mean."

"Milord, de man call to speak about de burgundy you order, milord," said Champfort, who came into the room with a sly, inquisitive face.

"Tell him I'll see him immediately—show him into the parlour, and give him a newspaper to read."

"Yes, milord—milord has it in his pocket since he dress."

"Here it is," said his lordship; and as Champfort came forward to receive the newspaper, his eye glanced at the bank-notes, and then at Miss Portman.

"Here," continued Lord Delacour, as Champfort had left the room, "here are your two hundred guineas, Miss Portman; and as I am going to this man about my burgundy, and shall be out all the rest of the day, let me trouble you the next time you see Lady Delacour to give her this pocket-book from me. I should be sorry that Miss Portman, from any thing that has passed, should run away with the idea that I am a niggardly husband, or a tyrant, though I certainly like to be master in my own house. What are you doing, madam?—that is your note, that does not go into the pocket-book, you know."

"Permit me to put it in, my lord," said Belinda, returning the pocket-book to him, "and to beg you will give Lady Delacour the pleasure of seeing you: she has inquired several times whether your lordship were at home. I will run up to her dressing-room, and tell her that you are here."

"How lightly she goes on the wings of good-nature!" said Lord Delacour. "I can do no less than follow her; for though I like to be treated with respect in my own house, there is a time for every thing. I would not give Lady Delacour the trouble of coming down here to me with her sprained ankle, especially as she has inquired for me several times."

His lordship's visit was not of unseasonable length; for he recollected that the man who came about the burgundy was waiting for him. But, perhaps, the shortness of the visit rendered it the more pleasing, for Lady Delacour afterward said to Belinda, "My dear, would you believe it, my Lord Delacour was absolutely a perfect example of the useful and agreeable this morning—who knows but he may become the sublime and beautiful in time? En attendant here are your two hundred guineas, my dear Belinda: a thousand thanks for the thing, and a million for the manner—manner is all in all in conferring favours. My lord, who, to do him justice, has too much honesty to pretend to more delicacy than he really possesses, told me that he had been taking a lesson from Miss Portman this morning in the art of obliging; and really, for a grown gentleman, and for the first lesson, he comes on surprisingly. I do think, that by the time he is a widower his lordship will be quite another thing, quite an agreeable man—not a genius, not a Clarence Hervey—that you cannot expect. Apropos, what is the reason that we have seen so little of Clarence Hervey lately? He has certainly some secret attraction elsewhere. It cannot be that girl Sir Philip mentioned; no, she's nothing new. Can it be at Lady Anne Percival's?—or where can it be? Whenever he sees me, I think he asks when we go to Harrowgate. Now Oakly-park is within a few miles of Harrowgate. I will not go there, that's decided. Lady Anne is an exemplary matron, so she is out of the case; but I hope she has no sister excellence, no niece, no cousin, to entangle our hero."

"Ours!" said Belinda.

"Well, yours, then," said Lady Delacour.

"Mine!"

"Yes, yours: I never in my life saw a better struggle between a sigh and a smile. But what have you done to poor Sir Philip Baddely? My Lord Delacour told me—you know all people who have nothing else to say, tell news quicker than others—my Lord Delacour told me, that he saw Sir Philip part from you this morning in a terrible bad humour. Come, whilst you tell your story, help me to string these pearls; that will save you from the necessity of looking at me, and will conceal your blushes: you need not be afraid of betraying Sir Philip's secrets; for I could have told you long ago, that he would inevitably propose for you—the fact is nothing new or surprising to me, but I should really like to hear how ridiculous the man made himself."

"And that," said Belinda, "is the only thing which I do not wish to tell your ladyship."

"Lord, my dear, surely it is no secret that Sir Philip Baddely is ridiculous; but you are so good-natured that I can't be out of humour with you. If you won't gratify my curiosity, will you gratify my taste, and sing for me once more that charming song which none but you can sing to please me?—I must learn it from you, absolutely."

Just as Belinda was beginning to sing, Marriott's macaw began to scream, so that Lady Delacour could not hear any thing else.

"Oh, that odious macaw!" cried her ladyship, "I can endure it no longer" (and she rang her bell violently): "it kept me from sleeping all last night—Marriott must give up this bird. Marriott, I cannot endure that macaw—you must part with it for my sake, Marriott. It cost you four guineas: I am sure I would give five with the greatest pleasure to get rid of it, for it is the torment of my life."

"Dear, my lady! I can assure you it is only because they will not shut the doors after them below, as I desire. I am certain Mr. Champfort never shut a door after him in his life, nor never will if he was to live to the days of Methuselah."

"That is very little satisfaction to me, Marriott," said Lady Delacour.

"And indeed, my lady, it is very little satisfaction to me, to hear my macaw abused as it is every day of my life, for Mr. Champfort's fault."

"But it cannot be Champfort's fault that I have ears."

"But if the doors were shut, my lady, you wouldn't or couldn't hear—as I'll prove immediately," said Marriott, and she ran directly and shut, according to her own account, "eleven doors which were stark staring wide open."—"Now, my lady, you can't hear a single syllable of the macaw."

"No, but one of the eleven doors will open presently," said Lady Delacour: "you will observe it is always more than ten to one against me."

A door opened, and the macaw was heard to scream. "The macaw must go, Marriott, that is certain," said her ladyship, firmly.

"Then I must go, my lady," said Marriott, angrily, "that is certain; for to part with my macaw is a thing I cannot do to please any body." Her eyes turned with indignation upon Belinda, from association merely; because the last time that she had been angry about her macaw, she had also been angry with Miss Portman, whom she imagined to be the secret enemy of her favourite.

"To stay another week in the house after my macaw's discarded in disgrace is a thing nothing shall prevail upon me to do." She flung out of the room in a fury.

"Good Heavens! am I reduced to this?" said Lady Delacour: "she thinks that she has me in her power. No; I can die without her: I have but a short time to live—I will not live a slave. Let the woman betray me, if she will. Follow her this moment, my dear generous friend; tell her never to come into this room again: take this pocket-book, pay her whatever is due to her in the first place, and give her fifty guineas—observe!—not as a bribe, but as a reward."

It was a delicate and difficult commission. Belinda found Marriott at first incapable of listening to reason. "I am sure there is nobody in the world that would treat me and my macaw in this manner, except my lady," cried she; "and somebody must have set her against me, for it is not natural to her: but since she can't bear me about her any longer, 'tis time I should be gone."

"The only thing of which Lady Delacour complained was the noise of this macaw," said Belinda; "it was a pretty bird—how long have you had it?"

"Scarcely a month," said Marriott, sobbing.

"And how long have you lived with your lady?"

"Six years!—And to part with her after all!—"

"And for the sake of a macaw! And at a time when your lady is so much in want of you, Marriott! You know she cannot live long, and she has much to suffer before she dies, and if you leave her, and if in a fit of passion you betray the confidence she has placed in you, you will reproach yourself for it ever afterward. This bird—or all the birds in the world—will not be able to console you; for you are of an affectionate disposition, I know, and sincerely attached to your poor lady."

"That I am!—and to betray her!—Oh, Miss Portman, I would sooner cut off my hand than do it. And I have been tried more than my lady knows of, or you either, for Mr. Champfort, who is the greatest mischief-maker in the world, and is the cause, by not shutting the door, of all this dilemma; for now, ma'am, I'm convinced, by the tenderness of your speaking, that you are not the enemy to me I supposed, and I beg your pardon; but I was going to say that Mr. Champfort, who saw the fracas between my lord and me, about the key and the door, the night of my lady's accident, has whispered it about at Lady Singleton's and every where—Mrs. Luttridge's maid, ma'am, who is my cousin, has pestered me with so many questions and offers, from Mrs. Luttridge and Mrs. Freke, of any money, if I would only tell who was in the boudoir—and I have always answered, nobody—and I defy them to get any thing out of me. Betray my lady! I'd sooner cut my tongue out this minute! Can she have such a base opinion of me, or can you, ma'am?"

"No, indeed, I am convinced that you are incapable of betraying her, Marriott; but in all probability after you have left her—"

"If my lady would let me keep my macaw," interrupted Marriott, "I should never think of leaving her."

"The macaw she will not suffer to remain in the house, nor is it reasonable that she should: it deprives her of sleep—it kept her awake three hours this morning."

Marriott was beginning the history of Champfort and the doors again; but Miss Portman stopped her by saying, "All this is past now. How much is due to you, Mrs. Marriott? Lady Delacour has commissioned me to pay you every thing that is due to you."

"Due to me! Lord bless me, ma'am, am I to go?"

"Certainly, it was your own desire—it is consequently your lady's: she is perfectly sensible of your attachment to her, and of your services, but she cannot suffer herself to be treated with disrespect. Here are fifty guineas, which she gives you as a reward for your past fidelity, not as a bribe to secure your future secrecy. You are at liberty, she desires me to say, to tell her secret to the whole world, if you choose to do so."

"Oh, Miss Portman, take my macaw—do what you will with it—only make my peace with my lady," cried Marriott, clasping her hands, in an agony of grief: "here are the fifty guineas, ma'am, don't leave them with me—I will never be disrespectful again—take my macaw and all! No, I will carry it myself to my lady."

Lady Delacour was surprised by the sudden entrance of Marriott, and her macaw. The chain which held the bird Marriott put into her ladyship's hand without being able to say any thing more than, "Do what you please, my lady, with it—and with me."

Pacified by this submission, Lady Delacour granted Marriott's pardon, and she most sincerely rejoiced at this reconciliation.

The next day Belinda asked the dowager Lady Boucher, who was going to a bird-fancier's, to take her with her, in hopes that she might be able to meet with some bird more musical than a macaw, to console Marriott for the loss of her screaming favourite. Lady Delacour commissioned Miss Portman to go to any price she pleased. "If I were able, I would accompany you myself, my dear, for poor Marriott's sake, though I would almost as soon go to the Augean stable."

There was a bird-fancier in High Holborn, who had bought several of the hundred and eighty beautiful birds, which, as the newspapers of the day advertised, had been "collected, after great labour and expense, by Mons. Marten and Co. for the Republican Museum at Paris, and lately landed out of the French brig Urselle, taken on her voyage from Cayenne to Brest, by His Majesty's Ship Unicorn."

When Lady Boucher and Belinda arrived at this bird-fancier's, they were long in doubt to which of the feathered beauties they should give the preference. Whilst the dowager was descanting upon their various perfections, a lady and three children came in; she immediately attracted Belinda's attention, by her likeness to Clarence Hervey's description of Lady Anne Percival—it was Lady Anne, as Lady Boucher, who was slightly acquainted with her, informed Belinda in a whisper.

The children were soon eagerly engaged looking at the birds.

"Miss Portman," said Lady Boucher, "as Lady Delacour is so far from well, and wishes to have a bird that will not make any noise in the house, suppose you were to buy for Mrs. Marriott this beautiful pair of green parroquets; or, stay, a goldfinch is not very noisy, and here is one that can play a thousand pretty tricks. Pray, sir, make it draw up water in its little bucket for us."

"Oh, mamma!" said one of the little boys, "this is the very thing that is mentioned in Bewick's History of Birds. Pray look at this goldfinch, Helena, now it is drawing up its little bucket—but where is Helena? here's room for you, Helena."

Whilst the little boys were looking at the goldfinch, Belinda felt somebody touch her gently: it was Helena Delacour.

"Can I speak a few words to you?" said Helena.

Belinda walked to the farthest end of the shop with her.

"Is my mamma better?" said she, in a timid tone. "I have some gold fish, which you know cannot make the least noise: may I send them to her? I heard that lady call you Miss Portman: I believe you are the lady who wrote such a kind postscript to me in mamma's last letter—that is the reason I speak so freely to you now. Perhaps you would write to tell me if mamma will see me; and Lady Anne Percival would take me at any time, I am sure—but she goes to Oakly-park in a few days. I wish I might be with mamma whilst she is ill; I would not make the least noise. But don't ask her, if you think it will be troublesome— only let me send the gold fish."

Belinda was touched by the manner in which this affectionate little girl spoke to her. She assured her that she would say all she wished to her mother, and she begged Helena to send the gold fish whenever she pleased.

"Then," said Helena, "I will send them as soon as I go home as soon as I go back to Lady Anne Percival's, I mean." Belinda, when she had finished speaking to Helena, heard the man who was showing the birds, lament that he had not a blue macaw, which Lady Anne Percival was commissioned to procure for Mrs. Margaret Delacour.

"Red macaws, my lady, I have in abundance; but unfortunately, a blue macaw I really have not at present; nor have I been able to get one, though I have inquired amongst all the bird-fanciers in town; and I went to the auction at Haydon-square on purpose, but could not get one."

Belinda requested Lady Boucher would tell her servants to bring in the cage that contained Marriott's blue macaw; and as soon as it was brought she gave it to Helena, and begged that she would carry it to her Aunt Delacour.

"Lord, my dear Miss Portman," said Lady Boucher, drawing her aside, "I am afraid you will get yourself into a scrape; for Lady Delacour is not upon speaking terms with this Mrs. Margaret Delacour—she cannot endure her; you know she is my Lord Delacour's aunt."

Belinda persisted in sending the macaw, for she was in hopes that these terrible family quarrels might be made up, if either party would condescend to show any disposition to oblige the other.

Lady Anne Percival understood Miss Portman's civility as it was meant.

"This is a bird of good omen," said she; "it augurs family peace."

"I wish you would do me the favour, Lady Boucher, to introduce me to Miss Portman," continued Lady Anne.

"The very thing I wished!" cried Helena.

A few minutes' conversation passed afterward upon different subjects, and Lady Anne Percival and Belinda parted with a mutual desire to see more of each other.

CHAPTER XIII — SORTES VIRGILIANAE

When Belinda got home, Lady Delacour was busy in the library looking over a collection of French plays with the ci-devant Count de N—; a gentleman who possessed such singular talents for reading dramatic compositions, that many people declared that they would rather hear him read a play than see it performed at the theatre. Even those who were not judges of his merit, and who had little taste for literature, crowded to hear him, because it was the fashion. Lady Delacour engaged him for a reading party at her house, and he was consulting with her what play would be most amusing to his audience. "My dear Belinda! I am glad you are come to give us your opinion," said her ladyship; "no one has a better taste: but first I should ask you what you have done at your bird-fancier's; I hope you have brought home some horned cock, or some monstrously beautiful creature for Marriott. If it has not a voice like the macaw I shall be satisfied; but even if it be the bird of paradise, I question whether Marriott will like it as well as its screaming predecessor."

"I am sure she will like what is coming for her," said Belinda, "and so will your ladyship; but do not let me interrupt you and monsieur le Comte." And as she spoke, she took up a volume of plays which lay upon the table.

"Nanine, or La Prude, which shall we have?" said Lady Delacour: "or what do you think of L'Ecossaise?"

"The scene of L'Ecossaise is laid in London," said Belinda; "I should think with an English audience it would therefore be popular."

"Yes! so it will," said Lady Delacour: "then let it be L'Ecossaise. M. le Comte I am sure will do justice to the character of Friport the Englishman, 'qui scait donner, mais qui ne scait pas vivre.' My dear, I forgot to tell you that Clarence Hervey has been here: it is a pity you did not come a little sooner, you would have heard a charming scene of the School for Scandal read by him. M. le Comte was quite delighted; but Clarence was in a great hurry, he would only give us one scene, he was going to Mr. Percival's on business. I am sure what I told you the other day is true: but, however, he has promised to come back to dine with me—M. le Comte, you will dine with us, I hope?"

The count was extremely sorry that it was impossible—he was engaged. Belinda suddenly recollected that it was time to dress for dinner; but just as the count took his leave, and as she was going up stairs, a footman met her, and told her that Mr. Hervey was in the drawing-room, and wished to speak to her. Many conjectures were formed in Belinda's mind as she passed on to the drawing-room; but the moment that she opened the door, she knew the nature of Mr. Hervey's business, for she saw the glass globe containing Helena Delacour's gold fishes standing on the table beside him. "I have been commissioned to present these to you for Lady Delacour," said Mr. Hervey, "and I have seldom received a commission that has given me so much pleasure. I perceive that Miss Portman is indeed a real friend to Lady Delacour—how happy she is to have such a friend!"

After a pause Mr. Hervey went on speaking of Lady Delacour, and of his earnest desire to see her as happy in domestic life as she appeared to be in public. He frankly confessed, that when he was first acquainted with her ladyship, he had looked upon her merely as a dissipated woman of fashion, and he had considered only his own amusement in cultivating her society: "But," continued he, "of late I have formed a different opinion of her character; and I think, from what I have observed, that Miss Portman's ideas on this subject agree with mine. I had laid a plan for making her ladyship acquainted with Lady Anne Percival, who appears to me one of the most amiable and one of the happiest of women. Oakly-park is but a few miles from Harrowgate.—But I am disappointed in this scheme; Lady Delacour has changed her mind, she says, and will not go there. Lady Anne, however, has just told me, that, though it is July, and though she loves the country, she will most willingly stay in town a month longer, as she thinks that, with your assistance, there is some probability of her effecting a reconciliation between Lady Delacour and her husband's relations, with some of whom Lady Anne is intimately acquainted. To begin with my friend, Mrs. Margaret Delacour: the macaw was most graciously received, and I flatter myself that I have prepared Mrs. Delacour to think somewhat more favourably of her niece than she was wont to do. All now depends upon Lady Delacour's conduct towards her daughter: if she continues to treat her with neglect, I shall be convinced that I have been mistaken in her character."

Belinda was much pleased by the openness and the unaffected good-nature with which Clarence Hervey spoke, and she certainly was not sorry to hear from his own lips a distinct explanation of his views and sentiments. She assured him that no effort that she could make with propriety should be wanting to effect the desirable reconciliation between her ladyship and her family, as she perfectly agreed with him in thinking that Lady Delacour's character had been generally misunderstood by the world.

"Yes," said Mr. Hervey, "her connexion with that Mrs. Freke hurt her more in the eyes of the world than she was aware of. It is tacitly understood by the public, that every lady goes bail for the character of her female friends. If Lady Delacour had been so fortunate as to meet with such a friend as Miss Portman in her early life, what a different woman she would have been! She once said some such thing to me herself, and she never appeared to me so amiable as at that moment."

Mr. Hervey pronounced these last words in a manner more than usually animated; and whilst he spoke, Belinda stooped to gather a sprig from a myrtle, which stood on the hearth. She perceived that the myrtle, which was planted in a large china vase, was propped up on one side with the broken bits of Sir Philip Baddely's little stick: she took them up, and threw them out of the window. "Lady Delacour stuck those fragments there this morning," said Clarence smiling, "as trophies. She told me of Miss Portman's victory over the heart of Sir Philip Baddely; and Miss Portman should certainly have allowed them to remain there, as indisputable evidence in favour of the baronet's taste and judgment."

Clarence Hervey appeared under some embarrassment, and seemed to be restrained by some secret cause from laying open his real feelings: his manner varied continually. Belinda could not avoid seeing his perplexity—she had recourse again to the gold fishes and to Helena: upon these subjects they could both speak very fluently. Lady Delacour made her appearance by the time that Clarence had finished repeating the Abbé Nollet's experiments, which he had heard from his friend Doctor X—.

"Now, Miss Portman, the transmission of sound in water," said Clarence—

"Deep in philosophy, I protest!" said Lady Delacour, as she came in. "What is this about the transmission of sound in water?—Ha! whence come these pretty gold fishes?"

"These gold fishes," said Belinda, "are come to console Marriott for the loss of her macaw."

"Thank you, my dear Belinda, for these mute comforters," said her ladyship; "the very best things you could have chosen."

"I have not the merit of the choice," said Belinda, "but I am heartily glad that you approve of it."

"Pretty creatures," said Lady Delacour: "no fish were ever so pretty since the days of the prince of the Black Islands in the Arabian Tales. And am I obliged to you, Clarence, for these subjects?"

"No; I have only had the honour of bringing them to your ladyship from—"

"From whom?—Amongst all my numerous acquaintance, have I one in the world who cares a gold fish about me?—Stay, don't tell me, let me guess—Lady Newland?—No; you shake your heads. I guessed her ladyship, merely because I know she wants to bribe me some way or other to go to one of her stupid entertainments; she wants to pick out of me taste enough to spend a fortune. But you say it was not Lady Newland?—Mrs. Hunt then perhaps? for she has two daughters whom she wants me to ask to my concerts. It was not Mrs. Hunt?—Well, then, it was Mrs. Masterson; for she has a mind to go with me to Harrowgate, where, by-the-bye, I shall not go; so I won't cheat her out of her gold fishes; it was Mrs. Masterson, hey?"

"No. But these little gold fishes came from a person who would be very glad to go with you to Harrowgate!" said Clarence Hervey. "Or who would be very glad to stay with you in town," said Belinda: "from a person who wants nothing from you but—your love."

"Male or female?" said Lady Delacour.

"Female."

"Female? I have not a female friend in the world but yourself, my dear Belinda; nor do I know another female in the world, whose love I should think about for half an instant. But pray tell me the name of this unknown friend of mine, who wants nothing from me but love."

"Excuse me," said Belinda; "I cannot tell her name, unless you will promise to see her."

"You have really made me impatient to see her," said Lady Delacour: "but I am not able to go out, you know, yet; and with a new acquaintance, one must go through the ceremony of a morning visit. Now, en conscience, is it worth while?"

"Very well worth while," cried Belinda and Clarence Hervey, eagerly.

"Ah, pardi! as M. le Comte exclaims continually, Ah, pardi! You are both wonderfully interested in this business. It is some sister, niece, or cousin of Lady Anne Percival's; or—no, Belinda looks as if I were wrong. Then, perhaps, it is Lady Anne herself?—Well, take me where you please, my dear Belinda, and introduce me where you please: I depend on your taste and judgment in all things; but I really am not yet able to pay morning visits."

"The ceremony of a morning visit is quite unnecessary here," said Belinda: "I will introduce the unknown friend to you to-morrow, if you will let me invite her to your reading-party."

"With pleasure. She is some charming émigrée of Clarence Hervey's acquaintance. But where did you meet with her this morning? You have both of you conspired to puzzle me. Take it upon yourselves, then, if this new acquaintance should not, as Ninon de l'Enclos used to say, quit cost. If she be half as agreeable and graceful, Clarence, as Madame la Comtesse de Pomenars, I should not think her acquaintance too dearly purchased by a dozen morning visits."

Here the conversation was interrupted by a thundering knock at the door.

"Whose carriage is it?" said Lady Delacour. "Oh! Lady Newland's ostentatious livery; and here is her ladyship getting out of her carriage as awkwardly as if she had never been in one before. Overdressed, like a true city dame! Pray, Clarence, look at her, entangled in her bale of gold muslin, and conscious of her bulse of diamonds!—'Worth, if I'm worth a farthing, five hundred thousand pounds bank currency!' she says or seems to say, whenever she comes into a room. Now let us see her entrée—"

"But, my dear," cried Lady Delacour, starting at the sight of Belinda, who was still in her morning dress, "absolutely below par!—Make your escape to Marriott, I conjure you, by all your fears of the contempt of a lady, who will at the first look estimate you, au juste, to a farthing a yard."

As she left the room, Belinda heard Clarence Hervey repeat to Lady Delacour—

"Give me a look, give me a face,
That makes simplicity a grace;
Robes loosely flowing, hair as free—"

He paused—but Belinda recollected the remainder of the stanza—

"Such sweet neglect more taketh me
Than all th'adulteries of art,
That strike mine eyes, but not mine heart."

It was observed, that Miss Portman dressed herself this day with the most perfect simplicity.

Lady Delacour's curiosity was raised by the description which Belinda and Clarence Hervey had given of the new acquaintance who sent her the gold fishes, and who wanted nothing from her but her love.

Miss Portman told her that the unknown would probably come half an hour earlier to the reading-party than any of the rest of the company. Her ladyship was alone in the library, when Lady Anne Percival brought Helena, in consequence of a note from Belinda.

Miss Portman ran down stairs to the hall to receive her: the little girl took her hand in silence. "Your mother was much pleased with the pretty gold fishes," said Belinda, "and she will be still more pleased, when she knows that they came from you:—she does not know that yet."

"I hope she is better to-day? I will not make the least noise," whispered Helena, as she went up stairs on tiptoe.

"You need not be afraid to make a noise—you need not walk on tiptoe, nor shut the doors softly; for Lady Delacour seems to like all noises except the screaming of the macaw. This way, my dear."

"Oh, I forgot—it is so long since!—Is mamma up and dressed?"

"Yes. She has had concerts and balls since her illness. You will hear a play read to-night," said Belinda, "by that French gentleman whom Lady Anne Percival mentioned to me yesterday."

"But there is a great deal of company, then, with mamma?"

"Nobody is with her now: so come into the library with me," said Belinda. "Lady Delacour, here is the young lady who sent you the gold fishes."

"Helena!" cried Lady Delacour.

"You must, I am sure, acknowledge that Mr. Hervey was in the right, when he said that the lady was a striking resemblance of your ladyship."

"Mr. Hervey knows how to flatter. I never had that ingenuous countenance, even in my best days: but certainly the hair of her head is like mine—and her hands and arms. But why do you tremble, Helena? Is there any thing so very terrible in the looks of your mother?"

"No, only—"

"Only what, my dear?"

"Only—I was afraid—you might not like me."

"Who has filled your little foolish head with these vain fears? Come, simpleton, kiss me, and tell me how comes it that you are not at Oakly-hall, or—What's the name of the place?—Oakly-park?"

"Lady Anne Percival would not take me out of town, she said, whilst you were ill; because she thought that you might wish—I mean she thought that I should like to see you—if you pleased."

"Lady Anne is very good—very obliging—very considerate."

"She is very good-natured," said Helena.

"You love this Lady Anne Percival, I perceive."

"Oh, yes, that I do. She has been so kind to me! I love her as if she were—"

"As if she were—What? finish your sentence."

"My mother," said Helena, in a low voice, and she blushed.

"You love her as well as if she were your mother," repeated Lady Delacour: "that is intelligible: speak intelligibly whatever you say, and never leave a sentence unfinished."

"No, ma'am."

"Nothing can be more ill-bred, nor more absurd; for it shows that you have the wish without the power to conceal your sentiments. Pray, my dear," continued Lady Delacour, "go to Oakly-park immediately—all farther ceremony towards me may be spared."

"Ceremony, mamma!" said the little girl, and the tears came into her eyes. Belinda sighed; and for some moments there was a dead silence.

"I mean only to say, Miss Portman," resumed Lady Delacour, "that I hate ceremony: but I know that there are people in the world who love it, who think all virtue, and all affection, depend on ceremony—who are

'Content to dwell in decencies for ever.'

I shall not dispute their merits. Verily, they have their reward in the good opinion and good word of all little minds, that is to say, of above half the world. I envy them not their hard-earned fame. Let ceremony curtsy to ceremony with Chinese decorum; but, when ceremony expects to be paid with affection, I beg to be excused."

"Ceremony sets no value upon affection, and therefore would not desire to be paid with it," said Belinda.

"Never yet," continued lady Delacour, pursuing the train of her own thoughts without attending to Belinda, "never yet was any thing like real affection won by any of these ceremonious people."

"Never," said Miss Portman, looking at Helena; who, having quickness enough to perceive that her mother aimed this tirade against ceremony at Lady Anne Percival, sat in the most painful embarrassment, her eyes cast down, and her face and neck colouring all over. "Never yet," said Miss Portman, "did mere ceremonious person win any thing like real affection; especially from children, who are often excellent, because unprejudiced, judges of character."

"We are all apt to think, that an opinion that differs from our own is a prejudice," said Lady Delacour: "what is to decide?"

"Facts, I should think," said Belinda.

"But it is so difficult to get at facts, even about the merest trifles," said Lady Delacour. "Actions we see, but their causes we seldom see—an aphorism worthy of Confucius himself: now to apply. Pray, my dear Helena, how came you by the pretty gold fishes that you were so good as to send to me yesterday?"

"Lady Anne Percival gave them to me, ma'am."

"And how came her ladyship to give them to you, ma'am?"

"She gave them to me," said Helena, hesitating.

"You need not blush, nor repeat to me that she gave them to you; that I have heard already—that is the fact: now for the cause—unless it be a secret. If it be a secret which you have been desired to keep, you are quite right to keep it. I make no doubt of its being necessary, according to some systems of education, that children should be taught to keep secrets; and I am convinced (for Lady Anne Percival is, I have heard, a perfect judge of propriety) that it is peculiarly proper that a daughter should know how to keep secrets from her mother: therefore, my dear, you need not trouble yourself to blush or hesitate any more—I shall ask no farther questions: I was not aware that there was any secret in the case."

"There is no secret in the world in the case, mamma," said Helena; "I only hesitated because—"

"You hesitated only because, I suppose you mean. I presume Lady Anne Percival will have no objection to your speaking good English?"

"I hesitated only because I was afraid it would not be right to praise myself. Lady Anne Percival one day asked us all—"

"Us all?"

"I mean Charles, and Edward, and me, to give her an account of some experiments, on the hearing of fishes, which Dr. X— had told to us: she promised to give the gold fishes, of which we were all very fond, to whichever of us should give the best account of them—Lady Anne gave the fishes to me."

"And is this all the secret? So it was real modesty made her hesitate, Belinda? I beg your pardon, my dear, and Lady Anne's: you see how candid I am, Belinda. But one question more, Helena: Who put it into your head to send me your gold fishes?"

"Nobody, mamma; no one put it into my head. But I was at the bird-fancier's yesterday, when Miss Portman was trying to get some bird for Mrs. Marriott, that could not make any noise to disturb you; so I thought my fishes would be the nicest things for you in the world; because they cannot make the least noise, and they are as pretty as any birds in the world—prettier, I think—and I hope Mrs. Marriott thinks so too."

"I don't know what Marriott thinks about the matter, but I can tell you what I think," said Lady Delacour, "that you are one of the sweetest little girls in the world, and that you would make me love you if I had a heart of stone, which I have not, whatever some people may think.—Kiss me, my child!"

The little girl sprang forwards, and threw her arms round her mother, exclaiming, "Oh, mamma, are you in earnest?" and she pressed close to her mother's bosom, clasping her with all her force.

Lady Delacour screamed, and pushed her daughter away.

"She is not angry with you, my love," said Belinda, "she is in sudden and violent pain—don't be alarmed—she will be better soon. No, don't ring the bell, but try whether you can open these window-shutters, and throw up the sash."

Whilst Belinda was supporting Lady Delacour, and whilst Helena was trying to open the window, a servant came into the room to announce the Count de N—.

"Show him into the drawing-room," said Belinda. Lady Delacour, though in great pain, rose and retired to her dressing-room. "I shall not be able to go down to these people yet," said she; "you must make my excuses to the count and to every body; and tell poor Helena I was not angry, though I pushed her away. Keep her below stairs: I will come as soon as I am able. Send Marriott. Do not forget, my dear, to tell Helena I was not angry."

The reading party went on, and Lady Delacour made her appearance as the company were drinking orgeat, between the fourth and fifth act. "Helena, my dear," said she, "will you bring me a glass of orgeat?"

Clarence Hervey looked at Belinda with a congratulatory smile: "do not you think," whispered he, "that we shall succeed? Did you see that look of Lady Delacour's?"

Nothing tends more to increase the esteem and affection of two people for each other than their having one and the same benevolent object. Clarence Hervey and Belinda seemed to know one another's thoughts and feelings this evening better than they had ever done before during the whole course of their acquaintance.

After the play was over, most of the company went away; only a select party of beaux esprits stayed to supper; they were standing at the table at which the count had been reading: several volumes of French plays and novels were lying there, and Clarence Hervey, taking up one of them, cried, "Come, let us try our fate by the Sortes Virgilianae."

Lady Delacour opened the book, which was a volume of Marmontel's Tales.

"La femme comme il y en a peu!" exclaimed Hervey.

"Who will ever more have faith in the Sortes Virgilianae?" said Lady Delacour, laughing; but whilst she laughed she went closer to a candle, to read the page which she had opened. Belinda and Clarence Hervey followed her. "Really, it is somewhat singular, Belinda, that I should have opened upon this passage," continued she, in a low voice, pointing it out to Miss Portman.

It was a description of the manner in which la femme comme il y en a peu managed a husband, who was excessively afraid of being thought to be governed by his wife. As her ladyship turned over the page, she saw a leaf of myrtle which Belinda, who had been reading the story the preceding day, had put into the book for a mark.

"Whose mark is this? Yours, Belinda, I am sure, by its elegance," said Lady Delacour. "So! this is a concerted plan between you two, I see," continued her ladyship, with an air of pique: "you have contrived prettily de me dire des vérités! One says, 'Let us try our fate by the Sortes Virgilianae;' the other has dexterously put a mark in the book, to make it open upon a lesson for the naughty child."

Belinda and Mr. Hervey assured her that they had used no such mean arts, that nothing had been concerted between them.

"How came this leaf of myrtle here, then?" said Lady Delacour.

"I was reading that story yesterday, and left it as my mark."

"I cannot help believing you, because you never yet deceived me, even in the merest trifle: you are truth itself, Belinda. Well, you see that you were the cause of my drawing such an extraordinary lot; the book would not have opened here but for your mark. My fate, I find, is in your hands: if Lady Delacour is ever to be la femme comme il y en a peu, which is the most improbable thing in the world, Miss Portman will be the cause of it."

"Which is the most probable thing in the world," said Clarence Hervey. "This myrtle has a delightful perfume," added he, rubbing the leaf between his fingers.

"But, after all," said Lady Delacour, throwing aside the book, "This heroine of Marmontel's is not la femme comme il y en a peu, but la femme comme il n'y en a point."

"Mrs. Margaret Delacour's carriage, my lady, for Miss Delacour," said a footman to her ladyship.

"Helena stays with me to-night—my compliments," said Lady Delacour.

"How pleased the little gipsy looks!" added she, turning to Helena, who heard the message; "and how handsome she looks when she is pleased!—Do these auburn locks of yours, Helena, curl naturally or artificially?"

"Naturally, mamma."

"Naturally! so much the better: so did mine at your age."

Some of the company now took notice of the astonishing resemblance between Helena and her mother; and the more Lady Delacour considered her daughter as a part of herself, the more she was inclined to be pleased with her. The glass globe containing the gold fishes was put in the middle of the table at supper; and Clarence Hervey never paid her ladyship such respectful attention in his life as he did this evening.

The conversation at supper turned upon a magnificent and elegant entertainment which had lately been given by a fashionable duchess, and some of the company spoke in high terms of the beauty and accomplishments of her grace's daughter, who had for the first time appeared in public on that occasion.

"The daughter will eclipse, totally eclipse, the mother," said Lady Delacour. "That total eclipse has been foretold by many knowing people," said Clarence Hervey; "but how can there be an eclipse between two bodies which never cross one another and that I understand to be the case between the duchess and her daughter."

This observation seemed to make a great impression upon Lady Delacour. Clarence Hervey went on, and with much eloquence expressed his admiration of the mother who had stopped short in the career of dissipation to employ her inimitable talents in the education of her children; who had absolutely brought Virtue into fashion by the irresistible powers of wit and beauty.

"Really, Clarence," said Lady Delacour, rising from table, "vous parlez avec beaucoup d'onction. I advise you to write a sentimental comedy, a comédie larmoyante, or a drama on the German model, and call it The School for Mothers, and beg her grace of — to sit for your heroine."

"Your ladyship, surely, would not be so cruel as to send a faithful servant a begging for a heroine?" said Clarence Hervey.

Lady Delacour smiled at first at the compliment, but a few minutes afterwards she sighed bitterly. "It is too late for me to think of being a heroine," said she.

"Too late?" cried Hervey, following her eagerly as she walked out of the supper-room; "too late? Her grace of — is some years older than your ladyship."

"Well, I did not mean to say too late," said Lady Delacour; "but let us go on to something else. Why were you not at the fête champêtre the other day? and where were you all this morning? And pray can you tell me when your friend doctor X— returns to town?"

"Mr. Horton is getting better," said Clarence, "and I hope that we shall have Dr. X— soon amongst us again. I hear that he is to be in town in the course of a few days."

"Did he inquire for me?—Did he ask how I did?"

"No. I fancy he took it for granted that your ladyship was quite well; for I told him you were getting better every day, and that you were in charming spirits."

"Yes," said Lady Delacour, "but I wear myself out with these charming spirits. I am very nervous still, I assure you, and sitting up late is not good for me: so I shall wish you and all the world a good night. You see I am absolutely a reformed rake."

CHAPTER XIV — THE EXHIBITION

Two hours after her ladyship had retired to her room, as Belinda was passing by the door to go to her own bedchamber, she heard Lady Delacour call to her.

"Belinda, you need not walk so softly; I am not asleep. Come in, will you, my dear? I have something of consequence to say to you. Is all the world gone?"

"Yes; and I thought that you were asleep. I hope you are not in pain."

"Not just at present, thank you; but that was a terrible embrace of poor little Helena's. You see to what accidents I should be continually exposed, if I had that child always about me; and yet she seems of such an affectionate disposition, that I wish it were possible to keep her at home. Sit down by my bedside, my dear Belinda, and I will tell you what I have resolved upon."

Belinda sat down, and Lady Delacour was silent for some minutes.

"I am resolved," said she, "to make one desperate effort for my life. New plans, new hopes of happiness, have opened to my imagination, and, with my hopes of being happy, my courage rises. I am determined to submit to the dreadful operation which alone can radically cure me—you understand me; but it must be kept a profound secret. I know of a person who could be got to perform this operation with the utmost secrecy."

"But, surely," said Belinda, "safety must be your first object!"

"No, secrecy is my first object. Nay, do not reason with me; it is a subject on which I cannot, will not, reason. Hear me—I will keep Helena with me for a few days; she was surprised by what passed in the library this evening—I must remove all suspicion from her mind."

"There is no suspicion in her mind," said Belinda.

"So much the better: she shall go immediately to school, or to Oakly-park. I will then stand my trial for life or death; and if I live I will be, what I have never yet been, a mother to Helena. If I die, you and Clarence Hervey will take care of her; I know you will. That young man is worthy of you, Belinda. If I die, I charge you to tell him that I knew his value; that I had a soul capable of being touched by the eloquence of virtue." Lady Delacour, after a pause, said, in an altered tone, "Do you think, Belinda, that I shall survive this operation?"

"The opinion of Dr. X—," said Belinda, "must certainly be more satisfactory than mine;" and she repeated what the doctor had left with her in writing upon this subject. "You see," said Belinda, "that Dr. X—is by no means certain that you have the complaint which you dread."

"I am certain of it," said Lady Delacour, with a deep sigh. Then, after a pause, she resumed: "So it is the doctor's opinion, that I shall inevitably destroy myself if, from a vain hope of secrecy, I put myself into ignorant hands? These are his own words, are they? Very strong; and he is prudent to leave that opinion in writing. Now, whatever happens, he cannot be answerable for 'measures which he does not guide:' nor you either, my dear; you have done all that is prudent and proper. But I must beg you to recollect, that I am neither a child nor a fool; that I am come to years of discretion, and that I am not now in the delirium of a fever; consequently, there can be no pretence for managing me. In this particular I must insist upon managing myself. I have confidence in the skill of the person whom I shall employ: Dr. X—, very likely, would have none, because the man may not have a diploma for killing or curing in form. That is nothing to the purpose. It is I that am to undergo the operation: it is my health, my life, that is risked; and if I am satisfied, that is enough. Secrecy, as I told you before, is my first object."

"And cannot you," said Belinda, "depend with more security upon the honour of a surgeon who is at the head of his profession, and who has a high reputation at stake, than upon a vague promise of secrecy from some obscure quack, who has no reputation to lose?"

"No," said Lady Delacour: "I tell you, my dear, that I cannot depend upon any of these 'honourable men.' I have taken means to satisfy myself on this point: their honour and foolish delicacy would not allow them to perform such an operation for a wife, without the knowledge, privity, consent, &c. &c. &c. of her husband. Now Lord Delacour's knowing the thing is quite out of the question."

"Why, my dear Lady Delacour, why?" said Belinda, with great earnestness. "Surely a husband has the strongest claim to be consulted upon such an occasion! Let me entreat you to tell Lord Delacour your intention, and then all will be right. Say Yes, my dear friend! let me prevail upon you," said Belinda, taking her ladyship's hand, and pressing it between both of hers with the most affectionate eagerness.

Lady Delacour made no answer, but fixed her eyes upon Belinda's.

"Lord Delacour," continued Miss Portman, "deserves this from you, by the great interest, the increasing interest, that he has shown of late about your health: his kindness and handsome conduct the other morning certainly pleased you, and you have now an opportunity of showing that confidence in him, which his affection and constant attachment to you merit."

"I trouble myself very little about the constancy of Lord Delacour's attachment to me," said her ladyship coolly, withdrawing her hand from Belinda; "whether his lordship's affection for me has of late increased or diminished, is an object of perfect indifference to me. But if I were inclined to reward him for his late attentions, I should apprehend that we might hit upon some better reward than you have pitched upon. Unless you imagine that Lord Delacour has a peculiar taste for surgical operations, I cannot conceive how his becoming my confidant upon this occasion could have an immediate tendency to increase his affection for me—about which affection I don't care a straw, as you, better than any one else, must know; for I am no hypocrite. I have laid open my whole heart to you, Belinda."

"For that very reason," said Miss Portman, "I am eager to use the influence which I know I have in your heart for your happiness. I am convinced that it will be absolutely impossible that you should carry on this scheme in the house with your husband without its being discovered. If he discover it by accident, he will feel very differently from what he would do if he were trusted by you."

"For Heaven's sake, my dear," cried Lady Delacour, "let me hear no more about Lord Delacour's feelings."

"But allow me then to speak of my own," said Belinda: "I cannot be concerned in this affair, if it is to be concealed from your husband."

"You will do about that as you think proper," said Lady Delacour haughtily. "Your sense of propriety towards Lord Delacour is, I observe, stronger than your sense of honour towards me. But I make no doubt that you act upon principle—just principle. You promised never to abandon me; but when I most want your assistance, you refuse it, from consideration for Lord Delacour. A scruple of delicacy absolves a person of nice feelings, I find, from a positive promise—a new and convenient code of morality!"

Belinda, though much hurt by the sarcastic tone in which her ladyship spoke, mildly answered, that the promise she had made to stay with her ladyship during her illness was very different from an engagement to assist her in such a scheme as she had now in contemplation.

Lady Delacour suddenly drew the curtain between her and Belinda, saying, "Well, my dear, at all events, I am glad to hear you don't forget your promise of staying with me. You are, perhaps, prudent to refuse me your assistance, all circumstances considered. Good night: I have kept you up too long—good night!"

"Good night!" said Belinda, drawing aside the curtain, "You will not be displeased with me, when you reflect coolly."

"The light blinds me," said Lady Delacour; and she turned her face away from Miss Portman, and added, in a drowsy voice, "I will think of what has been said some time or other: but just now I would rather go to sleep than say or hear any more; for I am more than half asleep already."

Belinda closed the curtains and left the room. But Lady Delacour, notwithstanding the drowsy tone in which she pronounced these last words, was not in the least inclined to sleep. A passion had taken possession of her mind, which kept her broad awake the remainder of the night—the passion of jealousy. The extreme eagerness with which Belinda had urged her to consult Lord Delacour, and to trust him with her secret, displeased her; not merely as an opposition to her will, and undue attention to his lordship's feelings, but as "confirmation strong" of a hint which had been dropped by Sir Philip Baddely, but which never till now had appeared to her worthy of a moment's consideration. Sir Philip had observed, that, "if a young lady had any hopes of being a viscountess, it was no wonder she thought a baronet beneath her notice." "Now," thought Lady Delacour, "this is not impossible. In the first place, Belinda Portman is niece to Mrs. Stanhope; she may have all her aunt's art, and the still greater art to conceal it under the mask of openness and simplicity: Volto sciolto, pensieri stretti, is the grand maxim of the Stanhope school." The moment Lady Delacour's mind turned to suspicion, her ingenuity rapidly supplied her with circumstances and arguments to confirm and justify her doubts.

"Miss Portman fears that my husband is growing too fond of me: she says, he has been very attentive to me of late. Yes, so he has; and on purpose to disgust him with me, she immediately urges me to tell him that I have a loathsome disease, and that I am about to undergo a horrid operation. How my eyes have been blinded by her artifice! This last stroke was rather too bold, and has opened them effectually, and now I see a thousand things that escaped me before. Even to-night, the Sortes Virgilianae, the myrtle leaf, Miss Portman's mark, left in the book exactly at the place where Marmontel gives a receipt for managing a husband of Lord Delacour's character. Ah, ah! By her own confession, she had been reading this: studying it. Yes, and she has studied it to some purpose; she has made that poor weak lord of mine think her an angel. How he ran on in her praise the other day, when he honoured me with a morning visit! That morning visit, too, was of her suggestion; and the bank-notes, as he, like a simpleton, let out in the course of the conversation, had been offered to her first. She, with a delicacy that charmed my short-sighted folly, begged that they might go through my hands. How artfully managed! Mrs. Stanhope herself could not have done better. So, she can make Lord Delacour do whatever she pleases; and she condescends to make him behave prettily to me, and desires him to bring me peace-offerings of bank-notes! She is, in fact, become my banker; mistress of my house, my husband, and myself! Ten days I have been confined to my room. Truly, she has made a good use of her time: and I, fool that I am, have been thanking her for all her disinterested kindness!

"Then her attention to my daughter! disinterested, too, as I thought!—But, good Heavens, what an idiot I have been! She looks forward to be the step-mother of Helena; she would win the simple child's affections even before my face, and show Lord Delacour what a charming wife and mother she would make! He said some such thing to me, as well as I remember, the other day. Then her extreme prudence! She never coquets, not she, with any of the young men who come here on purpose to see her. Is this natural? Absolutely unnatural—artifice! artifice! To contrast herself with me in Lord Delacour's opinion is certainly her object. Even to Clarence Hervey, with whom she was, or pretended to be, smitten, how cold and reserved she is grown of late; and how haughtily she rejected my advice, when I hinted that she was not taking the way to win him! I could not comprehend her; she had no designs on Clarence Hervey, she assured me. Immaculate purity! I believe you.

"Then her refusal of Sir Philip Baddely!—a baronet with fifteen thousand a year to be refused by a girl who has nothing, and merely because he is a fool! How could I be such a fool as to believe it? Worthy niece of Mrs. Stanhope, I know you now! And now I recollect that extraordinary letter of Mrs. Stanhope's which I snatched out of Miss Portman's hands some months ago, full of blanks, and inuendoes, and references to some letter which Belinda had written about my disputes with my husband! From that moment to this, Miss Portman has never let me see another of her aunt's letters. So I may conclude they are all in the same style; and I make no doubt that she has instructed her niece, all this time, how to proceed. Now I know why she always puts Mrs. Stanhope's letters into her pocket the moment she receives them, and never opens them in my presence. And I have been laying open my whole heart, telling my whole history, confessing all my faults and follies, to this girl! And I have told her that I am dying! I have taught her to look forward with joy and certainty to the coronet, on which she has fixed her heart.

"On my knees I conjured her to stay with me to receive my last breath. Oh, dupe, miserable dupe, that I am! could nothing warn me? In the moment that I discovered the treachery of one friend, I went and prostrated myself to the artifices of another—of another a thousand times more dangerous—ten thousand times more beloved! For what was Harriot Freke in comparison with Belinda Portman? Harriot Freke, even whilst she diverted me most, I half despised. But Belinda!—Oh, Belinda! how entirely have I loved—trusted—admired—adored—respected—revered you!"

Exhausted by the emotions to which she had worked herself up by the force of her powerful imagination, Lady Delacour, after passing several restless hours in bed, fell asleep late in the morning; and when she awaked, Belinda was standing by her bedside. "What could you be dreaming of?" said Belinda, smiling. "You started, and looked at me with such horror, when you opened your eyes, as if I had been your evil genius." It is not in human nature, thought Lady Delacour, suddenly overcome by the sweet smile and friendly tone of Belinda, it is not in human nature to be so treacherous; and she stretched out both her arms to Belinda, saying, "You my evil genius? No. My guardian angel, my dearest Belinda, kiss me, and forgive me."

"Forgive you for what?" said Belinda; "I believe you are dreaming still, and I am sorry to awaken you; but I am come to tell you a wonderful thing—that Lord Delacour is up, and dressed, and actually in the breakfast-room; and that he has been talking to me this half hour—of what do you think?—of Helena. He was quite surprised, he said, to see her grown such a fine girl, and he declares that he no longer regrets that she was not a boy; and he says that he will dine at home to-day, on purpose to drink Helena's health in his new burgundy; and, in short, I never saw him in such good spirits, or so agreeable: I always thought he was one of the best-natured men I had ever seen. Will not you get up to breakfast? Lord Delacour has asked for you ten times within these five minutes."

"Indeed!" said Lady Delacour, rubbing her eyes. "All this is vastly wonderful; but I wish you had not awakened me so soon."

"Nay, nay," said Belinda, "I know by the tone of your voice, that you do not mean what you say; I know you will get up, and come down to us directly—so I will send Marriott."

Lady Delacour got up, and went down to breakfast, in much uncertainty what to think of Miss Portman; but ashamed to let her into her mind, and still more afraid that Lord Delacour should suspect her of doing him the honour to be jealous, Belinda had not the least guess of what was really passing in her ladyship's heart; she implicitly believed her expressions of complete indifference to her lord; and jealousy was the last feeling which Miss Portman would have attributed to Lady Delacour, because she unfortunately was not sufficiently aware that jealousy can exist without love. The idea of Lord Delacour as an object of attachment, or of a coronet as an object of ambition, or of her friend's death as an object of joy, were so foreign to Belinda's innocent mind, that it was scarcely possible she could decipher Lady Delacour's thoughts. Her ladyship affected to be in "remarkable good spirits this morning," declared that she had never felt so well since her illness, ordered her carriage as soon as breakfast was over, and said she would take Helena to Maillardet's, to see the wonders of his little conjuror and his singing-bird. "Nothing equal to Maillardet's singing-bird has ever been seen or heard of, my dear Helena, since the days of Aboulcasem's peacock in the Persian Tales. Since Lady Anne Percival has not shown you these charming things, I must."

"But I hope you won't tire yourself, mamma," said the little girl.

"I'm afraid you will," said Belinda. "And you know, my dear," added Lord Delacour, "that Miss Portman, who is so very obliging and good-natured, could go just as well with Helena; and I am sure, would, rather than that you should tire yourself, or give yourself an unnecessary trouble."

"Miss Portman is very good," answered Lady Delacour, hastily; "but I think it no unnecessary trouble to give my daughter any pleasure in my power. As to its tiring me, I am neither dead, nor dying, yet; for the rest, Miss Portman, who understands what is proper, blushes for you, as you see, my lord, when you propose that she, who is not yet a married woman, should chaperon a young lady. It is quite out of rule; and Mrs. Stanhope would be shocked if her niece could, or would, do such a thing to oblige any body."

Lord Delacour was too much in the habit of hearing sarcastic, and to him incomprehensible speeches from her ladyship, to take any extraordinary notice of this; and if Belinda blushed, it was merely from the confusion into which she was thrown by the piercing glance of Lady Delacour's black eyes—a glance which neither guilt nor innocence could withstand. Belinda imagined that her ladyship still retained some displeasure from the conversation that had passed the preceding night, and the first time that she was alone with Lady Delacour, she again touched upon the subject, in hopes of softening or convincing her. "At all events, my dear friend," said she, "you will not, I hope, be offended by the sincerity with which I speak—I can have no object but your safety and happiness."

"Sincerity never offends me," was her ladyship's cold answer. And all the time that they were out together, she was unusually ceremonious to Miss Portman; and there would have been but little conversation, if Helena had not been present, to whom her mother talked with fluent gaiety. When they got to Spring Gardens, Helena exclaimed, "Oh! there's Lady Anne Percival's carriage, and Charles and Edward with her—they are going to the same place that we are, I dare say, for I heard Charles ask Lady Anne to take him to see Maillardet's little bird—Mr. Hervey mentioned it to us, and he said it was a curious piece of machinery."

"I wish you had told me sooner that Lady Anne was likely to be there—I don't wish to meet her so awkwardly: I am not well enough yet, indeed, to go to these odious, hot, close places; and, besides, I hate seeing sights."

Helena, with much good humour, said that she would rather give up seeing the sight than be troublesome to her mother. When they came to Maillardet's, however, Lady Delacour saw Mrs. — getting out of her carriage, and to her she consigned Helena and Miss Portman, saying that she would take a turn or two in the park, and call for them in half an hour. When the half hour was over, and her ladyship returned, she carelessly asked, as they were going home, whether they had been pleased with their visit to the bird and the conjuror. "Oh, yes, mamma!" said Helena: "and do you know, that one of the questions that the people ask the conjuror is, Where is the happiest family to be found?" And Charles and Edward immediately said, "if he is a good conjuror, if he tells truth, he'll answer, 'At Oakly-park.'"

"Miss Portman, had you any conversation with Lady Anne Percival?" said Lady Delacour, coldly.

"A great deal," said Belinda, "and such as I am sure you would have liked: and so far from being a ceremonious person, I think I never saw any body who had such easy engaging manners."

"And did she ask you, Helena, again to go with her to that place where the happiest family in the world is to be found?"

"Oakly-park?—No, mamma; she said that she was very glad that I was with you; but she asked Miss Portman to come to see her whenever it was in her power."

"And could Miss Portman withstand such a temptation?"

"You know that I am engaged to your ladyship," said Belinda.

Lady Delacour bowed. "But from what passed last night," said she, "I was afraid that you might repent your engagement to me: and if so, I give up my bond. I should be miserable if I apprehended that any one, but more especially Miss Portman, felt herself a prisoner in my house."

"Dear Lady Delacour! I do not feel myself a prisoner; I have always till now felt myself a friend in your house; but we'll talk of this another time. Do not look at me with so much coldness; do not speak to me with so much politeness. I will not let you forget that I am your friend."

"I do not wish to forget it, Belinda," said Lady Delacour, with emotion; "I am not ungrateful, though I may seem capricious—bear with me."

"There now, you look like yourself again, and I am satisfied," cried Belinda. "As to going to Oakly-park, I give you my word I have not the most distant thoughts of it. I stay with you from choice, and not from compulsion, believe me."

"I do believe you," said Lady Delacour; and for a moment she was convinced that Belinda stayed with her for her own sake alone; but the next minute she suspected that Lord Delacour was the secret cause of her refusing to go to Oakly-park. His lordship dined at home this day, and two or three succeeding days, and he was not intoxicated from Monday till Thursday. These circumstances appeared to his lady very extraordinary. In fact, he was pleased and amused with his little daughter, Helena; and whilst she was yet almost a stranger to him, he wished to appear to her in the most agreeable and respectable light possible. One day after dinner, Lord Delacour, who was in a remarkably good humour, said to her ladyship, "My dear, you know that your new carriage was broken almost to pieces the night when you were overturned. Well, I have had it all set to rights again, and new painted, and it is all complete, except the hammer-cloth, which must have new fringe. What colour will you have the fringe?"

"What do you say, Miss Portman?" said her ladyship.

"Black and orange would look well, I think," said Belinda, "and would suit the lace of your liveries—would not it?"

"Certainly: black and orange then," said Lord Delacour, "it shall be."

"If you ask my opinion," said Lady Delacour, "I am for blue and white, to match the cloth of the liveries."

"Blue and white then it shall be," said Lord Delacour.

"Nay, Miss Portman has a better taste than I have; and she says black and orange, my lord."

"Then you'll have it black and orange, will you?" said Lord Delacour.

"Just as you please," said Lady Delacour, and no more passed.

Soon afterward a note came from Lady Anne Percival, with some trifles belonging to Helena, for which her mother had sent. The note was for Belinda—another pressing invitation to Oakly-park—and a very civil message from Mrs. Margaret Delacour, and thanks to Lady Delacour for the macaw. Ay, thought Lady Delacour, Miss Portman wants to ingratiate herself in time with all my husband's relations. "Mrs. Margaret Delacour should have addressed these thanks to you, Miss Portman, for I had not the grace to think of sending her the macaw." Lord Delacour, who was very fond of his aunt, immediately joined his thanks, and observed that Miss Portman was always considerate—always obliging—always kind. Then he drank her health in a bumper of burgundy, and insisted upon his little Helena's drinking her health. "I am sure you ought, my dear, for Miss Portman is very good—too good to you, child."

"Very good—not too good, I hope," said Lady Delacour. "Miss Portman, your health."

"And I hope," continued his lordship, after swallowing his bumper, "that my Lady Anne Percival does not mean to inveigle you away from us, Miss Portman. You don't think of leaving us, Miss Portman, I hope? Here's Helena would break her little heart;—I say nothing for my Lady Delacour, because she can say every thing so much better for herself; and I say nothing for myself, because I am the worst man in the world at making speeches, when I really have a thing at heart—as I have your staying with us, Miss Portman."

Belinda assured him that there was no occasion to press her to do what was perfectly agreeable to her, and said that she had no thoughts of leaving Lady Delacour. Her ladyship, with some embarrassment, expressed herself "extremely obliged, and gratified, and happy." Helena, with artless joy, threw her arms about Belinda, and exclaimed, "I am glad you are not going; for I never liked any body so much, of whom I knew so little."

"The more you know of Miss Portman the more you will like her, child—at least I have found it so," said Lord Delacour.

"Clarence Hervey would, I am sure, have given the Pigot diamond, if it were in his gift, for such a smile as you bestowed on Lord Delacour just now," whispered Lady Delacour. For an instant Belinda was struck with the tone of pique and reproach, in which, her ladyship spoke. "Nay, my dear, I did not mean to make you blush so piteously," pursued her ladyship: "I really did not think it a blushing matter—but you know best. Believe me, I spoke without malice; we are so apt to judge from our own feelings—and I could as soon blush about the old man of the mountains as about my Lord Delacour."

"Lord Delacour!" said Belinda, with a look of such unfeigned surprise, that her ladyship instantly changed countenance, and, taking her hand with gaiety, said, "So, my little Belinda, I have caught you—the blush belongs then to Clarence Hervey? Well, any man of common sense would rather have one blush than a thousand smiles for his share: now we understand one another. And will you go with me to the exhibition to-morrow? I am told there are some charming pictures this year. Helena, who really has a genius for drawing, should see these things; and whilst she is with me, I will make her as happy as possible. You see the reformation is beginning—Clarence Hervey and Miss Portman can do wonders. If it be my fate, at last, to be la bonne mère, or la femme comme il y en a peu, how can I help it? There is no struggling against fate, my dear!"

Whenever Lady Delacour's suspicions of Belinda were suspended, all her affections returned with double force; she wondered at her own folly, she was ashamed that she could have let such ideas enter her mind, and she was beyond measure astonished that any thing relative to Lord Delacour could so far have interested her attention. "Luckily," said she to herself, "he has not the penetration of a blind beetle; and, besides, he has little snug jealousies of his own: so he will never find me out. It would be an excellent thing indeed, if he were to turn my 'master-torment' against myself—it would be a judgment upon me. The manes of poor Lawless would then be appeased. But it is impossible I should ever be a jealous wife: I am only a jealous friend, and I must satisfy myself about Belinda. To be a second time a dupe to the treachery of a friend would be too much for me—too much for my pride—too much for my heart."

The next day, when they came to the exhibition, Lady Delacour had an opportunity of judging of Belinda's real feelings. As they went up the stairs, they heard the voices of Sir Philip Baddely and Mr. Rochfort, who were standing upon the landing-place, leaning over the banisters, and running their little sticks along the iron rails, to try which could make the loudest noise.

"Have you been much pleased with the pictures, gentlemen?" said Lady Delacour, as she passed them.

"Oh, damme! no—'tis a cursed bore; and yet there are some fine pictures: one in particular—hey, Rochfort?—one damned fine picture!" said Sir Philip. And the two gentlemen laughing significantly, followed Lady Delacour and Belinda into the rooms.

"Ay, there's one picture that's worth all the rest, 'pon honour!" repeated Rochfort; "and we'll leave it to your ladyship's and Miss Portman's taste and judgment to find it out, mayn't we, Sir Philip?"

"Oh, damme! yes," said Sir Philip, "by all means." But he was so impatient to direct her eyes, that he could not keep himself still an instant.

"Oh, curse it! Rochfort, we'd better tell the ladies at once, else they may be all day looking and looking!"

"Nay, Sir Philip, may not I be allowed to guess? Must I be told which is your fine picture?—This is not much in favour of my taste."

"Oh, damn it! your ladyship has the best taste in the world, every body knows; and so has Miss Portman—and this picture will hit her taste particularly, I'm sure. It is Clarence Hervey's fancy; but this is a dead secret—dead—Clary no more thinks that we know it, than the man in the moon."

"Clarence Hervey's fancy! Then I make no doubt of its being good for something," said Lady Delacour, "if the painter have done justice to his imagination; for Clarence has really a fine imagination."

"Oh, damme! 'tis not amongst the history pieces," cried Sir Philip; "'tis a portrait."

"And a history piece, too, 'pon honour!" said Rochfort: "a family history piece, I take it, 'pon honour! it will turn out," said Rochfort; and both the gentlemen were, or affected to be, thrown into convulsions of laughter, as they repeated the words, "family history piece, 'pon honour!—family history piece, damme!"

"I'll take my oath as to the portrait's being a devilish good likeness," added Sir Philip; and as he spoke, he turned to Miss Portman: "Miss Portman has it! damme, Miss Portman has him!"

Belinda hastily withdrew her eyes from the picture at which she was looking. "A most beautiful creature!" exclaimed Lady Delacour.

"Oh, faith! yes; I always do Clary the justice to say, he has a damned good taste for beauty."

"But this seems to be foreign beauty," continued Lady Delacour, "if one may judge by her air, her dress, and the scenery about her—cocoa-trees, plantains: Miss Portman, what think you?"

"I think," said Belinda, (but her voice faltered so much that she could hardly speak,) "that it is a scene from Paul and Virginia. I think the figure is St. Pierre's Virginia."

"Virginia St. Pierre! ma'am," cried Mr. Rochfort, winking at Sir Philip. "No, no, damme! there you are wrong, Rochfort; say Hervey's Virginia, and then you have it, damme! or, may be, Virginia Hervey—who knows?"

"This is a portrait," whispered the baronet to Lady Delacour, "of Clarence's mistress." Whilst her ladyship leant her ear to this whisper, which was sufficiently audible, she fixed a seemingly careless, but most observing, inquisitive eye upon poor Belinda. Her confusion, for she heard the whisper, was excessive.

"She loves Clarence Hervey—she has no thoughts of Lord Delacour and his coronet: I have done her injustice," thought Lady Delacour, and instantly she despatched Sir Philip out of the room, for a catalogue of the pictures, begged Mr. Rochfort to get her something else, and, drawing Miss Portman's arm within hers, she said, in a low voice, "Lean upon me, my dearest Belinda: depend upon it, Clarence will never be such a fool as to marry the girl—Virginia Hervey she will never be!"

"And what will become of her? can Mr. Hervey desert her? she looks like innocence itself—and so young, too! Can he leave her for ever to sorrow, and vice, and infamy?" thought Belinda, as she kept her eyes fixed, in silent anguish, upon the picture of Virginia. "No, he cannot do this: if he could he would be unworthy of me, and I ought to think of him no more. No; he will marry her; and I must think of him no more."

She turned abruptly away from the picture, and she saw Clarence Hervey standing beside her.

"What do you think of this picture? is it not beautiful? We are quite enchanted with it; but you do not seem to be struck with it, as we were at the first glance," said Lady Delacour.

"Because," answered Clarence, gaily, "it is not the first glance I have had at that picture—I admired it yesterday, and admire it to-day."

"But you are tired of admiring it, I see. Well, we shall not force you to be in raptures with it—shall we, Miss Portman? A man may be tired of the most beautiful face in the world, or the most beautiful picture; but really there is so much sweetness, so much innocence, such tender melancholy in this countenance, that, if I were a man, I should inevitably be in love with it, and in love for ever! Such beauty, if it were in nature, would certainly fix the most inconstant man upon earth."

Belinda ventured to take her eyes for an instant from the picture, to see whether Clarence Hervey looked like the most inconstant man upon earth. He was intently gazing upon her; but as soon as she looked round, he suddenly exclaimed, as he turned to the picture—"A heavenly countenance, indeed!—the painter has done justice to the poet."

"Poet!" repeated Lady Delacour: "the man's in the clouds!"

"Pardon me," said Clarence; "does not M. de St. Pierre deserve to be called a poet? Though he does not write in rhyme, surely he has a poetical imagination."

"Certainly," said Belinda; and from the composure with which Mr. Hervey now spoke, she was suddenly inclined to believe, or to hope, that all Sir Philip's story was false. "M. de St. Pierre undoubtedly has a great deal of imagination, and deserves to be called a poet."

"Very likely, good people!" said Lady Delacour; "but what has that to do with the present purpose?"

"Nay," cried Clarence, "your ladyship certainly sees that this is St. Pierre's Virginia?"

"St. Pierre's Virginia! Oh, I know who it is, Clarence, as well as you do. I am not quite so blind, or so stupid, as you take me to be." Then recollecting her promise, not to betray Sir Philip's secret, she added, pointing to the landscape of the picture, "These cocoa trees, this fountain, and the words Fontaine de Virginie, inscribed on the rock—I must have been stupidity itself, if I had not found it out. I absolutely can read, Clarence, and spell, and put together. But here comes Sir Philip Baddely, who, I believe, cannot read, for I sent him an hour ago for a catalogue, and he pores over the book as if he had not yet made out the title."

Sir Philip had purposely delayed, because he was afraid of rejoining Lady Delacour whilst Clarence Hervey was with her, and whilst they were talking of the picture of Virginia.

"Here's the catalogue; here's the picture your ladyship wants. St. Pierre's Virginia: damme! I never heard of that fellow before—he is some new painter, damme! that is the reason I did not know the hand. Not a word of what I told you, Lady Delacour—you won't blow us to Clary," added he aside to her ladyship. "Rochfort keeps aloof; and so will I, damme!"

A gentleman at this instant beckoned to Mr. Hervey with an air of great eagerness. Clarence went and spoke to him, then returned with an altered countenance, and apologized to Lady Delacour for not dining with her, as he had promised. Business, he said, of great importance required that he should leave town immediately. Helena had just taken Miss Portman into a little room, where Westall's drawings were hung, to show her a group of Lady Anne Percival and her children; and Belinda was alone with the little girl, when Mr. Hervey came to bid her adieu. He was in much agitation.

"Miss Portman, I shall not, I am afraid, see you again for some time;—perhaps I may never have that— hem!—happiness. I had something of importance that I wished to say to you before I left town; but I am forced to go so suddenly, I can hardly hope for any moment but the present to speak to you, madam. May I ask whether you purpose remaining much longer with Lady Delacour?"

"Yes," said Belinda, much surprised. "I believe—I am not quite certain—but I believe I shall stay with her ladyship some time longer."

Mr. Hervey looked painfully embarrassed, and his eyes involuntarily fell upon little Helena. Helena drew her hand gently away from Belinda, left the room, and retired to her mother.

"That child, Miss Portman, is very fond of you," said Mr. Hervey. Again he paused, and looked round to see whether he could be overheard. "Pardon me for what I am going to say. This is not a proper place. I must be abrupt; for I am so circumstanced, that I have not a moment's time to spare. May I speak to you with the sincerity of a friend?"

"Yes. Speak to me with sincerity," said Belinda, "and you will deserve that I should think you my friend." She trembled excessively, but spoke and looked with all the firmness that she could command.

"I have heard a report," said Mr. Hervey, "which is most injurious to you."

"To me!"

"Yes. No one can escape calumny. It is whispered, that if Lady Delacour should die—."

At the word die, Belinda started.

"That if Lady Delacour should die, Miss Portman would become the mother of Helena!"

"Good Heavens! what an absurd report! Surely you could not for an instant believe it, Mr. Hervey?"

"Not for an instant. But I resolved, as soon as I heard it, to mention it to you; for I believe that half the miseries of the world arise from foolish mysteries—from the want of courage to speak the truth. Now that you are upon your guard, your own prudence will defend you sufficiently. I never saw any of your sex who appeared to me to have so much prudence, and so little art; but—farewell—I have not a moment to lose," added Clarence, suddenly checking himself; and he hurried away from Belinda, who stood fixed to the spot where he left her, till she was roused by the voices of several people who came into the room to see the drawings. She started as if from a dream, and went immediately in search of Lady Delacour.

Sir Philip Baddely was in earnest conversation with her ladyship; but he stopped speaking when Belinda came within hearing, and Lady Delacour turned to Helena, and said, "My dear, if you are satisfied, for mercy's sake let us be gone, for I am absolutely overcome with heat—and with curiosity," added she in a low voice to Belinda: "I long to hear how Clarence Hervey likes Westall's drawings."

As soon as they got home, Lady Delacour sent her daughter to practise a new lesson upon the piano forte. "And now sit down, my dear Belinda," said she, "and satisfy my curiosity. It is the curiosity of a friend, not of an impertinent busybody. Has Clarence declared himself? He chose an odd time and place; but that is no matter; I forgive him, and so do you, I dare say. But why do you tear that unfortunate carnation to pieces? Surely you cannot be embarrassed in speaking to me! What's the matter? I once did tell you, that I would not give up my claim to Clarence's adorations during my life; but I intend to live a few years longer after the amazonian operation is performed, you know; and I could not have the conscience to keep you waiting whole years. It is better to do things with a good grace, lest one should be forced at last to do them with an ill grace. Therefore I give up all manner of claim to every thing but—flattery! that of course you will allow me from poor Clarence. So now do not begin upon another flower; but, without any farther superfluous modesty, let me hear all the pretty things Clarence said or swore."

Whilst Belinda was pulling the carnation to pieces, she recollected what Mr. Hervey had said to her about mysteries: his words still sounded in her ear. "I believe that half the miseries of the world arise from foolish mysteries—from the want of courage to speak the truth." I will have the courage to speak the truth, thought she, whatever it may cost me.

"The only pretty thing that Mr. Hervey said was, that he never saw any woman who had so much prudence and so little art," said Belinda.

"A very pretty thing indeed, my dear! But it might have been said in open court by your grandfather, or your great-grandfather. I am sorry, if that was all, that Helena did not stay to hear such a charming moral compliment—Moralité à la glace. The last thing I should have expected in a tête-à-tête with Clarence Hervey. Was it worth while to pull that poor flower to pieces for such a pretty speech as this? And so that was all?"

"No, not all: but you overpower me with your wit; and I cannot stand the 'lightning of your eyes.'"

"There!" said her ladyship, letting down her veil over her face, "the fire of my eyes is not too much for you now."

"Helena was showing me Westall's drawing of Lady Anne Percival and her children—"

"And Mr. Hervey wished that he was the father of such a charming group of children, and you the mother—hey? was not that it? It was not put in such plain terms, but that was the purport, I presume?"

"No, not at all; he said nothing about Lady Anne Percival's children, but—"

"But—why then did you bring in her ladyship and her children? To gain time?—Bad policy!—Never, whilst you live, when you have a story to tell, bring in a parcel of people who have nothing to do with the beginning, the middle, or the end of it. How could I suspect you of such false taste! I really imagined these children were essential to the business; but I beg pardon for giving you these elements of criticism. I assure you I interrupt you, and talk on so fast, from pure good-nature, to give you time to recollect yourself; for I know you've the worst of memories, especially for what Clarence Hervey says. But come, my dear, dash into the middle of things at once, in the true Epic style."

"Then to dash into the midst of things at once," said Miss Portman, speaking very quick: "Mr. Hervey observed that Miss Delacour was growing very fond of me."

"Miss Delacour, did you say?" cried her ladyship: "Et puis?"

At this instant Champfort opened the door, looked in, and seeing Lady Delacour, immediately retired.

"Champfort, whom do you want—or what do you want?" said her ladyship.

"Miladi, c'est que—I did come from milord, to see if miladi and mademoiselle were visible. I did tink miladi was not at home."

"You see I am at home, though," said her ladyship. "Has Lord Delacour any business with me?"

"No, miladi: not with miladi," said Champfort; "it was with mademoiselle."

"With me, Monsieur Champfort? then you will be so good as to tell Lord Delacour I am here."

"And that I am not here, Champfort; for I must be gone to dress."

She rose hastily to leave the room, but Miss Portman caught her hand: "You won't go, I hope, Lady Delacour," said she, "till I have finished my long story?" Lady Delacour sat down again, ashamed of her own embarrassment.

Whether this be art, innocence, or assurance, thought she, I cannot tell; but we shall see.

Lord Delacour now came in, with a half-unfolded newspaper, and a packet of letters in his hand. He came to apologize to Miss Portman for having, by mistake, broken the seal of a letter to her, which had been sent under cover to him. He had simply asked Champfort whether the ladies were at home, that he might not have the trouble of going up stairs if they were out. Monsieur Champfort possessed, in an eminent degree, the mischievous art of appearing mysterious about the simplest things in the world.

"Though I was so thoughtless as to break the seal before I looked at the direction of the letter," said Lord Delacour, "I assure you I went no farther than the first three words; for I knew 'my dear niece' could not possibly mean me." He gave Miss Portman the letter, and left the room. This explanation was perfectly satisfactory to Belinda; but Lady Delacour, prejudiced by the hesitation of Champfort, could not help suspecting that this letter was merely the ostensible cause of his lordship's visit.

"From my aunt Stanhope," said Miss Portman, as she opened her letter. She folded it up again after glancing over the first page, and put it into her pocket, colouring deeply.

All Lady Delacour's suspicions about Mrs. Stanhope's epistolary counsels and secrets instantly recurred, with almost the force of conviction to her mind.

"Miss Portman," said she, "I hope your politeness to me does not prevent you from reading your letter? Some ceremonious people think it vastly rude to read a letter in company; but I am not one of them: I can write whilst you read, for I have fifty notes and more to answer. So pray read your letter at your ease."

Belinda had but just unfolded her letter again, when Lord Delacour returned, followed by Champfort, who brought with him a splendid hammer-cloth.

"Here, my dear Lady Delacour," said his lordship, "is a little surprise for you: here is a new hammer-cloth, of my bespeaking and taste, which I hope you will approve of."

"Very handsome, upon my word!" said Lady Delacour, coldly, and she fixed her eyes upon the fringe, which was black and orange: "Miss Portman's taste, I see!"

"Did you not say black and orange fringe, my dear?"

"No. I said blue and white, my lord."

His lordship declared he did not know how the mistake had happened; it was merely a mistake:—but her ladyship was convinced that it was done on purpose. And she said to herself, "Miss Portman will order my liveries next! I have not even the shadow of power left in my own house! I am not treated with even a decent show of respect! But this shall go on till I have full conviction of her views."

Dissembling her displeasure, she praised the hammer-cloth, and especially the fringe. Lord Delacour retired satisfied; and Miss Portman sat down to read the following letter from her aunt Stanhope.

"Crescent, Bath, July—Wednesday.

"MY DEAR NIECE,

"I received safely the bank notes for my two hundred guineas, enclosed in your last. But you should never trust unnecessarily in this manner to the post—always, when you are obliged to send bank notes by post, cut them in two, and send half by one post and half by another. This is what is done by all prudent people. Prudence, whether in trifles or in matters of consequence, can be learned only by experience (which is often too dearly bought), or by listening, which costs nothing, to the suggestions of those who have a thorough knowledge of the world.

"A report has just reached me concerning you and a certain lord, which gives me the most heartfelt concern. I always knew, and told you, that you were a great favourite with the person in question. I depended on your prudence, delicacy, and principles, to understand this hint properly, and I trusted that you would conduct yourself accordingly. It is too plain, (from the report alluded to,) that there has been some misconduct or mis-management somewhere. The misconduct I cannot—the mis-management I must, attribute to you, my dear; for let a man's admiration for any woman be ever so great, unless she suffer herself to be dazzled by vanity, or unless she be naturally of an inconsiderate temper, she can surely prevent his partiality from becoming so glaring as to excite envy: envy is always to be dreaded by handsome young women, as being, sooner or later, infallibly followed by scandal. Of this, I fear, you have not been sufficiently aware, and you see the consequences—consequences which, to a female of genuine delicacy or of real good sense, must be extremely alarming. Men of contracted minds and cold tempers, who are absolutely incapable of feeling generous passion for our sex, are often unaccountably ambitious to gain the reputation of being well with any woman whose beauty, accomplishments, or connexions, may have brought her into fashion. Whatever affection may be pretended, this is frequently the ultimate and sole object of these selfish creatures. Whether or not the person I have in my eye deserves to be included in this class, I will not presume positively to determine; but you, who have personal opportunities of observation, may decide this point (if you have any curiosity on the subject) by observing whether he most affects to pay his devoirs to you in public or in private. If the latter be the case, it is the most dangerous; because a man even of the most contracted understanding has always sense or instinct enough to feel that the slightest taint in the reputation of the woman who is, or who is to be, his wife, would affect his own private peace, or his honour in the eyes of the world. A husband who has in a first marriage been, as it is said, in constant fear both of matrimonial subjugation and disgrace, would, in his choice of a second lady, be peculiarly nice, and probably tardy. Any degree of favour that might have been shown him, any report that may have been raised, and above all, any restraint he might feel himself under from implied engagement, or from the discovery or reputation of superior understanding and talents in the object beloved, would operate infallibly against her, to the confusion of all her plans, and the ruin at once of her reputation, her peace of mind, and her hopes of an establishment. Nay, supposing the best that could possibly happen—that, after playing with the utmost dexterity this desperate game, the pool were absolutely your own; yet, if there were any suspicions of unfair play buzzed about amongst the by-standers, you would not in the main be a gainer; for my dear, without character, what is even wealth, or all that wealth can bestow? I do not mean to trouble you with stale wise sayings, which young people hate; nor musty morality, which is seldom fit for use in the world, or which smells too much of books to be brought into good company. This is not my way of giving advice; but I only beg you to observe what actually passes before your eyes in the circle in which we live. Ladies of the best families, with rank and fortune, and beauty and fashion, and every thing in their favour, cannot (as yet in this country) dispense with the strictest observance of the rules of virtue and decorum. Some have fancied themselves raised so high above the vulgar as to be in no danger from the thunder and lightning of public opinion; but these ladies in the clouds have found themselves mistaken—they have been blasted, and have fallen nobody knows where! What is become of Lady —, and the Countess of —, and others I could mention, who were as high as envy could look? I remember seeing the Countess of —, who was then the most beautiful creature my eyes ever beheld, and the most admired that ever was heard of, come into the Opera-house, and sit the whole night in her box without any woman's speaking or courtesying to her, or taking any more notice of her than you would of a post, or a beggar-woman. Even a coronet cannot protect a woman, you see, from disgrace: if she falls, she and it, and all together, are trampled under foot. But why should I address all this to my dear niece? Whither have the terror and confusion I was thrown into by this strange report about you and Lord — led me? And yet one cannot be too cautious—'Ce n'est que le premier mot qui coute'—Scandal never stops after the first word, unless she be instantly gagged by a dexterous hand. Nothing shall be wanting on my part, but you alone are the person who can do any thing effectual Do not imagine that I would have you quit Lady—; that is the first idea, I know, that will come into your silly little head, but put it out directly. If you were upon this attack to quit the field of battle, you yield the victory to your enemies. To leave Lady—'s house would be folly and madness. As long as she is your friend, or appears such, all is safe; but any coolness on her part would, in the present circumstances, be death to your reputation. And, even if you were to leave her on the best terms possible, the malicious world would say that you left her on the worst, and would assign as a reason the report alluded to. People who have not yet believed it would then conclude that it must be true; and thus by your cowardice you would furnish an incontrovertible argument against your innocence. I therefore desire that you will not, upon any account, think of coming home to me at present; indeed, I hope your own good sense would prevent you from wishing it, after the reasons that I have given. Far from quitting Lady — from false delicacy, it is your business, from consideration for her peace, as well as your own, to redouble your attentions to her in private, and, above all things, to appear as much as possible with her in public. I am glad to hear her health is so far reestablished, that she can appear again in public; her spirits, as you may hint, will be the better for a little amusement. Luckily, you have it completely in your power to convince her and all the world of the correctness of your mind. I believe I certainly should have fainted, my dear, when I first heard this shocking report, if I had not just afterward received a letter from Sir Philip Baddely which revived me. His proposal at this crisis for you, my dear, is a charming thing. You have nothing to do but to encourage his addresses immediately,—the report dies away of itself, and all is just as your best friends wish. Such an establishment for you, my dear, is indeed beyond their most sanguine expectations. Sir Philip hints in his letter, that my influence might be wanting with you in his favour; but this surely cannot be. As I have told him, he has merely mistaken becoming female reserve for a want of sensibility on your part, which would be equally unnatural and absurd. Do you know, my dear, that Sir Philip Baddely has an estate of fifteen thousand a-year in Wiltshire? and his uncle Barton's estate in Norfolk will, in due time, pay his debts. Then, as to family—look in the lists of baronets in your pocket-book; and surely, my love, an old baronetage in actual possession is worth something more than the reversion of a new coronet; supposing that such a thing could properly be thought of, which Heaven forbid! So I see no possible objection to Sir Philip, my dear Belinda! and I am sure you have too much candour and good sense to make any childish or romantic difficulties. Sir Philip is not, I know, a man of what you call genius. So much the better, my dear—those men of genius are dangerous husbands; they have so many oddities and eccentricities, there is no managing them, though they are mighty pleasant men in company to enliven conversation; for example, your favourite, Clarence Hervey. As it is well known he is not a marrying man, you never can have thought of him. You are not a girl to expose yourself to the ridicule, &c., of all your female acquaintance by romance and nonsense. I cannot conceive that a niece of mine could degrade herself by a mean prepossession for a man who has never made any declaration of his attachment to her, and who, I am sure, feels no such attachment. That you may not deceive yourself, it is fit I should tell you, what otherwise it might not be so proper to mention to a young lady, that he keeps and has kept a mistress for some years; and those who are most intimately in his confidence have assured me that, if ever he marries any body, he will marry this girl; which is not impossible, considering that she is, they say, the most beautiful young creature that ever was seen, and he a man of genius. If you have any sense or spirit, I have said enough. So adieu!—Let me hear, by return of the post, that every thing is going on as it should do. I am impatient to write to your sister Tollemache this good news. I always foretold that my Belinda would marry better than her sister, or any of her cousins, and take place of them all. Are not you obliged to me for sending you this winter to town to Lady —? It was an admirable hit. Pray tell Lady Delacour, with my best compliments, that our aloe friend (her ladyship will understand me) cheated a gentleman of my acquaintance the other day, at casino, out of seventy guineas. He hates the sight of her odious red wig as much now as we always did. I knew, and told Lady D—, as she will do me the justice to remember, that Mrs.—cheated at play. What a contemptible character!—Pray, my dear, do not forget to tell Lady Delacour, that I have a charming anecdote for her, about another friend of ours, who has lately gone over to the enemy. Has her ladyship seen a manuscript that is handed about as a great secret, and said to be by —, a parallel between our friend and the Chevalier d'Eon? It is done with infinite wit and humour, in the manner of Plutarch. I would send a copy, but am afraid my frank would be too heavy if I began upon another sheet. So once more adieu, my dear niece! Write to me without fail, and mention Sir Philip. I have written to him to give my approbation, &c.

"Yours sincerely,

"SELINA STANHOPE."

"Mrs. Stanhope seems to have written you a volume instead of a letter, Miss Portman," cried Lady Delacour, as Belinda turned over the sheets of her aunt's long epistle. She did not attempt to read it regularly through: some passages here and there were sufficient to astonish and shock her extremely. "No bad news, I hope?" said Lady Delacour, again looking up from her writing at Belinda, who sat motionless, leaning her head upon her hand, as if deep in thought, Mrs. Stanhope's unfolded letter hanging from her hand. In the midst of the variety of embarrassing, painful, and alarming feelings excited by this letter, she had sufficient strength of mind to adhere to her resolution of speaking the exact truth to Lady Delacour. When she was roused by her ladyship's question, "No bad news, I hope, Miss Portman?" she instantly answered, with all the firmness she could command. "Yes. My aunt has been alarmed by a strange report which I heard myself for the first time this morning from Mr. Hervey. I am sure I am much obliged to him for having the courage to speak the truth to me." Here she repeated what Mr. Hervey had said to her. Lady Delacour never raised her eyes whilst Belinda spoke, but went on scratching out some words in what she was writing. Through the mask of paint which she wore no change of colour could be visible; and as Belinda did not see the expression of her ladyship's eyes, she could not in the least judge of what was passing in her mind.

"Mr. Hervey has acted like a man of honour and sense," said Lady Delacour; "but it is a pity, for your sake, he did not speak sooner—before this report became so public—before it reached Bath, and your aunt. Though it could not surprise her much, she has such a perfect knowledge of the world, and —"

Lady Delacour uttered these broken sentences in a voice of suppressed anger; cleared her throat several times, and at last, unable to speak, stopped short, and then began with much precipitation to put wafers into several notes that she had been writing. So it has reached Bath, thought she—the report is public! I never till now heard a hint of any such thing except from Sir Philip Baddely; but it has doubtless been the common talk of the town, and I am laughed at as a dupe and an idiot, as I am. And now, when the thing can he concealed no longer, she comes to me with that face of simplicity, and knowing my generous temper, throws herself on my mercy, and trusts that her speaking to me with this audacious plainness will convince me of her innocence. "You have acted in the most prudent manner possible, Miss Portman," said her ladyship, as she went on sealing her notes, "by speaking at once to me of this strange, scandalous, absurd report. Do you act from your aunt Stanhope's advice, or entirely from your own judgment and knowledge of my character?"

"From my own judgment and knowledge of your character, in which I hope—I am not—I cannot be mistaken," said Belinda, looking at her with a mixture of doubt and astonishment.

"No—you calculated admirably—'twas the best, the only thing you could do. Only," said her ladyship, falling back in her chair with an hysteric laugh, "only the blunder of Champfort, and the entrance of my Lord Delacour, and the hammercloth with the orange and black fringe—forgive me, my dear; for the soul of me I can't help laughing—it was rather unlucky; so awkward, such a contretemps! But you," added she, wiping her eyes, as if recovering from laughter, "you have such admirable presence of mind, nothing disconcerts you! You are equal to all situations, and stand in no need of such long letters of advice from your aunt Stanhope," pointing to the two folio sheets which lay at Belinda's feet.

The rapid, unconnected manner in which Lady Delacour spoke, the hurry of her motions, the quick, suspicious, angry glances of her eye, her laugh, her unintelligible words, all conspired at this moment to give Belinda the idea that her intellects were suddenly disordered. She was so firmly persuaded of her ladyship's utter indifference to Lord Delacour, that she never conceived the possibility of her being actuated by the passion of jealousy—by the jealousy of power—a species of jealousy which she had never felt, and could not comprehend. But she had sometimes seen Lady Delacour in starts of passion that seemed to border on insanity, and the idea of her losing all command of her reason now struck Belinda with irresistible force. She felt the necessity of preserving her own composure; and with all the calmness that she could assume, she took up her aunt Stanhope's letter, and looked for the passage in which Mrs. Luttridge and Harriot Freke were mentioned. If I can turn the course of Lady Delacour's mind, thought she, or catch her attention, perhaps she will recover herself. "Here is a message to you, my dear Lady Delacour," cried she, "from my aunt Stanhope, about—about Mrs. Luttridge."

Miss Portman's hand trembled as she turned over the pages of the letter. "I am all attention," said Lady Delacour, with a composed voice; "only take care, don't make a mistake: I'm in no hurry; don't read any thing Mrs. Stanhope might not wish. It is dangerous to garble letters, almost as dangerous as to snatch them out of a friend's hand, as I once did, you know—but you need not now be under the least alarm."

Conscious that this letter was not fit for her ladyship to see, Belinda neither offered to show it to her, nor attempted any apology for her reserve and embarrassment, but hastily began to read the message relative to Mrs. Luttridge; her voice gaining confidence as she went on, as she observed that she had fixed Lady Delacour's attention, who now sat listening to her, calm and motionless. But when Miss Portman came to the words, "Do not forget to tell Lady D —, that I have a charming anecdote for her about another friend of hers, who lately went over to the enemy," her ladyship exclaimed with great vehemence, "Friend!—Harriot Freke!—Yes, like all other friends—Harriot Freke!—What was she compared to? 'Tis too much for me—too much!" and she put her hand to her head.

"Compose yourself, my dear friend," said Belinda, in a calm, gentle tone; and she went toward her with an intention of soothing her by caresses; but, at her approach, Lady Delacour pushed the table on which she had been writing from her with violence, started up, flung back the veil which fell over her face as she rose, and darted upon Belinda a look, which fixed her to the spot where she stood. It said, "Come not a step nearer, at your peril!" Belinda's blood ran cold—she had no longer any doubt that this was insanity. She shut the penknife which lay upon the table, and put it into her pocket.

"Cowardly creature!" cried Lady Delacour, and her countenance changed to the expression of ineffable contempt; "what is it you fear?"

"That you should injure yourself. Sit down—for Heaven's sake listen to me, to your friend, to Belinda!"

"My friend! my Belinda!" cried Lady Delacour, and she turned from her, and walked away some steps in silence; then suddenly clasping her hands, she raised her eyes to heaven with a fervent but wild expression of devotion, and exclaimed, "Great God of heaven, my punishment is just! the death of Lawless is avenged. May the present agony of my soul expiate my folly! Of guilt—deliberate guilt—of hypocrisy—treachery—I have not—oh, never may I have—to repent!"

She paused—her eyes involuntarily returned upon Belinda. "Oh, Belinda! You, whom I have so loved—so trusted!"

The tears rolled fast down her painted cheeks; she wiped them hastily away, and so roughly, that her face became a strange and ghastly spectacle. Unconscious of her disordered appearance, she rushed past Belinda, who vainly attempted to stop her, threw up the sash, and stretching herself far out of the window, gasped for breath. Miss Portman drew her back, and closed the window, saying, "The rouge is all off your face, my dear Lady Delacour; you are not fit to be seen. Sit down upon this sofa, and I will ring for Marriott, and get some fresh rouge. Look at your face in this glass—you see—"

"I see," interrupted Lady Delacour, looking full at Belinda, "that she who I thought had the noblest of souls has the meanest! I see that she is incapable of feeling. Rouge! not fit to be seen!—At such a time as this, to talk to me in this manner! Oh, niece of Mrs. Stanhope!—dupe!—dupe that I am!" She flung herself upon the sofa, and struck her forehead with her hand violently several times. Belinda catching her arm, and holding it with all her force, cried in a tone of authority, "Command yourself, Lady Delacour, I conjure you, or you will go out of your senses; and if you do, your secret will be discovered by the whole world."

"Hold me not—you have no right," cried Lady Delacour, struggling to free her hand. "All-powerful as you are in this house, you have no longer any power over me! I am not going out of my senses! You cannot get me into Bedlam, all-powerful, all-artful as you are. You have done enough to drive me mad—but I am not mad. No wonder you cannot believe me—no wonder you are astonished at the strong expression of feelings that are foreign to your nature—no wonder that you mistake the writhings of the heart, the agony of a generous soul, for madness! Look not so terrified; I will do you no injury. Do not you hear that I can lower my voice?—do not you see that I can be calm? Could Mrs. Stanhope herself—could you, Miss Portman, speak in a softer, milder, more polite, more proper tone than I do now? Are you pleased, are you satisfied?"

"I am better satisfied—a little better satisfied," said Belinda.

"That's well; but still you tremble. There's not the least occasion for apprehension—you see I can command myself, and smile upon you."

"Oh, do not smile in that horrid manner!"

"Why not?—'Horrid!—Don't you love deceit?"

"I detest it from my soul."

"Indeed!" said Lady Delacour, still speaking in the same low, soft, unnatural voice: "then why do you practise it, my love?"

"I never practised it for a moment—I am incapable of deceit. When you are really calm, when you can really command yourself, you will do me justice, Lady Delacour; but now it is my business, if I can, to bear with you."

"You are goodness itself, and gentleness, and prudence personified. You know perfectly how to manage a friend, whom you fear you have driven just to the verge of madness. But tell me, good, gentle, prudent Miss Portman, why need you dread so much that I should go mad? You know, if I went mad, nobody would mind, nobody would believe whatever I say—I should be no evidence against you, and I should be out of your way sufficiently, shouldn't I? And you would have all the power in your own hands, would not you? And would not this be almost as well as if I were dead and buried? No; your calculations are better than mine. The poor mad wife would still be in your way, would yet stand between you and the fond object of your secret soul—a coronet!"

As she pronounced the word coronet, she pointed to a coronet set in diamonds on her watch-case, which lay on the table. Then suddenly seizing the watch, she dashed it upon the marble hearth with all her force—"Vile bauble!" cried she; "must I lose my only friend for such a thing as you? Oh, Belinda! do you see that a coronet cannot confer happiness?"

"I have seen it long: I pity you from the bottom of my soul," said Belinda, bursting into tears.

"Pity me not. I cannot endure your pity, treacherous woman!" cried Lady Delacour, and she stamped with a look of rage—"most perfidious of women!"

"Yes, call me perfidious, treacherous—stamp at me—say, do what you will; I can and will bear it all—all patiently; for I am innocent, and you are mistaken and unhappy," said Belinda. "You will love me when you return to your senses; then how can I be angry with you?"

"Fondle me not," said Lady Delacour, starting back from Belinda's caresses: "do not degrade yourself to no purpose—I never more can be your dupe. Your protestations of innocence are wasted on me—I am not so blind as you imagine—dupe as you think me, I have seen much in silence. The whole world, you find, suspects you now. To save your reputation, you want my friendship—you want—"

"I want nothing from you, Lady Delacour," said Belinda. "You have suspected me long in silence! then I have mistaken your character—I can love you no longer. Farewell for ever! Find another—a better friend."

She walked away from Lady Delacour with proud indignation; but, before she reached the door, she recollected her promise to remain with this unfortunate woman.

Is a dying woman, in the paroxysm of insane passion, a fit object of indignation? thought Belinda, and she stopped short. "No, Lady Delacour," cried she, "I will not yield to my humour—I will not listen to my pride. A few words said in the heat of passion shall not make me forget myself or you. You have given me your confidence; I am grateful for it. I cannot, will not desert you: my promise is sacred."

"Your promise!" said Lady Delacour, contemptuously. "I absolve you from your promise. Unless you find it convenient to yourself to remember it, pray let it be forgotten; and if I must die—"

At this instant the door opened suddenly, and little Helena came in singing—

"'Merrily, merrily shall we live now,
Under the blossom that hangs on the bough.'
What comes next, Miss Portman?"

Lady Delacour dragged her veil across her face, and rushed out of the room.

"What is the matter?—Is mamma ill?"

"Yes, my dear," said Belinda. But at this instant she heard the sound of Lord Delacour's voice upon the stairs; she broke from the little girl, and with the greatest precipitation retreated to her own room.

She had not been alone above an hour before Marriott knocked at the door.

"Miss Portman, you don't know how late it is. Lady Singleton and the Miss Singletons are come. But, merciful heaven!" exclaimed Marriott, as she entered the room, "what is all this packing up? What is this trunk?"

"I am going to Oakly-park with Lady Anne Percival," said Belinda, calmly.

"I thought there was something wrong; my mind misgave me all the time I was dressing my lady,—she was in such a flutter, and never spoke to me. I'd lay my life this is, some way or other, Mr. Champfort's doings. But, good dear Miss Portman, can you leave my poor lady when she wants you so much; and I'll take upon me to say, ma'am, loves you so much at the bottom of her heart? Dear me, how your face is flushed! Pray let me pack up these things, if it must be. But I do hope, if it be possible, that you should stay. However, I've no business to speak. I beg pardon for being so impertinent: I hope you won't take it ill,—it is only from regard to my poor lady I ventured to speak."

"Your regard to your lady deserves the highest approbation, Marriott," said Belinda. "It is impossible that I should stay with her any longer. When I am gone, good Marriott, and when her health and strength decline, your fidelity and your services will be absolutely necessary to your mistress; and from what I have seen of the goodness of your heart, I am convinced that the more she is in want of you, the more respectful will be your attention."

Marriott answered only by her tears, and went on packing up in a great hurry.

Nothing could equal Lady Delacour's astonishment when she learnt from Marriott that Miss Portman was actually preparing to leave the house. After a moment's reflection, however, she persuaded herself that this was only a new artifice to work upon her affections; that Belinda did not mean to leave her; but that she would venture all lengths, in hopes of being at the last moment pressed to stay. Under this persuasion, Lady Delacour resolved to disappoint her expectations: she determined to meet her with that polite coldness which would best become her own dignity, and which, without infringing the laws of hospitality, would effectually point out to the world that Lady Delacour was no dupe, and that Miss Portman was an unwelcome inmate in her house.

The power of assuming gaiety when her heart was a prey to the most poignant feelings, she had completely acquired by long practice. With the promptitude of an actress, she could instantly appear upon the stage, and support a character totally foreign to her own. The loud knocks at the door, which announced the arrival of company, were signals that operated punctually upon her associations; and to this species of conventional necessity her most violent passions submitted with magical celerity. Fresh rouged, and beautifully dressed, she was performing her part to a brilliant audience in her drawing-room when Belinda entered. Belinda beheld her with much astonishment, but more pity.

"Miss Portman," said her ladyship, turning carelessly towards her, "where do you buy your rouge?—Lady Singleton, would you rather at this moment be mistress of the philosopher's stone, or have a patent for rouge that will come and go like Miss Portman's?—Apropos! have you read St. Leon?" Her ladyship was running on to a fresh train of ideas, when a footman announced the arrival of Lady Anne Percival's carriage; and Miss Portman rose to depart.

"You dine with Lady Anne, Miss Portman, I understand?—My compliments to her ladyship, and my duty to Mrs. Margaret Delacour, and her macaw. Au revoir! Though you talk of running away from me to Oakly-park, I am sure you will do no such cruel thing. I am, with all due humility, so confident of the irresistible attractions of this house, that I defy Oakly-park and all its charms. So, Miss Portman, instead of adieu, I shall only say, au revoir!"

"Adieu, Lady Delacour!" said Belinda, with a look and tone which struck her ladyship to the heart. All her suspicions, all her pride, all her affected gaiety vanished; her presence of mind forsook her, and for some moments she stood motionless and powerless. Then recollecting herself, she flew after Miss Portman, abruptly stopped her at the head of the stairs, and exclaimed, "My dearest Belinda, are you gone?—My best, my only friend!—Say you are not gone for ever!—Say you will return!"

"Adieu!" repeated Belinda. It was all she could say; she broke from Lady Delacour, and hurried out of the house with the strongest feeling of compassion for this unhappy woman, but with an unaltered sense of the propriety and necessity of her own firmness.

There was an air of benevolence and perfect sincerity in the politeness with which Lady Anne Percival received Belinda, that was peculiarly agreeable to her agitated and harassed mind.

"You see, Lady Anne," said Belinda, "that I come to you at last, after having so often refused your kind invitations."

"So you surrender yourself at discretion, just when I was going to raise the siege in despair," said Lady Anne: "now I may make my own terms; and the only terms I shall impose are, that you will stay at Oakly-park with us, as long as we can make it agreeable to you, and no longer. Whether those who cease to please, or those who cease to be pleased, are most to blame, it may sometimes be difficult to determine; so difficult, that when this becomes a question between two friends, they perhaps had better part than venture upon the discussion."

Lady Anne Percival could not avoid suspecting that something disagreeable had passed between Lady Delacour and Belinda; but she was not troubled with the disease of idle curiosity, and her example prevailed upon Mrs. Margaret Delacour, who dined with her, to refrain from all questions and comments.

The prejudice which this lady had conceived against our heroine, as being a niece of Mrs. Stanhope's, had lately been vanquished by the favourable representations of her conduct which she had heard from her nephew, and by the kindness that Belinda had shown to little Helena.

"Madam," said Mrs. Delacour, addressing herself to Miss Portman with some formality, but much dignity, "permit me, as one of my Lord Delacour's nearest relations now living, to return you my thanks for having, as my nephew informs me, exerted your influence over Lady Delacour for the happiness of his family. My little Helena, I am sure, feels her obligations towards you, and I rejoice that I have had an opportunity of expressing, in person, my sense of what our family owes to Miss Portman. As to the rest, her own heart will reward her. The praise of the world is but an inferior consideration. However, it deserves to be mentioned, as an instance of the world's candour, and for the singularity of the case, that every body agrees in speaking well even of so handsome a young lady as Miss Portman."

"She must have had extraordinary prudence," said Lady Anne; "and the world does justly to reward it with extraordinary esteem."

Belinda, with equal pleasure and surprise, observed that all this was said sincerely, and that the report, which she had feared was public, had never reached Mrs. Delacour or Lady Anne Percival.

In fact, it was known and believed only by those who had been prejudiced by the malice or folly of Sir Philip Baddely. Piqued by the manner in which his addresses had been received by Belinda, he readily listened to the comfortable words of his valet de chambre, who assured him that he had it from the best possible authority (Lord Delacour's own gentleman, Mr. Champfort), that his lordship was deeply taken with Miss Portman—that the young lady managed every thing in the house—that she had been very prudent, to be sure, and had refused large presents—but that there was no doubt of her becoming Lady Delacour, if ever his lordship should be at liberty. Sir Philip was the person who mentioned this to Clarence Hervey, and Sir Philip was the person who hinted it to Mrs. Stanhope, in the very letter which he wrote to implore her influence in favour of his own proposal. This manoeuvring lady represented this report as being universally known and believed, in hopes of frightening her niece into an immediate match with the baronet. In the whole extent of Mrs. Stanhope's politic imagination, she had never foreseen the possibility of her niece's speaking the simple truth to Lady Delacour, and she had never guarded against this danger. She never thought of Belinda's mentioning this report to her ladyship, because she would never have dealt so openly, had she been in the place of her niece. Thus her art and falsehood operated against her own views, and produced consequences diametrically opposite to her expectations. It was her exaggerations that made Lady Delacour believe, when Belinda repeated what she had said, that this report was universally known and credited; her own suspicions were by these means again awakened, and her jealousy and rage were raised to such a pitch, that, no longer mistress of herself, she insulted her friend and guest. Miss Portman was then obliged to do the very thing that Mrs. Stanhope most dreaded—to leave Lady Delacour's house and all its advantages. As to Sir Philip Baddely, Belinda never thought of him from the moment she read her aunt's letter, till after she had left her ladyship; her mind was firmly decided upon this subject; yet she could not help fearing that her aunt would not understand her reasons, or approve her conduct. She wrote to Mrs. Stanhope in the most kind and respectful manner; assured her that there had been no foundation whatever for the report which had produced so much uneasiness; that Lord Delacour had always treated her with politeness and good-nature, but that such thoughts or views as had been attributed to him, she was convinced had never entered his lordship's mind; that hearing of the publicity of this report had, however, much affected Lady D—. "I have, therefore," said Belinda, "thought it prudent to quit her ladyship, and to accept of an invitation from Lady Anne Percival to Oakly-park. I hope, my dear aunt, that you will not be displeased by my leaving town without seeing Sir Philip Baddely again. Our meeting could indeed answer no purpose, as it is entirely out of my power to return his partiality. Of his character, temper, and manners, I know enough to be convinced, that our union could tend only to make us both miserable. After what I have seen, nothing can ever tempt me to marry from any of the common views of interest or ambition."

On this subject Belinda, though she declared her own sentiments with firm sincerity, touched as slightly as she could, because she anxiously wished to avoid all appearance of braving the opinions of an aunt to whom she was under obligations. She was tempted to pass over in silence all that part of Mrs. Stanhope's letter which related to Clarence Hervey; but upon reflection, she determined to conquer her repugnance to speak of him, and to make perfect sincerity the steady rule of her conduct. She therefore acknowledged to her aunt, that of all the persons she had hitherto seen, this gentleman was the most agreeable to her; but at the same time she assured her, that the refusal of Sir Philip Baddely was totally independent of all thoughts of Mr. Hervey—that, before she had received her aunt's letter, circumstances had convinced her that Mr. Hervey was attached to another woman. She concluded by saying, that she had neither romantic hopes nor wishes, and that her affections were at her own command.

Belinda received the following angry answer from Mrs. Stanhope:—

"Henceforward, Belinda, you may manage your own affairs as you think proper; I shall never more interfere with my advice. Refuse whom you please—go where you please—get what friends, and what admirers, and what establishment you can—I have nothing more to do with it—I will never more undertake the management of young people. There's your sister Tollemache has made a pretty return for all my kindness! she is going to be parted from her husband, and basely throws all the blame upon me. But 'tis the same with all of you. There's your cousin Joddrell refused me a hundred guineas last week, though the piano-forte and harp I bought for her before she was married stood me in double that sum, and are now useless lumber on my hands; and she never could have had Joddrell without them, as she knows as well as I do. As for Mrs. Levit, she never writes to me, and takes no manner of notice of me. But this is no matter, for her notice can be of no consequence now to any body. Levit has run out every thing he had in the world!—All his fine estates advertised in to-day's paper—an execution in the House, I'm told. I expect that she will have the assurance to come to me in her distress: but she shall find my doors shut, I promise her. Your cousin Valleton's match has, through her own folly, turned out like all the rest. She, her husband, and all his relations are at daggers-drawing; and Valleton will die soon, and won't leave her a farthing in his will, I foresee, and all the fine Valleton estate goes to God knows whom!

"If she had taken my advice after marriage as before, it would have been all her own at this instant. But the passions run away with people, and they forget every thing—common sense, gratitude, and all—as you do, Belinda. Clarence Hervey will never think of you, and I give you up!—Now manage for yourself as you please, and as you can! I'll have nothing more to do with the affairs of young ladies who will take no advice.

"SELINA STANHOPE.

"P. S. If you return directly to Lady Delacour's, and marry Sir Philip Baddely, I will forgive the past."

The regret which Belinda felt at having grievously offended her aunt was somewhat alleviated by the reflection that she had acted with integrity and prudence. Thrown off her guard by anger, Mrs. Stanhope had inadvertently furnished her niece with the best possible reasons against following her advice with regard to Sir Philip Baddely, by stating that her sister and cousins, who had married with mercenary views, had made themselves miserable, and had shown their aunt neither gratitude nor respect.

The tranquillity of Belinda's mind was gradually restored by the society that she enjoyed at Oakly-park. She found herself in the midst of a large and cheerful family, with whose domestic happiness she could not forbear to sympathize. There was an affectionate confidence, an unconstrained gaiety in this house, which forcibly struck her, from its contrast with what she had seen at Lady Delacour's. She perceived that between Mr. Percival and Lady Anne there was a union of interests, occupations, taste, and affection. She was at first astonished by the openness with which they talked of their affairs in her presence; that there were no family secrets, nor any of those petty mysteries which arise from a discordance of temper or struggle for power. In conversation, every person expressed without constraint their wishes and opinions; and wherever these differed, reason and the general good were the standards to which they appealed. The elder and younger part of the family were not separated from each other; even the youngest child in the house seemed to form part of the society, to have some share and interest in the general occupations or amusements The children were treated neither as slaves nor as playthings, but as reasonable creatures; and the ease with which they were managed, and with which they managed themselves, surprised Belinda; for she heard none of that continual lecturing which goes forward in some houses, to the great fatigue and misery of all the parties concerned, and of all the spectators. Without force or any factitious excitements, the taste for knowledge, and the habits of application, were induced by example, and confirmed by sympathy. Mr. Percival was a man of science and literature, and his daily pursuits and general conversation were in the happiest manner instructive and interesting to his family. His knowledge of the world, and his natural gaiety of disposition, rendered his conversation not only useful, but in the highest degree amusing. From the merest trifles he could lead to some scientific fact, some happy literary allusion, or philosophical investigation.

Lady Anne Percival had, without any pedantry or ostentation, much accurate knowledge, and a taste for literature, which made her the chosen companion of her husband's understanding, as well as of his heart. He was not obliged to reserve his conversation for friends of his own sex, nor was he forced to seclude himself in the pursuit of any branch of knowledge; the partner of his warmest affections was also the partner of his most serious occupations; and her sympathy and approbation, and the daily sense of her success in the education of their children, inspired him with a degree of happy social energy, unknown to the selfish solitary votaries of avarice and ambition.

In this large and happy family there was a variety of pursuits. One of the boys was fond of chemistry, another of gardening; one of the daughters had a talent for painting, another for music; and all their acquirements and accomplishments contributed to increase their mutual happiness, for there was no envy or jealousy amongst them.

Those who unfortunately have never enjoyed domestic happiness, such as we have just described, will perhaps suppose the picture to be visionary and romantic; there are others—it is hoped many others—who will feel that it is drawn from truth and real life. Tastes that have been vitiated by the stimulus of dissipation might, perhaps, think these simple pleasures insipid.

Every body must ultimately judge of what makes them happy, from the comparison of their own feelings in different situations. Belinda was convinced by this comparison, that domestic life was that which could alone make her really and permanently happy. She missed none of the pleasures, none of the gay company, to which she had been accustomed at Lady Delacour's. She was conscious, at the end of each day, that it had been agreeably spent; yet there were no extraordinary exertions made to entertain her; every thing seemed in its natural course, and so did her mind. Where there was so much happiness, no want of what is called pleasure was ever experienced. She had not been at Oakly-park a week before she forgot that it was within a few miles of Harrowgate, and she never once recollected her vicinity to this fashionable water-drinking place for a month afterwards.

"Impossible!" some young ladies will exclaim. We hope others will feel that it was perfectly natural. But to deal fairly with our readers, we must not omit to mention a certain Mr. Vincent, who came to Oakly-park during the first week of Belinda's visit, and who stayed there during the whole succeeding month of felicity. Mr. Vincent was a creole; he was about two-and-twenty: his person and manners were striking and engaging; he was tall, and remarkably handsome; he had large dark eyes, an aquiline nose, fine hair, and a manly sunburnt complexion; his countenance was open and friendly, and when he spoke upon any interesting subject, it lighted up, and became full of fire and animation. He used much gesture in conversation; he had not the common manners of young men who are, or who aim at being thought, fashionable, but he was perfectly at ease in company, and all that was uncommon about him appeared foreign. He had a frank, ardent temper, incapable of art or dissimulation, and so unsuspicious of all mankind, that he could scarcely believe falsehood existed in the world, even after he had himself been its dupe. He was in extreme astonishment at the detection of any species of baseness in a gentleman; for he considered honour and generosity as belonging indefeasibly, if not exclusively, to the privileged orders. His notions of virtue were certainly aristocratic in the extreme, but his ambition was to entertain such only as would best support and dignify an aristocracy. His pride was magnanimous, not insolent; and his social prejudices were such as, in some degree, to supply the place of the power and habit of reasoning, in which he was totally deficient. One principle of philosophy he practically possessed in perfection; he enjoyed the present, undisturbed by any unavailing regret for the past, or troublesome solicitude about the future. All the goods of life he tasted with epicurean zest; all the evils he bore with stoical indifference. The mere pleasure of existence seemed to keep him in perpetual good humour with himself and others; and his never-failing flow of animal spirits exhilarated even the most phlegmatic. To persons of a cold and reserved temper he sometimes appeared rather too much of an egotist: for he talked with fluent enthusiasm of the excellent qualities and beauties of whatever he loved, whether it were his dog, his horse, or his country: but this was not the egotism of vanity; it was the overflowing of an affectionate heart, confident of obtaining sympathy from his fellow-creatures, because conscious of feeling it for all that existed.

He was as grateful as he was generous; and though high-spirited and impatient of restraint, he would submit with affectionate gentleness to the voice of a friend, or listen with deference to the counsel of those in whose superior judgment he had confidence. Gratitude, respect, and affection, all conspired to give Mr. Percival the strongest power over his soul. Mr. Percival had been a guardian and a father to him. His own father, an opulent merchant, on his death-bed requested that his son, who was then about eighteen, might be immediately sent to England for the advantages of a European education. Mr. Percival, who had a regard for the father, arising from circumstances which it is not here necessary to explain, accepted the charge of young Vincent, and managed so well, that his ward when he arrived at the age of twenty-one did not feel relieved from any restraint. On the contrary, his attachment to his guardian increased from that period, when the laws gave him full command over his fortune and his actions. Mr. Vincent had been at Harrowgate for some time before Mr. Percival came into the country; but as soon as he heard of Mr. Percival's arrival, he left half finished a game of billiards, of which, by-the-bye, he was extremely fond, to pay his respects at Oakly-park. At the first sight of Belinda, he did not seem much struck with her appearance; perhaps, from his thinking that there was too little languor in her eyes, and too much colour in her cheeks; he confessed that she was graceful, but her motions were not quite slow enough to please him.

It is somewhat singular that Lady Delacour's faithful friend, Harriot Freke, should be the cause of Mr. Vincent's first fixing his favourable attention on Miss Portman.

He had a black servant of the name of Juba, who was extremely attached to him: he had known Juba from a boy, and had brought him over with him when he first came to England, because the poor fellow begged so earnestly to go with young massa. Juba had lived with him ever since, and accompanied him wherever he went. Whilst he was at Harrowgate, Mr. Vincent lodged in the same house with Mrs. Freke. Some dispute arose between their servants, about the right to a coach-house, which each party claimed as exclusively their own. The master of the house was appealed to by Juba, who sturdily maintained his massa's right; he established it, and rolled his massa's curricle into the coach-house in triumph. Mrs. Freke, who heard and saw the whole transaction from her window, said, or swore, that she would make Juba repent of what she called his insolence. The threat was loud enough to reach his ears, and he looked up in astonishment to hear such a voice from a woman; but an instant afterwards he began to sing very gaily, as he jumped into the curricle to turn the cushions, and then danced himself up and down by the springs, as if rejoicing in his victory. A second and a third time Mrs. Freke repeated her threat, confirming it by an oath, and then violently shut down the window and disappeared. Mr. Vincent, to whom Juba, with much simplicity, expressed his aversion of the man-woman who lived in the house with them, laughed at the odd manner in which the black imitated her voice and gesture, but thought no more of the matter. Some time afterward, however, Juba's spirits forsook him; he was never heard to sing or to whistle, he scarcely ever spoke even to his master, who was much surprised by this sudden change from gaiety and loquacity to melancholy taciturnity. Nothing could draw from the poor fellow any explanation of the cause of this alteration in his humour; and though he seemed excessively grateful for the concern which his master showed about his health, no kindness or amusement could restore him to his wonted cheerfulness. Mr. Vincent knew that he was passionately fond of music; and having heard him once express a wish for a tambourine, he gave him one: but Juba never played upon it, and his spirits seemed every day to grow worse and worse. This melancholy lasted during the whole time that he remained at Harrowgate, but from the first day of his arrival at Oakly-park he began to mend: after he had been there a week, he was heard to sing, and whistle, and talk as he used to do, and his master congratulated him upon his recovery. One evening his master asked him to go back to Harrowgate for his tambourine, as little Charles Percival wished to hear him play upon it. This simple request had a wonderful effect upon poor Juba; he began to tremble from head to foot, his eyes became fixed, and he stood motionless; after some time, he suddenly clasped his hands, fell upon his knees, and exclaimed:

"Oh, massa, Juba die! If Juba go back, Juba die!" and he wiped away the drops that stood upon his forehead. "But me will go, if massa bid—me will die!"

Mr. Vincent began to imagine that the poor fellow was out of his senses. He assured him, with the greatest kindness, that he would almost as soon hazard his own life as that of such a faithful, affectionate servant; but he pressed him to explain what possible danger he dreaded from returning to Harrowgate. Juba was silent, as if afraid to speak—"Don't fear to speak to me," said Mr. Vincent; "I will defend you: if anybody have injured you, or if you dread that any body will injure you, trust to me; I will protect you."

"Ah, massa, you no can! Me die, if me go back! Me no can say word more;" and he put his finger upon his lips, and shook his head. Mr. Vincent knew that Juba was excessively superstitious; and convinced, that, if his mind were not already deranged, it would certainly become so, were any secret terror thus to prey upon his imagination, he assumed a very grave countenance, and assured him, that he should be extremely displeased if he persisted in this foolish and obstinate silence. Overcome by this, Juba burst into tears, and answered:

"Den me will tell all."

This conversation passed before Miss Portman and Charles Percival, who were walking in the park with Mr. Vincent, at the time he met Juba and asked him to go for the tambourine. When he came to the words, "Me will tell all," he made a sign that he wished to tell it to his master alone. Belinda and the little boy walked on, to leave him at liberty to speak; and then, though with a sort of reluctant horror, he told that the figure of an old woman, all in flames, had appeared to him in his bedchamber at Harrowgate every night, and that he was sure she was one of the obeah-women of his own country, who had pursued him to Europe to revenge his having once, when he was a child, trampled upon an egg-shell that contained some of her poisons. The extreme absurdity of this story made Mr. Vincent burst out a laughing; but his humanity the next instant made him serious; for the poor victim of superstitious terror, after having revealed what, according to the belief of his country, it is death to mention, fell senseless on the ground. When he came to himself, he calmly said, that he knew he must now die, for that the obeah-women never forgave those that talked of them or their secrets; and, with a deep groan, he added, that he wished he might die before night, that he might not see her again. It was in vain to attempt to reason him out of the idea that he had actually seen this apparition: his account of it was, that it first appeared to him in the coach-house one night, when he went thither in the dark—that he never afterwards went to the coach-house in the dark—but that the same figure of an old woman, all in flames, appeared at the foot of his bed every night whilst he stayed at Harrowgate; and that he was then persuaded she would never let him escape from her power till she had killed him. That since he had left Harrowgate, however, she had not tormented him, for he had never seen her, and he was in hopes that she had forgiven him; but that now he was sure of her vengeance for having spoken of her.

Mr. Vincent knew the astonishing power which the belief in this species of sorcery has over the minds of the Jamaica negroes; they pine and actually die away from the moment they fancy themselves under the malignant influence of these witches. He almost gave poor Juba over for lost. The first person that he happened to meet after his conversation was Belinda, to whom he eagerly related it, because he had observed, that she had listened with much attention and sympathy to the beginning of the poor fellow's story. The moment that she heard of the flaming apparition, she recollected having seen a head drawn in phosphorus, which one of the children had exhibited for her amusement, and it occurred to her that, perhaps, some imprudent or ill-natured person might have terrified the ignorant negro by similar means. When she mentioned this to Mr. Vincent, he recollected the threat that had been thrown out by Mrs. Freke, the day that Juba had taken possession of the disputed coach-house; and from the character of this lady, Belinda judged that she would be likely to play such a trick, and to call it, as usual, fun or frolic. Miss Portman suggested that one of the children should show him the phosphorus, and should draw some ludicrous figure with it in his presence. This was done, and it had the effect that she expected. Juba, familiarized by degrees with the object of his secret horror, and convinced that no obeah-woman was exercising over him her sorceries, recovered his health and spirits. His gratitude to Miss Portman, who was the immediate cause of his cure, was as simple and touching as it was lively and sincere. This was the circumstance which first turned Mr. Vincent's attention towards Belinda. Upon examining the room in which the negro used to sleep at Harrowgate, the strong smell of phosphorus was perceived, and part of the paper was burnt on the very spot where he had always seen the figure, so that he was now perfectly convinced that this trick had been purposely played to frighten him, in revenge for his having kept possession of the coach-house.

Mrs. Freke, when she found herself detected, gloried in the jest, and told the story as a good joke wherever she went—triumphing in the notion, that it was she who had driven both master and man from Harrowgate.

The exploit was, however, by no means agreeable in its consequences to her friend Mrs. Luttridge, who was now at Harrowgate. For reasons of her own, she was very anxious to fix Mr. Vincent in her society, and she was much provoked by Mrs. Freke's conduct. The ladies came to high words upon the occasion, and an irreparable breach would have ensued had not Mrs. Freke, in the midst of her rage, recollected Mrs. Luttridge's electioneering interest: and suddenly changing her tone, she declared that "she was really sorry to have driven Mr. Vincent from Harrowgate; that her only intention was to get rid of his black; she would lay any wager, that, with Mrs. Luttridge's assistance, they could soon get the gentleman back again;" and she proposed, as a certain method of fixing Mr. Vincent in Mrs. Luttridge's society, to invite Belinda to Harrowgate.

"You may be sure," said Mrs. Freke, "that she must by this time be cursedly tired of her visit to those stupid good people at Oakly-park, and never woman wanted an excuse to do any thing she liked: so trust to her own ingenuity to make some decent apology to the Percivals for running away from them. As to Vincent, you may be sure Belinda Portman is his only inducement for staying with that precious family-party; and if we have her we have him. Now we can be sure of her, for she has just quarrelled with our dear Lady Delacour. I had the whole story from my maid, who had it from Champfort. Lady Delacour and she are at daggers-drawing, and it will be delicious to her to hear her ladyship handsomely abused. We are the declared enemies of her enemy, so we must be her friends. Nothing unites folk so quickly and so solidly, as hatred of some common foe."

This argument could not fail to convince Mrs. Luttridge, and the next day Mrs. Freke commenced her operations. She drove in her unicorn to Oakly-park to pay Miss Portman a visit. She had no acquaintance either with Mr. Percival or Lady Anne, and she had always treated Belinda, when she met her in town, rather cavalierly, as an humble companion of Lady Delacour. But it cost Mrs. Freke nothing to change her tone: she was one of those ladies who can remember or forget people, be perfectly familiar or strangely rude, just as it suits the convenience, fashion, or humour of the minute.

CHAPTER XVII — RIGHTS OF WOMAN

Belinda was alone, and reading, when Mrs. Freke dashed into the room.

"How do, dear creature?" cried she, stepping up to her, and shaking hands with her boisterously—"How do?—Glad to see you, faith!—Been long here?—Tremendously hot to-day!"

She flung herself upon the sofa beside Belinda, threw her hat upon the table, and then continued speaking.

"And how d'ye go on here, poor child?—Gad! I'm glad you're alone—expected to find you encompassed by a whole host of the righteous. Give me credit for my courage in coming to deliver you out of their hands. Luttridge and I had such compassion upon you, when we heard you were close prisoner here! I swore to set the distressed damsel free, in spite of all the dragons in Christendom; so let me carry you off in triumph in my unicorn, and leave these good people to stare when they come home from their sober walk, and find you gone. There's nothing I like so much as to make good people stare—I hope you're of my way o' thinking—you don't look as if you were, though; but I never mind young ladies' looks—always give the lie to their thoughts. Now we talk o' looks—never saw you look so well in my life—as handsome as an angel! And so much the better for me. Do you know, I've a bet of twenty guineas on your head—on your face, I mean. There's a young bride at Harrowgate, Lady H—, they're all mad about her; the men swear she's the handsomest woman in England, and I swear I know one ten times as handsome. They've dared me to make good my word, and I've pledged myself to produce my beauty at the next ball, and to pit her against their belle for any money. Most votes carry it. I'm willing to double my bet since I've seen you again. Come, had not we best be off? Now don't refuse me and make speeches—you know that's all nonsense—I'll take all the blame upon myself."

Belinda, who had not been suffered to utter a word whilst Mrs. Freke ran on in this strange manner, looked in unfeigned astonishment; but when she found herself seized and dragged towards the door, she drew back with a degree of gentle firmness that astonished Mrs. Freke. With a smiling countenance, but a steady tone, she said, "that she was sorry Mrs. Freke's knight-errantry should not be exerted in a better cause, for that she was neither a prisoner, nor a distressed damsel."

"And will you make me lose my bet?" cried Mrs. Freke "Oh, at all events, you must come to the ball!—I'm down for it. But I'll not press it now, because you're frightened out of your poor little wits, I see, at the bare thoughts of doing any thing considered out of rule by these good people. Well, well! it shall be managed for you—leave that to me: I'm used to managing for cowards. Pray tell me—you and Lady

Delacour are off, I understand?—Give ye joy!—She and I were once great friends; that is to say, I had over her 'that power which strong minds have over weak ones,' but she was too weak for me—one of those people that have neither courage to be good, nor to be bad."

"The courage to be bad," said Belinda, "I believe, indeed, she does not possess."

Mrs. Freke stared. "Why, I heard you had quarrelled with her!"

"If I had," said Belinda, "I hope that I should still do justice to her merits. It is said that people are apt to suffer more by their friends than their enemies. I hope that will never be the case with Lady Delacour, as I confess that I have been one of her friends."

"'Gad, I like your spirit—you don't want courage, I see, to fight even for your enemies. You are just the kind of girl I admire. I see you have been prejudiced against me by Lady Delacour; but whatever stories she may have trumped up, the truth of the matter is this, there's no living with her, she's so jealous—so ridiculously jealous—of that lord of hers, for whom all the time she has the impudence to pretend not to care more than I do for the sole of my boot," said Mrs. Freke, striking it, with her whip; "but she hasn't the courage to give him tit for tat: now this is what I call weakness. Pray, how do she and Clarence Hervey go on together?—Are they out o' the hornbook of platonics yet?"

"Mr. Hervey was not in town when I left it," said Belinda.

"Was not he?—Ho! ho!—He's off then!—Ay, so I prophesied; she's not the thing for him: he has some strength of mind—some soul—above vulgar prejudices; so must a woman be to hold him. He was caught at first by her grace and beauty, and that sort of stuff; but I knew it could not last—knew she'd dilly dally with Clary, till he would turn upon his heel and leave her there."

"I fancy that you are entirely mistaken both with respect to Mr. Hervey and Lady Delacour," Belinda very seriously began to say. But Mrs. Freke interrupted her, and ran on; "No! no! no! I'm not mistaken; Clarence has found her out. She's a very woman—that he could forgive her, and so could I; but she's a mere woman—and that he can't forgive—no more can I."

There was a kind of drollery about Mrs. Freke, which, with some people, made the odd things she said pass for wit. Humour she really possessed; and when she chose it, she could be diverting to those who like buffoonery in women. She had set her heart upon winning Belinda over to her party. She began by flattery of her beauty; but as she saw that this had no effect, she next tried what could be done by insinuating that she had a high opinion of her understanding, by talking to her as an esprit fort.

"For my part," said she, "I own I should like a strong devil better than a weak angel."

"You forget," said Belinda, "that it is not Milton, but Satan, who says,

'Fallen spirit, to be weak is to be miserable.'"

"You read, I see!—I did not know you were a reading girl. So was I once; but I never read now. Books only spoil the originality of genius: very well for those who can't think for themselves—but when one has made up one's opinion, there is no use in reading."

"But to make them up," replied Belinda, "may it not be useful?"

"Of no use upon earth to minds of a certain class. You, who can think for yourself, should never read."

"But I read that I may think for myself."

"Only ruin your understanding, trust me. Books are full of trash—nonsense, conversation is worth all the books in the world."

"And is there never any nonsense in conversation?"

"What have you here?" continued Mrs. Freke, who did not choose to attend to this question; exclaiming, as she reviewed each of the books on the table in their turns, in the summary language of presumptuous ignorance, "Smith's Theory of Moral Sentiments—milk and water! Moore's Travels— hasty pudding! La Bruyère—nettle porridge! This is what you were at when I came in, was it not?" said she, taking up a book in which she saw Belinda's mark: "Against Inconsistency in our Expectations. Poor thing! who bored you with this task?"

"Mr. Percival recommended it to me, as one of the best essays in the English language."

"The devil! they seem to have put you in a course of the bitters—a course of the woods might do your business better. Do you ever hunt?—Let me take you out with me some morning—you'd be quite an angel on horseback; or let me drive you out some day in my unicorn."

Belinda declined this invitation, and Mrs. Freke strode away to the window to conceal her mortification, threw up the sash, and called out to her groom, "Walk those horses about, blockhead!"

Mr. Percival and Mr. Vincent at this instant came into the room.

"Hail, fellow! well met!" cried Mrs. Freke, stretching out her hand to Mr. Vincent.

It has been remarked, that an antipathy subsists between creatures, who, without being the same, have yet a strong external resemblance. Mr. Percival saw this instinct rising in Mr. Vincent, and smiled.

"Hail, fellow! well met! I say. Shake hands and be friends, man! Though I'm not in the habit of making apologies, if it will be any satisfaction to you, I beg your pardon for frightening your poor devil of a black."

Then turning towards Mr. Percival, she measured him with her eye, as a person whom she longed to attack. She thought, that if Belinda's opinion of the understanding of these Percivals could be lowered, she should rise in her esteem: accordingly, she determined to draw Mr. Percival into an argument.

"I've been talking treason, I believe, to Miss Portman," cried she; "for I've been opposing some of your opinions, Mr. Percival."

"If you opposed them all, madam," said Mr. Percival, "I should not think it treason."

"Vastly polite!—But I think all our politeness hypocrisy: what d'ye say to that?"

"You know that best, madam!"

"Then I'll go a step farther; for I'm determined you shall contradict me: I think all virtue is hypocrisy."

"I need not contradict you, madam," said Mr. Percival, "for the terms which you make use of contradict themselves."

"It is my system," pursued Mrs. Freke, "that shame is always the cause of the vices of women."

"It is sometimes the effect," said Mr. Percival; "and, as cause and effect are reciprocal, perhaps you may, in some instances, be right."

"Oh! I hate qualifying arguers—plump assertion or plump denial for me: you sha'n't get off so. I say shame is the cause of all women's vices."

"False shame, I suppose you mean?" said Mr. Percival.

"Mere play upon words! All shame is false shame—we should be a great deal better without it. What say you, Miss Portman?—Silent, hey? Silence that speaks."

"Miss Portman's blushes," said Mr. Vincent, "speak for her."

"Against her," said Mrs. Freke: "women blush because they understand."

"And you would have them understand without blushing?" said Mr. Percival. "I grant you that nothing can be more different than innocence and ignorance. Female delicacy—"

"This is just the way you men spoil women," cried Mrs. Freke, "by talking to them of the delicacy of their sex, and such stuff. This delicacy enslaves the pretty delicate dears."

"No; it enslaves us," said Mr. Vincent.

"I hate slavery! Vive la liberté!" cried Mrs. Freke. "I'm a champion for the Rights of Woman."

"I am an advocate for their happiness," said Mr. Percival, "and for their delicacy, as I think it conduces to their happiness."

"I'm an enemy to their delicacy, as I am sure it conduces to their misery."

"You speak from experience?" said Mr. Percival.

"No, from observation. Your most delicate women are always the greatest hypocrites; and, in my opinion, no hypocrite can or ought to be happy."

"But you have not proved the hypocrisy," said Belinda. "Delicacy is not, I hope, an indisputable proof of it? If you mean false delicacy—"

"To cut the matter short at once," cried Mrs. Freke, "why, when a woman likes a man, does not she go and tell him so honestly?"

Belinda, surprised by this question from a woman, was too much abashed instantly to answer.

"Because she's a hypocrite. That is and must be the answer."

"No," said Mr. Percival; "because, if she be a woman of sense, she knows that by such a step she would disgust the object of her affection."

"Cunning!—cunning!—cunning!—the arms of the weakest."

"Prudence! prudence!—the arms of the strongest. Taking the best means to secure our own happiness without injuring that of others is the best proof of sense and strength of mind, whether in man or woman. Fortunately for society, the same conduct in ladies which best secures their happiness most increases ours."

Mrs. Freke beat the devil's tattoo for some moments, and then exclaimed, "You may say what you will, but the present system of society is radically wrong:—whatever is, is wrong."

"How would you improve the state of society?" asked Mr. Percival, calmly.

"I'm not tinker-general to the world," said she.

"I'm glad of it," said Mr. Percival; "for I have heard that tinkers often spoil more than they mend."

"But if you want to know," said Mrs. Freke, "what I would do to improve the world, I'll tell you: I'd have both sexes call things by their right names."

"This would doubtless be a great improvement," said Mr. Percival; "but you would not overturn society to attain it, would you? Should we find things much improved by tearing away what has been called the decent drapery of life?"

"Drapery, if you ask me my opinion," cried Mrs. Freke, "drapery, whether wet or dry, is the most confoundedly indecent thing in the world."

"That depends on public opinion, I allow," said Mr. Percival. "The Lacedaemonian ladies, who were veiled only by public opinion, were better covered from profane eyes than some English ladies are in wet drapery."

"I know nothing of the Lacedaemonian ladies: I took my leave of them when I was a schoolboy—girl, I should say. But pray, what o'clock is it by you? I've sat till I'm cramped all over," cried Mrs. Freke, getting up and stretching herself so violently that some part of her habiliments gave way. "Honi soit qui mal y pense!" said she, bursting into a horse laugh.

Without sharing in any degree that confusion which Belinda felt for her, she strode out of the room, saying, "Miss Portman, you understand these things better than I do; come and set me to rights."

When she was in Belinda's room, she threw herself into an arm-chair, and laughed immoderately.

"How I have trimmed Percival this morning!" said she.

"I am glad you think so," said Belinda; "for I really was afraid he had been too severe upon you."

"I only wish," continued Mrs. Freke, "I only wish his wife had been by. Why the devil did not she make her appearance? I suppose the prude was afraid of my demolishing and unrigging her."

"There seems to have been more danger of that for you than for any body else," said Belinda, as she assisted to set Mrs. Freke's rigging, as she called it, to rights.

"I do of all things delight in hauling good people's opinions out of their musty drawers, and seeing how they look when they're all pulled to pieces before their faces! Pray, are those Lady Anne's drawers or yours?" said Mrs. Freke, pointing to a chest of drawers.

"Mine."

"I'm sorry for it; for if they were hers, to punish her for shirking me, by the Lord, I'd have every rag she has in the world out in the middle of the floor in ten minutes! You don't know me—I'm a terrible person when provoked—stop at nothing!"

As Mrs. Freke saw no other chance left of gaining her point with Belinda, she tried what intimidating her would do.

"I stop at nothing," repeated she, fixing her eyes upon Miss Portman, to fascinate her by terror. "Friend or foe! peace or war! Take your choice. Come to the ball at Harrowgate, I win my bet, and I'm your sworn friend. Stay away, I lose my bet, and am your sworn enemy."

"It is not in my power, madam," said Belinda, calmly, "to comply with your request."

"Then you'll take the consequences," cried Mrs. Freke. She rushed past her, hurried down stairs, and called out, "Bid my blockhead bring my unicorn."

She, her unicorn, and her blockhead, were out of sight in a few minutes.

Good may be drawn from evil. Mrs. Freke's conversation, though at the time it confounded Belinda, roused her, upon reflection, to examine by her reason the habits and principles which guided her conduct. She had a general feeling that they were right and necessary; but now, with the assistance of Lady Anne and Mr. Percival, she established in her own understanding the exact boundaries between right and wrong upon many subjects. She felt a species of satisfaction and security, from seeing the demonstration of those axioms of morality, in which she had previously acquiesced. Reasoning gradually became as agreeable to her as wit; nor was her taste for wit diminished, it was only refined by this process. She now compared and judged of the value of the different species of this brilliant talent.

Mrs. Freke's wit, thought she, is like a noisy squib, the momentary terror of passengers; Lady Delacour's like an elegant firework, which we crowd to see, and cannot forbear to applaud; but Lady Anne Percival's wit is like the refulgent moon, we

"Love the mild rays, and bless the useful light."

"Miss Portman," said Mr. Percival, "are not you afraid of making an enemy of Mrs. Freke, by declining her invitation to Harrowgate?"

"I think her friendship more to be dreaded than her enmity," replied Belinda.

"Then you are not to be terrified by an obeah-woman?" said Mr. Vincent.

"Not in the least, unless she were to come in the shape of a false friend," said Belinda.

"Till lately," said Mr. Vincent, "I was deceived in the character of Mrs. Freke. I thought her a dashing, free-spoken, free-hearted sort of eccentric person, who would make a staunch friend and a jolly companion. As a mistress, or a wife, no man of any taste could think of her. Compare that woman now with one of our Creole ladies."

"But why with a creole?" said Mr. Percival.

"For the sake of contrast, in the first place: our creole women are all softness, grace, delicacy—"

"And indolence," said Mr. Percival.

"Their indolence is but a slight, and, in my judgment, an amiable defect; it keeps them out of mischief, and it attaches them to domestic life. The activity of a Mrs. Freke would never excite their emulation; and so much the better."

"So much the better, no doubt," said Mr. Percival. "But is there no other species of activity that might excite their ambition with propriety? Without diminishing their grace, softness, or delicacy, might not they cultivate their minds? Do you think ignorance, as well as indolence, an amiable defect, essential to the female character?"

"Not essential. You do not, I hope, imagine that I am so much prejudiced in favour of my countrywomen, that I can neither see nor feel the superiority in some instances of European cultivation? I speak only in general."

"And in general," said Lady Anne Percival, "does Mr. Vincent wish to confine our sex to the bliss of ignorance?"

"If it be bliss," said Mr. Vincent, "what reason would they have for complaint?"

"If," said Belinda; "but that is a question which you have not yet decided."

"And how can we decide it?" said Mr. Vincent, "The taste and feelings of individuals must be the arbiters of their happiness."

"You leave reason quite out of the question, then," said Mr. Percival, "and refer the whole to taste and feeling? So that if the most ignorant person in the world assert that he is happier than you are, you are bound to believe him."

"Why should not I?" said Mr. Vincent.

"Because," said Mr. Percival, "though he can judge of his own pleasures, he cannot judge of yours; his are common to both, but yours are unknown to him. Would you, at this instant, change places with that ploughman yonder, who is whistling as he goes for want of thought? or, would you choose to go a step higher in the bliss of ignorance, and turn savage?"

Mr. Vincent laughed, and protested that he should be very unwilling to give up his title to civilized society; and that, instead of wishing to have less knowledge, he regretted that he had not more. "I am sensible," said he, "that I have many prejudices;—Miss Portman has made me ashamed of some of them."

There was a degree of candour in Mr. Vincent's manner and conversation, which interested every body in his favour; Belinda amongst the rest. She was perfectly at ease in Mr. Vincent's company, because she considered him as a person who wished for her friendship, without having any design to engage her affections. From several hints that dropped from him, from Mr. Percival, and from Lady Anne, she was persuaded that he was attached to some creole lady; and all that he said in favour of the elegant softness and delicacy of his countrywomen confirmed this opinion.

Miss Portman was not one of those young ladies who fancy that every gentleman who converses freely with them will inevitably fall a victim to the power of their charms, and will see in every man a lover, or nothing.

CHAPTER XVIII — A DECLARATION

"I've found it!—I've found it, mamma!" cried little Charles Percival, running eagerly into the room with a plant in his hand. "Will you send this in your letter to Helena Delacour, and tell her that is the thing that gold fishes are so fond of? And tell her that it is called lemna, and that it may be found in any ditch or pool."

"But how can she find ditches and pools in Grosvenor-square, my dear?"

"Oh, I forgot that. Then will you tell her, mamma, that I will send her a great quantity?"

"How, my dear?"

"I don't know, mamma, yet—but I will find out some way."

"Would it not be as well, my dear," said his mother, smiling, "to consider how you can perform your promises before you make them?"

"A gentleman," said Mr. Vincent, "never makes a promise that he cannot perform."

"I know that very well," said the boy, proudly: "Miss Portman, who is very good-natured, will, I am sure, be so good, when she goes back to Lady Delacour, as to carry food for the gold fishes to Helena—you see that I have found out a way to keep my promise."

"No, I'm afraid not," said Belinda; "for I am not going back to Lady Delacour's."

"Then I am very glad of it!" said the boy, dropping the weed, and clapping his hands joyfully; "for then I hope you will always stay here, don't you, mamma?—don't you, Mr. Vincent? Oh, you do, I am sure, for I heard you say so to papa the other day! But what makes you grow so red?"

His mother took him by the hand, as he was going to repeat the question, and leading him out of the room, desired him to show her the place where he found the food for the gold fishes.

Belinda, to Mr. Vincent's great relief, seemed not to take any notice of the child's question, nor to have any sympathy in his curiosity; she was intently copying Westall's sketch of Lady Anne Percival and her family, and she had been roused, by the first mention of Helena Delacour's name, to many painful and some pleasing recollections. "What a charming woman, and what a charming family!" said Mr. Vincent, as he looked at the drawing; "and how much more interesting is this picture of domestic happiness than all the pictures of shepherds and shepherdesses, and gods and goddesses, that ever were drawn!"

"Yes," said Belinda, "and how much more interesting this picture is to us, from our knowing that it is not a fancy-piece; that the happiness is real, not imaginary: that this is the natural expression of affection in the countenance of the mother; and that these children, who crowd round her, are what they seem to be—the pride and pleasure of her life!"

"There cannot," exclaimed Mr. Vincent, with enthusiasm, "be a more delightful picture! Oh, Miss Portman, is it possible that you should not feel what you can paint so well?"

"Is it possible, sir," said Belinda, "that you should suspect me of such wretched hypocrisy, as to affect to admire what I am incapable of feeling?"

"You misunderstand—you totally misunderstand me. Hypocrisy! No; there is not a woman upon earth whom I believe to be so far above all hypocrisy, all affectation. But I imagined—I feared—"

As he spoke these last words he was in some confusion, and hastily turned over the prints in a portfolio which lay upon the table. Belinda's eye was caught by an engraving of Lady Delacour in the character of the comic muse. Mr. Vincent did not know the intimacy that had subsisted between her ladyship and Miss Portman—she sighed from the recollection of Clarence Hervey, and of all that had passed at the masquerade.

"What a contrast!" said Mr. Vincent, placing the print of Lady Delacour beside the picture of Lady Anne Percival. "What a contrast! Compare their pictures—compare their characters—compare—"

"Excuse me," interrupted Belinda; "Lady Delacour was once my friend, and I do not like to make a comparison so much to her disadvantage. I have never seen any woman who would not suffer by a comparison with Lady Anne Percival."

"I have been more fortunate, I have seen one—one equally worthy of esteem—admiration—love."

Mr. Vincent's voice faltered in pronouncing the word love; yet Belinda, prepossessed by the idea that he was attached to some creole lady, simply answered, without looking up from her drawing, "You are indeed very fortunate—peculiarly fortunate. Are the West-Indian ladies—"

"West-Indian ladies!" interrupted Mr. Vincent. "Surely, Miss Portman cannot imagine that I am at this instant thinking of any West-Indian lady!" Belinda looked up with an air of surprise. "Charming Miss Portman," continued he, "I have learnt to admire European beauty, European excellence! I have acquired new ideas of the female character—ideas—feelings that must henceforward render me exquisitely happy or exquisitely miserable."

Miss Portman had been too often called "charming" to be much startled or delighted by the sound: the word would have passed by unnoticed, but there was something so impassioned in Mr. Vincent's manner, that she could no longer mistake it for common gallantry, and she was in evident confusion. Now for the first time the idea of Mr. Vincent as a lover came into her mind: the next instant she accused herself of vanity, and dreaded that he should read her thoughts. "Exquisitely miserable!" said she, in a tone of raillery: "I should not suppose, from what I have seen of Mr. Vincent, that any thing could make him exquisitely miserable."

"Then you do not know my character—you do not know my heart: it is in your power to make me exquisitely miserable. Mine is not the cold, hackneyed phrase of gallantry, but the fervid language of passion," cried he, seizing her hand.

At this instant one of the children came in with some flowers to Belinda; and, glad of the interruption, she hastily put up her drawings and left the room, observing that she should scarcely have time to dress before dinner. However, as soon as she found herself alone, she forgot how late it was; and though she sat down before the glass to dress, she made no progress in the business, but continued for some time motionless, endeavouring to recollect and to understand all that had passed. The result of her reflections was the conviction that her partiality for Clarence Hervey was greater than she ever had till this moment suspected. "I have told my aunt Stanhope," thought she, "that the idea of Mr. Hervey had no influence in my refusal of Sir Philip Baddely; I have said that my affections are entirely at my own command: then why do I feel this alarm at the discovery of Mr. Vincent's views? Why do I compare him with one whom I thought I had forgotten?—And yet how are we to judge of character? How can we form any estimate of what is amiable, of what will make us happy or miserable, but by comparison? Am I to blame for perceiving superiority? Am I to blame if one person be more agreeable, or seem to be more agreeable, than another? Am I to blame if I cannot love Mr. Vincent?"

Before Belinda had answered these questions to her satisfaction, the dinner-bell rang. There happened to dine this day at Mr. Percival's a gentleman who had just arrived from Lisbon, and the conversation turned upon the sailors' practice of stilling the waves over the bar of Lisbon by throwing oil upon the water. Charles Percival's curiosity was excited by this conversation, and he wished to see the experiment. In the evening his father indulged his wishes. The children were delighted at the sight, and little Charles insisted upon Belinda's following him to a particular spot, where he was well convinced that she could see better than any where else in the world. "Take care," cried Lady Anne, "or you will lead your friend into the river, Charles." The boy paused, and soon afterwards asked his father several questions about swimming and drowning, and bringing people to life after they had been drowned. "Don't you remember, papa," said he, "that Mr. Hervey, who was almost drowned in the Serpentine river in London?"—Belinda coloured at hearing unexpectedly the name of the person of whom she was at that instant thinking, and the child continued—"I liked that Mr. Hervey very much—I liked him from the first day I saw him. What a number of entertaining things he told us at dinner! We used to call him the good-natured gentleman: I like him very much—I wish he was here this minute. Did you ever see him, Miss Portman? Oh, yes, you must have seen him; for it was he who carried Helena's gold fishes to her mother, and he used often to be at Lady Delacour's—was not he?"

"Yes, my dear, often."

"And did not you like him very much?"—This simple question threw Belinda into inexpressible confusion: but fortunately the crimson on her face was seen only by Lady Anne Percival. To Belinda's great satisfaction, Mr. Vincent forbore this evening any attempt to renew the conversation of the morning; he endeavoured to mix, with his usual animation and gaiety, in the family society; and her embarrassment was much lessened when she heard the next day, at breakfast, that he was gone to Harrowgate. Lady Anne Percival took notice that she was this morning unusually sprightly.

After breakfast, as they were passing through the hall to take a walk in the park, one of the little boys stopped to look at a musical instrument which hung up against the wall.

"What is this, mamma?—It is not a guitar, is it?"

"No, my dear, it is called a banjore; it is an African instrument, of which the negroes are particularly fond. Mr. Vincent mentioned it the other day to Miss Portman, and I believe she expressed some curiosity to see one. Juba went to work immediately to make a banjore, I find. Poor fellow! I dare say that he was very sorry to go to Harrowgate, and to leave his African guitar half finished; especially as it was intended for an offering to Miss Portman. He is the most grateful, affectionate creature I ever saw."

"But why, mamma," said Charles Percival, "is Mr. Vincent gone away? I am sorry he is gone; I hope he will soon come back. In the mean time, I must run and water my carnations."

"His sorrow for his friend Mr. Vincent's departure does not seem to affect his spirits much," said Lady Anne. "People who expect sentiment from children of six years old will be disappointed, and will probably teach them affectation. Surely it is much better to let their natural affections have time to expand. If we tear the rosebud open we spoil the flower." Belinda smiled at this parable of the rosebud, which, she said, might be applied to men and women, as well as to children.

"And yet, upon reflection," said Lady Anne, "the heart has nothing in common with a rosebud. Nonsensical allusions pass off very prettily in conversation. I mean, when we converse with partial friends: but we should reason ill, and conduct ourselves worse, if we were to trust implicitly to poetical analogies. Our affections," continued Lady Anne, "arise from circumstances totally independent of our will."

"That is the very thing I meant to say," interrupted Belinda, eagerly.

"They are excited by the agreeable or useful qualities that we discover in things or in persons."

"Undoubtedly," said Belinda.

"Or by those which our fancies discover," said Lady Anne.

Belinda was silent; but, after a pause, she said, "That it was certainly very dangerous, especially for women, to trust to fancy in bestowing their affections." "And yet," said Lady Anne, "it is a danger to which they are much exposed in society. Men have it in their power to assume the appearance of every thing that is amiable and estimable, and women have scarcely any opportunities of detecting the counterfeit."

"Without Ithuriel's spear, how can they distinguish the good from the evil?" said Belinda. "This is a common-place complaint, I know; the ready excuse that we silly young women plead, when we make mistakes for which our friends reproach us, and for which we too often reproach ourselves."

"The complaint is common-place precisely because it is general and just," replied Lady Anne. "In the slight and frivolous intercourse, which fashionable belles usually have with those fashionable beaux who call themselves their lovers, it is surprising that they can discover any thing of each other's real character. Indeed they seldom do; and this probably is the cause why there are so many unsuitable and unhappy marriages. A woman who has an opportunity of seeing her lover in private society, in domestic life, has infinite advantages; for if she has any sense, and he has any sincerity, the real character of both may perhaps be developed."

"True," said Belinda (who now suspected that Lady Anne alluded to Mr. Vincent); "and in such a situation a woman would readily be able to decide whether the man who addressed her would suit her taste or not; so she would be inexcusable if, either from vanity or coquetry, she disguised her real sentiments."

"And will Miss Portman, who cannot, by any one to whom she is known, be suspected of vanity or coquetry, permit me to speak to her with the freedom of a friend?"

Belinda, touched by the kindness of Lady Anne's manner, pressed her hand, and exclaimed, "Yes, dear Lady Anne, speak to me with freedom—you cannot do me a greater favour. No thought of my mind, no secret feeling of my heart, shall be concealed from you."

"Do not imagine that I wish to encroach upon the generous openness of your temper," said Lady Anne; "tell me when I go too far, and I will be silent. One who, like Miss Portman, has lived in the world, has seen a variety of characters, and probably has had a variety of admirers, must have formed some determinate idea of the sort of companion that would make her happy, if she were to marry—unless," said Lady Anne, "she has formed a resolution against marriage."

"I have formed no such resolution," said Belinda. "Indeed, since I have seen the happiness which you and Mr. Percival enjoy in your own family, I have been much more disposed to think that a union—that a union such as yours, would increase my happiness. At the same time, my aversion to the idea of marrying from interest, or convenience, or from any motives but esteem and love, is increased almost to horror. O Lady Anne! there is nothing that I would not do to please the friends to whom I am under obligations, except sacrificing my peace of mind, or my integrity, the happiness of my life, by—"

Lady Anne, in a gentle tone, assured her, that she was the last person in the world who would press her to any union which would make her unhappy. "You perceive that Mr. Vincent has spoken to me of what passed between you yesterday. You perceive that I am his friend, but do not forget that I am also yours.

If you fear undue influence from any of your relations in favour of Mr. Vincent's large fortune, &c. let his proposal remain a secret between ourselves, till you can decide, from farther acquaintance with him, whether it will be in your power to return his affection."

"I fear, my dear Lady Anne," cried Belinda, "that it is not in my power to return his affection."

"And may I ask your objections?"

"Is it not a sufficient objection, that I am persuaded I cannot love him?"

"No; for you may be mistaken in that persuasion. Remember what we said a little while ago, about fancy and spontaneous affections. Does Mr. Vincent appear to you defective in any of the qualities which you think essential to happiness? Mr. Percival has known him from the time he was a man, and can answer for his integrity and his good temper. Are not these the first points you would consider? They ought to be, I am sure, and I believe they are. Of his understanding I shall say nothing, because you have had full opportunities of judging of it from his conversation."

"Mr. Vincent appears to have a good understanding," said Belinda.

"Then to what do you object?—Is there any thing disgusting to you in his person or manners?"

"He is very handsome, he is well bred, and his manners are unaffected," said Belinda; "but—do not accuse me of caprice—altogether he does not suit my taste; and I cannot think it sufficient not to feel disgust for a husband—though I believe this is the fashionable doctrine."

"It is not mine, I assure you," said Lady Anne. "I am not one of those who think it 'safest to begin with a little aversion;' but since you acknowledge that Mr. Vincent possesses the essential good qualities that entitle him to your esteem, I am satisfied. We gradually acquire knowledge of the good qualities of those who endeavour to please us; and if they are really amiable, their persons become agreeable to us by degrees, when we become accustomed to them."

"Accustomed!" said Belinda, smiling: "one does grow accustomed even to disagreeable things certainly; but at this rate, my dear Lady Anne, I do not doubt but one might grow accustomed to Caliban."

"My belief in the reconciling power of custom does not go quite so far," said Lady Anne. "It does not extend to Caliban, or even to the hero of La Belle et La Bête; but I do believe, that, in a mind so well regulated as yours, esteem may certainly in time be improved into love. I will tell Mr. Vincent so, my dear."

"No, my dear Lady Anne! no; you must not—indeed you must not. You have too good an opinion of me—my mind is not so well regulated—I am much weaker, much sillier, than you imagine—than you can conceive," said Belinda.

Lady Anne soothed her with the most affectionate expressions, and concluded with saying, "Mr. Vincent has promised not to return from Harrowgate, to torment you with his addresses, if you be absolutely determined against him. He is of too generous, and perhaps too proud a temper, to persecute you with vain solicitations; and however Mr. Percival and I may wish that he could obtain such a wife, we shall have the common, or uncommon, sense and good-nature to allow our friends to be happy their own way."

"You are very good—too good. But am I then to be the cause of banishing Mr. Vincent from all his friends—from Oakly-park?"

"Will he not do what is most prudent, to avoid the charming Miss Portman," said Lady Anne, smiling, "if he must not love her? This was at least the advice I gave him, when he consulted us yesterday evening. But I will not sign his writ of banishment lightly. Nothing but the assurance that the heart is engaged can be a sufficient cause for despair; nothing else could, in my eyes, justify you, my dear Belinda, from the charge of caprice."

"I can give you no such assurance, I hope—I believe," said Belinda, in great confusion; "and yet I would not for the world deceive you: you have a right to my sincerity." She paused; and Lady Anne said with a smile, "Perhaps I can spare you the trouble of telling me in words what a blush told me, or at least made me suspect, yesterday evening, when we were standing by the river side, when little Charles asked you—"

"Yes, I remember—I saw you look at me."

"Undesignedly, believe me."

"Undesignedly, I am sure; but I was afraid you would think—"

"The truth."

"No; but more than the truth. The truth you shall hear; and the rest I will leave to your judgment and to your kindness."

Belinda gave a full account of her acquaintance with Clarence Hervey; of the variations in his manner towards her; of his excellent conduct with respect to Lady Delacour (of this, by-the-by, she spoke at large). But she was more concise when she touched upon the state of her own heart; and her voice almost failed when she came to the history of the lock of beautiful hair, the Windsor incognita, and the picture of Virginia. She concluded by expressing her conviction of the propriety of forgetting a man, who was in all probability attached to another, and she declared it to be her resolution to banish him from her thoughts. Lady Anne said, "that nothing could be more prudent or praiseworthy than forming such a resolution—except keeping it." Lady Anne had a high opinion of Mr. Hervey; but she had no doubt, from Belinda's account, and from her own observations on Mr. Hervey, and from slight circumstances which had accidentally come to Mr. Percival's knowledge, that he was, as Belinda suspected, attached to another person. She wished, therefore, to confirm Miss Portman in this belief, and to turn her thoughts towards one who, beside being deserving of her esteem and love, felt for her the most sincere affection. She did not, however, press the subject farther at this time, but contented herself with requesting that Belinda would take three days (the usual time given for deliberation in fairy tales) before she should decide against Mr. Vincent.

The next day they went to look at a porter's lodge, which Mr. Percival had just built; it was inhabited by an old man and woman, who had for many years been industrious tenants, but who, in their old age, had been reduced to poverty, not by imprudence, but by misfortune. Lady Anne was pleased to see them comfortably settled in their new habitation; and whilst she and Belinda were talking to the old couple, their grand-daughter, a pretty looking girl of about eighteen, came in with a basket of eggs in her hand. "Well, Lucy," said Lady Anne, "have you overcome your dislike to James Jackson?" The girl reddened, smiled, and looked at her grand-mother, who answered for her in an arch tone, "Oh, yes, my lady! We are not afraid of Jackson now; we are grown very great friends. This pretty cane chair for my good man was his handiwork, and these baskets he made for me. Indeed, he's a most industrious, ingenious, good-natured youth; and our Lucy takes no offence at his courting her now, my lady, I can assure you. That necklace, which is never off her neck now, he turned for her, my lady; it is a present of his. So I tell him he need not be discouraged, though so be she did not take to him at the first; for she's a good girl, and a sensible girl—I say it, though she's my own; and the eyes are used to a face after a time, and then it's nothing. They say, fancy's all in all in love: now in my judgment, fancy's little or nothing with girls that have sense. But I beg pardon for prating at this rate, more especially when I am so old as to have forgot all the little I ever knew about such things."

"But you have the best right in the world to speak about such things, and your grand-daughter has the best reason in the world to listen to you," said Lady Anne, "because, in spite of all the crosses of fortune, you have been an excellent and happy wife, at least ever since I can remember."

"And ever since I can remember, that's more; no offence to your ladyship," said the old man, striking his crutch against the ground. "Ever since I can remember, she has made me the happiest man in the whole world, in the whole parish, as every body knows, and I best of all!" cried he, with a degree of enthusiasm that lighted up his aged countenance, and animated his feeble voice.

"And yet," said the honest dame, "if I had followed my fancy, and taken up with my first love, it would not ha' been with he, Lucy. I had a sort of a fancy (since my lady's so good as to let me speak), I had a sort of a fancy for an idle young man; but he, very luckily for me, took it into his head to fall in love with another young woman, and then I had leisure enough left me to think of your grandfather, who was not so much to my taste like at first. But when I found out his goodness and cleverness, and joined to all, his great tenderness for me, I thought better of it, Lucy (as who knows but you may do, though there shall not be a word said on my part to press you, for poor Jackson?); and my thinking better is the cause why I have been so happy ever since, and am so still in my old age. Ah, Lucy! dear, what a many years that same old age lasts, after all! But young folks, for the most part, never think what's to come after thirty or forty at farthest. But I don't say this for you, Lucy; for you are a good girl, and a sensible girl, though my own grand-daughter, as I said before, and therefore won't be run away with by fancy, which is soon past and gone: but make a prudent choice, that you won't never have cause to repent of. But I'll not say a word more; I'll leave it all to yourself and James Jackson."

"You do right," said Lady Anne: "good morning to you! Farewell, Lucy! That's a pretty necklace, and is very becoming to you—fare ye well!"

She hurried out of the cottage with Belinda, apprehensive that the talkative old dame might weaken the effect of her good sense and experience by a farther profusion of words.

"One would think," said Belinda, with an ingenuous smile, "that this lesson upon the dangers of fancy was intended for me: at any rate, I may turn it to my own advantage!"

"Happy those who can turn all the experience of others to their own advantage!" said Lady Anne: "this would be a more valuable privilege than the power of turning every thing that is touched to gold."

They walked on in silence for a few minutes; and then Miss Portman, pursuing the train of her own thoughts, and unconscious that she had not explained them to Lady Anne, abruptly exclaimed, "But if I should be entangled, so as not to be able to retract!—and if it should not be in my power to love him at last, he will think me a coquette, a jilt, perhaps: he will have reason to complain of me, if I waste his time, and trifle with his affections. Then is it not better that I should avoid, by a decided refusal, all possibility of injury to Mr. Vincent, and of blame to myself?"

"There is no danger of Mr. Vincent's misunderstanding or misrepresenting you. The risk that he runs is by his voluntary choice; and I am sure that if, after farther acquaintance with him, you find it impossible to return his affection, he will not consider himself as ill-used by your refusal."

"But after a certain time—after the world suspects that two people are engaged to each other, it is scarcely possible for the woman to recede: when they come within a certain distance, they are pressed to unite, by the irresistible force of external circumstances. A woman is too often reduced to this dilemma: either she must marry a man she does not love, or she must be blamed by the world—either she must sacrifice a portion of her reputation, or the whole of her happiness."

"The world is indeed often too curious, and too rash in these affairs," said Lady Anne. "A young woman is not in this respect allowed sufficient time for freedom of deliberation. She sees, as Mr. Percival once said, 'the drawn sword of tyrant custom suspended over her head by a single hair.'"

"And yet, notwithstanding you are so well aware of the danger, your ladyship would expose me to it?" said Belinda.

"Yes; for I think the chance of happiness, in this instance, overbalances the risk," said Lady Anne. "As we cannot alter the common law of custom, and as we cannot render the world less gossiping, or less censorious, we must not expect always to avoid censure; all we can do is, never to deserve it—and it would be absurd to enslave ourselves to the opinion of the idle and ignorant. To a certain point, respect for the opinion of the world is prudence; beyond that point, it is weakness. You should also consider that the world at Oakly-park and in London are two different worlds. In London if you and Mr. Vincent were seen often in each other's company, it would be immediately buzzed about that Miss Portman and Mr. Vincent were going to be married; and if the match did not take place, a thousand foolish stories might be told to account for its being broken off. But here you are not surrounded by busy eyes and busy tongues. The butchers, bakers, ploughmen, and spinsters, who compose our world, have all affairs of their own to mind. Besides, their comments can have no very extensive circulation; they are used to see Mr. Vincent continually here; and his staying with us the remainder of the autumn will not appear to them any thing wonderful or portentous."

Their conversation was interrupted. Mr. Vincent returned to Oakly-park—but upon the express condition that he should not make his attachment public by any particular attentions, and that he should draw no conclusions in his favour from Belinda's consenting to converse with him freely upon every common subject. To this treaty of amity Lady Anne Percival was guarantee.

CHAPTER XIX — A WEDDING

Belinda and Mr. Vincent could never agree in their definition of the-word flattery; so that there were continual complaints on the one hand of a breach of treaty, and, on the other, solemn protestations of the most scrupulous adherence to his compact. However this might be, it is certain that the gentleman gained so much, either by truth or fiction, that, in the course of some weeks, he got the lady as far as "gratitude and esteem."

One evening, Belinda was playing with little Charles Percival at spillikins. Mr. Vincent, who found pleasure in every thing that amused Belinda, and Mr. Percival, who took an interest in every thing which entertained his children, were looking on at this simple game.

"Mr. Percival," said Belinda, "condescending to look at a game of jack-straws!"

"Yes," said Lady Anne; "for he is of Dryden's opinion, that, if a straw can be made the instrument of happiness, he is a wise man who does not despise it."

"Ah! Miss Portman, take care!" cried Charles, who was anxious that she should win, though he was playing against her. "Take care! don't touch that knave."

"I would lay a hundred guineas upon the steadiness of Miss Portman's hand," cried Mr. Vincent.

"I'll lay you sixpence, though," cried Charles, eagerly, "that she'll stir the king, if she touches that knave—I'll lay you a shilling."

"Done! done!" cried Mr. Vincent.

"Done! done!" cried the boy, stretching out his hand, but his father caught it.

"Softly! softly, Charles!—No betting, if you please, my dear. Done and done sometimes ends in—undone."

"It was my fault—it was I who was in the wrong," cried Vincent immediately.

"I am sure you are in the right, now," said Mr. Percival; "and, what is better than my saying so, Miss Portman thinks so, as her smile tells me."

"You moved, Miss Portman!" cried Charles:—"Oh, indeed! the king's head stirred, the very instant papa spoke. I knew it was impossible that you could get that knave clear off without shaking the king. Now, papa, only look how they were balanced."

"I grant you," said Mr. Vincent, "I should have made an imprudent bet. So it is well I made none; for now I see the chances were ten to one, twenty to one, a hundred to one against me."

"It does not appear to me to be a matter of chance," said Mr. Percival. "This is a game of address, not chance, and that is the reason I like it."

"Oh, papa! Oh, Miss Portman! look how nicely these are balanced. There! my breath has set them in motion. Look, they shake, shake, shake, like the great rocking-stones at Brimham Crags."

"That is comparing small things to great, indeed!" said Mr. Percival.

"By-the-by," cried Mr. Vincent, "Miss Portman has never seen those wonderful rocking-stones—suppose we were to ride to see them to-morrow?"

The proposal was warmly seconded by the children, and agreed to by every one. It was settled, that after they had seen Brimham Crags they should spend the remainder of the day at Lord C—'s beautiful place in the neighbourhood.

The next morning was neither too hot nor too cold, and they set out on their little party of pleasure; the children went with their mother, to their great delight, in the sociable; and Mr. Vincent, to his great delight, rode with Belinda. When they came within sight of the Crags, Mr. Percival, who was riding with them, exclaimed—"What is that yonder, on the top of one of the great rocking-stones?"

"It looks like a statue," said Vincent. "It has been put up since we were here last."

"I fancy it has got up of itself," said Belinda, "for it seems to be getting down of itself. I think I saw it stoop. Oh! I see now, it is a man who has got up there, and he seems to have a gun in his hand, has not he? He is going through his manual exercise for his diversion—for the diversion of the spectators below, I perceive—there is a party of people looking at him."

"Him!" said Mr. Percival.

"I protest it is a woman!" said Vincent.

"No, surely," said Belinda: "it cannot be a woman!"

"Not unless it be Mrs. Freke," replied Mr. Percival.

In fact it was Mrs. Freke, who had been out shooting with a party of gentlemen, and who had scrambled upon this rocking-stone, on the summit of which she went through the manual exercise at the word of command from her officer. As they rode nearer to the scene of action, Belinda heard the shrill screams of a female voice, and they descried amongst the gentlemen a slight figure in a riding habit.

"Miss Moreton, I suppose," said Mr. Vincent.

"Poor girl! what are they doing with her?" cried Belinda.

"They seem to be forcing her up to the top of that place, where she has no mind to go. Look how Mrs. Freke drags her up by the arm!"

As they drew nearer, they heard Mrs. Freke laughing loud as she rocked this frightened girl upon the top of the stone.

"We had better keep out of the way, I think," said Belinda: "for perhaps, as she has vowed vengeance against me, she might take a fancy to setting me upon that pinnacle of glory."

"She dare not," cried Vincent, his eyes flashing with anger: "you may trust to us to defend you."

"Certainly!—But I will not run into danger on purpose to give you the pleasure of defending me," said Belinda; and as she spoke, she turned her horse another way.

"You won't turn back, Miss Portman?" cried Vincent eagerly, laying his hand on her bridle.—"Good Heavens, ma'am! we can't run away!—We came here to look at these rocking-stones!—We have not half seen them. Lady Anne and the children will be here immediately. You would not deprive them of the pleasure of seeing these things!"

"I doubt whether they would have much pleasure in seeing some of these things! and as to the rest, if I disappoint the children now, Mr. Percival will, perhaps, have the goodness to bring them some other day."

"Certainly," said Mr. Percival: "Miss Portman shows her usual prudence."

"The children are so good tempered, that I am sure they will forgive me," continued Belinda; "and Mr. Vincent will be ashamed not to follow their example, though he seems to be rather angry with me at present for obliging him to turn back—out of the path of danger."

"You must not be surprised at that," said Mr. Percival, laughing; "for Mr. Vincent is a lover and a hero. You know it is a ruled case, in all romances, that when a lover and his mistress go out riding together, some adventure must befal them. The horse must run away with the lady, and the gentleman must catch her in his arms just as her neck is about to be broken. If the horse has been too well trained for the heroine's purpose, 'some footpad, bandit fierce, or mountaineer,' some jealous rival must make his appearance quite unexpectedly at the turn of a road, and the lady must be carried off—robes flying—hair streaming—like Bürger's Leonora. Then her lover must come to her rescue just in the proper moment. But if the damsel cannot conveniently be run away with, she must, as the last resource, tumble into a river to make herself interesting, and the hero must be at least half drowned in dragging her out, that she may be under eternal obligations to him, and at last be forced to marry him out of pure gratitude."

"Gratitude!" interrupted Mr. Vincent: "he is no hero, to my mind, who would be content with gratitude, instead of love."

"You need not alarm yourself: Miss Portman does not seem inclined to put you to the trial, you see," said Mr. Percival, smiling. "Now it is really to be regretted, that she deprived you of an opportunity of fighting some of the gentlemen in Mrs. Freke's train, or of delivering her from the perilous height of one of those rocking-stones. It would have been a new incident in a novel."

"How that poor girl screamed!" said Belinda. "Was her terror real or affected?"

"Partly real, partly affected, I fancy," said Mr. Percival.

"I pity her," said Mr. Vincent; "for Mrs. Freke leads her a weary life."

"She is certainly to be pitied, but also to be blamed," said Mr. Percival. "You do not know her history. Miss Moreton ran away from her friends to live with this Mrs. Freke, who has led her into all kinds of mischief and absurdity. The girl is weak and vain, and believes that every thing becomes her which Mrs.

Freke assures her is becoming. At one time she was persuaded to go to a public ball with her arms as bare as Juno's, and her feet as naked as Mad. Tallien's. At another time Miss Moreton (who unfortunately has never heard the Greek proverb, that half is better than the whole,) was persuaded by Mrs. Freke to lay aside, her half boots, and to equip herself in men's whole boots; and thus she rode about the country, to the amazement of all the world. These are trifles; but women who love to set the world at defiance in trifles seldom respect its opinion in matters of consequence. Miss Moreton's whole boots in the morning, and her bare feet in the evening, were talked of by every body, till she gave them more to talk of about her attachment to a young officer. Mrs. Freke, whose philosophy is professedly latitudinarian in morals, laughed at the girl's prejudice in favour of the ceremony of marriage. So did the officer; for Miss Moreton had no fortune. It is suspected that the young lady did not feel the difficulty, which philosophers are sometimes said to find in suiting their practice to their theory. The unenlightened world reprobated the theory much, and the practice more. I am inclined, in spite of scandal, to think the poor girl was only imprudent: at all events, she repents her folly too late. She has now no friend upon earth but Mrs. Freke, who is, in fact, her worst enemy, and who tyrannizes over her without mercy. Imagine what it is to be the butt of a buffoon!"

"What a lesson to young ladies in the choice of female friends!" said Belinda. "But had Miss Moreton no relations, who could interfere to get her out of Mrs. Freke's hands?"

"Her father and mother were old, and, what is more contemptible, old-fashioned: she would not listen to their advice; she ran away from them. Some of her relations were, I believe, willing that she should stay with Mrs. Freke, because she was a dashing, fashionable woman, and they thought it might be what is called an advantage to her. She had one relation, indeed, who was quite of a different opinion, who saw the danger of her situation, and remonstrated in the strongest manner—but to no purpose. This was a cousin of Miss Moreton's, a respectable clergyman. Mrs. Freke was so much incensed by his insolent interference, as she was pleased to call it, that she made an effigy of Mr. Moreton dressed in his canonicals, and hung the figure up as a scarecrow in a garden close by the high road. He was so much beloved and respected for his benevolence and unaffected piety, that Mrs. Freke totally failed in her design of making him ridiculous; her scarecrow was torn to pieces by his parishioners; and though, in the true spirit of charity, he did all he could to moderate their indignation against his enemy, the lady became such an object of detestation, that she was followed with hisses and groans whenever she appeared, and she dared not venture within ten miles of the village.

"Mrs. Freke now changed the mode of her persecution: she was acquainted with a nobleman from whom our clergyman expected a living, and she worked upon his lordship so successfully, that he insisted upon having an apology made to the lady. Mr. Moreton had as much dignity of mind as gentleness of character; his forbearance was that of principle, and so was his firmness: he refused to make the concessions that were required. His noble patron bullied. Though he had a large family to provide for, the clergyman would not degrade himself by any improper submission. The incumbent died, and the living was given to a more compliant friend. So ends the history of one of Mrs. Freke's numerous frolics."

"This was the story," said Mr. Vincent, "which effectually changed my opinion of her. Till I heard it, I always looked upon her as one of those thoughtless, good-natured people, who, as the common saying is, do nobody any harm but themselves."

"It is difficult in society," said Mr. Percival, "especially for women, to do harm to themselves, without doing harm to others. They may begin in frolic, but they must end in malice. They defy the world—the world in return excommunicates them—the female outlaws become desperate, and make it the business and pride of their lives to disturb the peace of their sober neighbours. Women who have lowered themselves in the public opinion cannot rest without attempting to bring others to their own level."

"Mrs. Freke, notwithstanding the blustering merriment that she affects, is obviously unhappy," said Belinda; "and since we cannot do her any good, either by our blame or our pity, we had better think of something else."

"Scandal," said Mr. Vincent, "does not seem to give you much pleasure, Miss Portman. You will be glad to hear that Mrs. Freke's malice against poor Mr. Moreton has not ruined him. Do you know Mr. Percival, that he has just been presented to a good living by a generous young man, who heard of his excellent conduct?"

"I am extremely glad of it," said Mr. Percival. "Who is this generous young man? I should like to be acquainted with him."

"So should I," said Mr. Vincent: "he is a Mr. Hervey."

"Clarence Hervey, perhaps?"

"Yes, Clarence was his name."

"No man more likely to do a generous action than Clarence Hervey," said Mr. Percival.

"Nobody more likely to do a generous action than Mr. Hervey," repeated Belinda, in rather a low tone. She could now praise Clarence Hervey without blushing, and she could think even of his generosity without partiality, though not without pleasure. By strength of mind, and timely exertion, she had prevented her prepossession from growing into a passion that might have made her miserable. Proud of this conquest over herself, she was now disposed to treat Mr. Vincent with more favour than usual. Self-complacency generally puts us in good-humour with our friends.

After spending some pleasant hours in Lord C—'s beautiful grounds, where the children explored to their satisfaction every dingle and bushy dell, they returned home in the cool of the evening. Mr. Vincent thought it the most delightful evening he had ever felt.

"What! as charming as a West Indian evening?" said Mr. Percival. "This is more than I expected ever to hear you acknowledge in favour of England. Do you remember how you used to rave of the climate and of the prospects of Jamaica?"

"Yes, but my taste has quite changed."

"I remember the time," said Mr. Percival, "when you thought it impossible that your taste should ever change; when you told me that taste, whether for the beauties of animate or inanimate nature, was immutable."

"You and Miss Portman have taught me better sense. First loves are generally silly things," added he, colouring a little. Belinda coloured also.

"First loves," continued Mr. Percival, "are not necessarily more foolish than others; but the chances are certainly against them. From poetry or romance, young people usually form their earlier ideas of love, before they have actually felt the passion; and the image which they have in their own minds of the beau ideal is cast upon the first objects they afterward behold. This, if I may be allowed the expression, is Cupid's Fata Morgana. Deluded mortals are in ecstasy whilst the illusion lasts, and in despair when it vanishes."

Mr. Percival appeared to be unconscious that what he was saying was any way applicable to Belinda. He addressed himself to Mr. Vincent solely, and she listened at her ease.

"But," said she, "do not you think that this prejudice, as I am willing to allow it to be, in favour of first loves, may in our sex be advantageous? Even when a woman may be convinced—that she ought not to indulge a first love, should she not be prevented by delicacy from thinking of a second?"

"Delicacy, my dear Miss Portman, is a charming word, and a still more charming thing, and Mrs. Freke has probably increased our affection for it; but even delicacy, like all other virtues, must be judged of by the test of utility. We should run into romance, and error, and misery, if we did not constantly refer to this standard. Our reasonings as to the conduct of life, as far as moral prudence is concerned, must depend ultimately upon facts. Now, of the numbers of people in this world, how many do you think have married their first loves? Probably not one out of ten. Then, would you have nine out of ten pine all their lives in celibacy, or fret in matrimony, because they cannot have the persons who first struck their fancy?"

"I acknowledge this would not add to the happiness of society," said Belinda.

"Nor to its virtue," said Mr. Percival. "I scarcely know an idea more dangerous to domestic happiness than this belief in the unextinguishable nature of a first flame. There are people who would persuade us that, though it may be smothered for years, it must break out at last, and blaze with destructive fury. Pernicious doctrine! false as it is pernicious!—The struggles between duty and passion may be the charm of romance, but must be the misery of real life. The woman who marries one man, and loves another, who, in spite of all that an amiable and estimable husband can do to win her confidence and affection, nourishes in secret a fatal prepossession for her first love, may perhaps, by the eloquence of a fine writer, be made an interesting heroine;—but would any man of sense or feeling choose to be troubled with such a wife?—Would not even the idea that women admired such conduct necessarily tend to diminish our confidence, if not in their virtue, at least in their sincerity? And would not this suspicion destroy our happiness? Husbands may sometimes have delicate feelings as well as their wives, though they are seldom allowed to have any by these unjust novel writers. Now, could a husband who has any delicacy be content to possess the person without the mind?—the duty without the love?— Could he be perfectly happy, if, in the fondest moments, he might doubt whether he were an object of disgust or affection?—whether the smiles of apparent joy were only the efforts of a suffering martyr?— Thank Heaven! I am not married to one of these charming martyrs. Let those live with them who admire them. For my part, I admire and love the wife, who not only seems but is happy—as I," added Mr. Percival smiling, "have the fond credulity to believe. If I have spoken too long or too warmly upon the chapter of first loves, I have at least been a perfectly disinterested declaimer; for I can assure you, Miss Portman, that I do not suspect Lady Anne Percival of sighing in secret for some vision of perfection, any more than she suspects me of pining for the charming Lady Delacour, who, perhaps, you may have heard was my first love. In these days, however, so few people marry with even the pretence to love of any sort, that you will think I might have spared this tirade. No; there are ingenuous minds which will never be enslaved by fashion or interest, though they may be exposed to be deceived by romance, or by the delicacy of their own imaginations."

"I hear," said Belinda, smiling, "I hear and understand the emphasis with which you pronounce that word delicacy. I see you have not forgotten that I used it improperly half an hour ago, as you have convinced me."

"Happy they," said Mr. Percival, "who can be convinced in half an hour! There are some people who cannot be convinced in a whole life, and who end where they began, with saying—'This is my opinion—I always thought so, and always shall.'"

Mr. Vincent at all times loved Mr. Percival; but he never felt so much affection for him as he did this evening, and his arguments appeared to him unanswerable. Though Belinda had never mentioned to Mr. Vincent the name of Clarence Hervey till this day, and though he did not in the least suspect from her manner that this gentleman ever possessed any interest in her heart; yet, with her accustomed sincerity, she had confessed to him that an impression had been made upon her mind before she came to Oakly-park.

After this conversation with Mr. Percival, Mr. Vincent perceived that he gained ground more rapidly in her favour; and his company grew every day more agreeable to her taste: he was convinced that, as he possessed her esteem, he should in time secure her affections.

"In time," repeated Lady Anne Percival: "you must allow her time, or you will spoil all."

It was with some difficulty that Mr. Vincent restrained his impatience, even though he was persuaded of the prudence of his friend's advice. Things went on in this happy, but as he thought slow, state of progression till towards the latter end of September.

One fine morning Lady Anne Percival came into Belinda's room with a bridal favour in her hand. "Do you know," said she, "that we are to have a wedding to-day? This favour has just been sent to my maid. Lucy, the pretty girl whom you may remember to have seen some time ago with that prettily turned necklace, is the bride, and James Jackson is the bridegroom. Mr. Vincent has let them a very pretty little farm in the neighbourhood, and—hark! there's the sound of music."

They looked out of the window, and they saw a troop of villagers, gaily dressed, going to the wedding. Lady Anne, who was always eager to promote innocent festivity, sent immediately to have a tent pitched in the park; and all the rural company were invited to a dance in the evening: it was a very cheerful spectacle. Belinda heard from all sides praises of Mr. Vincent's generosity; and she could not be insensible to the simple but enthusiastic testimony which Juba bore to his master's goodness. Juba had composed, in his broken dialect, a little song in honour of his master, which he sang to his banjore with the most touching expression of joyful gratitude. In some of the stanzas Belinda could distinguish that her own name was frequently repeated. Lady Anne called him, and desired to have the words of this song. They were a mixture of English and of his native language; they described in the strongest manner what had been his feelings whilst he was under the terror of Mrs. Freke's fiery obeah-woman, then his joy on being relieved from these horrors, with the delightful sensations of returning health;—and thence he suddenly passed to his gratitude to Belinda, the person to whom he owed his recovery. He concluded with wishing her all sorts of happiness, and, above all, that she might be fortunate in her love; which

Juba thought the highest degree of felicity. He had no sooner finished his song, which particularly touched and pleased Miss Portman, than he begged his master to offer to her the little instrument, which he had made with much pains and ingenuity. She accepted the banjore with a smile that enchanted Mr. Vincent; but at this instant they were startled by the sound of a carriage driving rapidly into the park. Belinda looked up, and between the heads of the dancers she just caught a glimpse of a well-known livery. "Good heavens!" she exclaimed, "Lady Delacour's carriage!—Can it be Lady Delacour?"

The carriage stopped, and Marriott hastily jumped out of it. Belinda pressed forward to meet her; poor Marriott was in great agitation:—"Oh, Miss Portman! my poor lady is very ill—very ill, indeed. She has sent me for you—here's her letter. Dear Miss Portman, I hope you won't refuse to come; she has been very ill, and is very ill; but she would be better, if she could see you again. But I'll tell every thing, ma'am, when we are by ourselves, and when you have read your letter."

Miss Portman immediately accompanied Marriott towards the house; and as they walked thither, she learned that Lady Delacour had applied to the quack-doctor in whom she had such implicit faith, and had in vain endeavoured to engage him to perform for her the operation to which she had determined to submit. He was afraid to hazard it, and he prevailed upon her to give up the scheme, and to try some new external remedy from which he promised wonders. No one knew what his medicines were, but they affected her head in the most alarming manner.

In her delirium she called frequently upon Miss Portman; sometimes accusing her of the basest treachery, sometimes addressing her as if she were present, and pouring forth the warmest expressions of friendship. "In her lucid intervals, ma'am," continued Marriott, "she for some weeks scarcely ever mentioned your name, nor could bear to hear me mention it. One day, when I was saying how much I wished that you were with her again, she darted at me the most terrible look that ever I beheld.

"'When I am in my grave, Marriott,' cried my lady, 'it will be time enough for Miss Portman again to visit this house, and you may then express your attachment to her with more propriety than at present.' These were my lady's own words—I shall never forget them: they struck and astonished me, ma'am, so much, I stood like one stupified, and then left the room to think them over again by myself, and make sense of them, if I could. Well, ma'am, to be sure, it then struck me like a flash of lightning, that my lady was jealous—and, begging your pardon, ma'am—of you. This seemed to me the most unnatural thing in the world, considering how easy my lady had always seemed to be about my lord; but it was now clear to me, that this was the cause of your leaving us so suddenly, ma'am. Well, I was confident that Mr. Champfort was at the bottom of the business from the first; and now that I knew what scent to go upon, I went to work with fresh spirit to find him out, which was a thing I was determined upon—and what I'm determined upon, I generally do, ma'am. So I put together things about Miss Portman and my lord, that had dropped at odd times from Sir Philip Baddely's gentleman; and I, partly serious and partly flirting, which in a good cause is no sin, drew from him (for he pretends to be a little an admirer of mine, ma'am, though I never gave him the smallest encouragement) all he knew or suspected, or had heard reported, or whispered; and out it came, ma'am, that Mr. Champfort was the original of all; and that he had told a heap of lies about some bank-notes that my lord had given you, and that you and my lord were to be married as soon as my lady was dead; and I don't know what, which he maliciously circulated through Sir Philip's gentleman to Sir Philip himself, and so round again to my lady. Now, Sir Philip's man behaved like a gentleman upon the occasion, which I shall ever be free to acknowledge and remember: and when I represented things properly, and made him sensible of the mischief, which, he assured me, was done purely with an eye to serve Sir Philip, his master, he very candidly offered to assist me to unmask that villain Champfort, which he could easily do with the assistance of a few bottles of claret, and a few fair words; which, though I can't abide hypocrisy, I thought quite allowable upon such an occasion. So, ma'am, when Mr. Champfort was thrown off his guard by the claret, Sir Philip's gentleman began to talk of my lord and my lady, and Miss Portman; and he observed that my lord and my lady were coming together more than they used to be since Miss Portman left the house. To which Champfort replied with an oath, like an unmannered reprobate as he is, and in his gibberish, French and English, which I can't speak; but the sense of it was this:—'My lord and lady shall never come together, if I can help it. It was to hinder this I got Miss Portman banished; for my lord was quite another man after she got Miss Helena into the house; and I don't doubt but he might have been brought to leave off his burgundy, and set up for a sober, regular man; which would not suit me at all. If my lady once was to get power over him again, I might go whistle—so (with another reprobate oath) my lord and my lady shall never come together again whilst I live.'

"Well, ma'am," continued Marriott, "as soon as I was in possession of this precious speech, I carried it and a letter of Sir Philip Baddely's gentleman vouching it to my lady. My lady was thunderstruck, and so vexed to have been, as she said, a dupe, that she sent for my lord directly, and insisted upon his giving up Mr. Champfort. My lord demurred, because my lady spoke so high, and said insist. He would have done it, I'm satisfied, of his own accord with the greatest pleasure, if my lady had not, as it were, commanded it. But he answered at last, 'My Lady Delacour, I'm not a man to be governed by a wife—I shall keep or part with my own servants in my own house, according to my own pleasure;' and saying so, he left the room. I never saw my lady so angry as she was at this refusal of my lord to part with him. The house was quite in a state of distraction for some days. I never would sit down to the same table, ma'am, with Mr. Champfort, nor speak to him, nor look at him, and parties ran high above and below stairs. And at last my lady, who had been getting better, took to her bed again with a nervous fever, which brought her almost to death's door; she having been so much weakened before by the quack medicines and convulsions, and all her sufferings in secret. She would not see my lord on no account, and Champfort persuaded him her illness was pretence, to bring him to her purpose; which was the more readily believed, because nobody was ever let into my lady's bedchamber but myself. All this time she never mentioned your name, ma'am; but once, when I was sitting by her bedside, as she was asleep, she started suddenly, and cried out, 'Oh, my dearest Belinda! are you come back to me?'—She awakened herself with the start; and raising herself quite up in her bed, she pulled back the curtains, and looked all round the room. I'm sure she expected to see you; and when she found it was a dream, she gave a heavy sigh, and sank down upon her pillow. I then could not forbear to speak, and this time my lady was greatly touched when I mentioned your name:—she shed tears, ma'am; and you know it is not a little thing that can draw tears from my lady. But when I said something about sending for you, she answered, she was sure you would not return to her, and that she would never condescend to ask a favour in vain, even from you. Then I replied that I was sure you loved her still, and as well as ever: and that the proof of that was, that Mrs. Luttridge and Mrs. Freke together, by all their wiles, could not draw you over to their party at Harrowgate, and that you had affronted Mrs. Freke by defending her ladyship. My lady was all surprise at this, and eagerly asked how I came to know it. Now, ma'am, I had it all by a post letter from Mrs. Luttridge's maid, who is my cousin, and knows every thing that's going on. My lady from this moment forward could scarce rest an instant without wishing for you, and fretting for you as I knew by her manner. One day my lord met me on the stairs as I was coming down from my poor lady's room, and he asked me how she was, and why she did not send for a physician. 'The best physician, my lord, she could send for,' said I, 'would be Miss Portman; for she'll never be well till that good young lady comes back again, in my humble opinion.'

"'And what should prevent that good young lady from coming back again? Not I, surely,' rejoined my lord, 'for I wish she were here with all my heart.'

"'It is not easy to suppose, my lord,' said I, 'after all that has passed, that the young lady would choose to return, or that my lady would ask her, whilst Mr. Champfort remains paramount in the house.' 'If that's all,' cried my lord, 'tell your lady I'll part with Champfort upon the spot; for the rascal has just had the insolence to insist upon it, that a pair of new boots are not too tight for me, when I said they were. I'll show him I can be master, and will, in my own house.' Ma'am, my heart leaped for joy within me at hearing these words, and I ran up to my lady with them. I easily concluded in my own mind, that my lord was glad of the pretence of the boots, to give up handsomely after his standing out so long. To be sure, my lord's mightily jealous of being master, and mighty fond of his own way; but I forgive him every thing for doing as I would have him at last, and dismissing that prince of mischief-makers, Mr. Champfort. My lady called for her writing-desk directly, and sat up in her bed, and with her trembling hand, as you see by the writing, ma'am, wrote a letter to you as fast as ever she could, and the postchaise was ordered. I don't know what fancy seized her—but if you remember, ma'am, the hammercloth to her new carriage had orange and black fringe at first: she would not use it, till this had been changed to blue and white. Well, ma'am, she recollected this on a sudden, as I was getting ready to come for you; and she set the servants at work directly to take off the blue and white, and put on the black and orange fringe again, which she said must be done before your coming. And my lady ordered her own footman to ride along with me; and I have come post, and have travelled night and day, and will never rest till I get back. But, ma'am, I won't keep you any longer from reading your letter, only to say, that I hope to Heaven you will not refuse to return to my poor lady, if it be only to put her mind at ease before she dies. She cannot have long to live."

As Marriott finished these words they reached the house, and Belinda went to her own room to read Lady Delacour's letter. It contained none of her customary 'éloquence du billet,' no sprightly wit, no real, no affected gaiety; her mind seemed to be exhausted by bodily suffering, and her high spirit subdued. She expressed the most poignant anguish for having indulged such unjust suspicions and intemperate passions. She lamented having forfeited the esteem and affection of the only real friend she had ever possessed—a friend of whose forbearance, tenderness, and fidelity, she had received such indisputable proofs. She concluded by saying, "I feel my end fast approaching, and perhaps, Belinda, your humanity will induce you to grant my last request, and to let me see you once more before I die."

Belinda immediately decided to return to Lady Delacour—though it was with real regret that she thought of leaving Lady Anne Percival, and the amiable and happy family to whom she had become so much attached. The children crowded round her when they heard that she was going, and Mr. Vincent stood in silent sorrow—but we spare our readers this parting scene Miss Portman promised to return to Oakly-park as soon as she possibly could. Mr. Vincent anxiously requested permission to follow her to town: but this she positively refused; and he submitted with as good a grace as a lover can submit to any thing that crosses his passion.

CHAPTER XX — RECONCILIATION

Aware that her remaining in town at such an unusual season of the year would appear unaccountable to her fashionable acquaintance, Lady Delacour contrived for herself a characteristic excuse; she declared that there was no possibility of finding pleasure in any thing but novelty, and that the greatest novelty to her would be to remain a whole summer in town. Most of her friends, amongst whom she had successfully established a character for caprice, were satisfied that this was merely some new whim, practised to signalize herself by singularity. The real reason that detained her was her dependence upon the empiric, who had repeatedly visited and constantly prescribed for her. Convinced, however, by the dreadful situation to which his prescriptions had lately reduced her that he was unworthy of her confidence, she determined to dismiss him: but she could not do this, as she had a considerable sum to pay him, till Marriott's return, because she could not trust any one but Marriott to let him up the private staircase into the boudoir.

During Marriott's absence, her ladyship suffered no one to attend her but a maid who was remarkable for her stupidity. She thought that she could have nothing to fear from this girl's spirit of inquiry, for never was any human being so destitute of curiosity. It was about noon when Belinda and Marriott arrived. Lady Delacour, who had passed a restless night, was asleep. When she awoke, she found Marriott standing beside her bed.

"Then it is all in vain, I see," cried her ladyship: "Miss Portman is not with you?—Give me my laudanum."

"Miss Portman is come, my lady," said Marriott; "she is in the dressing-room: she would not come in here with me, lest she should startle you."

"Belinda is come, do you say? Admirable Belinda!" cried Lady Delacour, and she clasped her hands with ecstasy.

"Shall I tell her, my lady, that you are awake?"

"Yes—no—stay—Lord Delacour is at home. I will get up immediately. Let my lord be told that I wish to speak with him—that I beg he will breakfast with me in my dressing-room half an hour hence. I will dress immediately."

Marriott in vain represented that she ought not to hurry herself in her present weak state. Intent upon her own thoughts, she listened to nothing that was said, but frequently urged Marriott to be expeditious. She put on an unusual quantity of rouge: then looking at herself in the glass, she said, with a forced smile, "Marriott, I look so charmingly, that Miss Portman, perhaps, will be of Lord Delacour's opinion, and think that nothing is the matter with me. Ah! no; she has been behind the scenes—she knows the truth too well!—Marriott, pray did she ask you many questions about me?—Was not she very sorry to leave Oakly-park?—Were not they all extremely concerned to part with her?—Did she ask after Helena?—Did you tell her that I insisted upon my lord's parting with Champfort?"

At the word Champfort, Marriott's mouth opened eagerly, and she began to answer with her usual volubility. Lady Delacour waited not for any reply to the various questions which, in the hurry of her mind, she had asked; but, passing swiftly by Marriott, she threw open the door of her dressing-room. At the sight of Belinda she stopped short; and, totally overpowered, she would have sunk upon the floor, had not Miss Portman caught her in her arms, and supported her to a sofa. When she came to herself, and heard the soothing tone of Belinda's voice, she looked up timidly in her face for a few moments without being able to speak.

"And are you really here once more, my dear Belinda?" cried she at last; "and may I still call you my friend?—and do you forgive me?—Yes, I see you do—and from you I can endure the humiliation of being forgiven. Enjoy the noble sense of your own superiority."

"My dear Lady Delacour," said Belinda, "you see all this in too strong a light: you have done me no injury—I have nothing to forgive."

"I cannot see it in too strong a light.—Nothing to forgive!—Yes, you have; that which it is the most difficult to forgive—injustice. Oh, how you must have despised me for the folly, the meanness of my suspicions! Of all tempers that which appears to me, and I am sure to you, the most despicable, the most intolerable, is a suspicious temper. Mine was once open, generous as your own—you see how the best dispositions may be depraved—what am I now? Fit only

'To point a moral, or adorn a tale'—
a mismatched, misplaced, miserable, perverted being."

"And now you have abused yourself till you are breathless, I may have some chance," said Belinda, "of being heard in your defence. I perfectly agree with you in thinking that a suspicious temper is despicable and intolerable; but there is a vast difference between an acute fit of jealousy, as our friend Dr. X— would say, and a chronic habit of suspicion. The noblest natures may be worked up to suspicion by designing villany; and then a handkerchief, or a hammercloth, 'trifles as light as air'—"

"Oh, my dear, you are too good. But my folly admits of no excuse, no palliation," interrupted Lady Delacour; "mine was jealousy without love."

"That indeed would admit of no excuse," said Belinda; "therefore you will pardon me if I think it incredible—especially as I have detected you in feeling something like affection for your little daughter, after you had done your best, I mean your worst, to make me believe that you were a monster of a mother."

"That was quite another affair, my dear. I did not know Helena was worth loving. I did not imagine my little daughter could love me. When I found my mistake, I changed my tone. But there is no hope of mistake with my poor husband. Your own sense must show you, that Lord Delacour is not a man to beloved."

"That could not always have been your ladyship's opinion," said Belinda, with an arch smile.

"Lord! my dear," said Lady Delacour, a little embarrassed, "in the highest paroxysm of my madness, I never suspected that you could love Lord Delacour; I surely only hinted that you were in love with his coronet. That was absurd enough in all conscience—don't make me more absurd than I am."

"Is it then the height of absurdity to love a husband?"

"Love! Nonsense!—Impossible!—Hush! here he comes, with his odious creaking shoes. What man can ever expect to be loved who wears creaking shoes?" pursued her ladyship, as Lord Delacour entered the room, his shoes creaking at every step; and assuming an air of levity, she welcomed him as a stranger to her dressing-room. "No speeches, my lord! no speeches, I beseech you," cried she, as he was beginning to speak to Miss Portman. "Believe me, that explanations always make bad worse. Miss Portman is here, thank Heaven! and her; and Champfort is gone, thank you—or your boots. And now let us sit down to breakfast, and forget as soon as possible every thing that is disagreeable."

When Lady Delacour had a mind to banish painful recollections, it was scarcely possible to resist the magical influence of her conversation and manners; yet her lord's features never relaxed to a smile during this breakfast. He maintained an obstinate silence, and a profound solemnity—till at last, rising from table, he turned to Miss Portman, and said, "Of all the caprices of fine ladies, that which surprises me the most is the whim of keeping their beds without being sick. Now, Miss Portman, you would hardly suppose that my Lady Delacour, who has been so lively this morning, has kept her bed, as I am informed, a fortnight—is not this astonishing?"

"Prodigiously astonishing, that my Lord Delacour, like all the rest of the world, should be liable to be deceived by appearances," cried her ladyship. "Honour me with your attention for a few minutes, my lord, and perhaps I may increase your astonishment."

His lordship, struck by the sudden change of her voice from gaiety to gravity, fixed his eyes upon her and returned to his seat. She paused—then addressing herself to Belinda, "My incomparable friend," said she, "I will now give you a convincing proof of the unlimited power you have over my mind. My lord, Miss Portman has persuaded me to the step which I am now going to take. She has prevailed upon me to make a decisive trial of your prudence and kindness. She has determined me to throw myself on your mercy."

"Mercy!" repeated Lord Delacour; and a confused idea, that she was now about to make a confession of the justice of some of his former suspicions, took possession of his mind: he looked aghast.

"I am going, my lord, to confide to you a secret of the utmost importance—a secret which is known to but three people in the world—Miss Portman, Marriott, and a man whose name I cannot reveal to you."

"Stop, Lady Delacour!" cried his lordship, with a degree of emotion and energy which he had never shown till now: "stop, I conjure, I command you, madam! I am not sufficiently master of myself—I once loved you too well to hear such a stroke. Trust me with no such secret—say no more—you have said enough—too much. I forgive you, that is all I can do: but we must part, Lady Delacour!" said he, breaking from her with agony expressed in his countenance.

"The man has a heart, a soul, I protest! You knew him better than I did, Miss Portman. Nay, you are not gone yet, my lord! You really love me, I find."

"No, no, no," cried he, vehemently: "weak as you take me to be, Lady Delacour, I am incapable of loving a woman who has disgraced me, disgraced herself, her family, her station, her high endowments, her—" His utterance failed.

"Oh, Lady Delacour!" cried Belinda, "how can you trifle in this manner?"

"I meant not," said her ladyship, "to trifle: I am satisfied. My lord, it is time that you should be satisfied. I can give you the most irrefragable proof, that whatever may have been the apparent levity of my conduct, you have had no serious cause for jealousy. But the proof will shock—disgust you. Have you courage to know more?—Then follow me."

He followed her.—Belinda heard the boudoir door unlocked.—In a few minutes they returned.—Grief, and horror, and pity, were painted in Lord Delacour's countenance, as he passed hastily through the room.

"My dearest friend, I have taken your advice: would to Heaven I had taken it sooner!" said Lady Delacour to Miss Portman. "I have revealed to Lord Delacour my real situation. Poor man! he was shocked beyond expression. He behaved incomparably well. I am convinced that he would, as he said, let his hand be cut off to save my life. The moment his foolish jealousy was extinguished, his love for me revived in full force. Would you believe it? he has promised me to break with odious Mrs. Luttridge. Upon my charging him to keep my secret from her, he instantly, in the handsomest manner in the world, declared he would never see her more, rather than give me a moment's uneasiness. How I reproach myself for having been for years the torment of this man's life!"

"You may do better than reproach yourself, my dear Lady Delacour," said Belinda; "you may yet live for years to be the blessing and pride of his life. I am persuaded that nothing but your despair of obtaining domestic happiness has so long enslaved you to dissipation; and now that you find a friend in your husband, now that you know the affectionate temper of your little Helena, you will have fresh views and fresh hopes; you will have the courage to live for yourself, and not for what is called the world."

"The world!" cried Lady Delacour, with a tone of disdain: "how long has that word enslaved a soul formed for higher purposes!" She paused, and looked up towards heaven with an expression of fervent devotion, which Belinda had once, and but once, before seen in her countenance. Then, as if forgetful even that Belinda was present, she threw herself upon a sofa, and fell, or seemed to fall, into a profound reverie. She was roused by the entrance of Marriott, who came into the room to ask whether she would now take her laudanum. "I thought I had taken it," said she in a feeble voice; and as she raised her eyes and saw Belinda, she added, with a faint smile, "Miss Portman, I believe, has been laudanum to me this morning: but even that will not do long, you see; nothing will do for me now but this," and she stretched out her hand for the laudanum. "Is not it shocking to think," continued she, after she had swallowed it, "that in laudanum alone I find the means of supporting existence?"

She put her hand to her head, as if partly conscious of the confusion of her own ideas: and ashamed that Belinda should witness it, she desired Marriott to assist her to rise, and to support her to her bedchamber. She made a sign to Miss Portman not to follow her. "Do not take it unkindly, but I am quite exhausted, and wish to be alone; for I am grown fond of being alone some hours in the day, and perhaps I shall sleep."

Marriott came out of her lady's room about a quarter of an hour afterward, and said that her lady seemed disposed to sleep, but that she desired to have her hook left by her bedside. Marriott searched among several which lay upon the table, for one in which a mark was put. Belinda looked over them along with Marriott, and she was surprised to find that they had almost all methodistical titles. Lady Delacour's mark was in the middle of Wesley's Admonitions. Several pages in other books of the same description Miss Portman found marked in pencil, with reiterated lines, which she knew to be her ladyship's customary mode of distinguishing passages that she particularly liked. Some were highly oratorical, but most of them were of a mystical cast, and appeared to Belinda scarcely intelligible. She had reason to be astonished at meeting with such books in the dressing-room of a woman of Lady Delacour's character. During the solitude of her illness, her ladyship had first begun to think seriously on religious subjects, and the early impressions that had been made on her mind in her childhood, by a methodistical mother, recurred. Her understanding, weakened perhaps by disease, and never accustomed to reason, was incapable of distinguishing between truth and error; and her temper, naturally enthusiastic, hurried her from one extreme to the other—from thoughtless scepticism to visionary credulity. Her devotion was by no means steady or permanent; it came on by fits usually at the time when the effect of opium was exhausted, or before a fresh dose began to operate. In these intervals she was low-spirited—bitter reflections on the manner in which she had thrown away her talents and her life obtruded themselves; the idea of the untimely death of Colonel Lawless, of which she reproached herself as the cause, returned; and her mind, from being a prey to remorse, began to sink in these desponding moments under the most dreadful superstitious terrors—terrors the more powerful as they were secret. Whilst the stimulus of laudanum lasted, the train of her ideas always changed, and she was amazed at the weak fears and strange notions by which she had been disturbed; yet it was not in her power entirely to chase away these visions of the night, and they gained gradually a dominion over her, of which she was heartily ashamed. She resolved to conceal this weakness, as in her gayer moments she thought it, from Belinda, from whose superior strength of understanding she dreaded ridicule or contempt. Her experience of Miss Portman's gentleness and friendship might reasonably have prevented or dispelled such apprehensions; but Lady Delacour was governed by pride, by sentiment, by whim, by enthusiasm, by passion—by any thing but reason.

When she began to revive after her fit of languor, and had been refreshed by opium and sleep, she rang for Marriott, and inquired for Belinda. She was much provoked when Marriott, by way of proving to her that Miss Portman could not have been tired of being left alone, told her that she had been in the dressing-room rummaging over the books.

"What books?" cried Lady Delacour. "I forgot that they were left there. Miss Portman is not reading them still, I suppose? Go for them, and let them be locked up in my own bookcase, and bring me the key."

Her ladyship appeared in good spirits when she saw Belinda again. She rallied her upon the serious studies she had chosen for her morning's amusements. "Those methodistical books, with their strange quaint titles," said she, "are, however, diverting enough to those who, like myself, can find diversion in the height of human absurdity."

Deceived by the levity of her manner, Belinda concluded that the marks of approbation in these books were ironical, and she thought no more of the matter; for Lady Delacour suddenly gave a new turn to the conversation by exclaiming, "Now we talk of the height of human absurdity, what are we to think of Clarence Hervey?"

"Why should we think of him at all?" said Belinda.

"For two excellent reasons, my dear: because we cannot help it, and because he deserves it. Yes, he deserves it, believe me, if it were only for having written these charming letters," said Lady Delacour, opening a cabinet, and taking out a small packet of letters, which she put into Belinda's hands. "Pray, read them; you will find them amazingly edifying, as well as entertaining. I protest I am only puzzled to know whether I shall bind them up with Sterne's Sentimental Journey or Fordyce's Sermons for Young Women. Here, my love, if you like description," continued her ladyship, opening one of the letters, "here is a Radcliffean tour along the picturesque coasts of Dorset and Devonshire. Why he went this tour, unless for the pleasure and glory of describing it, Heaven knows! Clouds and darkness rest over the tourist's private history: but this, of course, renders his letters more piquant and interesting. All who have a just taste either for literature or for gallantry, know how much we are indebted to the obscure for the sublime; and orators and lovers feel what felicity there is in the use of the fine figure of suspension."

"Very good description, indeed!" said Belinda, without raising her eyes from the letter, or seeming to pay any attention to the latter part of Lady Delacour's speech; "very good description, certainly!"

"Well, my dear; but here is something better than pure description—here is sense for you: and pray mark the politeness of addressing sense to a woman—to a woman of sense, I mean—and which of us is not? Then here is sentiment for you," continued her ladyship, spreading another letter before Belinda; "a story of a Dorsetshire lady, who had the misfortune to be married to a man as unlike Mr. Percival, and as like Lord Delacour, as possible; and yet, oh, wonderful! they make as happy a couple as one's heart could wish. Now, I am truly candid and good-natured to admire this letter; for every word of it is a lesson to me, and evidently was so intended. But I take it all in good part, because, to do Clarence justice, he describes the joys of domestic Paradise in such elegant language, that he does not make me sick. In short, my dear Belinda, to finish my panegyric, as it has been said of some other epistles, if ever there were letters calculated to make you fall in love with the writer of them, these are they."

"Then," said Miss Portman, folding up the letter which she was just going to read, "I will not run the hazard of reading them."

"Why, my dear," said Lady Delacour, with a look of mingled concern, reproach, and raillery, "have you actually given up my poor Clarence, merely on account of this mistress in the wood, this Virginia St. Pierre? Nonsense! Begging your pardon, my dear, the man loves you. Some entanglement, some punctilio, some doubt, some delicacy, some folly, prevents him from being just at this moment, where, I confess, he ought to be—at your feet; and you, out of patience, which a young lady ought never to be if she can help it, will go and marry—I know you will—some stick of a rival, purely to provoke him."

"If ever I marry," said Belinda, with a look of proud humility, "I shall certainly marry to please myself, and not to provoke any body else; and, at all events, I hope I shall never marry a stick."

"Pardon me that word," said Lady Delacour. "I am convinced you never will—but one is apt to judge of others by one's self. I am willing to believe that Mr. Vincent—"

"Mr. Vincent! How did you know—" exclaimed Belinda.

"How did I know? Why, my dear, do you think I am so little interested about you, that I have not found out some of your secrets? And do you think that Marriott could refrain from telling me, in her most triumphant tone, that 'Miss Portman has not gone to Oakly-park for nothing; that she has made a conquest of a Mr. Vincent, a West Indian, a ward, or lately a ward, of Mr. Percival's, the handsomest man that ever was seen, and the richest, &c. &c. &c.?' Now simple I rejoiced at the news; for I took it for granted you would never seriously think of marrying the man."

"Then why did your ladyship rejoice?"

"Why? Oh, you novice at Cupid's chess-board! do not you see the next move? Check with your new knight, and the game is your own. Now, if your aunt Stanhope saw your look at this instant, she would give you up for ever—if she have not done that already. In plain, unmetaphorical prose, then, cannot you comprehend, my straight-forward Belinda, that if you make Clarence Hervey heartily jealous, let the impediments to your union be what they may, he will acknowledge himself to be heartily in love with you? I should make no scruple of frightening him within an inch of his life, for his good. Sir Philip Baddely was not the man to frighten him; but this Mr. Vincent, by all accounts, is just the thing."

"And do you imagine that I could use Mr. Vincent so ill?—And can you think me capable of such double dealing?"

"Oh! in love and war, you know, all stratagems are allowable. But you take the matter so seriously, and you redden with such virtuous indignation, that I dare not say a word more—only—may I ask—are you absolutely engaged to Mr. Vincent?"

"No. We have had the prudence to avoid all promises, all engagements."

"There's my good girl!" cried Lady Delacour, kissing her: "all may yet turn out well. Read those letters—take them to your room, read them, read them; and depend upon it, my dearest Belinda! you are not the sort of woman that will, that can be happy, if you make a mere match of convenience. Forgive me—I love you too well not to speak the truth, though it may offend for a moment."

"You do not offend, but you misunderstand me," said Belinda. "Have patience with me, and you shall find that I am incapable of making a mere match of convenience."

Then Miss Portman gave Lady Delacour a simple but full account of all that had passed at Oakly-park relative to Mr. Vincent. She repeated the arguments by which Lady Anne Percival had first prevailed upon her to admit of Mr. Vincent's addresses. She said, that she had been convinced by Mr. Percival, that the omnipotence of a first love was an idea founded in error, and realized only in romance; and that to believe that none could be happy in marriage, except with the first object of their fancy or their affections, would be an error pernicious to individuals and to society. When she detailed the arguments used by Mr. Percival on this subject, Lady Delacour sighed, and observed that Mr. Percival was certainly right, judging from his own experience, to declaim against the folly of first loves; "and for the same reason," added she, "perhaps I may be pardoned if I retain some prejudice in their favour." She turned aside her head to hide a starting tear, and here the conversation dropped. Belinda, recollecting the circumstances of her ladyship's early history, reproached herself for having touched on this tender subject, yet at the same time she felt with increased force, at this moment, the justice of Mr. Percival's observations; for, evidently, the hold which this prejudice had kept in Lady Delacour's mind had materially injured her happiness, by making her neglect, after her marriage, all the means of content that were in her reach. Her incessant comparisons between her first love and her husband excited perpetual contempt and disgust in her mind for her wedded lord, and for many years precluded all perception of his good qualities, all desire to live with him upon good terms, and all idea of securing that share of domestic happiness that was actually in her power. Belinda resolved at some future moment, whenever she could, with propriety and with effect, to suggest these reflections to Lady Delacour, and in the mean time she was determined to turn them to her own advantage. She perceived that she should have need of all her steadiness to preserve her judgment unbiassed by her ladyship's wit and persuasive eloquence on the one hand, and on the other by her own high opinion of Lady Anne Percival's judgment, and the anxious desire she felt to secure her approbation. The letters from Clarence Hervey she read at night, when she retired to her own room; and they certainly raised not only Belinda's opinion of his talents, but her esteem for his character. She saw that he had, with great address, made use of the influence he possessed over Lady Delacour, to turn her mind to every thing that could make her amiable, estimable, and happy—she saw that Clarence, so far from attempting, for the sake of his own vanity, to retain his pre-eminence in her ladyship's imagination, used on the contrary "his utmost skill" to turn the tide of her affections toward her husband and her daughter. In one of his letters, and but in one, he mentioned Belinda. He expressed great regret in hearing from Lady Delacour that her friend, Miss Portman, was no longer with her. He expatiated on the inestimable advantages and happiness of having such a friend—but this referred to Lady Delacour, not to himself. There was an air of much respect and some embarrassment in all he said of Belinda, but nothing like love. A few words at the end of this paragraph were cautiously obliterated, however; and, without any obvious link of connexion, the writer began a new sentence with a general reflection upon the folly and imprudence of forming romantic projects. Then he enumerated some of the various schemes he had formed in his early youth, and humorously recounted how they had failed, or how they had been abandoned. Afterward, changing his tone from playful wit to serious philosophy, he observed the changes which these experiments had made in his own character.

"My friend, Dr. X—," said he, "divides mankind into three classes: those who learn from the experience of others—they are happy men; those who learn from their own experience—they are wise men; and, lastly, those who learn neither from their own nor from other people's experience—they are fools. This class is by far the largest. I am content," continued Clarence, "to be in the middle class—perhaps you will say because I cannot be in the first: however, were it in my power to choose my own character, I should, forgive me the seeming vanity of the speech, still be content to remain in my present station upon this principle—the characters of those who are taught by their own experience must be progressive in knowledge and virtue. Those who learn from the experience of others may become stationary, because they must depend for their progress on the experiments that we brave volunteers, at whose expense they are to live and learn, are pleased to try. There may be much safety in thus snugly fighting, or rather seeing the battle of life, behind the broad shield of a stouter warrior; yet it seems to me to be rather an ignominious than an enviable situation.

"Our friend, Dr. X—, would laugh at my insisting upon being amongst the class of learners by their own experience. He would ask me, whether it be the ultimate end of my philosophy to try experiments, or to be happy. And what answer should I make? I have none ready. Common sense stares me in the face, and my feelings, even at this instant, alas! confute my system. I shall pay too dear yet for some of my experiments. 'Sois grand homme, et sois malheureux,' is, I am afraid, the law of nature, or rather the decree of the world. Your ladyship will not read this without a smile; for you will immediately infer, that I think myself a great man; and as I detest hypocrisy yet more than vanity, I shall not deny the charge. At all events, I feel that I am at present—however gaily I talk of it—in as fair a way to be unhappy for life, as if I were, in good earnest, the greatest man in Europe.

"Your ladyship's most respectful admirer, and sincere friend,

"CLARENCE HERVEY."

"P. S.—Is there any hope that your friend, Miss Portman, may spend the winter in town?"

Though Lady Delacour had been much fatigued by the exertion of her spirits during the day, she sat up at night to write to Mr. Hervey. Her love and gratitude to Miss Portman interested her most warmly for her happiness, and she was persuaded that the most effectual way to secure it would be to promote her union with her first love. Lady Delacour, who had also the best opinion of Clarence Hervey, and the most sincere friendship for him, thought she was likewise acting highly for his interest; and she felt that she had some merit in at once parting with him from the train of her admirers, and urging him to become a dull, married man. Besides these generous motives, she was, perhaps, a little influenced by jealousy of the superior power which Lady Anne Percival had in so short a time acquired over Belinda's mind. "Strange," thought she, "if love and I be not a match for Lady Anne Percival and reason!" To do Lady Delacour justice, it must be observed, that she took the utmost care in her letter not to commit her friend; she wrote with all the delicate address of which she was mistress. She began by rallying her correspondent on his indulging himself so charmingly in the melancholy of genius; and she prescribed as a cure to her malheureux imaginaire, as she called him, those joys of domestic life which he so well knew how to paint.

"Précepte commence, exemple achève," said her ladyship. "You will never see me la femme comme il y en a peu, till I see you le bon mari. Belinda Portman has this day returned to me from Oakly-park, fresh, blooming, wise, and gay, as country air, flattery, philosophy, and love can make her. It seems that she has had full employment for her head and heart. Mr. Percival and Lady Anne, by right of science and reason, have taken possession of the head, and a Mr. Vincent, their ci-devant ward and declared favourite, has laid close siege to the heart, of which he is in a fair way, I think, to take possession, by the right of conquest. As far as I can understand—for I have not yet seen le futur—he deserves my Belinda; for besides being as handsome as any hero of romance, ancient or modern, he has a soul in which neither spot nor blemish can be found, except the amiable weakness of being desperately in love—a weakness which we ladies are apt to prefer to the most philosophic stoicism: apropos of philosophy— we may presume, that notwithstanding Mr. V— is a creole, he has been bred up by his guardian in the class of men who learn by the experience of others. As such, according to your system, he has a right to expect to be a happy man, has not he? According to Mrs. Stanhope's system, I am sure that he has: for his thousands and tens of thousands, as I am credibly informed, pass the comprehension of the numeration table.

"But these will weigh not a grain in the estimation of her truly disinterested and noble-minded niece. Mrs. Stanhope knows nothing of Mr. Vincent's proposals; and it is well for him she does not, for her worldly good word would mar the whole. Not so as to Lady Anne and Mr. Percival's approbation—their opinion is all in all with my friend. How they have contrived it, I know not, but they have gained over Belinda's mind a degree of power almost equal to parental authority; so you may guess that the doubtful beam will not much longer nod from side to side: indeed it seems to me scarcely necessary to throw in the sword of authority to turn the scale.

"If you can persuade yourself to finish your picturesque tour before the ides of the charming month of November, do, my dear Clarence! make haste and come back to us in time for Belinda's wedding—and do not forget my commission about the Dorsetshire angel; bring me one in your right hand with a gold ring upon her taper finger—so help you, Cupid! or never more expect a smile

"From your sincere friend and admirer,

"T.C.H. DELACOUR."

"P.S. Observe, my good sir, that I am not in such a desperate hurry to congratulate you on your marriage, that I should be satisfied with an ordinary Mrs. Hervey: so do not, under pretence of obliging me, or for any other consideration, yoke yourself to some damsel that you will be ashamed to produce. For one woman worthy to be Clarence Hervey's wife, I have seen, at a moderate computation, a hundred fit to be his mistress. If he should, on this subject, mistake the fitness of things or of persons, he would indeed be in a fair way to be unhappy for life.

"The substance of a lady's letter, it has been said, always is comprised in the postscript."

After Lady Delacour had finished this letter, which she had no doubt would bring Clarence immediately to town, she left it with Marriott, with orders to have it sent by the next post. Much fatigued, she then retired to rest, and was not visible the next day till near dinner-time. When Miss Portman returned the packet of Mr. Hervey's letters, her ladyship was dissatisfied with the measured terms of Belinda's approbation, and she said, with a sarcastic smile, "So, they have made a complete philosopher of you at Oakly-park! You are perfect in the first lesson—not to admire. And is the torch of Cupid to be extinguished on the altar of Reason?"

"Rather to be lighted there, if possible," said Belinda; and she endeavoured to turn the conversation to what she thought must be more immediately interesting to Lady Delacour—her own health. She assured her, with perfect truth, that she was at present more intent upon her situation than upon Cupid or his torch.

"I believe you, my generous Belinda!" said Lady Delacour; "and for that very reason I am interested in your affairs, I am afraid, even to the verge of impertinence. May I ask why this preux chevalier of yours did not attend you, or follow you to town?"

"Mr. Vincent?—He knew that I came to attend your ladyship. I told him that you had been confined by a nervous fever, and that it would be impossible for me to see him at present; but I promised, when you could spare me, to return to Oakly-park."

Lady Delacour sighed, and opened Clarence Hervey's letters one after another, looking over them without seeming well to know what she was about. Lord Delacour came into the room whilst these letters were still in her hand. He had been absent since the preceding morning, and he now seemed as if he were just come home, much fatigued. He began in a tone of great anxiety to inquire after Lady Delacour's health. She was piqued at his having left home at such a time, and, merely bowing her head to him, she went on reading. His eyes glanced upon the letters which she held in her hand; and when he saw the well-known writing of Clarence Hervey, his manner immediately altered, and, stammering out some common-place phrases, he threw himself into an arm-chair by the fireside, protesting that he was tired to death—that he was half dead—that he had been in a post-chaise for three hours, which he hated—had ridden fifty miles since yesterday; and he muttered that he was a fool for his pains—an observation which, though it reached her ladyship's ears, she did not think proper to contradict.

His lordship had then recourse to his watch, his never-failing friend in need, which he always pulled out with a particular jerk when he was vexed.

"It is time for me to be gone—I shall be late at Studley's."

"You dine with his lordship then?" said Lady Delacour, in a careless tone.

"Yes; and his good burgundy, I hope, will wind me up again," said he, stretching himself, "for I am quite down."

"Quite down? Then we may conclude that my friend Mrs. Luttridge is not yet come to Rantipole. Rantipole, my dear," continued Lady Delacour, turning to Miss Portman, "is the name of Harriot Freke's villa in Kent. However strange it may sound to your ears and mine, I can assure you the name has made fortune amongst a certain description of wits. And candour must allow that, if not elegant, it is appropriate; it gives a just idea of the manners and way of life of the place, for every thing at Rantipole is rantipole. But I am really concerned, my lord, you should have ridden yourself down in this way for nothing. Why did not you get better intelligence before you set out? I am afraid you feel the loss of Champfort. Why did not you contrive to learn for certain, my dear good lord, whether the Luttridge was at Rantipole, before you set out on this wild goose chase?"

"My dear good lady," replied Lord Delacour, assuming a degree of spirit which startled her as much as it became him, "why do you not get better intelligence before you suspect me of being a brute and a liar? Did not I promise you yesterday, that I would break with the Luttridge, as you call her? and how could you imagine that the instant afterwards, just at the time I was wrung to the soul, as you know I was— how could you imagine I would leave you to go to Rantipole, or to any woman upon earth?"

"Oh, my lord! I beg your pardon, I beg your pardon a thousand times," cried Lady Delacour, rising with much emotion; and, going towards him with a sudden impulse, she kissed his forehead.

"And so you ought to beg my pardon," said Lord Delacour, in a faltering voice, but without moving his posture.

"You will acknowledge you left me, however, my lord? That is clear."

"Left you! Yes, so I did; to ride all over the country in search of a house that would suit you. For what else did you think I could leave you at such a time as this?"

Lady Delacour again stooped, and leaned her arm upon his shoulder.

"I wish to Heaven, my dear," said his lordship, shrinking as he put away her hand, which still held Clarence Hervey's letters, "I wish to Heaven, my dear, you would not hold those abominable perfumed papers just under my very nose. You know I cannot stand perfumes."

"Are they perfumed? Ay; so every thing is that I keep in that cabinet of curiosities. Thank you, my dear Miss Portman," said her ladyship, as Belinda rose to take the letters from her hand. "Will you have the goodness to put them back into their cabinet, if you can endure to touch them, if the perfume has not overcome you as well as my lord? After all, it is only ottar of roses, to which few people's olfactory nerves have an antipathy."

"I have the honour to be one of the few," said his lordship, rising from his seat with so sudden a motion as to displace Lady Delacour's arm which leaned upon him. "For my part," continued he, taking down one of the Argand lamps from the chimney-piece, and trimming it, "I would rather a hundred to one snuff up the oil of this cursed lamp."

Whilst his lordship applied himself to trimming the lamp with great earnestness, Lady Delacour negligently walked away to the farthest end of the room, where stood the cabinet, which Belinda was trying to unlock.

"Stay, my love; it has a secret lock, which I alone can manage."

"Oh, my dear Lady Delacour!" whispered Belinda, holding her hand as she gave her the key, "I never can love or esteem you if you use Lord Delacour ill now."

"Ill now? ill now? This lock is spoilt, I do believe," said she aloud.

"Nay, you understand me, Lady Delacour! You see what is passing in his mind."

"To be sure: I am not a fool, though he is. I see he is jealous, though he has had such damning proof that all's right—the man's a fool, that's all. Are you sure this is the key I gave you, my dear?"

"And can you think him a fool," pursued Belinda, in a still more earnest whisper, "for being more jealous of your mind than of your person? Fools have seldom so much penetration, or so much delicacy."

"But, Lord! what would you have me do? what would you have me say? That Lord Delacour writes better letters than these?"

"Oh, no! but show him these letters, and you will do justice to him, to yourself, to Cla—, to every body."

"I am sure I should be happy to do justice to every body."

"Then pray do this very instant, my dearest Lady Delacour! and I shall love you for it all my life."

"Done!—for who can withstand that offer?—Done!" said her ladyship. Then turning to Lord Delacour, "My lord, will you come here and tell us what can be the matter with this lock?"

"If the lock be spoiled, Lady Delacour, you had better send for a locksmith," replied his lordship, who was still employed about the wick of the Argand: "I am no locksmith—I do not pretend to understand locks—especially secret locks."

"But you will not desert us at our utmost need, I am sure, my lord," said Belinda, approaching him with a conciliatory smile.

"You want the light, I believe, more than I do," said his lordship, advancing with the lamp to meet her. "Well! what is the matter with this confounded lock of yours, Lady Delacour? I know I should be at Studley's by this time—but how in the devil's name can you expect me to open a secret lock when I do not know the secret, Lady Delacour?"

"Then I will tell you the secret, Lord Delacour—that there is no secret at all in the lock, or in the letters. Here, if you can stand the odious smell of ottar of roses, take these letters and read them, foolish man; and keep them till the shocking perfume is gone off."

Lord Delacour could scarcely believe his senses; he looked in Lady Delacour's eyes to see whether he had understood her rightly.

"But I am afraid," said she, smiling, "that you will find the perfume too overcoming."

"Not half so overcoming," cried he, seizing her hand, and kissing it often with eager tenderness, "not half so overcoming as this confidence, this kindness, this condescension from you."

"Miss Portman will think us both a couple of old fools," said her ladyship, making a slight effort to withdraw her hand. "But she is almost as great a simpleton herself, I think," continued she, observing that the tears stood in Belinda's eyes.

"My lord," said a footman who came in at this instant, "do you dress? The carriage is at the door, as you ordered, to go to Lord Studley's."

"I'd see Lord Studley at the devil, sir, and his burgundy along with him, before I'd go to him to-day; and you may tell him so, if you please," cried Lord Delacour.

"Very well, my lord," said the footman.

"My lord dines at home—they may put up the carriage—that's all," said Lady Delacour: "only let us have dinner directly," added she, as the servant shut the door. "Miss Portman will be famished amongst us: there is no living upon sentiment."

"And there is no living with such belles without being something more of a beau," said Lord Delacour, looking at his splashed boots. "I will be ready for dinner before dinner is ready for me." With activity very unusual to him, he hurried out of the room to change his dress.

"O day of wonders!" exclaimed Lady Delacour. "And, O night of wonders! if we can get him through the evening without the help of Lord Studley's wine. You must give us some music, my good Belinda, and make him accompany you with his flute. I can tell you he has really a very pretty taste for music, and knows fifty times more of the matter than half the dilettanti, who squeeze the human face divine into all manner of ridiculous shapes, by way of persuading you that they are in ecstasy! And, my dear, do not forget to show us the charming little portfolio of drawings that you have brought from Oakly-park. Lord Delacour was with me at Harrowgate in the days of his courtship: he knows the charming views that you have been taking about Knaresborough and Fountain's Abbey, and all those places. I will answer for it, he remembers them a hundred times better than I do. And, my love, I assure you he is a better judge of drawing than many whom we saw ogling Venus rising from the sea, in the Orleans gallery. Lord Delacour has let his talents go to sleep in a shameless manner; but really he has talents, if they could be wakened. By-the-by, pray make him tell you the story of Lord Studley's original Titian: he tells that story with real humour. Perhaps you have not found it out, but Lord Delacour has a vast deal of drollery in his own way, and—"

"Dinner's ready, my lady!"

"That is a pity!" whispered Lady Delacour; "for if they had let me go on in my present humour, I should have found out that my lord has every accomplishment under the sun, and every requisite under the moon, to make the marriage state happy."

With the assistance of Belinda's portfolio and her harp, and the good-humour and sprightliness of Lady Delacour's wit, his lordship got through the evening much to his own satisfaction. He played on the flute, he told the story of Studley's original Titian, and he detected a fault that had escaped Mr. Percival in the perspective of Miss Portman's sketch of Fountain's Abbey. The perception that his talents were called out, and that he appeared to unusual advantage, made him excellent company: he found that the spirits can be raised by self-complacency even more agreeably than by burgundy.

Whilst they were at breakfast the next morning in Lady Delacour's dressing-room, Marriott knocked at the door, and immediately opening it, exclaimed in a joyful tone, "Miss Portman, they're eating it! Ma'am, they're eating it as fast as ever they can!"

"Bring them in; your lady will give you leave, Marriott, I fancy," said Miss Portman. Marriott brought in her gold fishes; some green leaves were floating on the top of the water in the glass globe.

"See, my lady," said she, "what Miss Portman has been so good as to bring from Oakly-park for my poor gold fishes, who, I am sure, ought to be much obliged to her, as well as myself." Marriott set the globe beside her lady, and retired.

"From Oakly-park! And by what name impossible to pronounce must I call these green leaves, to please botanic ears?" said Lady Delacour.

"This," replied Belinda, "is what

'Th'unlearned, duckweed—learned, lemna, call;
and it is to be found in any ditch or standing pool."

"And what possessed you, my dear, for the sake of Marriott and her gold fishes, to trouble yourself to bring such stuff a hundred and seventy miles?"

"To oblige little Charles Percival," said Miss Portman. "He was anxious to keep his promise of sending it to your Helena. She found out in some book that she was reading with him last summer, that gold fishes are fond of this plant; and I wish," added Belinda, in a timid voice, "that she were here at this instant to see them eat it."

Lady Delacour was silent for some minutes, and kept her eye steadily upon the gold fishes. At length she said, "I never shall forget how well the poor little creature behaved about those gold fishes. I grew amazingly fond of her whilst she was with me. But you know, circumstanced as I was, after you left me, I could not have her at home."

"But now I am here," said Belinda, "will she he any trouble to you? And will she not make your home more agreeable to you, and to Lord Delacour, who was evidently very fond of her?"

"Ah, my dear!" said Lady Delacour, "you forget, and so do I at times, what I have to go through. It is in vain to talk, to think of making home, or any place, or any thing, or any person, agreeable to me now. What am I? The outside rind is left—the sap is gone. The tree lasts from day to day by miracle—it cannot last long. You would not wonder to hear me talk in this way, if you knew the terrible time I had last night after we parted. But I have these nights constantly now. Let us talk of something else. What have you there—a manuscript?"

"Yes, a little journal of Edward Percival's, which he sent for the entertainment of Helena."

Lady Delacour stretched out her hand for it. "The boy will write as like his father as possible," said she, turning over the leaves. "I wish to have this poor girl with me—but I have no spirits. And you know, whenever Lord Delacour can find a house that will suit us, we shall leave town, and I could not take Helena with me. But this may be the last opportunity I may ever have of seeing her; and I can refuse you nothing, my dear. So will you go for her? She can stay with us a few days. Lady Boucher, that most convenient dowager, who likes going about, no matter where, all the morning, will go with you to Mrs. Dumont's academy in Sloane-street. I would as soon go to a bird-fancier's as to a boarding-school for young ladies: indeed, I am not well enough to go any where. So I will throw myself upon a sofa, and read this child's journal. I wonder how that or any thing else can interest me now."

Belinda, who had been used to the variations of Lady Delacour's spirits, was not much alarmed by the despondent strain in which she now spoke, especially when she considered that the thoughts of the dreadful trial this unfortunate woman was soon to go through must naturally depress her courage. Rejoiced at the permission that she had obtained to go for Helena, Miss Portman sent immediately to Lady Boucher, who took her to Sloane-street.

"Now, my dear, considerate Miss Portman," said Lady Boucher, "I must beg, and request that you will hurry Miss Delacour into the carriage as fast as possible. I have not a moment to spare; for I am to be at a china auction at two, that I would not miss for the whole world. Well, what's the matter with the people? Why does not James knock at the door? Can't the man read? Can't the man see?" cried the purblind dowager. "Is not that Mrs. Dumont's name on the door before his eyes?"

"No, ma'am, I believe this name is Ellicot," said Belinda.

"Ellicot, is it? Ay, true. But what's the man stopping for, then? Mrs. Dumont's is the next door, tell the blind dunce. Mercy on us! To waste one's time in this way! I shall, as sure as fate, be too late for the china auction. What upon earth stops us?"

"Nothing but a little covered cart, which stands at Mrs. Dumont's door. There, now it is going; an old man is drawing it out of the way as fast as he can."

"Open the coach-door, James!" cried Lady Boucher the moment that they had drawn up. "Now, my dear, considerate Miss Portman, remember the auction, and don't let Miss Delacour stay to change her dress or any thing."

Belinda promised not to detain her ladyship a minute. The door at Mrs. Dumont's was open, and a servant was assisting an old man to carry in some geraniums and balsams out of the covered cart which had stopped the way. In the hall a crowd of children were gathered round a high stand, on which they were eagerly arranging their flower-pots; and the busy hum of voices was so loud, that when Miss Portman first went in, she could neither hear the servant, nor make him hear her name. Nothing was to be heard but "Oh, how beautiful! Oh, how sweet! That's mine! That's yours! The great rose geranium for Miss Jefferson! The white Provence rose for Miss Adderly! No, indeed, Miss Pococke, that's for Miss Delacour; the old man said so."

"Silence, silence, mesdemoiselles!" cried the voice of a French woman, and all was silence. The little crowd looked towards the hall door; and from the midst of her companions, Helena Delacour, who now caught a glimpse of Belinda, sprang forward, throwing down her white Provence rose as she passed.

"Lady Boucher's compliments, ma'am," said the servant to Mrs. Dumont; "she's in indispensable haste, and she begs you won't let Miss Delacour think of changing her dress."

It was the last thing of which Miss Delacour was likely to think at this instant. She was so much overjoyed, when she heard that Belinda was come by her mamma's desire to take her home, that she would scarcely stay whilst Mrs. Dumont was tying on her straw hat, and exhorting her to let Lady Delacour know how it happened that she was "so far from fit to be seen."

"Yes, ma'am; yes, ma'am, I'll remember; I'll be sure to remember," said Helena, tripping down the steps. But just as she was getting into the carriage she stopped at the sight of the old man, and exclaimed, "Oh, good old man! I must not forget you."

"Yes, indeed, you must, though, my dear Miss Delacour," said Lady Boucher, pulling her into the carriage: "'tis no time to think of good old men now."

"But I must. Dear Miss Portman, will you speak for me? I must pay—I must settle—and I have a great deal to say."

Miss Portman desired the old man to call in Berkley-square at Lady Delacour's; and this satisfying all parties, they drove away.

When they arrived in Berkley-square, Marriott told them that her lady was just gone to lie down. Edward Percival's little journal, which she had been reading, was left on the sofa, and Belinda gave it to Helena, who eagerly began to look over it.

"Thirteen pages! Oh, how good he has been to write so much for me!" said she; and she had almost finished reading it before her mother came into the room.

Lady Delacour shrunk back as her daughter ran towards her; for she recollected too well the agony she had once suffered from an embrace of Helena's. The little girl appeared more grieved than surprised at this; and after kissing her mother's hand, without speaking, she again looked down at the manuscript.

"Does that engross your attention so entirely, my dear," said Lady Delacour, "that you can neither spare one word nor one look for your mother?"

"Oh, mamma! I only tried to read, because I thought you were angry with me."

"An odd reason for trying to read, my dear!" said Lady Delacour with a smile: "have you any better reason for thinking I was angry with you?"

"Ah, I know you are not angry now, for you smile," said Helena; "but I thought at first that you were, mamma, because you gave me only your hand to kiss."

"Only my hand! The next time, simpleton, I'll give you only my foot to kiss," said her ladyship, sitting down, and holding out her foot playfully.

Her daughter threw aside the book, and kneeling down kissed her foot, saying, in a low voice, "Dear mamma, I never was so happy in my life; for you never looked so very, very kindly at me before."

"Do not judge always of the kindness people feel for you, child, by their looks; and remember that it is possible a person might have felt more than you could guess by their looks. Pray now, Helena, you are such a good judge of physiognomy, should you guess that I was dying, by my looks?"

The little girl laughed, and repeated "Dying? Oh, no, mamma."

"Oh, no! because I have such a fine colour in my cheeks, hey?"

"Not for that reason, mamma," said Helena, withdrawing her eyes from her mother's face.

"What, then you know rouge already when you see it?—You perceive some difference, for instance, between Miss Portman's colour and mine? Upon my word, you are a nice observer. Such nice observers are sometimes dangerous to have near one."

"I hope, mother," said Helena, "that you do not think I would try to find out any thing that you wish, or that I imagined you wished, I should not know."

"I do not understand you, child," cried Lady Delacour, raising herself suddenly upon the sofa, and looking full in her daughter's face.

Helena's colour rose to her temples; but, with a firmness that surprised even Belinda, she repeated what she had said nearly in the same words.

"Do you understand her, Miss Portman?" said Lady Delacour.

"She expresses, I think," said Belinda, "a very honourable sentiment, and one that is easily understood."

"Ay, in general, certainly," said Lady Delacour, checking herself; "but I thought that she meant to allude to something in particular—that was what I did not understand. Undoubtedly, my dear, you have just expressed a very honourable sentiment, and one that I should scarcely have expected from a child of your age.

"Helena, my dear," said her mother, after a silence of some minutes, "did you ever read the Arabian Tales?—'Yes, mamma,' I know must be the answer. But do you remember the story of Zobeide, who carried the porter home with her on condition that, let him hear or see what he might, he would ask no questions?"

"Yes, mamma."

"On the same conditions should you like to stay with me for a few days?"

"Yes. On any conditions, mamma, I should like to stay with you."

"Agreed, then, my dear!" said Lady Delacour. "Now let us go to the gold fishes, and see them eat lemna, or whatever you please to call it."

While they were looking at the gold fishes, the old man, who had been desired by Miss Portman to call, arrived. "Who is this fine, gray-haired old man?" said Lady Delacour. Helena, who did not know the share which Belinda's aunt and her own mother had in the transaction, began with great eagerness to tell the history of the poor gardener, who had been cheated by some fine ladies out of his aloe, &c. She then related how kind Lady Anne Percival and her Aunt Margaret had been to him; that they had gotten him a place as a gardener at Twickenham; and that he had pleased the family to whom he was recommended so much by his good behaviour, that, as they were leaving their house, and obliged to part with him, they had given him all the geraniums and balsams out of the green-house of which he had the care, and these he had been this day selling to the young ladies at Mrs. Dumont's. "I received the money for him, and I was just going to pay him," said Helena, "when Miss Portman came; and that put every thing else out of my head. May I go and give him his money now, mamma?"

"He can wait a few minutes," said Lady Delacour, who had listened to this story with much embarrassment and impatience. "Before you go, Helena, favour us with the names of the fine ladies who cheated this old gardener out of his aloe."

"Indeed, mamma, I don't know their names."

"No!—Did you never ask Lady Anne Percival, or your aunt Margaret?—Look in my face, child! Did they never inform you?"

"No, ma'am, never. I once asked Lady Anne, and she said that she did not choose to tell me; that it would be of no use to me to know."

"I give Lady Anne Percival more credit and more thanks for this," cried Lady Delacour, "than for all the rest. I see she has not attempted to lower me in my child's opinion. I am the fine lady, Helena—I was the cause of his being cheated—I was intent upon the noble end of outshining a certain Mrs. Luttridge—the noble means I left to others, and the means have proved worthy of the end. I deserve to be brought to shame for my folly; yet my being ashamed will do nobody any good but myself. Restitution is in these cases the best proof of repentance. Go, Helena, my love! settle your little affairs with this old man, and bid him call here again to-morrow. I will see what we can do for him."

Lord Delacour had this very morning sent home to her ladyship a handsome diamond ring, which had been intended as a present for Mrs. Luttridge, and which he imagined would therefore be peculiarly acceptable to his lady. In the evening, when his lordship asked her how she liked the ring, which he desired the jeweller to leave for her to look at it, she answered, that it was a handsome ring, but that she hoped he had not purchased it for her.

"It is not actually bought, my dear," said his lordship; "but if it suits your fancy, I hope you will do me the honour to wear it for my sake."

"I will wear it for your sake, my lord," said Lady Delacour, "if you desire it; and as a mark of your regard it is agreeable: but as to the rest—

'My taste for diamonds now is o'er,
The sparkling baubles please no more.'

If you wish to do me a kindness, I will tell you what I should like much better than diamonds, though I know it is rather ungracious to dictate the form and fashion of a favour. But as my dictatorship in all human probability cannot last much longer—"

"Oh, my dear Lady Delacour! I must not hear you talk in this manner: your dictatorship, as you call it, will I hope last many, many happy years. But to the point—what should you like better, my dear, than this foolish ring?"

Her ladyship then expressed her wish that a small annuity might be settled upon a poor old man, whom she said she had unwittingly injured. She told the story of the rival galas and the aloe, and concluded by observing, that her lord was in some measure called upon to remedy part of the unnumbered ills which had sprung from her hatred of Mrs. Luttridge, as he had originally been the cause of her unextinguishable ire. Lord Delacour was flattered by this hint, and the annuity was immediately promised to the old gardener.

In talking to this old man afterward, Lady Delacour found, that the family in whose service he lately lived had a house at Twickenham that would just answer her purpose. Lord Delacour's inquiries had hitherto been unsuccessful; he was rejoiced to find what he wanted just as he was giving up the search. The house was taken, and the old man hired as gardener—a circumstance which seemed to give him almost as much pleasure as the annuity; for there was a morello cherry-tree in the garden which had succeeded the aloe in his affection: "it would have grieved him sorely," he said, "to leave his favourite tree to strangers, after all the pains he had been at in netting it to keep off the birds."

As the period approached when her fate was to be decided, Lady Delacour's courage seemed to rise; and at the same time her anxiety, that her secret should not be discovered, appeared to increase.

"If I survive this business," said she, "it is my firm intention to appear in a new character, or rather to assert my real character. I will break through the spell of dissipation—I will at once cast off all the acquaintance that are unworthy of me—I will, in one word, go with you, my dear Belinda, to Mr. Percival's. I can bear to be mortified for my good; and I am willing, since I find that Lady Anne Percival has behaved generously to me, with regard to Helena's affections, I am willing that the recovery of my moral health should be attributed to the salubrious air of Oakly-park. But it would be inexpressible, intolerable mortification to me, to have it said or suspected in the world of fashion, that I retreated from the ranks disabled instead of disgusted. A voluntary retirement is graceful and dignified; a forced retreat is awkward and humiliating. You must be sensible that I could not endure to have it whispered—'Lady Delacour now sets up for being a prude, because she can no longer be a coquette.' Lady Delacour would become the subject of witticisms, epigrams, caricatures without end. It would just be the very thing for Mrs. Luttridge; then she would revenge herself without mercy for the ass and her panniers. We should have 'Lord and Lady D—, or the Domestic Tête-à-tête,' or 'The Reformed Amazon,' stuck up in a print-shop window! Oh, my dear, think of seeing such a thing! I should die with vexation; and of all deaths, that is the death I should like the least."

Though Belinda could not entirely enter into those feelings, which thus made Lady Delacour invent wit against herself, and anticipate caricatures; yet she did every thing in her power to calm her ladyship's apprehension of a discovery.

"My dear," said Lady Delacour, "I have perfect confidence in Lord Delacour's promise, and in his good-nature, of which he has within these few days given me proofs that are not lost upon my heart; but he is not the most discreet man in the world. Whenever he is anxious about any thing, you may read it a mile off in his eyes, nose, mouth, and chin. And to tell you all my fears in one word, Marriott informed me this morning, that the Luttridge, who came from Harrowgate to Rantipole, to meet Lord Delacour, finding that there was no drawing him to her, has actually brought herself to town.

"To town!—At this strange time of year! How will my lord resist this unequivocal, unprecedented proof of passion? If she catch hold of him again, I am undone. Or, even suppose him firm as a rock, her surprise, her jealousy, her curiosity, will set all engines at work, to find out by what witchcraft I have taken my husband from her. Every precaution that prudence could devise against her malicious curiosity I have taken. Marriott, you know, is above all temptation. That vile wretch (naming the person whose quack medicines had nearly destroyed her), that vile wretch will be silent from fear, for his own sake. He is yet to be paid and dismissed. That should have been done long ago, but I had not money both for him and Mrs. Franks the milliner. She is now paid: and Lord Delacour—I am glad to tell his friend how well he deserves her good opinion—Lord Delacour in the handsomest manner supplied me with the means of satisfying this man. He is to be here at three o'clock to-day; and this is the last interview he will ever have with Lady Delacour in the mysterious boudoir."

The fears which her ladyship expressed of Mrs. Luttridge's malicious curiosity were not totally without foundation. Champfort was at work for her and for himself. The memorable night of Lady Delacour's overturn, and the bustle that Marriott made about the key of the boudoir, were still fresh in his memory; and he was in hopes that, if he could discover the mystery, he should at once regain his power over Lord Delacour, reinstate himself in his lucrative place, and obtain a handsome reward, or, more properly speaking, bribe, from Mrs. Luttridge. The means of obtaining information of all that passed in Lady Delacour's family were, he thought, still in his power, though he was no longer an inmate of the house. The stupid maid was not so stupid as to be impenetrable to the voice of flattery, or, as Mr. Champfort called it, the voice of love. He found it his interest to court, and she her pleasure to be courted. On these "coquettes of the second table," on these underplots in the drama, much of the comedy, and some of the tragedy, of life depend. Under the unsuspected mask of stupidity this worthy mistress of our intriguing valet-de-chambre concealed the quick ears of a listener, and the demure eyes of a spy. Long, however, did she listen, and long did she spy in vain, till at last Mr. Champfort gave her notice in writing that his love would not last another week, unless she could within that time contrive to satisfy his curiosity; and that, in short, she must find out the reason why the boudoir was always locked, and why Mrs. Marriott alone was to be trusted with the key. Now it happened that this billet-doux was received on the very day appointed for Lady Delacour's last interview with the quack surgeon in the mysterious boudoir. Marriott, as it was her custom upon such occasions, let the surgeon in, and showed him up the back stairs into the boudoir, locked the door, and bade him wait there till her lady came. The man had not been punctual to the hour appointed; and Lady Delacour, giving up all expectation of his coming till the next day, had retired to her bedchamber, where she of late usually at this hour secluded herself to read methodistical books, or to sleep. Marriott, when she went up to let her lady know that the person, as she always called him, was come, found her so fast asleep that she thought it a pity to waken her, as she had not slept at all the preceding night. She shut the door very softly, and left her lady to repose. At the bottom of the stairs she was met by the stupid maid, whom she immediately despatched with orders to wash some lace: "Your lady's asleep," said she, "and pray let me have no running up and down stairs." The room into which the stupid maid went was directly underneath the boudoir; and whilst she was there she thought that she heard the steps of a man's foot walking over head. She listened more attentively—she heard them again. She armed herself with a glass of jelly in her hand, for my lady, and hurried up stairs instantly to my lady's room. She was much surprised to see my lady fast asleep. Her astonishment at finding that Mrs. Marriott had told her the truth was such, as for a moment to bereave her of all presence of mind, and she stood with the door ajar in her hand. As thus she stood she was roused by the sound of some one clearing his throat very softly in the boudoir—his throat; for she recollected the footsteps she had heard before, and she was convinced it could be no other than a masculine throat. She listened again, and stooped down to try whether any feet could be seen under the door. As she was in this attitude, her lady suddenly turned on her bed, and the book which she had been reading fell from the pillow to the floor with a noise, that made the listener start up instantaneously in great terror. The noise, however, did not waken Lady Delacour, who was in that dead sleep which is sometimes the effect of opium. The noise was louder than what could have been made by the fall of a book alone, and the girl descried a key that had fallen along with the book. It occurred to her that this might possibly be the key of the boudoir. From one of those irresistible impulses which some people make an excuse for doing whatever they please, she seized it, resolved at all hazards to open the mysterious door. She was cautiously putting the key into the key-hole, so as not to make the least noise, when she was suddenly startled by a voice behind her, which said, "Who gave you leave to open that door?"

She turned, and saw Helena standing at the half open bedchamber door.

"Mercy, Miss Delacour! who thought of seeing you? For God's sake, don't make a noise to waken my lady!"

"Did my mother desire you to go into that room?" repeated Helena.

"Dear me! no, miss," said the maid, putting on her stupid face; "but I only thought to open the door, to let in a little air to freshen the room, which my lady always likes, and bids me to do—and I thought—"

Helena took the key gently from her hand without listening to any more of her thoughts, and the woman left the room muttering something about jelly and my lady, Helena went to the side of her mother's bed, determined to wait there till she awakened, then to give her the key, and tell her the circumstance. Notwithstanding the real simplicity of this little girl's character, she was, as her mother had discovered, a nice observer, and she had remarked that her mother permitted no one but Marriott to go into the boudoir. This remark did not excite her to dive into the mystery: on the contrary, she carefully repressed all curiosity, remembering the promise she had given to her mother when she talked of Zobeide and the porter. She had not been without temptation to break this promise; for the maid who usually attended her toilette had employed every art in her power to stimulate her curiosity. As she was dressing Helena this morning, she had said to her, "The reason I was so late calling you, miss, this morning, was because I was so late myself last night; for I went to the play, miss, last night, which was Bluebeard. Lord bless us! I'm sure, if I had been Bluebeard's wife, I should have opened the door, if I'd died for it; for to have the notion of living all day long, and all night too, in a house in which there was a room that one was never to go into, is a thing I could not put up with." Then after a pause, and after waiting in vain for some reply from Helena, she added, "Pray, Miss Delacour, did you ever go into that little room within my lady's bedchamber, that Mrs. Marriott keeps the key of always?"

"No," said Helena.

"I've often wondered what's in it: but then that's only because I'm a simpleton. I thought to be sure, you knew."

Observing that Helena looked much displeased, she broke off her speech, hoping that what she had said would operate in due time, and that she should thus excite the young lady to get the secret from Marriott, which she had no doubt afterward of worming from Miss Delacour.

In all this she calculated ill; for what she had said only made Helena distrust and dislike her. It was the recollection of this conversation that made her follow the maid to her mother's bedchamber, to see what detained her there so long. Helena had heard Marriott say, that "she ought not to run up and down stairs, because her lady was asleep," and it appeared extraordinary that but a few minutes after this information she should have gone into the room with a glass of jelly in her hand.

"Ah, mamma!" thought Helena, as she stood beside her mother's bed, "you did not understand, and perhaps you did not believe me, when I said that I would not try to find out any thing that you wished me not to know. Now I hope you will understand me better."

Lady Delacour opened her eyes: "Helena," cried she, starting up, "how came you by that key?"

"Oh, mother! don't look as if you suspected me." She then told her mother how the key came into her hands.

"My dear child, you have done me an essential service," said Lady Delacour: "you know not its importance, at least in my estimation. But what gives me infinitely more satisfaction, you have proved yourself worthy of my esteem—my love."

Marriott came into the room, and whispered a few words to her lady.

"You may speak out, Marriott, before my Helena," said Lady Delacour, rising from the bed as she spoke: "child as she is, Helena has deserved my confidence; and she shall be convinced that, where her mother has once reason to confide, she is incapable of suspicion. Wait here for a few minutes, my dear."

She went to her boudoir, paid and dismissed the surgeon expeditiously, then returned, and taking her daughter by the hand, she said, "You look all simplicity, my dear! I see you have no vulgar, school-girl curiosity. You will have all your mother's strength of mind; may you never have any of her faults, or any of her misfortunes! I speak to you not as to a child, Helena, for you have reason far above your years; and you will remember what I now say to you as long as you live. You will possess talents, beauty, fortune; you will be admired, followed, and flattered, as I have been: but do not throw away your life as I have thrown away mine—to win the praise of fools. Had I used but half the talents I possess, as I hope you will use yours, I might have been an ornament to my sex—I might have been a Lady Anne Percival."

Here Lady Delacour's voice failed; but commanding her emotion, she in a few moments went on speaking.

"Choose your friends well, my dear daughter! It was my misfortune, my folly, early in life to connect myself with a woman, who under the name of frolic led me into every species of mischief. You are too young, too innocent, to hear the particulars of my history now; but you will hear them all at a proper time from my best friend, Miss Portman. I shall leave you to her care, my dear, when I die."

"When you die!—Oh, mother!" said Helena, "but why do you talk of dying?" and she threw her arms round her mother.

"Gently, my love!" said Lady Delacour, shrinking back; and she seized this moment to explain to her daughter why she shrunk in this manner from her caresses, and why she talked of dying.

Helena was excessively shocked.

"I wished, my dear," resumed her mother, calmly, "I wished to have spared you the pain of knowing all this. I have given you but little pleasure in my life; it is unjust to give you so much pain. We shall go to Twickenham to-morrow, and I will leave you with your Aunt Margaret, my dear, till all is over. If I die, Belinda will take you with her immediately to Oakly-park—you shall have as little sorrow as possible. If you had shown me less of your affectionate temper, you would have spared yourself the anguish that you now feel, and you would have spared me—"

"My dear, kind mother," interrupted Helena, throwing herself on her knees at her mother's feet, "do not send me away from you—I don't wish to go to my Aunt Margaret—I don't wish to go to Oakly-park—I wish to stay with you. Do not send me away from you; for I shall suffer ten times more if I am not with you, though I know I can be of no use."

Overcome by her daughter's entreaties, Lady Delacour at last consented that she should remain with her, and that she should accompany her to Twickenham.

The remainder of this day was taken up in preparations for their departure. The stupid maid was immediately dismissed. No questions were asked, and no reasons for her dismissal assigned, except that Lady Delacour had no farther occasion for her services. Marriott alone was to attend her lady to Twickenham. Lord Delacour, it was settled, should stay in town, lest the unusual circumstance of his attending his lady should excite public curiosity. His lordship, who was naturally a good-natured man, and who had been touched by the kindness his wife had lately shown him, was in extreme agitation during the whole of this day, which he thought might possibly be the last of her existence. She, on the contrary, was calm and collected; her courage seemed to rise with the necessity for its exertion.

In the morning, when the carriage came to the door, as she parted with Lord Delacour, she put into his hand a paper that contained some directions and requests with which, she said, she hoped that he would comply, if they should prove to be her last. The paper contained only some legacies to her servants, a provision for Marriott, and a bequest to her excellent and beloved friend, Belinda Portman, of the cabinet in which she kept Clarence Hervey's letters.

Interlined in this place, Lady Delacour had written these words: "My daughter is nobly provided for; and lest any doubt or difficulty should arise from the omission, I think it necessary to mention that the said cabinet contains the valuable jewels left to me by my late uncle, and that it is my intention that the said jewels should be part of my bequest to the said Belinda Portman.—If she marry a man of good fortune, she will wear them for my sake: if she do not marry an opulent husband, I hope she will sell the jewels without scruple, as they are intended for her convenience, and not as an ostentatious bequest. It is fit that she should be as independent in her circumstances as she is in her mind."

Lord Delacour with much emotion looked over this paper, and assured her ladyship that she should be obeyed, if—he could say no more.

"Farewell, then, my lord!" said she: "keep up your spirits, for I intend to live many years yet to try them."

CHAPTER XXII — A SPECTRE

The surgeon who was to attend Lady Delacour was prevented from going to her on the day appointed; he was one of the surgeons of the queen's household, and his attendance was required at the palace. This delay was extremely irksome to Lady Delacour, who had worked up her courage to the highest point, but who had not prepared herself to endure suspense. She spent nearly a week at Twickenham in this anxious state, and Belinda observed that she every day became more and more thoughtful and reserved. She seemed as if she had some secret subject of meditation, from which she could not bear to be distracted. When Helena was present, she exerted herself to converse in her usual sprightly strain; but as soon as she could escape, as she thought, unobserved, she would shut herself up in her own apartment, and remain there for hours.

"I wish to Heaven, Miss Portman," said Marriott, coming one morning into her room with a portentous face, "I wish to Heaven, ma'am, that you could any way persuade my lady not to spend so many hours of the day and night as she does in reading those methodistical books that she keeps to herself!—I'm sure that they do her no good, but a great deal of harm, especially now when her spirits should be kept up as much as possible. I am sensible, ma'am, that 'tis those books that have made my lady melancholy of a sudden. Ma'am, my lady has let drop very odd hints within these two or three days, and she speaks in a strange disconnected sort of style, and at times I do not think she is quite right in her head."

When Belinda questioned Marriott more particularly about the strange hints which her lady had let fall, she with looks of embarrassment and horror declined repeating the words that had been said to her; yet persisted in asserting that Lady Delacour had been very strange for these two or three days. "And I'm sure, ma'am, you'd be shocked if you were to see my lady in a morning, when she wakens, or rather when I first go into the room—for, as to wakening, that's out of the question. I am certain she does not sleep during the whole night. You'll find, ma'am, it is as I tell you, those books will quite turn her poor head, and I wish they were burnt. I know the mischief that the same sort of things did to a poor cousin of my own, who was driven melancholy mad by a methodist preacher, and came to an untimely end. Oh, ma'am! if you knew as much as I do, you'd be as much alarmed for my lady as I am."

It was impossible to prevail upon Marriott to explain herself more distinctly. The only circumstances that could be drawn from her seemed to Belinda so trifling as to be scarcely worth mentioning. For instance, that Lady Delacour, contrary to Marriott's advice, had insisted on sleeping in a bedchamber upon the ground floor, and had refused to let a curtain be put up before a glass door that was at the foot of her bed. "When I offered to put up the curtain, ma'am," said Marriott, "my lady said she liked the moonlight, and that she would not have it put up till the fine nights were over. Now, Miss Portman, to hear my lady talk of the moon, and moonlights, and liking the moon, is rather extraordinary and unaccountable; for I never heard her say any thing of the sort in her life before; I question whether she ever knew there was a moon or not from one year's end to another. But they say the moon has a great deal to do with mad people; and, from my own experience, I'm perfectly sensible, ma'am, it had in my own cousin's case; for, before he came to the worst, he took a prodigious fancy to the moon, and was always for walking by moonlight, and talking to one of the beauty of the moon, and such melancholy nonsense, ma'am."

Belinda could not forbear smiling at this melancholy nonsense; though she was inclined to be of Marriott's opinion about the methodistical books, and she determined to talk to Lady Delacour on the subject. The moment that she made the attempt, her ladyship, commanding her countenance, with her usual ability, replied only by cautious, cold monosyllables, and changed the conversation as soon as she could.

At night, when they were retiring to rest, Marriott, as she lighted them to their rooms, observed that she was afraid her lady would suffer from sleeping in so cold a bedchamber, and Belinda pressed her friend to change her apartment.

"No, my dear," replied Lady Delacour, calmly. "I have chosen this for my bedchamber, because it is at a distance from the servants' rooms; and when the operation, which I have to go through, shall be performed, my cries, if I should utter any, will not be overheard. The surgeon will be here in a few days, and it is not worth while to make any change."

The next day, towards evening, the surgeon and Dr. X— arrived. Belinda's blood ran cold at the sight of them.

"Will you be so kind, Miss Portman," said Marriott, "as to let my lady know that they are come? for I am not well able to go, and you can speak more composed to her than I can."

Miss Portman went to Lady Delacour's bedchamber. The door was bolted. As Lady Delacour opened it, she fixed her eyes upon Belinda, and said to her with a mild voice, "You are come to tell me that the surgeon is arrived. I knew that by the manner in which you knocked at the door. I will see him this moment," continued she, in a firm tone; and she deliberately put a mark in the book which she had been reading, walked leisurely to the other end of the room, and locked it up in her book-case. There was an air of determined dignity in all her motions. "Shall we go? I am ready," said she, holding out her hand to Belinda, who had sunk upon a chair.

"One would think that you were the person that was going to suffer. But drink this water, my dear, and do not tremble for me; you see that I do not tremble for myself. Listen to me, dearest Belinda! I owe it to your friendship not to torment you with unnecessary apprehensions. Your humanity shall be spared this dreadful scene."

"No," said Belinda, "Marriott is incapable of attending you. I must—I will—I am ready now. Forgive me one moment's weakness. I admire, and will imitate, your courage. I will keep my promise."

"Your promise was to be with me in my dying moments, and to let me breathe my last in your arms."

"I hope that I shall never be called upon to perform that promise."

Lady Delacour made no answer, but walked on before her with steady steps into the room where Dr. X— and the surgeon were waiting. Without adverting in the least to the object of their visit, she paid her compliments to them, as if they came on a visit of mere civility. Without seeming to notice the serious countenances of her companions, she talked of indifferent subjects with the most perfect ease, occupying herself all the time with cleaning a seal, which she unhooked from her watch-chain. "This seal," said she, turning to Dr. X—, "is a fine onyx—it is a head of Esculapius. I have a great value for it. It was given to me by your friend, Clarence Hervey; and I have left it in my will, doctor," continued she, smiling, "to you, as no slight token of my regard. He is an excellent young man; and I request," said she, drawing Dr. X— to a window, and lowering her voice, "I request, when you see him again, and when I am out of the way, that you will tell him such were my sentiments to the hour of my death. Here is a letter which you will have the goodness to put into his hands, sealed with my favourite seal. You need have no scruple to take charge of it; it relates not to myself. It expresses only my opinion concerning a lady who stands almost as high in your esteem, I believe, as she does in mine. My affection and my gratitude have not biassed my judgment in the advice which I have ventured to give to Mr. Hervey."

"But he will soon be here," interrupted Dr. X—, "and then—"

"And then I shall be gone," said Lady Delacour, coolly,

"'To that undiscover'd country,
From whose bourn no traveller returns.'"

Dr. X— was going to interrupt her, but she continued rapidly, "And now, my dear doctor, tell me candidly, have you seen any symptoms of cowardice in my manner this evening?"

"None," replied he. "On the contrary, I have admired your calm self-possession."

"Then do not suspect me of want of fortitude, when I request that this operation may not be performed to-day. I have changed my mind within these few hours. I have determined, for a reason which I am sure that you would feel to be sufficient, to postpone this affair till to-morrow. Believe me, I do not act from caprice."

She saw that Dr. X— did not yield assent to her last assertion, and that he looked displeased.

"I will tell you my reason," said she; "and then you will have no right to be displeased if I persist, as I shall inflexibly, in my determination. It is my belief that I shall die this night. To submit to a painful operation to-day would be only to sacrifice the last moments of my existence to no purpose. If I survive this night, manage me as you please! But I am the best judge of my own feelings—I shall die to-night."

Dr. X— looked at her with a mixture of astonishment and compassion. Her pulse was high, she was extremely feverish, and he thought that the best thing which he could do was to stay with her till the next day, and to endeavour to divert her mind from this fancy, which he considered as an insane idea. He prevailed upon the surgeon to stay with her till the next morning; and he communicated his intentions to Belinda, who joined with him in doing all that was possible to entertain and interest her by conversation during the remainder of the day. She had sufficient penetration to perceive that they gave not the least faith to her prognostic, and she never said one word more upon the subject; but appeared willing to be amused by their attempts to divert her, and resolute to support her courage to the last moment. She did not affect trifling gaiety: on the contrary, there was in all she said more strength and less point than usual.

The evening passed away, and Lady Delacour seemed totally to have forgotten her own prophecy respecting the event of the ensuing night; so much so, that she spoke of several things that she intended to do the next day. Helena knew nothing of what had passed, and Belinda imagined that her friend put this constraint upon herself to avoid alarming her daughter. Yet, after Helena retired, her mother's manner continued to be so much the same, that Dr. X— began to believe that her ladyship was actuated merely by caprice. In this opinion she confirmed him by bursting out a laughing when he proposed that some one should sit up with her during the night.

"My sage sir," said she, "have you lived to this time without ever having been duped by a woman before? I wanted a day's reprieve, and I have gained it—gained a day, spent in most agreeable conversation, for which I thank you. To-morrow," said she, turning to the surgeon, "I must invent some new excuse for my cowardice; and though I give you notice of it beforehand, as Harrington did when he picked the man's pocket, yet, nevertheless, I shall succeed. Good night!"

She hurried to her own apartment, leaving them all in astonishment and perplexity. Belinda was persuaded that she only affected this gaiety to prevent Dr. X— from insisting upon sitting up in her room, as he had proposed. Doctor X—, judging, as he said, from her ladyship's general character, attributed the whole to caprice; and the surgeon, judging, as he said, from human nature in general, was decided in his belief that she had been influenced, as she herself declared, by cowardice. After having all expressed their opinions, without making any impression upon one another, they retired to rest.

Belinda's bedchamber was next to Helena's; and after she had been in bed about an hour, she fancied that she heard some one walking softly in the next room. She rose, and found Lady Delacour standing beside her daughter's bed. She started at the sight of Belinda, but only said in a low voice, as she pointed to her child, "Don't waken her." She then looked at her for some moments in silence. The moon shone full upon her face. She stooped over Helena, parted the ringlets of hair upon her forehead, and kissed her gently.

"You will be good to this poor girl when I am gone, Belinda!" said she, turning away from her as she spoke: "I only came to look at her for the last time."

"Are you then serious, my dear Lady Delacour?"

"Hush! Don't waken her," said Lady Delacour, putting her finger on her lips; and walking slowly out of the room, she forbade Belinda to follow.

"If my fears be vain," said she, "why should I disturb you with them? If they be just, you will hear my bell ring, and then come to me."

For some time afterward all was perfectly silent in the house. Belinda did not go to bed, but sat waiting and listening anxiously. The clock struck two; and as she heard no other sound, she began to hope that she had suffered herself to be falsely alarmed by a foolish imagination, and she lay down upon her bed, resolving to compose herself to rest. She was just sinking to sleep, when she thought she heard the faint sound of a bell. She was not sure whether she was dreaming or awake. She started up and listened. All was silent. But in a few minutes Lady Delacour's bell rang violently. Belinda flew to her room. The surgeon was already there; he had been sitting up in the next room to write letters, and he had heard the first sound of the bell. Lady Delacour was senseless, supported in the surgeon's arms. Belinda, by his directions, ran immediately for Doctor X—, who was at the other end of the house. Before she returned, Lady Delacour had recovered her senses. She begged that the surgeon would leave the room, and that neither Dr. X— nor Marriott might be yet admitted, as she had something of importance to communicate to Miss Portman. The surgeon withdrew, and she beckoned to Belinda, who sat down upon the side of her bed. Lady Delacour held out her hand to her; it was covered with a cold dew.

"My dear friend," said she, "my prophecy is accomplishing—I know I must die."

"The surgeon said that you were not in the least danger, my dear Lady Delacour; that it was merely a fainting fit. Do not suffer a vain imagination thus to overpower your reason."

"It is no vain imagination—I must die," said Lady Delacour.

'I hear a voice you cannot hear,
Which says I must not stay;
I see a hand you cannot see,
Which beckons me away.'

"You perceive that I am in my perfect senses, my dear, or I could not quote poetry. I am not insane—I am not delirious."

She paused—"I am ashamed to tell you what I know will expose me to your ridicule."

"Ridicule!" cried Belinda: "can you think me so cruel as to consider your sufferings a subject for ridicule?"

Lady Delacour was overcome by the tenderness with which Belinda spoke.

"I will then speak to you," said she, "without reserve. Inconsistent as it is with the strength of mind which you might expect from me, I cannot resist the impression which has been made on my mind by— a vision."

"A vision!"

"Three times," continued Lady Delacour, "it has appeared to me about this hour. The first night after we came here I saw it; last night it returned; and to-night I have beheld it for the third time. I consider it as a warning to prepare for death. You are surprised—you are incredulous. I know that this must appear to you extravagant; but depend upon it that what I tell you is true. It is scarcely a quarter of an hour since I beheld the figure of —, that man for whose untimely death I am answerable. Whenever I close my eyes the same form appears before me."

"These visions," said Belinda, "are certainly the effects of opium."

"The forms that flit before my eyes when I am between sleeping and waking," said Lady Delacour, "I am willing to believe, are the effects of opium; but, Belinda, it is impossible I should be convinced that my senses have deceived me with respect to what I have beheld when I have been as broad awake, and in as perfect possession of my understanding as I am at this instant. The habits of my life, and the natural gaiety, not to say levity, of my temper, have always inclined me rather to incredulity than to superstition. But there are things which no strength of mind, no temerity can resist. I repeat it—this is a warning to me to prepare for death. No human means, no human power can save me!"

Here they were interrupted by Marriott, who could no longer be restrained from bursting into the room. Dr. X— followed, and going calmly to the side of Lady Delacour's bed, took her hand to feel her pulse.

"Mrs. Marriott, you need not alarm yourself in this manner," said he: "your lady is at this instant in as little danger as I am."

"You think she'll live! Oh, my lady! why did you terrify us in this manner?"

Lady Delacour smiled, and calmly said, as Doctor X— still continued to count her pulse, "The pulse may deceive you, doctor, but I do not. Marriott, you may—"

Belinda heard no more; for at this instant, as she was standing alone, near the glass-door that was opposite to the bed, she saw at a distance in the garden the figure which Lady Delacour had described. Lady Delacour was now so intent upon speaking to Dr. X—, that she saw nothing but him. Belinda had the presence of mind to be perfectly silent. The figure stood still for some moments. She advanced a few steps nearer to the window, and the figure vanished. She kept her eye steadily fixed upon the spot where it had disappeared, and she saw it rise again and glide quickly behind some bushes. Belinda beckoned to Dr. X—, who perceived by the eagerness of her manner, that she wished to speak to him immediately. He resigned his patient to Marriott, and followed Miss Portman out of the room. She told him what she had just seen, said it was of the utmost consequence to Lady Delacour to have the truth ascertained, and requested that Dr. X—would go with some of the men-servants and search the garden, to discover whether any one was there concealed, or whether any footsteps could be traced. The doctor did not search long before he perceived footsteps in the borders opposite to the glass-door of Lady Delacour's bedchamber; he was carefully following their track, when he heard a loud cry, which seemed to come from the other side of the garden wall. There was a breach in the wall over which he scrambled with some difficulty. The screams continued with redoubled violence. As he was making his way to the spot from which they proceeded, he was met by the old gardener, who was crossing one of the walks with a lantern in his hand.

"Ho! ho!" cried the gardener, "I take it that we have the thief at last. I fancy that the fellow whose footsteps I traced, and who has been at my morello cherry-tree every night, has been caught in the trap. I hope his leg is not broke, though!-This way, sir—this way!"

The gardener led the doctor to the place, and there they found a man, whose leg had actually been caught in the spring-trap which had been set for the defence of the cherry-tree. The man had by this time fallen into a swoon; they extricated him as fast as possible, and Doctor X— had him brought to Lady Delacour's, in order that the surgeon, who was there, might see his leg.

As they were carrying him across the hall, Belinda met them. She poured out a glass of water for the man, who was just recovering from his swoon; but as she went nearer to give it him, she was struck with his wonderful resemblance to Harriot Freke.

"It must be Mrs. Freke herself!" whispered she to Marriott, whose wide opening eyes, at this instant, fixed themselves upon her.

"It must be Mrs. Freke herself, ma'am!" repeated Marriott.

And so in fact it was.

There is a certain class of people, who are incapable of generous confidence in their equals, but who are disposed to yield implicit credit to the underhand information of mean emissaries. Through the medium of Champfort and the stupid maid, Mrs. Freke had learned a confused story of a man's footsteps having been heard in Lady Delacour's boudoir, of his being let in by Marriott secretly, of his having remained locked up there for several hours, and of the maid's having been turned away, merely because she innocently went to open the door whilst the gentleman was in concealment. Mrs. Freke was farther informed by the same unquestionable authority, that Lady Delacour had taken a house at Twickenham, for the express purpose of meeting her lover: that Miss Portman and Marriott were the only persons who were to be of this party of pleasure.

Upon the faith of this intelligence, Mrs. Freke, who had accompanied Mrs. Luttridge to town, immediately repaired to Twickenham, to pay a visit to a third cousin, that she might have an opportunity of detecting the intrigues, and afterwards of publishing the disgrace, of her former friend. The desire of revenging herself upon Miss Portman, for having declined her civilities at Harrowgate, had also a powerful influence in stimulating her malicious activity. She knew that if it were proved that Belinda was the confidante of Lady Delacour's intrigues, her reputation must be materially injured, and that the Percivals would then be as desirous to break off as they now were anxious to promote the match with Mr. Vincent. Charmed with this hope of a double triumph, the vindictive lady commenced her operations, nor was she ashamed to descend to the character of a spy. The general and convenient name of frolic, she thought, would cover every species of meanness. She swore that "it was charming fun to equip herself at night in men's clothes, and to sally forth to reconnoitre the motions of the enemy."

By an unfrequented path she used to gain the window that looked into Lady Delacour's bedchamber. This was the figure which appeared at night at a certain hour, and which, to her ladyship's disturbed imagination, seemed to be the form of Colonel Lawless. There was, indeed, a resemblance in their size and persons, which favoured the delusion. For several nights Mrs. Freke paid these visits without obtaining any satisfaction; but this night she thought herself overpaid for her exertions, by the charming discovery which she fancied she had made. She mistook the surgeon for a lover of Lady Delacour's; and she was hurrying home with the joyful intelligence, when she was caught in the gardener's trap. The agony that she suffered was at first intense, but in a few hours the pain somewhat subsided; and in this interval of rest she turned to Belinda, and with a malicious smile said,—"Miss Portman, 'tis fair I should pay for my peeping; but I shall not pay quite so dear for it as some of my friends."

Miss Portman did not in the least comprehend her, till she added, "I'm sure you'll allow that 'tis better for a lady to lose her leg than her reputation—and for my part I'd rather be caught in a man trap, than have a man caught in my bedchamber. My service to your friend, Lady Delacour, and tell her so."

"And do you know who that gentleman was, that you saw in her ladyship's room?"

"Not I, not yet; but I'll make it my business to find out. I give you fair notice; I'm a very devil when provoked. Why didn't you make me your friend when you could?—You'll not baffle me. I have seen all I wanted, and I am capable of painting all I saw. As to who the man might be, that's no matter; one Lothario is as good as another for my purpose."

Longer had Mrs. Freke spoken with malignant triumph, had she not been interrupted by a burst of laughter from the surgeon. Her vexation was indescribable when he informed her, that he was the man whom she had seen in Lady Delacour's bedchamber, and whom she had mistaken for a favoured lover.

Mrs. Freke's leg was much cut and bruised; and now that she was no longer supported by the hopes of revenge, she began to lament loudly and incessantly the injury that she had sustained. She impatiently inquired how long it was probable that she should be confined by this accident; and she grew quite outrageous when it was hinted, that the beauty of her legs would be spoiled, and that she would never more be able to appear to advantage in man's apparel. The dread of being seen by Lady Delacour in the deplorable yet ludicrous situation to which she had reduced herself operated next upon her mind, and every time the door of the apartment opened, she looked with terror towards it, expecting to see her ladyship appear. But though Lady Delacour heard from Marriott immediately the news of Mrs. Freke's disaster, she never disturbed her by her presence. She was too generous to insult a fallen foe.

Early in the morning Mrs. Freke was by her own desire conveyed to her cousin's house, where without regret we shall leave her to suffer the consequences of her frolic.

"A false prophetess! Nowithstanding all my visions, I have outlived the night, you see," said Lady Delacour, to Miss Portman when they met in the morning. "I have heard, my dear Belinda, and I believe, that the passion of love, which can endure caprice, vice, wrinkles, deformity, poverty, nay, disease itself, is notwithstanding so squeamish as to be instantaneously disgusted by the perception of folly in the object beloved. I hope friendship, though akin to love, is of a more robust constitution, else what would become of me? My folly, and my visions, and my spectre—oh, that I had not exposed myself to you in this manner! Harriot Freke herself is scarcely more contemptible. Spies and cowards are upon an equal footing. Her malice and her frolic are consistent with her character, but my fears and my superstition are totally inconsistent with mine. Forget the nonsense I talked to you last night, my dear, or fancy that I was then under the dominion of laudanum. This morning you shall see Lady Delacour herself again. Is Dr. X—, is the surgeon ready? Where are they? I am prepared. My fortitude shall redeem me in your opinion, Belinda, and in my own."

Doctor X— and the surgeon immediately obeyed her summons.

Helena heard them go into Lady Delacour's room, and she saw by Marriott's countenance, who followed, that her mother was going to submit to the operation. She sat down trembling on the steps which led to her mother's room, and waited there a long time, as she thought, in the most painful suspense. At last she heard some one call Helena. She looked up, and saw her father close to her.

"Helena," said he, "how is your mother?"

"I don't know. Oh, papa, you cannot go in there now," said Helena, stopping him as he was pressing forwards.

"Why did not you or Miss Portman write to me yesterday, as you promised?" said Lord Delacour, in a voice that showed he was scarcely able to ask the question.

"Because, papa, we had nothing to tell you: nothing was done yesterday. But the surgeon is now there," said Helena, pointing towards her mother's room.

Lord Delacour stood motionless for an instant; then suddenly seizing his daughter's hand, "Let us go," said he: "if we stay here, we shall hear her screams;" and he was hurrying her away, when the door of Lady Delacour's apartment opened, and Belinda appeared, her countenance radiant with joy.

"Good news, dear Helena! Oh, my lord! you are come in a happy moment—I give you joy."

"Joy! joy! joy!" cried Marriott, following.

"Is it all over?" said Lord Delacour.

"And without a single shriek!" said Helena. "What courage!"

"There's no need of shrieks, or courage either, thank God," said Marriott. "Dr. X— says so, and he is the best man in the world, and the cleverest. And I was right from the first; I said it was impossible my lady should have such a shocking complaint as she thought she had. There's no such thing at all in the case, my lord! I said so always, till I was persuaded out of my senses by that villainous quack, who contradicted me for this own 'molument. And Doctor X— says, if my lady will leave off the terrible quantities of laudanum she takes, he'll engage for her recovery."

The surgeon and Dr. X— now explained to Lord Delacour that the unprincipled wretch to whom her ladyship had applied for assistance had persuaded her that she had a cancer, though in fact her complaint arose merely from the bruise which she had received. He knew too well how to make a wound hideous and painful, and so continue her delusion for his own advantage. Dr. X— observed, that if Lady Delacour would have permitted either the surgeon or him to have examined sooner into the real state of the case, it would have saved herself infinite pain, and them all anxiety. Belinda at this moment felt too much to speak.

"I'm morally certain," cried Marriott, "Mr. Champfort would die with vexation, if he could see the joy that's painted in my lord's face this minute. And we may thank Miss Portman for this, for 'twas she made every thing go right, and I never expected to live to see so happy a day."

Whilst Marriott ran on in this manner with all the volubility of joy, Lord Delacour passed her with some difficulty, and Helena was in her mother's arms in an instant.

Lady Delacour, struck to the heart by their affectionate looks and words, burst into tears. "How little have I deserved this kindness from you, my lord! or from you, my child! But my feelings," added she, wiping away her tears, "shall not waste themselves in tears, nor in vain thanks. My actions, the whole course of my future life, shall show that I am not quite a brute. Even brutes are won by kindness. Observe, my lord," continued she, smiling, "I said won, not tamed!—A tame Lady Delacour would be a sorry animal, not worth looking at. Were she even to become domesticated, she would fare the worse."

"How so?—How so, my dear?" said Lord Delacour and Belinda almost in the same breath.

"How so?—Why, if Lady Delacour were to wash off her rouge, and lay aside her air, and be as gentle, good, and kind as Belinda Portman, for instance, her lord would certainly say to her,

'So alter'd are your face and mind,
'Twere perjury to love you now.'"

In some minds, emotions of joy are always connected with feelings of benevolence and generosity. Lady Delacour's heart expanded with the sensations of friendship and gratitude, now that she was relieved from those fears by which she had so long been oppressed.

"My dear daughter," said she to Helena, "have you at this instant any wish that I can gratify?—Ask any thing you please, the fairy Goodwill shall contrive to get it for you in a trice. You have thought of a wish at this moment, I know, by your eyes, by your blush. Nay, do not hesitate. Do you doubt me because I do not appear before you in the shape of a little ugly woman, like Cinderella's godmother? or do you despise me because you do not see a wand waving in my hand?—'Ah, little skilled of fairy lore!' know that I am in possession of a talisman that can command more than ever fairy granted. Behold my talisman," continued she, drawing out her purse, and showing the gold through the net-work. "Speak boldly, then," cried she to Helena, "and be obeyed."

"Ah, mamma," said Helena, "I was not thinking of what fairies or gold can give; but you can grant my wish, and if you will let me, I will whisper it to you."

Lady Delacour stooped to hear her daughter's whisper.

"Your wish is granted, my own grateful, charming girl," said her mother.

Helena's wish was, that her mother could be reconciled to her good aunt, Margaret Delacour.

Her ladyship sat down instantly, and wrote to Mrs. Delacour. Helena was the bearer of this letter, and Lady Delacour promised to wait upon this excellent old lady as soon as she should return to town.

In the meantime her ladyship's health rapidly improved under the skilful care of Dr. X—: it had been terribly injured by the ignorance and villany of the wretch to whom she had so long and so rashly trusted. The nostrums which he persuaded her to take, and the immoderate use of opium to which she accustomed herself, would have ruined her constitution, had it not been uncommonly strong. Dr. X— recommended it to her ladyship to abstain gradually from opium, and this advice she had the resolution to follow with uninterrupted perseverance.

The change in Lady Delacour's manner of life, in the hours and the company that she kept, contributed much to her recovery. She was no longer in continual anxiety to conceal the state of her health from the world. She had no secret to keep—no part to act; her reconciliation with her husband and with his friends restored her mind to ease and self-complacency. Her little Helena was a source of daily pleasure; and no longer conscious of neglecting her daughter, she no longer feared that the affections of her child should be alienated. Dr. X—, well aware that the passions have a powerful influence over the body, thought it full as necessary, in some cases, to attend to the mind as to the pulse. By conversing with Lady Delacour, and by combining hints and circumstances, he soon discovered what had lately been the course of her reading, and what impression it had made on her imagination. Mrs. Marriott, indeed, assisted him with her opinion concerning the methodistical books; and when he recollected the forebodings of death which her ladyship had felt, and the terror with which she had been seized on the night of Mrs. Freke's adventure, he was convinced that superstitious horrors hung upon his patient's spirits, and affected her health. To argue on religious subjects was not his province, much less his inclination; but he was acquainted with a person qualified by his profession and his character 'to minister to a mind diseased,' and he resolved on the first favourable opportunity to introduce this gentleman to her ladyship.

One morning Lady Delacour was complaining to Belinda, that the books in the library were in dreadful confusion. "My lord has really a very fine library," said she; "but I wish he had half as many books twice as well arranged: I never can find any thing I want. Dr. X—, I wish to heaven you could recommend a librarian to my lord—not a chaplain, observe."

"Why not a chaplain, may I ask your ladyship?" said the doctor.

"Oh, because we had once a chaplain, who gave me a surfeit of the whole tribe. The meanest sycophant, yet the most impertinent busy-body—always cringing, yet always intriguing—wanting to govern the whole family, and at the same time every creature's humble servant—fawning to my lord the bishop, insolent to the poor curate—anathematizing all who differed from him in opinion, yet without dignity to enforce the respect due to his faith or his profession—greedy for preferment, yet without a thought of the duties of his office. It was the common practice of this man to leap from his horse at the church door on a holiday, after following a pack of hounds, huddle on his surplice, and gabble over the service with the most indecent mockery of religion. Do I speak with acrimony? I have reason. It was this chaplain who first led my lord to Newmarket; it was he who first taught my lord to drink. Then he was a wit—an insufferable wit. His conversation after he had drank was such as no woman but Harriot Freke could understand, and such as few gentlemen could hear. I have never, alas! been thought a prude, but in the heyday of my youth and gaiety, this man always disgusted me. In one word, he was a buck parson. I hope you have as great a horror for this species of animal as I have?"

"Full as great," replied Dr. X—; "but I consider them as monsters, which belonging to no species, can disgrace none."

"They ought to be hunted by common consent out of civilized society," said Lady Delacour.

"They are by public opinion banished from all rational society; and your ladyship's just indignation proves, that they have no chance of being tolerated by fashion. But would it not allow such beings too much consequence, would it not extend their power to do mischief, if we perceived that one such person could disgust Lady Delacour with the whole race of chaplains?"

"It is uncommon," replied her ladyship, "to hear a physician earnest in the defence of the clergy—and a literary philosophic physician too! Shall we have an eulogium upon bishops as well as chaplains?"

"We have had that already," replied Dr. X—. "All ranks, persuasions, and descriptions of people, including, I hope, those stigmatized by the name of philosophers, have joined in admiration of the bishop of St. Pol de Leon. The conduct of the real martyrs to their faith amongst the French clergy, not even the most witty or brutal sceptic could ridicule."

"You surprise me, doctor!" said Lady Delacour; "for I assure you that you have the character of being very liberal in your opinions."

"I hope I am liberal in my opinions," replied the doctor, "and that I give your ladyship a proof of it."

"You would not then persecute a man or woman with ridicule for believing more than you do?" said Lady Delacour.

"Those who persecute, to overturn religion, can scarcely pretend to more philosophy, or more liberality, than those who persecute to support it," said Dr. X—.

"Perhaps, doctor, you are only speaking popularly?"

"I believe what I now say to be true," said Dr. X—, "and I always endeavour to make truth popular."

"But possibly these are only truths for ladies. Doctor X— may be such an ungallant philosopher, as to think that some truths are not fit for ladies. He may hold a different language with gentlemen."

"I should not only be an ungallant but a weak philosopher," said Dr. X—, "if I thought that truth was not the same for all the world who can understand it. And who can doubt Lady Delacour's being of that number?"

Lady Delacour, who, at the beginning of this conversation, had spoken guardedly, from the fear of lowering the doctor's opinion of her understanding, was put at her ease by the manner in which he now spoke; and, half laying aside the tone of raillery, she said to him, "Well, doctor! seriously, I am not so illiberal as to condemn all chaplains for one, odious as he was. But where to find his contrast in these degenerate days? Can you, who are a defender of the faith, and so forth, assist me? Will you recommend a chaplain to my lord?"

"Willingly," said Dr. X—; "and that is what I would not say for a world of fees, unless I were sure of my man."

"What sort of a man is he?"

"Not a buck parson."

"And I hope not a pedant, not a dogmatist, for that would be almost as bad. Before we domesticate another chaplain, I wish to know all his qualities, and to have a full and true description of him."

"Shall I then give you a full and true description of him in the words of Chaucer?"

"In any words you please. But Chaucer's chaplain must be a little old-fashioned by this time, I should think."

"Pardon me. Some people, as well as some things, never grow old-fashioned. I should not be ashamed to produce Chaucer's parish priest at this day to the best company in England—I am not ashamed to produce him to your ladyship; and if I can remember twenty lines in his favour, I hope you will give me credit for being a sincere friend to the worthy part of the clergy. Observe, you must take them as I can patch them together; I will not promise that I can recollect twenty lines de suite, and without missing a word; that is what I would not swear to do for His Grace the Archbishop of Canterbury."

"His Grace will probably excuse you from swearing; at least I will," said Lady Delacour, "on the present occasion: so now for your twenty lines in whatever order you please."

Doctor X—, with sundry intervals of recollection, which may be spared the reader, repeated the following lines:

"Yet has his aspect nothing of severe,
But such a face as promised him sincere.
Nothing reserved or sullen was to see,
But sweet regards, and pleasing sanctity,
Mild was his accent, and his action free.
With eloquence innate his tongue was arm'd,
Though harsh the precept, yet the preacher charm'd;
For, letting down the golden chain from high,
He drew his audience upwards to the sky.
He taught the Gospel rather than the law,
And forced himself to drive, but loved to draw.
The tithes his parish freely paid, he took;
But never sued, or curs'd with bell and book.
Wide was his parish, not contracted close
In streets—but here and there a straggling house.
Yet still he was at hand, without request,
To serve the sick, and succour the distressed.
The proud he tamed, the penitent he cheer'd,
Nor to rebuke the rich offender fear'd.
His preaching much, but more his practice wrought,
A living sermon of the truths he taught."

Lady Delacour wished that she could find a chaplain, who in any degree resembled this charming parish priest, and Dr. X—promised that he would the next day introduce to her his friend Mr. Moreton.

"Mr. Moreton!" said Belinda, "the gentleman of whom Mr. Percival spoke, Mrs. Freke's Mr. Moreton?"

"Yes," said Dr. X—, "the clergyman whom Mrs. Freke hanged in effigy, and to whom Clarence Hervey has given a small living."

These circumstances, even if he had not precisely resembled Chaucer's character of a benevolent clergyman, would have strongly interested Lady Delacour in his favour. She found him, upon farther acquaintance, a perfect contrast to her former chaplain; and he gradually acquired such salutary influence over her mind, that he relieved her from the terrors of methodism, and in their place substituted the consolations of mild and rational piety.

Her conscience was now at peace; her spirits were real and equable, and never was her conversation so agreeable. Animated with the new feelings of returning health, and the new hopes of domestic happiness, she seemed desirous to impart her felicity to all around her, but chiefly to Belinda, who had the strongest claims upon her gratitude, and the warmest place in her affections. Belinda never made her friend feel the weight of any obligation, and consequently Lady Delacour's gratitude was a voluntary pleasure—not an expected duty. Nothing could be more delightful to Miss Portman than thus to feel herself the object at once of esteem, affection, and respect; to see that she had not only been the means of saving her friend's life, but that the influence she had obtained over her mind was likely to be so permanently beneficial both to her and to her family.

Belinda did not take all the merit of this reformation to herself: she was most willing to share it, in her own imagination, not only with Dr. X—and Mr. Moreton, but with poor Clarence Hervey. She was pleased to observe that Lady Delacour never omitted any occasion of doing justice to his merit, and she loved her for that generosity, which sometimes passed the bounds of justice in her eulogiums. But Belinda was careful to preserve her consistency, and to guard her heart from the dangerous effect of these enthusiastic praises; and as Lady Delacour was now sufficiently re-established in her health, she announced her intention of returning immediately to Oakly-park, according to her promise to Lady Anne Percival and to Mr. Vincent.

"But, my dear," said Lady Delacour, "one week more is all I ask from you—may not friendship ask such a sacrifice from love?"

"You expect, I know," said Miss Portman, ingenuously, "that before the end of that time Mr. Hervey will be here."

"True. And have you no friendship for him?" said Lady Delacour with an arch smile, "or is friendship for every man in the creation, one Augustus Vincent always excepted, prohibited by the statutes of Oakly-park?"

"By the statutes of Oakly-park nothing is forbidden," said Belinda, "but what reason—"

"Reason! Oh, I have done if you go to reason! You are invulnerable to the light shafts of wit, I know, when you are cased in this heavy armour of reason; Cupid himself may strain his bow, and exhaust his quiver upon you in vain. But have a care—you cannot live in armour all your life—lay it aside but for a moment, and the little bold urchin will make it his prize. Remember, in one of Raphael's pictures, Cupid creeping into the armour of the conqueror of the world."

"I am sufficiently aware," said Belinda, smiling, "of the power of Cupid, and of his wiles. I would not brave his malice, but I will fly from it."

"It is so cowardly to fly!"

"Surely prudence, not courage, is the virtue of our sex; and seriously, my dear Lady Delacour, I entreat you not to use your influence over my mind, lest you should lessen my happiness, though you cannot alter my determination."

Moved by the earnest manner in which Belinda uttered these words, Lady Delacour rallied her no more, nor did she longer oppose her resolution of returning immediately to Oakly-park.

"May I remind you," said Miss Portman, "though it is seldom either politic or polite, to remind people of their promises,—but may I remind you of something like a promise you made, to accompany me to Mr. Percival's?"

"And would you have me behave so brutally to poor Lord Delacour, as to run away from him in this manner the moment I have strength to run?"

"Lord Delacour is included in this invitation," said Miss Portman, putting the last letter that she had received from Lady Anne Percival into her hands.

"When I recollect," said Lady Delacour, as she looked over the letter, "how well this Lady Anne of yours has behaved to me about Helena, when I recollect, that, though you have been with her so long, she has not supplanted me in your affections, and that she did not attempt to detain you when I sent Marriott to Oakly-park, and when I consider how much for my own advantage it will be to accept this invitation, I really cannot bring myself, from pride, or folly, or any other motive, to refuse it. So, my dear Belinda, prevail upon Lord Delacour to spend his Christmas at Oakly-park, instead of at Studley-manor (Rantipole, thank Heaven! is out of the question), and prevail upon yourself to stay a few days for me, and you shall take us all with you in triumph."

Belinda was convinced that, when Lady Delacour had once tasted the pleasures of domestic life, she would not easily return to that dissipation which she had followed from habit, and into which she had first been driven by a mixture of vanity and despair. All the connexions which she had imprudently formed with numbers of fashionable but extravagant and thoughtless women would insensibly be broken off by this measure; for Lady Delacour, who was already weary of their company, would be so much struck with the difference between their insipid conversation and the animated and interesting society in Lady Anne Percival's family, that she would afterwards think them not only burdensome but intolerable. Lord Delacour's intimacy with Lord Studley was one of his chief inducements to that intemperance, which injured almost equally his constitution and his understanding: for some weeks past he had abstained from all excess, and Belinda was well aware, that, when the immediate motive of humanity to Lady Delacour ceased to act upon him, he would probably return to his former habits, if he continued to visit his former associates. It was therefore of importance to break at once his connexion with Lord Studley, and to place him in a situation where he might form new habits, and where his dormant talents might be roused to exertion. She was convinced that his understanding was not so much below par as she had once been taught to think it: she perceived, also, that since their reconciliation, Lady Delacour was anxious to make him appear to advantage: whenever he said any thing that was worth hearing, she looked at Belinda with triumph; and whenever he happened to make a mistake in conversation, she either showed involuntary signs of uneasiness, or passed it off with that easy wit, by which she generally knew how "to make the worse appear the better reason." Miss Portman knew that Mr. Percival possessed the happy talent of drawing out all the abilities of those with whom he conversed, and that he did not value men merely for their erudition, science, or literature; he was capable of estimating the potential as well as the actual range of the mind. Of his generosity she could not doubt, and she was persuaded that he would take every possible means which good nature, joined to good sense, could suggest, to raise Lord Delacour in his lady's esteem, and to make that union happy which was indissoluble. All these reflections passed with the utmost rapidity in Belinda's mind, and the result of them was, that she consented to wait Lady Delacour's leisure for her journey.

CHAPTER XXIV — PEU À PEU

Things were in this situation, when one day Marriott made her appearance at her lady's toilette with a face which at once proclaimed that something had discomposed her, and that she was impatient to be asked what it was.

"What is the matter, Marriott?" said Lady Delacour; "for I know you want me to ask."

"Want you to ask! Oh, dear, my lady, no!—for I'm sure, it's a thing that goes quite against me to tell; for I thought, indeed, my lady, superiorly of the person in question; so much so, indeed, that I wished what I declare I should now be ashamed to mention, especially in the presence of Miss Portman, who deserves the best that this world can afford of every denomination. Well, ma'am, in one word," continued she, addressing herself to Belinda, "I am extremely rejoiced that things are as they are, though I confess that was not always my wish or opinion, for which I beg Mr. Vincent's pardon and yours; but I hope to be forgiven, since I'm now come entirely round to my Lady Anne Percival's way of thinking, which I learnt from good authority at Oakly-park; and I am now convinced and confident, Miss Portman, that every thing is for the best."

"Marriott will inform us, in due course of time, what has thus suddenly and happily converted her," said Lady Delacour to Belinda, who was thrown into some surprise and confusion by Marriott's address; but Marriott went on with much warmth—

Dear me! I'm sure I thought we had got rid of all double-dealers, when the house was cleared of Mr. Champfort; but, oh, mercy! there's not traps enough in the world for them all; I only wish they were all caught as finely as some people were. "Tis what all double-dealers, and Champfort at the head of the whole regiment, deserve—that's certain."

"We must take patience, my dear Belinda," said Lady Delacour, calmly, "till Marriott has exhausted all the expletives in and out of the English language; and presently, when she has fought all her battles with Champfort over again, we may hope to get at the fact."

"Dear! my lady, it has nothing to do with Mr. Champfort, nor any such style of personage, I can assure you; for, I'm positive, I'd rather think contemptibly of a hundred million Mr. Champforts than of one such gentleman as Mr. Clarence Hervey."

"Clarence Hervey!" exclaimed Lady Delacour: taking it for granted that Belinda blushed, her ladyship, with superfluous address, instantly turned, so as to hide her friend's face from Mrs. Marriott. "Well, Marriott, what of Mr. Hervey?"

"Oh, my lady, something you'll be surprised to hear, and Miss Portman, too. It is not, by any means, that I am more of a prude than is becoming, my lady: nor that I take upon me to be so innocent as not to know that young gentlemen of fortune will, if it be only for fashion's sake, have such things as kept mistresses (begging pardon for mentioning such trash); but no one that has lived in the world thinks any thing of that, except," added she, catching a glimpse of Belinda's countenance, "except, to be sure, ma'am, morally speaking, it's very wicked and shocking, and makes one blush before company, till one's used to it, and ought certainly to be put down by act of parliament, ma'am; but, my lady, you know, in point of surprising any body, or being discreditable in a young gentleman of Mr. Hervey's fortune and pretensions, it would be mere envy and scandal to deem it any thing—worth mentioning."

"Then, for mercy's sake, or mine," said Lady Delacour, "go on to something that is worth mentioning."

"Well, my lady, you must know, then, that yesterday I wanted some hempseed for my bullfinch—Miss Helena's bullfinch, I mean; for it was she found it by accident, you know, Miss Portman, the day after we came here. Poor thing! it got itself so entangled in the net over the morello cherry tree, in the garden, that it could neither get itself in nor out; but very luckily Miss Helena saw it, and saved, and brought it in: it was almost dead, my lady."

"Was it?—I mean I am very sorry for it: that is what you expect me to say. Now, go on—get us once past the bullfinch, or tell us what it has to do with Clarence Hervey."

"That is what I am aiming at, as fast as possible, my lady. So I sent for some hempseed for the bullfinch, and along with the hempseed they brought me wrapped round it, as it were, a printed handbill, as it might be, or advertisement, which I threw off, disregardingly, taking for granted it might have been some of those advertisements for lozenges or razor-strops, that meet one wherever one goes; but Miss Delacour picked it up, and found it was a kind of hue and cry after a stolen or strayed bullfinch. Ma'am, I was so provoked, I could have cried, when I learnt it was the exact description of our little Bobby to a feather—gray upon the back, and red on—"

"Oh! spare me the description to a feather. Well, you took the bird, bullfinch, or Bobby, as you call it, home to its rightful owner, I presume? Let me get you so far on your way."

"No, I beg your pardon, my lady, that is not the thing."

"Then you did not take the bird home to its owner—and you are a bird-stealer? With all my heart: be a dog-stealer, if you will—only go on."

"But, my lady, you hurry me so, it puts every thing topsy-turvy in my head; I could tell it as fast as possible my own way."

"Do so, then."

"I was ready to cry, when I found our little Bobby was claimed from us, to be sure; but Miss Delacour observed, that those with whom it had lived till it was grey must be sorrier still to part with it: so I resolved to do the honest and genteel thing by the lady who advertised for it, and to take it back myself, and to refuse the five guineas reward offered. The lady's name, according to the advertisement, was Ormond."

"Ormond!" repeated Lady Delacour, looking eagerly at Belinda: "was not that the name Sir Philip Baddely mentioned to us—you remember?"

"Yes, Ormond was the name, as well as I recollect," said Belinda, with a degree of steady composure that provoked her ladyship. "Go on, Marriott."

"And the words were, to leave the bird at a perfumer's in Twickenham, opposite to —; but that's no matter. Well, my lady, to the perfumer's I went with the bird, this morning. Now, I had my reasons for wishing to see this Mrs. Ormond myself, because, my lady, there was one thing rather remarkable about this bullfinch, that it sings a very particular tune, which I never heard any bullfinch, or any human creature, sing anything like before: so I determined, in my own cogitations, to ask this Mrs. Ormond to name the tunes her bullfinch could sing, before I produced it; and if she made no mention of its knowing any one out of the common way, I resolved to keep my bird to myself, as I might very conscientiously and genteelly too. So, my lady, when I got to the perfumer's, I inquired where Mrs. Ormond was to be found? I was told that she received no visits from any, at least from the female sex; and that I must leave the bird there till called for. I was considering what to do, and the strangeness of the information made about the female sex, when in there came, into the shop, a gentleman, who saved me all the indelicacy of asking particulars. The bullfinch was at this time piping away at a fine rate, and, as luck would have it, that very remarkable strange tune that I mentioned to you. Says the gentleman, as he came into the shop, fixing his eyes on the bullfinch as if they would have come fairly out of his head, 'How did that bird come here?'—'I brought it here, sir,' said I. Then he began to offer me mountains of gold in a very strange way, if I could tell him any tidings of the lady to whom it belonged. The shopman from behind the counter now bent forward, and whispered the gentleman that he could give him some information, if he would make it worth his while; and they both went together to a little parlour behind the shop, and I saw no more of them. But, my lady, very opportunely for me, that was dying with curiosity, out of the parlour they turned a young woman in, to attend the shop, who proved to be an acquaintance of mine, whom I had done some little favours to when in service in London. And this young woman, when I told her my distress about the advertisement and the bullfinch, let me into the whole of the affair. 'Ma'am,' said she, 'all that is known about Mrs. Ormond, in this house, or any where else, is from me; so there was no occasion for turning me out of the parlour. I lived with Mrs. Ormond, ma'am," says she, "'for half a year, in the very house she now occupies, and consequently nobody can be better informed than I am:'—to which I agreed. Then she told me that the reason that Mrs. Ormond never saw any company of any sort was, because she is not fit to see company—proper company—for she's not a proper woman. She has a most beautiful young creature there, shut up, who has been seduced, and is now deserted in a most cruel manner by a Mr. Hervey. Oh, my lady! how the name struck upon my ear! I hoped, however, it was not our Mr. Hervey; but it was the identical Mr. Clarence Hervey. I made the young woman describe him, for she had often and often seen him, when he visited the unfortunate creature; and the description could suit none but our Mr. Hervey, and besides it put it beyond a doubt, she told me his linen was all marked C. H. So our Mr. Hervey, ma'am," added Marriott, turning to Belinda, "it certainly proved to be, to my utter dismay and confusion."

"Oh, Marriott! my poor head!" exclaimed Lady Delacour, starting from under her hands: "that cruel comb went at least half an inch into my head—heads have feeling as well as hearts, believe me." And, as she spoke, she snatched out the comb with which Marriott had just fastened up her hair, and flung it on a sofa at some yards' distance. While Marriott went to fetch it, Lady Delacour thought that Belinda would have time to recover from that utter dismay and confusion into which she hoped that she must now be thrown. "Come, Marriott, make haste. I have done you at least a great favour, for you have all this hair to perform upon again, and you will have leisure to finish this story of yours—which, at all events, if it is not in any other respect wonderful, we must allow is wonderfully long."

"Well, my lady, to be short, then—I was more curious than ever, when I heard all this, to hear more; and asked my friend how she could ever think of staying in a house with ladies of such a description! Upon which she justified herself by assuring me, upon her honour, that at first she believed the young lady was married privately to Mr. Hervey, for that a clergyman came in secret, and read prayers, and she verily believes that the unfortunate young creature was deceived barbarously, and made to fancy herself married to all intents and purposes, till all at once Mr. Hervey threw off the mask, and left off visiting her, pretending a necessity to take a journey, and handing her over to that vile woman, that Mrs. Ormond, who bid her to be comforted, and all the things that are said by such women, on such occasions, by all accounts. But the poor deluded young thing saw how it was now too plain, and she was ready to break her heart; but not in a violent, common sort of way, ma'am, but in silent grief, pining and drooping. My friend could not stand the sight, nor endure to look upon Mrs. Ormond now she knew what she was; and so she left the house, without giving any reason, immediately. I forgot to mention, that the unfortunate girl's maiden name was St. Pierre, my lady: but her Christian name, which was rather an out o' the way name, I quite forget."

"No matter," said Lady Delacour; "we can live without it; or we can imagine it."

"To be sure—I beg pardon; such sort of people's names can't be of any consequence, and, I'm sure, I blame myself now for going to the house, after all I had heard."

"You did go to the house, then?"

"To my shame be it spoken; my curiosity got the better of me, and I went—but only on account of the bullfinch in the eyes of the world. It was a great while before I could get in: but I was so firm, that I would not give up the bird to no one but the lady herself, that I got in at last. Oh, never did my eyes light upon so beautiful a creature, nor so graceful, nor so innocent to look at!"—Belinda sighed—Marriott echoed the sigh, and continued "She was by herself, and in tears, when I was shown in, ma'am, and she started as if she had never seen any body before in her life. But when she saw the bullfinch, ma'am, she clapped her hands, and, smiling through her tears like a child, she ran up to me, and thanked me again and again, kissing the bird between times, and putting it into her bosom. Well, I declare, if she had talked to all eternity, she could never have made me pity her half so much as all this did, for it looked so much like innocence. I'm sure, nobody that was not—or, at least, that did not think themselves innocent, could have such ways, and such an innocent affection for a little bird. Not but what I know ladies of a certain description often have birds, but then their fondness is all affectation and fashion; but this poor thing was all nature. Ah! poor unfortunate girl, thought I—but it's no matter what I thought now," said Marriott, shutting her eyes, to hide the tears that came into them at this instant; "I was ashamed of myself, when I saw Mrs. Ormond just then come into the room, which made me recollect what sort of company I was in. La! my lady, how I detested the sight of her! She looked at me, too, more like a dragon than any thing else; though in a civil way, and as if she was frightened out of her wits, she asked Miss St. Pierre, as she called her, how I had got in (in a whisper), and she made all sorts of signs afterward to her, to go out of the room. Never having been in such a situation before, I was quite robbed of all fluency, and could not—what with the anger I felt for the one, and sorrow for the other— get out a word of common sense, or even recollect what pretence brought me into the room, till the bird very luckily put it into my head by beginning to sing; so then I asked, whether they could certify it to be theirs by any particular tune of its own? 'Oh, yes,' said Miss St. Pierre; and she sung the very same tune. I never heard so sweet a voice; but, poor thing, something came across her mind in the middle of it, and she stopped; but she thanked me again for bringing back the bird, which, she said, had been hers for a great many years, and that she loved it dearly. I stood, I believe, like one stupified, till I was roused by the woman's offering to put the five guineas reward, mentioned in the advertisement, into my hand. The touch of her gold made me start, as if it had been a snake, and I pushed it from me; and when she pressed it again, I threw it on the table, scarce knowing what I did; and just then, in her iniquitous hand, I saw a letter, directed to Clarence Hervey, Esq. Oh, how I hated the sight of his name, and every thing belonging to him, ma'am, at that minute! I'm sure, I could not have kept myself from saying something quite outrageous, if I had not taken myself out of the house, as I did, that instant.

"When there are women enough born and bred good for nothing, and ladies enough to flirt with, that would desire no better, that a gentleman like Mr. Clarence Hervey, ma'am, should set his wits, as one may say, to be the ruin of such a sweet, innocent-looking young creature, and then desert her in that barbarous way, after bringing a clergyman to deceive her with a mock ceremony, and all—oh! there is no fashion, nor nothing can countenance such wickedness! 'tis the worst of wickedness and cruelty—and I shall think and say so to the latest hour of my life."

"Well said, Marriott," cried Lady Delacour.

"And now you know the reason, ma'am," added Marriott, "that I said, I was glad things are as they are. To be sure I and every body once thought—but that's all over now—and I am glad things are as they are."

Lady Delacour once more turned her quick eyes upon Belinda, and was much pleased to see that she seemed to sympathize with Marriott's indignation.

In the evening, when they were alone, Lady Delacour touched upon the subject again, and observed, that as they should now, in all probability, see Mr. Hervey in a few days, they might be able to form a better judgment of this affair, which she doubted not had been exaggerated. "You should judge from the whole of Clarence's conduct and character, and not from any particular part," said her ladyship. "Do not his letters breathe a spirit of generosity?"

"But," interrupted Miss Portman, "I am not called upon to judge of Mr. Hervey's whole conduct and character, nor of any part of it; his letters and his generosity are nothing—"

"To you?" said Lady Delacour with a smile.

"This is no time, and no subject for raillery, my dear friend," said Belinda; "you assured me, and I believed you, that the idea of Mr. Hervey's return was entirely out of the question, when you prevailed upon me to delay my journey to Oakly-park. As I now understand that your ladyship has changed your mind, I must request your ladyship will permit me—"

"I will permit you to do what you please, dearest Belinda, except to call me your ladyship twice in one sentence. You shall go to Oakly-park the day after to-morrow: will that content you, my dear? I admire your strength of mind—you are much fitter to conduct yourself than I am to conduct you. I have done with raillery: my first, my only object, is your happiness. I respect and esteem as much as I love you, and I love you better than any thing upon earth—power excepted, you will say—power not excepted, believe me; and if you are one of those strange people that cannot believe without proof, you shall have proof positive upon the spot," added she, ringing the bell as she spoke. "I will no longer contend for power over your mind with your friends at Oakly-park. I will give orders, in your presence, to Marriott, to prepare for our march—I did not call it retreat; but there is nothing shows so much generalship as a good retreat, unless it be a great victory. I am, I confess, rather prejudiced in favour of victory."

"So am I," said Belinda, with a smile; "I am so strongly prejudiced in favour of victory, that rather than obtain no other, I would even be content with a victory over myself."

Scarcely had Belinda pronounced these words, when Lord Delacour, who had dined in town, entered the room, accompanied by Mr. Vincent.

"Give me leave, Lady Delacour, to introduce to you," said his lordship, "a young gentleman, who has a great, and, I am sure, a most disinterested desire to cultivate your ladyship's further acquaintance."

Lady Delacour received him with all the politeness imaginable; and even her prepossessions in favour of Clarence Hervey could not prevent her from being struck with his appearance. Il a infiniment l'air d'un héros de roman, thought she, and Belinda is not quite so great a philosopher as I imagined. In due time her ladyship recollected that she had orders to give to Marriott about her journey, that made it absolutely necessary she should leave Miss Portman to entertain Mr. Vincent, if possible, without her, for a few minutes; and Lord Delacour departed, contenting himself with the usual excuse of—letters to write.

"I ought to be delighted with your gallantry, Mr. Vincent," said Belinda, "in travelling so many miles, to remind me of my promise about Oakly-park; but on the contrary, I am sorry you have taken so much unnecessary trouble: Lady Delacour is, at this instant, preparing for our journey to Mr. Percival's. We intend to set out the day after to-morrow."

"I am heartily glad of it—I shall be infinitely overpaid for my journey, by having the pleasure of going back with you."

After some conversation upon different subjects, Mr. Vincent, with an air of frankness which was peculiarly pleasing to Belinda, put into her hands an anonymous letter, which he had received the preceding day.

"It is not worth your reading," said he; "but I know you too well to fear that it should give you any pain; and I hope you know me too well, to apprehend that it could make any impression on my mind."

Belinda read with some surprise:—

"Rash young man! beware of connecting yourself with the lady to whom you have lately been drawn in to pay your addresses: she is the most artful of women. She has been educated, as you may find upon inquiry, by one, whose successful trade it has been to draw in young men of fortune for her nieces, whence she has obtained the appellation of the match-maker general. The only niece whom she could not get rid of any other way, she sent to the most dissipated and unprincipled viscountess in town. The viscountess fell sick, and, as it was universally reported last winter, the young lady was immediately, upon her friend's death, to have been married to the viscount widower. But the viscountess detected the connexion, and the young lady, to escape from her friend's rage, and from public shame, was obliged to retreat to certain shades in the neighbourhood of Harrowgate; where she passed herself for a saint upon those who were too honourable themselves to be suspicious of others.

"At length the quarrel between her and the viscountess was made up, by her address and boldness in declaring, that if she was not recalled, she would divulge some secrets respecting a certain mysterious boudoir in her ladyship's house: this threat terrified the viscountess, who sent off express for her late discarded humble companion. The quarrel was hushed up, and the young lady is now with her noble friend at Twickenham. The person who used to be let up the private stairs into the boudoir, by Mrs. Marriott, is now more conveniently received at Twickenham."

Much more was said by the letter-writer in the same strain. The name of Clarence Hervey, in the last page, caught Belinda's eye; and with a trepidation which she did not feel at the beginning of this epistle, she read the conclusion.

"The viscount is not supposed to have been unrivalled in the young lady's favour. A young gentleman, of large fortune, great talents, and uncommon powers of pleasing, has, for some months, been her secret object; but he has been prudent enough to escape her matrimonial snares, though he carries on a correspondence with her, through the means of her friend the viscountess, to whom he privately writes. The noble lady has bargained to make over to her confidante all her interest in Hervey's heart. He is expected every day to return from his tour; and, if the schemes upon him can be brought to bear, the promised return to the neighbourhood of Harrowgate will never be thought of. Mr. Vincent will be left in the lurch; he will not even have the lady's fair hand—her fair heart is Clarence Hervey's, at all events. Further particulars shall be communicated to Mr. Vincent, if he pays due attention to this warning from

"A SINCERE FRIEND."

As soon as Belinda had finished this curious production, she thanked Mr. Vincent, with more kindness than she had ever before shown him, for the confidence he placed in her, and for the openness with which he treated her. She begged his permission to show this letter to Lady Delacour, though he had previously dreaded the effect which it might have upon her ladyship's feelings.

Her first exclamation was, "This is one of Harriot Freke's frolics;" but as her ladyship's indignation against Mrs. Freke had long since subsided into utter contempt, she did not waste another thought upon the writer of this horrible letter; but instantly the whole energy of her mind and fire of her eloquence burst forth in an eulogium upon her friend. Careless of all that concerned herself, she explained, without a moment's hesitation, every thing that could exalt Belinda: she described all the difficult circumstances in which her friend had been placed; she mentioned the secret with which she had been intrusted; the honour with which, even at the hazard of her own reputation, she had kept her promise of secrecy inviolable, when Lord Delacour, in a fit of intoxication and jealousy, had endeavoured to wrest from Marriott the key of the mysterious boudoir. She confessed her own absurd jealousy, explained how it had been excited by the artifices of Champfort and Sir Philip Baddely, how slight circumstances had worked her mind up almost to frenzy. "The temper, the dignity, the gentleness, the humanity, with which Belinda bore with me, during this paroxysm of madness," said Lady Delacour, "I never can forget; nor the spirit with which she left my house, when she saw me unworthy of her esteem, and ungrateful for her kindness; nor the magnanimity with which she returned to me, when I thought myself upon my death-bed: all this has made an impression upon my soul, which never, whilst I have life and reason, can be effaced. She has saved my life. She has made my life worth saving. She has made me feel my own value. She has made me know my own happiness. She has reconciled me to my husband. She has united me with my child. She has been my guardian angel.—She, the confidante of my intrigues!—she leagued with me in vice!—No, I am bound to her by ties stronger than vice ever felt; than vice, even in the utmost ingenuity of its depravity, can devise."

Exhausted by the vehemence with which she had spoken, Lady Delacour paused; but Vincent, who sympathized in her enthusiasm, kept his eyes fixed upon her, in hopes that she had yet more to say.

"I might, perhaps, you will think," continued she, smiling, "have spared you this history of myself, and of my own affairs, Mr. Vincent; but I thought it necessary to tell you the plain facts, which malice has distorted into the most odious form. This is the quarrel, this is the reconciliation, of which your anonymous friend has been so well informed. Now, as to Clarence Hervey."

"I have explained to Mr. Vincent," interrupted Belinda, "every thing that he could wish to know on that subject, and I now wish you to tell him that I faithfully remembered my promise to return to Oakly-park, and that we were actually preparing for the journey."

"Look here, sir," cried Lady Delacour, opening the door of her dressing-room, in which Marriott was upon her knees, locking a trunk, "here's dreadful note of preparation."

"You are a happier man than you yet know, Mr. Vincent," continued Lady Delacour; "for I can tell you, that some persuasion, some raillery, and some wit, I flatter myself, have been used, to detain Miss Portman from you."

"From Oakly-park," interrupted Belinda.

"From Oakly-park, &c. a few days longer. Shall I be frank with you, Mr. Vincent?—Yes, for I cannot help it—I am not of the nature of anonymous letter-writers; I cannot, either secretly or publicly, sign or say myself a sincere friend, without being one to the utmost extent of my influence. I never give my vote without my interest, nor my interest without my vote. Now Clarence Hervey is my friend. Start not at all, sir,—you have no reason; for if he is my friend, Miss Portman is yours: which has the better bargain? But, as I was going to tell you, Mr. Clarence Hervey is my friend, and I am his. My vote, interest, and influence, have consequently been all in his favour. I had reason to believe that he has long admired the dignity of Miss Portman's mind, and the simplicity of her character," continued her ladyship, with an arch look at Belinda; "and though he was too much a man of genius to begin with the present tense of the indicative mood, 'I love,' yet I was, and am, convinced, that he does love her."

"Can you, dear Lady Delacour," cried Belinda, "speak in this manner, and recollect all we heard from Marriott this morning? And to what purpose all this?"

"To what purpose, my dear? To convince your friend, Mr. Vincent, that I am neither fool nor knave; but that I deal fairly by you, by him, and by all the world. Mr. Hervey's conduct towards Miss Portman has, I acknowledge, sir, been undecided. Some circumstances have lately come to my knowledge which throw doubts upon his honour and integrity—doubts which, I firmly believe, he will clear up to my satisfaction at least, as soon as I see him, or as soon as it is in his power; with this conviction, and believing, as I do, that no man upon earth is so well suited to my friend,—pardon me, Mr. Vincent, if my wishes differ from yours: though my sincerity may give you present, it may save you from future, pain."

"Your ladyship's sincerity, whatever pain it may give me, I admire," said Mr. Vincent, with some pride in his manner; "but I see that I must despair of the honour of your ladyship's congratulations."

"Pardon me," interrupted Lady Delacour; "there you are quite mistaken: the man of Belinda's choice must receive my congratulations; he must do more—he must become my friend I would never rest till I had won his regard, nor should I in the least be apprehensive that he would not have sufficient greatness of mind to forgive my having treated him with a degree of sincerity which the common forms of politeness cannot justify, and at which common souls would be scandalized past recovery."

Mr. Vincent's pride was entirely vanquished by this speech; and with that frankness by which his manners were usually characterized, he thanked her for having distinguished him from common souls; and assured her that such sincerity as hers was infinitely more to his taste than that refined politeness of which he was aware no one was more perfect mistress than Lady Delacour.

Here their conversation ended, and Mr. Vincent, as it was now late, took his leave.

"Really, my dear Belinda," said Lady Delacour, when he was gone, "I am not surprised at your impatience to return to Oakly-park; I am not so partial to my knight, as to compare him, in personal accomplishments, with your hero. I acknowledge, also, that there is something vastly prepossessing in the frankness of his manners; he has behaved admirably well about this abominable letter; but, what is better than all in a lady's eyes he is éperdument amoureux."

"Not éperdument, I hope," said Belinda.

"Then, as you do not think it necessary for your hero to be éperdument amoureux, I presume," said Lady Delacour, "you do not think it necessary that a heroine should be in love at all. So love and marriage are to be separated by philosophy, as well as by fashion. This is Lady Anne Percival's doctrine! I give Mr. Percival joy. I remember the time, when he fancied love essential to happiness."

"I believe he not only fancies, but is sure of it now, from experience," said Belinda.

"Then he interdicts love only to his friends? He does not think it essential that you should know any thing about the matter. You may marry his ward, and welcome, without being in love with him."

"But not without loving him," said Belinda.

"I am not casuist enough in these matters to understand the subtle distinction you make, with the true Percival emphasis, between loving and falling in love. But I suppose I am to understand by loving, loving as half the world do when they marry."

"As it would be happy for half the world if they did," replied Belinda, mildly, but with a firmness of tone that her ladyship felt. "I should despise myself and deserve no pity from any human being, if, after all I have seen, I could think of marrying for convenience or interest."

"Oh! pardon me; I meant not to insinuate such an idea: even your worst enemy, Sir Philip Baddely, would acquit you there. I meant but to hint, my dear Belinda, that a heart such as yours is formed for love in its highest, purest, happiest state."

A pause ensued.

"Such happiness can be secured only," resumed Belinda, "by a union with a man of sense and virtue."

"A man of sense and virtue, I suppose, means Mr. Vincent," said Lady Delacour: "no doubt you have lately learned in the same sober style that a little love will suffice with a great deal of esteem."

"I hope I have learned lately that a great deal of esteem is the best foundation for a great deal of love."

"Possibly," said Lady Delacour; "but we often see people working at the foundation all their lives without getting any farther."

"And those who build their castles of happiness in the air," said Belinda, "are they more secure, wiser, or happier?"

"Wiser! I know nothing about that," said Lady Delacour; "but happier I do believe they are; for the castle-building is always a labour of love, but the foundation of drudgery is generally love's labour lost. Poor Vincent will find it so."

"Perhaps not," said Belinda; "for already his solid good qualities—"

"Solid good qualities!" interrupted Lady Delacour: "I beg your pardon for interrupting you, but, my dear, you know we never fall in love with good qualities, except, indeed, when they are joined to an aquiline nose—oh! that aquiline nose of Mr. Vincent's! I am more afraid of it than of all his solid good qualities. He has again, I acknowledge it, much the advantage of Clarence Hervey in personal accomplishments. But you are not a woman to be decided by personal accomplishments."

"And you will not allow me to be decided by solid good qualities," said Belinda. "So by what must I be determined?"

"By your heart, my dear; by your heart: trust your heart only."

"Alas!" said Belinda, "how many, many women have deplored their having trusted to their hearts only."

"Their hearts! but I said your heart: mind your pronouns, my dear; that makes all the difference. But, to be serious, tell me, do you really and bona fide, as my old uncle the lawyer used to say, love Mr. Vincent?"

"No," said Belinda, "I do not love him yet."

"But for that emphatic yet, how I should have worshipped you! I wish I could once clearly understand the state of your mind about Mr. Vincent, and then I should be able to judge how far I might indulge myself in raillery without being absolutely impertinent. So without intruding upon your confidence, tell me whatever you please."

"I will tell you all I know of my own mind," replied Belinda, looking up with an ingenuous countenance. "I esteem Mr. Vincent; I am grateful to him for the proofs he has given me of steady attachment, and of confidence in my integrity. I like his manners and the frankness of his temper; but I do not yet love him, and till I do, no earthly consideration could prevail upon me to marry him."

"Perfectly satisfactory, my dear Belinda; and yet I cannot be quite at ease whilst Mr. Vincent is present, and my poor Clarence absent: proximity is such a dangerous advantage even with the wisest of us. The absent lose favour so quickly in Cupid's court, as in all other courts; and they are such victims to false reports and vile slanderers!"

Belinda sighed.

"Thank you for that sigh, my dear," said Lady Delacour. "May I ask, would you, if you discovered that Mr. Vincent had a Virginia, discard him for ever from your thoughts?"

"If I discovered that he had deceived and behaved dishonourably to any woman, I certainly should banish him for ever from my regard."

"With as much ease as you banished Clarence Hervey?"

"With more, perhaps."

"Then you acknowledge—that's all I want—that you liked Clarence better than you do Vincent?"

"I acknowledge it," said Belinda, colouring up to her temples; "but that time is entirely past, and I never look back to it."

"But if you were forced to look back to it, my dear,—if Clarence Hervey proposed for you,—would not you cast a lingering look behind?"

"Let me beg of you, my dear Lady Delacour, as my friend," cried Belinda, speaking and looking with great earnestness; "let me beg of you to forbear. Do not use your powerful influence over my heart to make me think of what I ought not to think, or do what I ought not to do. I have permitted Mr. Vincent to address me. You cannot imagine that I am so base as to treat him with duplicity, or that I consider him only as a pis-aller; no—I have treated, I will treat him honourably. He knows exactly the state of my mind. He shall have a fair trial whether he can win my love; the moment I am convinced that he cannot succeed, I will tell him so decidedly: but if ever I should feel for him that affection which is necessary for my happiness and his, I hope I shall without fear, even of Lady Delacour's ridicule or displeasure, avow my sentiments, and abide by my choice."

"My dear, I admire you," said Lady Delacour; "but I am incorrigible; I am not fit to hear myself convinced. After all, I am impelled by the genius of imprudence to tell you, that, in spite of Mr. Percival's cure for first loves, I consider love as a distemper that can be had but once."

"As you acknowledge that you are not fit to hear yourself convinced," said Belinda, "I will not argue this point with you."

"But you will allow," said Lady Delacour, "as it is said or sung in Cupid's calendar, that—

'Un peu d'amour, un peu de soin,
Menent souvent un coeur bien loin;'"

and she broke off the conversation by singing that beautiful French air.

CHAPTER XXV — LOVE ME, LOVE MY DOG

The only interest that honest people can take in the fate of rogues is in their detection and punishment; the reader, then, will be so far interested in the fate of Mr. Champfort, as to feel some satisfaction at his being safely lodged in Newgate. The circumstance which led to this desirable catastrophe was the anonymous letter to Mr. Vincent. From the first moment that Marriott saw or heard of the letter, she was convinced, she said, that "Mr. Champfort was at the bottom of it." Lady Delacour was equally convinced that Harriot Freke was the author of the epistle; and she supported her opinion by observing, that Champfort could neither write nor spell English. Marriott and her lady were both right. It was a joint, or rather a triplicate performance. Champfort, in conjunction with the stupid maid, furnished the intelligence, which Mrs. Freke manufactured; and when she had put the whole into proper style and form, Mr. Champfort got her rough draught fairly copied at his leisure, and transmitted his copy to Mr. Vincent. Now all this was discovered by a very slight circumstance. The letter was copied by Mr. Champfort upon a sheet of mourning paper, off which he thought that he had carefully cut the edges; but one bit of the black edge remained, which did not escape Marriott's scrutinizing eye. "Lord bless my stars! my lady," she exclaimed, "this must be the paper—I mean may be the paper—that Mr. Champfort was cutting a quire of, the very day before Miss Portman left town. It's a great while ago, but I remember it as well as if it was yesterday. I saw a parcel of black jags of paper littering the place, and asked what had been going on? and was told, that it was only Mr. Champfort who had been cutting some paper; which, to be sure, I concluded my lord had given to him, having no further occasion for,—as my lord and you, my lady, were just going out of mourning at that time, as you may remember."

Lord Delacour, when the paper was shown to him, recognized it immediately by a private mark which he had put on the outside sheet of a division of letter paper, which, indeed, he had never given to Champfort, but which he had missed about the time Marriott mentioned. Between the leaves of this paper his lordship had put, as it was often his practice, some bank notes: they were notes but of small value, and when he missed them he was easily persuaded by Champfort that, as he had been much intoxicated the preceding night, he had thrown them away with some useless papers. He rummaged through his writing-desk in vain, and then gave up the search. It was true that on this very occasion he gave Champfort the remainder of some mourning paper, which he made no scruple, therefore, of producing openly. Certain that he could swear to his own private mark, and that he could identify his notes by their numbers, &c., of which he had luckily a memorandum, Lord Delacour, enraged to find himself both robbed and duped by a favourite servant, in whom he had placed implicit confidence, was effectually roused from his natural indolence: he took such active and successful measures, that Mr. Champfort was committed to gaol, to take his trial for the robbery. To make peace for himself, he confessed that he had been instigated by Mrs. Freke to get the anonymous letter written. This lady was now suffering just punishment for her frolics, and Lady Delacour thought her fallen so much below indignation, that she advised Belinda to take no manner of notice of her conduct, except by simply returning the letter to her, with "Miss Portman's, Mr. Vincent's, and Lord and Lady Delacour's, compliments and thanks to a sincere friend, who had been the means of bringing villany to justice."

So much for Mrs. Freke and Mr. Champfort, who, both together, scarcely deserve an episode of ten lines.

Now to return to Mr. Vincent. Animated by fresh hope, he pressed his suit with Belinda with all the ardour of his sanguine temper. Though little disposed to fear any future evil, especially in the midst of present felicity, yet he was aware of the danger that might ensue to him from Clarence Hervey's arrival; he was therefore impatient for the intermediate day to pass, and it was with heartfelt joy that he saw the carriages at last at the door, which were actually to convey them to Oakly-park. Mr. Vincent, who had all the West Indian love for magnificence, had upon this occasion an extremely handsome equipage. Lady Delacour, though she was disappointed by Clarence Hervey's not appearing, did not attempt to delay their departure. She contented herself with leaving a note, to be delivered to him on his arrival, which, she still flattered herself, would induce him immediately to go to Harrowgate. The trunks were fastened upon the carriages, the imperial was carrying out, Marriott was full of a world of business, Lord Delacour was looking at his horses as usual, Helena was patting Mr. Vincent's great dog, and Belinda was rallying her lover upon his taste for "the pomp, pride, and circumstance" of glorious travelling—when an express arrived from Oakly-park. It was to delay their journey for a few weeks. Mr. Percival and Lady Anne wrote word, that they were unexpectedly called from home by—. Lady Delacour did not stay to read by what, or by whom, she was so much delighted by this reprieve. Mr. Vincent bore the disappointment as well as could be expected; particularly when Belinda observed, to comfort him, that "the mind is its own place;" and that hers, she believed, would be the same at Twickenham as at Oakly-park. Nor did she give him any reason to regret that she was not immediately under the influence of his own friends. The dread of being unduly biassed by Lady Delacour, and the strong desire Belinda felt to act honourably by Mr. Vincent, to show him that she was not trifling with his happiness, and that she was incapable of the meanness of retaining a lover as a pis-aller, were motives which acted more powerfully in his favour than all that even Lady Anne Percival could have looked or said. The contrast between the openness and decision of his conduct towards her, and Clarence Hervey's vacillation and mystery; the belief that Mr. Hervey was or ought to be attached to another woman; the conviction that Mr. Vincent was strongly attached to her, and that he possessed many of the good qualities essential to her happiness, operated every day more and more strongly upon Belinda's mind.

Where was Clarence Hervey all this time? Lady Delacour, alas! could not divine. She every morning was certain that he would appear that day, and every night she was forced to acknowledge her mistake. No inquiries—and she had made all that could be made, by address and perseverance—no inquiries could clear up the mystery of Virginia and Mrs. Ormond; and her impatience to see her friend Clarence every hour increased. She was divided between her confidence in him and her affection for Belinda; unwilling to give him up, yet afraid to injure her happiness, or to offend her, by injudicious advice, and improper interference. One thing kept Lady Delacour for some time in spirits—Miss Portman's assurance that she would not bind herself by any promise or engagement to Mr. Vincent, even when decided in his favour; and that she should hold both him and herself perfectly free till they were actually married. This was according to Lady Anne and Mr. Percival's principles; and Lady Delacour was never tired of expressing directly or indirectly her admiration of the prudence and propriety of their doctrine.

Lady Delacour recollected her own promise, to give her sincere congratulations to the victorious knight; and she endeavoured to treat Mr. Vincent with impartiality. She was, however, now still less inclined to like him, from a discovery, which she accidentally made, of his being still upon good terms with odious Mrs. Luttridge. Helena, one morning, was playing with Mr. Vincent's large dog, of which he was excessively fond. It was called Juba, after his faithful servant.

"Helena, my dear," said Lady Delacour, "take care! don't trust your hand in that creature's monstrous mouth."

"I can assure your ladyship," cried Mr. Vincent, "that he is the very quietest and best creature in the world."

"No doubt," said Belinda, smiling, "since he belongs to you; for you know, as Mr. Percival tells you, every thing animate or inanimate that is under your protection, you think must be the best of its kind in the universe."

"But, really, Juba is the best creature in the world," repeated Mr. Vincent, with great eagerness. "Juba is, without exception, the best creature in the universe."

"Juba, the dog, or Juba, the man?" said Belinda: "you know, they cannot be both the best creatures in the universe."

"Well! Juba, the man, is the best man—and Juba, the dog, is the best dog, in the universe," said Mr. Vincent, laughing, with his usual candour, at his own foible, when it was pointed out to him. "But, seriously, Lady Delacour, you need not be in the least afraid to trust Miss Delacour with this poor fellow; for, do you know, during a whole month that I lent him to Mrs. Luttridge, at Harrowgate, she used constantly to let him sleep in the room with her; and now, whenever he sees her, he licks her hand as gently as if he were a lapdog; and it was but yesterday, when I had him there, she declared he was more gentle than any lapdog in London."

At the name of Luttridge, Lady Delacour changed countenance, and she continued silent for some time. Mr. Vincent, attributing her sudden seriousness to dislike or fear of his dog, took him out of the room.

"My dear Lady Delacour," said Belinda, observing that she still retained an air of displeasure, "I hope your antipathy to odious Mrs. Luttridge does not extend to every body who visits her."

"Tout au contraire," cried Lady Delacour, starting from her reverie, and assuming a playful manner: "I have made a general gaol-delivery of all my old hatreds; and even odious Mrs. Luttridge, though a hardened offender, must be included in this act of grace: so you need not fear that Mr. Vincent should fall under my royal displeasure for consorting with this state criminal. Though I can't sympathize with him, I forgive him, both for liking that great dog, and that little woman; especially, as I shrewdly suspect, that he likes the lady's E O table better than the lady."

"E O table! Good Heavens! you do not imagine Mr. Vincent—"

"Nay, my dear, don't look so terribly alarmed! I assure you, I did not mean to hint that there was any serious, improper attachment to the E O table; only a little flirtation, perhaps, to which his passion for you has, doubtless, put a stop."

"I'll ask him the moment I see him," cried Belinda, "if he is fond of play: I know he used to play at billiards at Oakly-park, but merely as an amusement. Games of address are not to be put upon a footing with games of hazard.'

"A man may, however, contrive to lose a good deal of money at billiards, as poor Lord Delacour can tell you. But I beseech you, my dear, do not betray me to Mr. Vincent; ten to one I am mistaken, for his great dog put me out of humour—"

"But with such a doubt upon my mind, unsatisfied—"

"It shall be satisfied; Lord Delacour shall make inquiries for me. Lord Delacour shall make inquiries, did I say?—will, I should have said. If Champfort had heard me, to what excellent account he might have turned that unlucky shall. What a nice grammarian a woman had need to be, who would live well with a husband inferior to her in understanding! With a superior or an equal, she might use shall and will as inaccurately as she pleases. Glorious privilege! How I shall envy it you, my dear Belinda! But how can you ever hope to enjoy it? Where is your superior? Where is your equal?"

Mr. Vincent, who had by this time seen his dog fed, which was one of his daily pleasures, returned, and politely assured Lady Delacour that Juba should not again intrude. To make her peace with Mr. Vincent, and to drive the E O table from Belinda's thoughts, her ladyship now turned the conversation from Juba the dog, to Juba the man. She talked of Harriot Freke's phosphoric Obeah woman, of whom, she said, she had heard an account from Miss Portman. From thence she went on to the African slave trade, by way of contrast, and she finished precisely where she intended, and where Mr. Vincent could have wished, by praising a poem called 'The dying Negro,' which he had the preceding evening brought to read to Belinda. This praise was peculiarly agreeable, because he was not perfectly sure of his own critical judgment, and his knowledge of English literature was not as extensive as Clarence Hervey's; a circumstance which Lady Delacour had discovered one morning, when they went to see Pope's famous villa at Twickenham. Flattered by her present confirmation of his taste, Mr. Vincent readily complied with a request to read the poem to Belinda. They were all deeply engaged by the charms of poetry, when they were suddenly interrupted by the entrance of—Clarence Hervey!

The book dropped from Vincent's hand the instant that he heard his name. Lady Delacour's eyes sparkled with joy. Belinda's colour rose, but her countenance maintained an expression of calm dignity. Mr. Hervey, upon his first entrance, appeared prepared to support an air of philosophic composure, which forsook him before he had walked across the room. He seemed overpowered by the kindness with which Lady Delacour received his congratulations on her recovery—struck by the reserve of Belinda's manner—but not surprised, or displeased, at the sight of Mr. Vincent. On the contrary, he desired immediately to be introduced to him, with the air of a man resolute to cultivate his friendship. Provoked and perplexed, Lady Delacour, in a tone of mingled reproach and astonishment, exclaimed, "Though you have not done me the honour, Mr. Hervey, to take any other notice of my last letter, I am to understand, I presume, by the manner in which you desire me to introduce you to our friend Mr. Vincent, that it has been received."

"Received! Good Heavens! have not you had my answer?" cried Clarence Hervey, with a voice and look of extreme surprise and emotion: "Has not your ladyship received a packet?"

"I have had no packet—I have had no letter. Mr. Vincent, do me the favour to ring the bell," cried Lady Delacour, eagerly: "I'll know, this instant, what's become of it."

"Your ladyship must have thought me—," and, as he spoke, his eye involuntarily glanced towards Belinda.

"No matter what I thought you," cried Lady Delacour, who forgave him every thing for this single glance; "if I did you a little injustice, Clarence, when I was angry, you must forgive me; for, I assure you, I do you a great deal of justice at other times."

"Did any letter, any packet, come here for me? Inquire, inquire," said she, impatiently, to the servant who came in. No letter or packet was to be heard of. It had been directed, Mr. Hervey now remembered, to her ladyship's house in town. She gave orders to have it immediately sent for; but scarcely had she given them, when, turning to Mr. Hervey, she laughed and said, "A very foolish compliment to you and your letter, for you certainly can speak as well as you can write; nay, better, I think—though you don't write ill, neither—but you can tell me, in two words, what in writing would take half a volume. Leave this gentleman and lady to 'the dying Negro,' and let me hear your two words in Lord Delacour's dressing-room, if you please," said she, opening the door of an adjoining apartment.

"Lord Delacour will not be jealous if he find you tête-à-tête with me, I promise you. But you shall not be compelled. You look—"

"I look," said Mr. Hervey, affecting to laugh, "as if I felt the impossibility of putting half a volume into two words. It is a long story, and—"

"And I must wait for the packet, whether I will or no—well, be it so," said Lady Delacour. Struck with the extreme perturbation into which he was thrown, she pressed him with no farther raillery, but instantly attempted to change the conversation to general subjects.

Again she had recourse to 'the dying Negro.' Mr. Vincent, to whom she now addressed herself, said, "For my part, I neither have, nor pretend to have, much critical taste; but I admire in this poem the manly, energetic spirit of virtue which it breathes." From the poem, an easy transition was made to the author; and Clarence Hervey, exerting himself to join in the conversation, observed, "that this writer (Mr. Day) was an instance that genuine eloquence must spring from the heart. Cicero was certainly right," continued he, addressing himself to Mr. Vincent, "in his definition of a great orator, to make it one of the first requisites, that he should be a good man."

Mr. Vincent coldly replied, "This definition would exclude too many men of superior talents, to be easily admitted."

"Perhaps the appearance of virtue," said Belinda, "might, on many occasions, succeed as well as the reality."

"Yes, if the man be as good an actor as Mr. Hervey," said, Lady Delacour, "and if he suit 'the action to the word'—'the word to the action.'"

Belinda never raised her eyes whilst her ladyship uttered these words; Mr. Vincent was, or seemed to be, so deeply engaged in looking for something in the book, which he held in his hand, that he could take no farther part in the conversation; and a dead silence ensued.

Lady Delacour, who was naturally impatient in the extreme, especially in the vindication of her friends, could not bear to see, as she did by Belinda's countenance, that she had not forgotten Marriott's story of Virginia St. Pierre; and though her ladyship was convinced that the packet would clear up all mysteries, yet she could not endure that even in the interim 'poor Clarence' should he unjustly suspected; nor could she refrain from trying an expedient, which just occurred to her, to satisfy herself and every body present. She was the first to break silence.

"To do ye justice, my friends, you are all good company this morning. Mr. Vincent is excusable, because he is in love; and Belinda is excusable, because—because—Mr. Hervey, pray help me to an excuse for Miss Portman's stupidity, for I am dreadfully afraid of blundering out the truth. But why do I ask you to help me? In your present condition, you seem totally unable to help yourself.—Not a word!—Run over the common-places of conversation—weather—fashion—scandal—dress—deaths— marriages.—Will none of these do? Suppose, then, you were to entertain me with other people's thoughts, since you have none of your own unpacked—Forfeit to arbitrary power," continued her ladyship, playfully seizing Mr. Vincent's book. "I have always observed that none submit with so good a grace to arbitrary power from our sex as your true men of spirit, who would shed the last drop of their blood to resist it from one of their own. Inconsistent creatures, the best of you! So read this charming little poem to us, Mr. Hervey, will you?"

He was going to begin immediately, but Lady Delacour put her hand upon the book, and stopped him.

"Stay; though I am tyrannical, I will not be treacherous. I warn you, then, that I have imposed upon you a difficult, a dangerous task. If you have any 'sins unwhipt of justice,' there are lines which I defy you to read without faltering—listen to the preface."

Her ladyship began as follows:

"Mr. Day, indeed, retained during all the period of his life, as might be expected from his character, a strong detestation of female seduction—Happening to see some verses, written by a young lady, on a recent event of this nature, which was succeeded by a fatal catastrophe—the unhappy young woman, who had been a victim to the perfidy of a lover, overpowered by her sensibility of shame, having died of a broken heart—he expresses his sympathy with the fair poetess in the following manner."

Lady Delacour paused, and fixed her eyes upon Clarence Hervey. He, with all the appearance of conscious innocence, received the book, without hesitation, from her hands, and read aloud the lines, to which she pointed.

"Swear by the dread avengers of the tomb,
By all thy hopes, by death's tremendous gloom,
That ne'er by thee deceived, the tender maid
Shall mourn her easy confidence betray'd,
Nor weep in secret the triumphant art,
With bitter anguish rankling in her heart;
So may each blessing, which impartial fate
Throws on the good, but snatches from the great,
Adorn thy favour'd course with rays divine,
And Heaven's best gift, a virtuous love, be thine!"

Mr. Hervey read these lines with so much unaffected, unembarrassed energy, that Lady Delacour could not help casting a triumphant look at Belinda, which said or seemed to say—you see I was right in my opinion of Clarence!

Had Mr. Vincent been left to his own observations, he would have seen the simple truth; but he was alarmed and deceived by Lady Delacour's imprudent expressions of joy, and by the significant looks that she gave her friend Miss Portman, which seemed to be looks of mutual intelligence. He scarcely dared to turn his eyes toward his mistress, or upon him whom he thought his rival: but he kept them anxiously fixed upon her ladyship, in whose face, as in a glass, he seemed to study every thing that was passing.

"Pray, have you ever played at chess, since we saw you last?" said Lady Delacour to Clarence. "I hope you do not forget that you are my knight. I do not forget it, I assure you—I own you as my knight to all the world, in public and private—do not I, Belinda?"

A dark cloud overspread Mr. Vincent's brow—he listened not to Belinda's answer. Seized with a transport of jealousy, he darted at Mr. Hervey a glance of mingled scorn and rage; and, after saying a few unintelligible words to Miss Portman and Lady Delacour, he left the room.

Clarence Hervey, who seemed afraid to trust himself longer with Belinda, withdrew a few minutes afterward.

"My dear Belinda," exclaimed Lady Delacour, the moment that he was out of the room, "how glad I am he is gone, that I may say all the good I think of him! In the first place, Clarence Hervey loves you. Never was I so fully convinced of it as this day. Why had we not that letter of his sooner? that will explain all to us: but I ask for no explanation, I ask for no letter, to confirm my opinion, my conviction—that he loves you: on this point I cannot be mistaken—he fondly loves you."

"He fondly loves her!—Yes, to be sure, I could have told you that news long ago," cried the dowager Lady Boucher, who was in the room before they were aware of her entrance; they had both been so eager, the one listening, and the other speaking.

"Fondly loves her!" repeated the dowager: "yes; and no secret, I promise you, Lady Delacour:" and then, turning to Belinda, she began a congratulatory speech, upon the report of her approaching marriage with Mr. Vincent. Belinda absolutely denied the truth of this report: but the dowager continued, "I distress you, I see, and it's quite out of rule, I am sensible, to speak in this sort of way, Miss Portman; but as I'm an old acquaintance, and an old friend, and an old woman, you'll excuse me. I can't help saying, I feel quite rejoiced at your meeting with such a match." Belinda again attempted to declare that she was not going to be married; but the invincible dowager went on: "Every way eligible, and every way agreeable. A charming young man, I hear, Lady Delacour: I see I must only speak to you, or I shall make Miss Portman sink to the centre of the earth, which I would not wish to do, especially at such a critical moment as this. A charming young man, I hear, with a noble West Indian fortune, and a noble spirit, and well connected, and passionately in love—no wonder. But I have done now, I promise you; I'll ask no questions: so don't run away, Miss Portman; I'll ask no questions, I promise you."

To ensure the performance of the promise, Lady Delacour asked what news there was in the world? This question, she knew, would keep the dowager in delightful employment. "I live quite out of the world here; but since Lady Boucher has the charity to come to see me, we shall hear all the 'secrets worth knowing,' from the best authority."

"Then, the first piece of news I have for you is, that my Lord and my Lady Delacour are absolutely reconciled; and that they are the happiest couple that ever lived."

"All very true," replied Lady Delacour.

"True!" repeated Lady Boucher: "why, my dear Lady Delacour, you amaze me!—Are you in earnest?— Was there ever any thing so provoking?—There have I been contradicting the report, wherever I went; for I was convinced that the whole story was a mistake, and a fabrication."

"The history of the reformation might not be exact, but the reformation itself your ladyship may depend upon, since you hear it from my own lips."

"Well, how amazing! how incredible!—Lord bless me! But your ladyship certainly is not in earnest? for you look just the same, and speak just in the same sort of way: I see no alteration, I confess."

"And what alteration, my good Lady Boucher, did you expect to see? Did you think that, by way of being exemplarily virtuous, I should, like Lady Q—, let my sentences come out of my mouth only at the rate of a word a minute?

'Like—minute—drops—from—off—the—eaves.'

Or did you expect that, in hopes of being a pattern for the rising generation, I should hold my features in penance, immoveably, thus—like some of the poor ladies of Antigua, who, after they have blistered their faces all over, to get a fine complexion, are forced, whilst the new skin is coming, to sit without speaking, smiling, or moving muscle or feature, lest an indelible wrinkle should be the consequence?"

Lady Boucher was impatient to have this speech finished, for she had a piece of news to tell. "Well!" cried she, "there's no knowing what to believe or disbelieve, one hears so many strange reports; but I have a piece of news for you, that you may all depend upon. I have one secret worth knowing, I can tell your ladyship—and one, your ladyship and Miss Portman, I'm sure, will be rejoiced to hear. Your friend, Clarence Hervey, is going to be married."

"Married! married!" cried Lady Delacour.

"Ay, ay, your ladyship may look as much astonished as you please, you cannot be more so than I was when I heard it. Clarence Hervey, Miss Portman, that was looked upon so completely, you know, as not a marrying man; and now the last man upon earth that your ladyship would suspect of marrying in this sort of way!"

"In what sort of way?—My dear Belinda, how can you stand this fire?" said Lady Delacour, placing a skreen, dexterously, to hide her face from the dowager's observation.

"Now only guess whom he is going to marry," continued Lady Boucher: "whom do you guess, Miss Portman?"

"An amiable woman, I should guess, from Mr. Hervey's general character," cried Lady Delacour.

"Oh, an amiable woman, I take for granted; every woman is amiable of course, as the newspapers tell us, when she is going to be married," said the dowager: "an amiable woman, to be sure; but that means nothing. I have not had a guess from Miss Portman."

"From general character," Belinda began, in a constrained voice.

"Do not guess from general character, my dear Belinda," interrupted Lady Delacour; "for there is no judging, in these cases, from general character, of what people will like or dislike."

"Then I will leave it to your ladyship to guess this time, if you please," said Belinda.

"You will neither of you guess till doomsday!" cried the dowager; "I must tell you. Mr. Hervey's going to marry—in the strangest sort of way!—a girl that nobody knows—a daughter of a Mr. Hartley. The father can give her a good fortune, it is true; but one should not have supposed that fortune was an object with Mr. Hervey, who has such a noble one of his own. It's really difficult to believe it."

"So difficult, that I find it quite impossible," said Lady Delacour, with an incredulous smile.

"Depend upon it, my dear Lady Delacour," said the dowager, laying the convincing weight of her arm upon her ladyship's, "depend upon it, my dear Lady Delacour, that my information is correct. Guess whom I had it from."

"Willingly. But first let me tell you, that I have seen Mr. Hervey within this half hour, and I never saw a man look less like a bridegroom."

"Indeed! well, I've heard, too, that he didn't like the match: but what a pity, when you saw him yourself this morning, that you didn't get all the particulars out of him. But let him look like what he will, you'll find that my information is perfectly correct. Guess whom I had it from—from Mrs. Margaret Delacour: it was at her house that Clarence Hervey first met Mr. Hartley, who, as I mentioned, is the father of the young lady. There was a charming scene, and some romantic story, about his finding the girl in a cottage, and calling her Virginia something or other, but I didn't clearly understand about that. However, this much is certain, that the girl, as her father told Mrs. Delacour, is desperately in love with Mr. Hervey, and they are to be married immediately. Depend upon it, you'll find my information correct. Good morning to you. Lord bless me! now I recollect, I once heard that Mr. Hervey was a great admirer of Miss Portman," said the dowager.

The inquisitive dowager, whose curiosity was put upon a new scent, immediately fastened her eyes upon Belinda's face; but from that she could make out nothing. Was it because she had not the best eyes, or because there was nothing to be seen? To determine this question, she looked through her glass, to take a clearer view; but Lady Delacour drew off her attention, by suddenly exclaiming—"My dear Lady Boucher, when you go back to town, do send me a bottle of concentrated anima of quassia."

"Ah! ah! have I made a convert of you at last?" said the dowager; and, satisfied with the glory of this conversion, she departed.

"Admire my knowledge of human nature, my dear Belinda," said Lady Delacour. "Now she will talk, at the next place she goes to, of nothing but of my faith in anima of quassia; and she will forget to make a gossiping story out of that most imprudent hint I gave her, about Clarence Hervey's having been an admirer of yours."

"Do not leave the room, Belinda; I have a thousand things to say to you, my dear."

"Excuse me, at present, my dear Lady Delacour; I am impatient to write a few lines to Mr. Vincent. He went away—"

"In a fit of jealousy, and I am glad of it."

"And I am sorry for it," said Belinda; "sorry that he should have so little confidence in me as to feel jealousy without cause—without sufficient cause, I should say; for certainly your ladyship gave pain, by the manner in which you received Mr. Hervey."

"Lord, my dear, you would spoil any man upon earth. You could not act more foolishly if the man were your husband. Are you privately married to him?—If you be not—for my sake—for your own—for Mr. Vincent's—do not write till we see the contents of Clarence Hervey's packet."

"It can make no alteration in what I write," said Belinda.

"Well, my dear, write what you please; but I only hope you will not send your letter till the packet arrives."

"Pardon me, I shall send it as soon as I possibly can: the 'dear delight of giving pain' does not suit my taste."

Lady Delacour, as soon as she was left alone, began to reconsider the dowager's story; notwithstanding her unbelieving smile, it alarmed her, for she could not refuse to give it some degree of credit, when she learnt that Mrs. Margaret Delacour was the authority from whom it came. Mrs. Delacour was a woman of scrupulous veracity, and rigid in her dislike to gossiping; so that it was scarcely probable a report originating with her, however it might be altered by the way, should prove to be totally void of foundation. The name of Virginia coincided with Sir Philip Baddely's hints, and with Marriott's discoveries: these circumstances considered, Lady Delacour knew not what opinion to form; and her eagerness to receive Mr. Hervey's packet every moment increased. She walked up and down the room—looked at her watch—fancied that it had stopped—held it to her ear—ran the bell every quarter of an hour, to inquire whether the messenger was not yet come back. At last, the long-expected packet arrived. She seized it, and hurried with it immediately to Belinda's room.

"Clarence Hervey's packet, my love!—Now, woe be to the person who interrupts us!" She bolted the door as she spoke—. rolled an arm-chair to the fire—"Now for it!" said she, seating herself. "The devil upon two sticks, if he were looking down upon me from the house-top, or Champfort, who is the worse devil of the two, would, if he were peeping through the keyhole, swear I was going to open a love-letter—and so I hope I am. Now for it!" cried she, breaking the seal.

"My dear friend," said Belinda, laying her hand upon Lady Delacour's, "before we open this packet, let me speak to you, whilst our minds are calm."

"Calm! It is the strangest time for your mind to be calm. But I must not affront you by my incredulity. Speak, then, but be quick, for I do not pretend to be calm; it not being, thank my stars, 'mon métier d'être philosophe.' Crack goes the last seal—speak now, or for ever after hold your tongue, my calm philosopher of Oakly-park: but do you wish me to attend to what you are going to say?"

"Yes," replied Belinda, smiling; "that is the usual wish of those who speak."

"Very true: and I can listen tolerably well, when I don't know what people are going to say; but when I know it all beforehand, I have an unfortunate habit of not being able to attend to one word. Now, my dear, let me anticipate your speech, and if my anticipation be wrong, then you shall rise to explain; and I will," said she, (putting her finger on her lips,) "listen to you, like Harpocrates, without moving an eyelash."

Belinda, as the most certain way of being heard, consented to hear before she spoke.

"I will tell you," pursued Lady Delacour, "if not what you are going to say to me, at least what you say to yourself, which is fully as much to the purpose. You say to yourself, 'Let this packet of Clarence Hervey contain what it may, it comes too late. Let him say, or let him do, 'tis all the same to me—because—(now for the reasoning)—because things have gone so far with Mr. Vincent, that Lady Anne Percival and all the world (at Oakly-park) will blame me, if I retract. In short, things have gone so far that I cannot recede; because—things have gone so far.' This is the rondeau of your argument. Nay, hear me out, then you shall have your turn, my dear, for an hour, if you please. Let things have gone ever so far, they can stop, and turn about again, cannot they? Lady Anne Percival is your friend, of course can wish only for your happiness. You think she is 'the thing that's most uncommon, a reasonable woman:' then she cannot be angry with you for being happy your own way. So I need not, as the orators say, labour this point any more. Now, as to your aunt. The fear of displeasing Mrs. Stanhope a little more or less is not to be put in competition with the hope of your happiness for life, especially as you have contrived to exist some months in a state of utter excommunication from her favour. After all, you know she will not grieve for any thing but the loss of Mr. Vincent's fortune; and Mr. Hervey's fortune might do as well, or almost as well: at least, she may compound with her pride for the difference, by considering that an English member of parliament is, in the eyes of the world (the only eyes with which she sees), a better connexion than the son of a West India planter, even though he may be a protégé of Lady Anne Percival.

"Spare me your indignation, my dear!—What a look was there!—Reasoning for Mrs. Stanhope, must not I reason as Mrs. Stanhope does?—Now I will put this stronger still. Suppose that you had actually acknowledged that Mr. Vincent had got beyond esteem with you; suppose that you had in due form consented to marry him; suppose that preparations were at this moment making for the wedding; even in that desperate case I should say to you, you are not a girl to marry because your wedding-gown is made up. Some few guineas are thrown away, perhaps; do not throw away your whole happiness after them—that would be sorry economy. Trust me, my dear, I should say, as I have to you, in time of need. Or, if you fear to be obliged to one who never was afraid of being obliged to you, ten to one the preparations for a wedding, though not the wedding, may be necessary immediately. No matter to Mrs. Franks who the bridegroom may be; so that her bill be paid, she would not care the turning of a feather whether it be paid by Mrs. Vincent or Mrs. Hervey. I hope I have convinced, I am sure I have made you blush, my dear, and that is some satisfaction. A blush at this moment is an earnest of victory. Lo, triumphe! Now I will open my packet; my hand shall not be held an instant longer."

"I absolve you from the penance of hearing me for an hour, but I claim your promise to attend to me for a few minutes, my dear friend," said Belinda: "I thank you most sincerely for your kindness; and let me assure you that I should not hesitate to accept from you any species of obligation."

"Thanks! thanks!—there's a dear good girl!—my own Belinda!"

"But indeed you totally misunderstand me; your reasoning—"

"Show me the fault of it: I challenge all the logic of all the Percivals."

"Your reasoning is excellent, if your facts were not taken for granted. You have taken it for granted, that Mr. Hervey is in love with me."

"No," said Lady Delacour; "I take nothing for granted, as you will find when I open this packet."

"You have taken it for granted," continued Belinda, "that I am still secretly attached to him; and you take it for granted that I am restrained only by fear of Lady Anne Percival, my aunt, and the world, from breaking off with Mr. Vincent: if you will read the letter, which I was writing to him when you came into the room, perhaps you will be convinced of your mistake."

"Read a letter to Mr. Vincent at such a time as this! then I will go and read my packet in my own room," cried Lady Delacour, rising hastily, with evident displeasure.

"Not even your displeasure, my dear friend," said Belinda, "can alter my determination to behave with consistency and openness towards Mr. Vincent; and I can bear your anger, for I know it arises from your regard for me."

"I never loved you so little as at this instant, Belinda."

"You will do me justice when you are cool."

"Cool!" repeated Lady Delacour, as she was about to leave the room, "I never wish to be as cool as you are, Belinda! So, after all, you love Mr. Vincent—you'll marry Mr. Vincent!"

"I never said so," replied Belinda: "you have not read my letter. Oh, Lady Delacour, at this instant—you should not reproach me."

"I did you injustice," cried Lady Delacour, as she now looked at Belinda's letter. "Send it—send it—you have said the very thing you ought; and now sit down with me to this packet of Clarence Hervey's—be just to him, as you are to Mr. Vincent, that's all I ask—give him a fair hearing:—now for it."

CHAPTER XXVI — VIRGINIA

Clarence Hervey's packet contained a history of his connexion with Virginia St. Pierre.

To save our hero from the charge of egotism, we shall relate the principal circumstances in the third person.

It was about a year before he had seen Belinda that Clarence Hervey returned from his travels; he had been in France just before the Revolution, when luxury and dissipation were at their height in Paris, and when a universal spirit of licentious gallantry prevailed. Some circumstances in which he was personally interested disgusted him strongly with the Parisian belles; he felt that women who were full of vanity, affectation, and artifice, whose tastes were perverted, and whose feelings were depraved, were equally incapable of conferring or enjoying real happiness. Whilst this conviction was full in his mind, he read the works of Rousseau: this eloquent writer's sense made its full impression upon Clarence's understanding, and his declamations produced more than their just effect upon an imagination naturally ardent. He was charmed with the picture of Sophia, when contrasted with the characters of the women of the world with whom he had been disgusted; and he formed the romantic project of educating a wife for himself. Full of this idea, he returned to England, determined to carry his scheme immediately into execution, but was some time delayed by the difficulty of finding a proper object for his purpose: it was easy to meet with beauty in distress, and ignorance in poverty; but it was difficult to find simplicity without vulgarity, ingenuity without cunning, or even ignorance without prejudice; it was difficult to meet with an understanding totally uncultivated, yet likely to reward the labour of late instruction; a heart wholly unpractised, yet full of sensibility, capable of all the enthusiasm of passion, the delicacy of sentiment, and the firmness of rational constancy. It is not wonderful that Mr. Hervey, with such high expectations, should not immediately find them gratified. Disappointed in his first search, he did not, however, relinquish his design; and at length, by accident, he discovered, or thought that he discovered, an object formed expressly for his purpose.

One fine evening in autumn, as he was riding through the New Forest, charmed with the picturesque beauties of the place, he turned out of the beaten road, and struck into a fresh track, which he pursued with increasing delight, till the setting sun reminded him that it was necessary to postpone his farther reflections on forest scenery, and that it was time to think of finding his way out of the wood. He was now in the most retired part of the forest, and he saw no path to direct him; but, as he stopped to consider which way he should turn, a dog sprang from a thicket, barking furiously at his horse: his horse was high-spirited, but he was master of him, and he obliged the animal to stand quietly till the dog, having barked himself hoarse, retreated of his own accord. Clarence watched to see which way he would go, and followed him, in hopes of meeting with the person to whom he belonged: he kept his guide in sight, till he came into a beautiful glade, in the midst of which was a neat but very small cottage, with numerous beehives in the garden, surrounded by a profusion of rose-trees which were in full blow. This cultivated spot was strikingly contrasted with the wildness of the surrounding scenery. As he came nearer, Mr. Hervey saw a young girl watering the rose-trees, which grew round the cottage, and an old woman beside her filling a basket with the flowers. The old woman was like most other old women, except that she had a remarkably benevolent countenance, and an air that had been acquired in better days; but the young girl did not appear to Clarence like any other young girl that he had ever seen. The setting sun shone upon her countenance, the wind blew aside the ringlets of her light hair, and the blush of modesty overspread her cheeks when she looked up at the stranger. In her large blue eyes there was an expression of artless sensibility with which Mr. Hervey was so powerfully struck that he remained for some moments silent, totally forgetting that he came to ask his way out of the forest. His horse had made so little noise upon the soft grass, that he was within a few yards of them before he was perceived by the old woman. As soon as she saw him, she turned abruptly to the young girl, put the basket of roses into her hand, and bid her carry them into the house. As she passed him, the girl, with a sweet innocent smile, held up the basket to Clarence, and offered him one of the roses.

"Go in, Rachell—go in, child," said the old woman, in so loud and severe a tone, that both Rachel and Mr. Hervey started; the basket was overturned, and the roses all scattered upon the grass. Clarence, though he attempted some apology, was by no means concerned for the accident, as it detained Rachel some instants longer to collect her flowers, and gave him an opportunity of admiring her finely shaped hands and arms, and the ease and natural grace of her motions.

"Go in, Rachel," repeated the old woman, in a still more severe tone; "leave the roses there—I can pick them up as well as you, child—go in."

The girl looked at the old woman with astonishment, her eyes filled with tears, and throwing down the roses that she held in her hand, she said, "I am going, grandmother." The door closed after her before Clarence recollected himself sufficiently to tell the old lady how he had lost his way, &c. Her severity vanished, as soon as her grand-daughter was safe in the house, and with much readiness she showed him the road for which he inquired.

As soon, however, as it was in his power, he returned thither; for he had taken such good note of the place, that he easily found his way to the spot, which appeared to him a terrestrial paradise. As he descended into the valley, he heard the humming of bees, but he saw no smoke rising from the cottage chimney—no dog barked—no living creature was to be seen—the house door was shut—the window-shutters closed—all was still. The place looked as if it had been deserted by all its inhabitants: the roses had not been watered, many of them had shed their leaves; and a basket half full of dead flowers was left in the middle of the garden. Clarence alighted, and tried the latch of the door, but it was fastened; he listened, but heard no sound; he walked round to the back of the house: a small lattice window was half open, and, as he went toward it, he thought he heard a low moaning voice; he gently pulled aside the curtain, and peeped in at the window. The room was darkened, his eyes had been dazzled by the sun, so that he could not, at first, see any object distinctly; but he heard the moaning repeated at intervals, and a soft voice at last said—

"Oh, speak to me!—speak to me once again—only once—only once again, speak to me!"

The voice came from a corner of the room, to which he had not yet turned his eyes: and as he drew aside more of the curtain, to let in more light, a figure started up from the side of a bed, at which she had been kneeling, and he saw the beautiful young girl, with her hair all dishevelled, and the strongest expression of grief in her countenance. He asked if he could do her any service. She beckoned to him to come in, and then, pointing to the bed, on which the old woman was stretched, said—

"She cannot speak to me—she cannot move one side—she has been so these three days—but she is not dead—she is not dead!"

The poor creature had been struck with the palsy. As Clarence went close to the bed, she opened her eyes, and fixing them upon him, she stretched out her withered hand, caught fast hold of her grand-daughter, and then raising herself, with a violent effort, she pronounced the word "Begone!" Her face grew black, her features convulsed, and she sunk down again in her bed, without power of utterance. Clarence left the house instantly, mounted his horse, and galloped to the next town for medical assistance. The poor woman was so far recovered by a skilful apothecary, that she could, in a few days, articulate so as to be understood. She knew that her end was approaching fast, and seemed piously resigned to her fate. Mr. Hervey went constantly to see her; but, though grateful to him for his humanity, and for the assistance he had procured for her, yet she appeared agitated when he was in the room, and frequently looked at him and at her grand-daughter with uncommon anxiety. At last, she whispered something to the girl, who immediately left the room; and she then beckoned to him to come closer to the arm-chair, in which she was seated.

"May be, sir," said she, "you thought me out of my right mind the day when I was lying on that bed, and said to you in such a peremptory tone, 'Begone!'—It was all I could say then; and, in truth, I cannot speak quite plain yet; nor ever shall again. But God's will be done. I had only one thing to say to you, sir, about that poor girl of mine—"

Clarence listened to her with eagerness. She paused, and then laying her cold hand upon his, she looked up earnestly in his face, and continued, "You are a fine young gentleman, and you look like a good gentleman; but so did the man who broke the heart of her poor mother. Her mother was carried off from a boarding-school, when she was scarcely sixteen, by a wretch, who, after privately marrying her, would not own his marriage, stayed with her but two years, then went abroad, left his wife and his infant, and has never been heard of since. My daughter died of a broken heart. Rachel was then between three and four years old; a beautiful child. God forgive her father!—God's will be done!"—She paused to subdue her emotion, and then, with some difficulty, proceeded.

"My only comfort is, I have bred Rachel up in innocence; I never sent her to a boarding-school. No, no; from the moment of her birth till now, I have kept her under my own eye. In this cottage she has lived with me, away from all the world. You are the first man she ever spoke to; the first man who ever was within these doors. She is innocence itself!—Oh, sir, as you hope for mercy when you are as I am now, spare the innocence of that poor child!—Never, never come here after her, when I am dead and gone! Consider, she is but a child, sir. God never made a better creature. Oh, promise me you will not be the ruin of my sweet innocent girl, and I shall die in peace!"

Clarence Hervey was touched. He instantly made the promise required of him; and, as nothing less would satisfy the poor dying woman, confirmed it by a solemn oath.

"Now I am easy," said she, "quite easy; and may God bless you for it! In the village here, there is a Mrs. Smith, a good farmer's wife, who knows us well; she will see to have me decently buried, and then has promised to sell all the little I have for my girl, and to take care of her. And you'll never come near her more?"

"I did not promise that," said Hervey.

The old woman again looked much disturbed.

"Ah, good young gentleman!" said she, "take my advice; it will be best for you both. If you see her again, you will love her, sir—you can't help it; and if she sees you—poor thing, how innocently she smiled when she gave you the rose!—oh, sir, never come near her when I am gone! It is too late for me now to get her out of your way. This night, I'm sure, will be my last in this world—oh, promise me you will never come here again!"

"After the oath I have taken," replied Clarence, "that promise would be unnecessary. Trust to my honour."

"Honour! Oh, that was the word the gentleman said that betrayed her poor mother, and left her afterwards to die.'—Oh, sir, sir—"

The violent emotion that she felt was too much for her—she fell back exhausted—never spoke more—and an hour afterwards she expired in the arms of her grand-daughter. The poor girl could not believe that she had breathed her last. She made a sign to the surgeon, and to Clarence Hervey, who stood beside her, to be silent; and listened, fancying that the corpse would breathe again. Then she kissed her cold lips, and the shrivelled cheeks, and the eyelids that were closed for ever. She warmed the dead fingers with her breath—she raised the heavy arm, and when it fell she perceived there was no hope: she threw herself upon her knees:—"She is dead!" she exclaimed; "and she has died without giving me her blessing! She can never bless me again."

They took her into the air, and Clarence Hervey sprinkled water upon her face. It was a fine night, and the fresh air soon brought her to her senses. He then said that he would leave her to the care of the surgeon, and ride to the village in search of that Mrs. Smith who had promised to be her friend.

"And so you are going away from me, too?" said she; and she burst into tears. At the sight of these tears Clarence turned away, and hurried from her. He sent the woman from the village, but returned no more that night.

Her simplicity, sensibility, and, perhaps more than he was aware, her beauty, had pleased and touched him extremely. The idea of attaching a perfectly pure, disinterested, unpractised heart, was delightful to his imagination: the cultivation of her understanding, he thought, would be an easy and a pleasing task: all difficulties vanished before his sanguine hopes.

"Sensibility," said he to himself, "is the parent of great talents and great virtues; and evidently she possesses natural feeling in an uncommon degree: it shall be developed with skill, patience, and delicacy; and I will deserve before I claim my reward."

The next day he returned to the cottage, accompanied by an elderly lady, a Mrs. Ormond; the same lady who afterward, to Marriott's prejudiced eyes, had appeared more like a dragon than any thing else, but who, to this simple, unsuspicious girl, seemed like what she really was, a truly good-natured, benevolent woman. She consented, most readily, to put herself under the protection of Mrs. Ormond, "provided Mrs. Smith would give her leave." There was no difficulty in persuading Mrs. Smith that it was for her advantage. Mrs. Smith, who was a plain farmer's wife, told all that she knew of Rachel's history; but all that she knew was little. She had heard only hints at odd times from the old woman: these agreed perfectly with what Mr. Hervey had already heard.

"The old gentlewoman," said Mrs. Smith, "as I believe I should call her by rights, has lived in the forest there, where you found her, these many a year—she earned her subsistence by tending bees and making rose-water—she was a good soul, but very particular, especially about her grand-daughter, which, considering all things, one cannot blame her for. She often told me she would never put Rachel to a boarding-school, which I approved, seeing she had no fortune; and it is the ruin of girls, to my mind, to be bred above their means—as it was of her mother, sir. Then she would never teach Rachel to write, for fear she should take to scrawling nonsense of love-letters, as her mother did before her. Now, sir, this I approved too, for I don't much mind about book-learning myself; and I even thought it would have been as well if the girl had not learnt to read; but that she did learn, and was always fond of, and I'm sure it was more plague than use too to her grandmother, for she was as particular about the books that the girl was to read as about all the rest. She went farther than all that, sir, for she never would let the girl speak to a man—not a man ever entered the doors of the house."

"So she told me."

"And she told you true enough. But there, I thought, she was quite wrong; for seeing the girl must, some time or other, speak to men, where was the use of her not learning to do it properly?—Lord, ma'am," continued Mrs. Smith, addressing herself to Mrs. Ormond, "Lord, ma'am, though it is a sin to be remembering so much of the particularities of the dead, I must say there never was an old lady who had more scrupulosities than the deceased. I verily thought, one day, she would have gone into fits about a picture of a man, that Rachel lit upon by accident, as if a picture had any sense to hurt a body! Now if it had been one of your naked pictures, there might have been some delicacy in her dislike to it; but it was no such thing, but a very proper picture.

"A picture, ma'am, of a young sea-officer, in his full uniform—quite proper, ma'am. It was his mother that left it with me, and I had it always in my own room, and the girl saw it, and was mightily taken with it, being the first thing of the kind she had ever lit upon, and the old lady comes in, and took on, till I verily thought she was crazed. Lord! I really could not but laugh; but I checked myself, when the poor old soul's eyes filled with tears, which made me know she was thinking of her daughter that was dead. When I thought on the cause of her particularity about Rachel, I could not laugh any more at her strangeness.

"I promised the good lady that day, in case of her death, to take care of her grand-daughter; and I thought in my own mind that, in time to come, if one of my boys should take a fancy to her, I should make no objections, because she was always a good, modest-behaved girl; and, I'm sure, would make a good wife, though too delicate for hard country work; but, as it pleases God to send you, madam, and the good gentleman, to take the charge of her off my hands, I am content it should be so, and I will sell every thing here for her honestly, and bring it to you, madam, for poor Rachel."

There was nothing that Rachel was anxious to carry away with her but a little bullfinch, of which she was very fond. One, and but one, circumstance about Rachel stopped the current of Clarence Hervey's imagination, and this, consequently, was excessively disagreeable to him—her name: the name of Rachel he could not endure, and he thought it so unsuited to her, that he could scarcely believe it belonged to her. He consequently resolved to change it as soon as possible. The first time that he beheld her, he was struck with the idea that she resembled the description of Virginia in M. de St. Pierre's celebrated romance; and by this name he always called her, from the hour that she quitted her cottage.

Mrs. Ormond, the lady whom he had engaged to take care of his Virginia, was a widow, the mother of a gentleman who had been his tutor at college. Her son died, and left her in such narrow circumstances, that she was obliged to apply to her friends for pecuniary assistance.

Mr. Hervey had been liberal in his contributions; from his childhood he had known her worth, and her attachment to him was blended with the most profound respect. She was not a woman of superior abilities, or of much information; but her excellent temper and gentle disposition won affection, though she had not any talents to excite admiration. Mr. Hervey had perfect confidence in her integrity; he believed that she would exactly comply with his directions, and he thought that her want of literature and ingenuity could easily be supplied by his own care and instructions. He took a house for her and his fair pupil at Windsor, and he exacted a solemn promise that she would neither receive nor pay any visits. Virginia was thus secluded from all intercourse with the world: she saw no one but Mrs. Ormond, Clarence Hervey, and Mr. Moreton, an elderly clergyman, whom Mr. Hervey engaged to attend every Sunday to read prayers for them at home. Virginia never expressed the slightest curiosity to see any other persons, or any thing beyond the walls of the garden that belonged to the house in which she lived; her present retirement was not greater than that to which she had long been accustomed, and consequently she did not feel her seclusion from the world as any restraint: with the circumstances that were altered in her situation she seemed neither to be dazzled nor charmed; the objects of convenience or luxury that were new to her she looked upon with indifference; but with any thing that reminded her of her former way of life, and of her grandmother's cottage, she was delighted.

One day Mr. Hervey asked her, whether she should like better to return to that cottage, or to remain where she was? He trembled for her answer. She innocently replied, "I should like best to go back to the cottage, if you would go with me—but I would rather stay here with you than live there without you."

Clarence was touched and flattered by this artless answer, and for some time he discovered every day fresh indications, as he thought, of virtue and abilities in his charming pupil. Her indifference to objects of show and ornament appeared to him an indisputable proof of her magnanimity, and of the superiority of her unprejudiced mind. What a difference, thought he, between this child of nature and the frivolous, sophisticated slaves of art!

To try and prove the simplicity of her taste, and the purity of her mind, he once presented to her a pair of diamond earrings and a moss rosebud, and asked her to take whichever she liked best. She eagerly snatched the rose, crying, "Oh! it puts me in mind of the cottage:—how sweet it smells!"

She placed it in her bosom, and then, looking at the diamonds, said, "They are pretty, sparkling things— what are they? of what use are they?" and she looked with more curiosity and admiration at the manner in which the earring shut and opened than at the diamonds. Clarence was charmed with her. When Mrs. Ormond told her that these things were to hang in her ears, she laughed and said, "How! how can I make them hang?"

"Have you never observed that I wear earrings?" said Mrs. Ormond.

"Ay! but yours are not like these, and—let me look—I never saw how you fastened them—let me look— oh! you have holes in your ears; but I have none in mine."

Mrs. Ormond told her that holes could easily be made in her ears, by running a steel pin through them. She shrunk back, defending her ear with one hand, and pushing the diamonds from her with the other, exclaiming, "Oh, no, no!—unless," added she, changing her tone, and turning to Clarence, "unless you wish it:—if you bid me, I will."

Clarence was scarcely master of himself at this instant; and it was with the utmost difficulty that he could reply to her with that dispassionate calmness which became his situation and hers. And yet there was more of ignorance and timidity, perhaps, than of sound sense or philosophy in Virginia's indifference to diamonds; she did not consider them as ornaments that would confer distinction upon their possessor, because she was ignorant of the value affixed to them by society. Isolated in the world, she had no excitements to the love of finery, no competition, no means of comparison, or opportunities of display; diamonds were consequently as useless to her as guineas were to Robinson Crusoe on his desert island. It could not justly be said that he was free from avarice, because he set no value on the gold; or that she was free from vanity, because she rejected the diamonds. These reflections could not possibly have escaped a man of Clarence Hervey's abilities, had he not been engaged in defence of a favourite system of education, or if his pupil had not been quite so handsome. Virginia's absolute ignorance of the world frequently gave an air of originality to her most trivial observations, which made her appear at once interesting and entertaining. All her ideas of happiness were confined to the life she had led during her childhood; and as she had accidentally lived in a beautiful situation in the New Forest, she appeared to have an instinctive taste for the beauties of nature, and for what we call the picturesque. This taste Mr. Hervey perceived, whenever he showed her prints and drawings, and it was a fresh source of delight and self-complacency to him. All that was amiable or estimable in Virginia had a double charm, from the secret sense of his penetration, in having discovered and appreciated the treasure. The affections of this innocent girl had no object but himself and Mrs. Ormond, and they were strong, perhaps, in proportion as they were concentrated. The artless familiarity of her manner, and her unsuspicious confidence, amounting almost to credulity, had irresistible power over Mr. Hervey's mind; he felt them as appeals at once to his tenderness and his generosity. He treated her with the utmost delicacy, and his oath was never absent from his mind: but he felt proudly convinced, that if he had not been bound by any such solemn engagement, no temptation could have made him deceive and betray confiding innocence.

Conscious that his views were honourable, anticipating the generous pleasure he should have in showing his superiority to all mercenary considerations and worldly prejudices, in the choice of a wife, he indulged, with a species of pride, his increasing attachment to Virginia; but he was not sensible of the rapid progress of the passion, till he was suddenly awakened by a few simple observations of Mrs. Ormond.

"This is Virginia's birthday—she tells me she is seventeen to-day."

"Seventeen!—is she only seventeen?" cried Clarence, with a mixture of surprise and disappointment in his countenance—"Only seventeen! Why she is but a child still."

"Quite a child," said Mrs. Ormond; "and so much the better."

"So much the worse, I think," said Clarence. "But are you sure she's only seventeen?—she must be mistaken—she must be eighteen, at least."

"God forbid!"

"God forbid!—Why, Mrs. Ormond?"

"Because, you know, we have a year more before us."

"That may be a very satisfactory prospect to you," said Mr. Hervey, smiling.

"And to you, surely," said Mrs. Ormond; "for, I suppose, you would be glad that your wife should, at least, know the common things that every body knows."

"As to that," said Clarence, "I should be glad that my wife were ignorant of what every body knows. Nothing is so tiresome to a man of any taste or abilities as what every body knows. I am rather desirous to have a wife who has an uncommon than a common understanding."

"But you would choose, would not you," said Mrs. Ormond, hesitating with an air of great deference, "that your wife should know how to write?"

"To be sure," replied Clarence, colouring. "Does not Virginia know how to write?"

"How should she?" said Mrs. Ormond: "it is no fault of hers, poor girl—she was never taught. You know it was her grandmother's notion that she should not learn to write, lest she should write love-letters."

"But you promised that she should be taught to write, and I trusted to you, Mrs. Ormond."

"She has been here only two months, and all that time, I am sure, I have done every thing in my power; but when a person comes to be sixteen or seventeen, it is up-hill work."

"I will teach her myself," cried Clarence: "I am sure she may be taught any thing."

"By you," said Mrs. Ormond, smiling; "but not by me."

"You have no doubts of her capacity, surely?"

"I am no judge of capacity, especially of the capacity of those I love; and I am grown very fond of Virginia; she is a charming, open-hearted, simple, affectionate creature. I rather think it is from indolence that she does not learn, and not from want of abilities."

"All indolence arises from want of excitement," said Clarence: "if she had proper motives, she would conquer her indolence."

"Why, I dare say, if I were to tell her that she would never have a letter from Mr. Hervey till she is able to write an answer, she would learn to write very expeditiously; but I thought that would not be a proper motive, because you forbade me to tell her your future views. And indeed it would be highly imprudent, on your account, as well as hers, to give her any hint of that kind: because you might change your mind, before she's old enough for you to think of her seriously, and then you would not know what to do with her; and after entertaining hopes of becoming your wife, she would be miserable, I am sure, with that affectionate tender heart of hers, if you were to leave her. Now that she knows nothing of the matter, we are all safe, and as we should be."

Though Clarence Hervey did not at this time foresee any great probability of his changing his mind, yet he felt the good sense and justice of Mrs. Ormond's suggestions; and he was alarmed to perceive that his mind had been so intoxicated as to suffer such obvious reflections to escape his attention. Mrs. Ormond, a woman whom he had been accustomed to consider as far his inferior in capacity, he now felt was superior to him in prudence, merely because she was undisturbed by passion. He resolved to master his own mind: to consider that it was not a mistress, but a wife he wanted in Virginia; that a wife without capacity or without literature could never be a companion suited to him, let her beauty or sensibility be ever so exquisite and captivating. The happiness of his life and of hers were at stake, and every motive of prudence and delicacy called upon him to command his affections. He was, however, still sanguine in his expectations from Virginia's understanding, and from his own power of developing her capacity. He made several attempts, with the greatest skill and patience; and his fair pupil, though she did not by any means equal his hopes, astonished Mrs. Ormond by her comparatively rapid progress.

"I always believed that you could make her any thing you pleased," said she. "You are a tutor who can work miracles with Virginia."

"I see no miracles," replied Clarence; "I am conscious of no such power. I should be sorry to possess any such influence, until I am sure that it would be for our mutual happiness."

Mr. Hervey then conjured Mrs. Ormond, by all her attachment to him and to her pupil, never to give Virginia the most distant idea that he had any intentions of making her his wife. She promised to do all that was in her power to keep this secret, but she could not help observing that it had already been betrayed, as plainly as looks could speak, by Mr. Hervey himself. Clarence in vain endeavoured to exculpate himself from this charge: Mrs. Ormond brought to his recollection so many instances of his indiscretion, that it was substantiated even in his own judgment, and he was amazed to find that all the time he had put so much constraint upon his inclinations, he had, nevertheless, so obviously betrayed them. His surprise, however, was at this time unmixed with any painful regret; he did not foresee the probability that he should change his mind; and notwithstanding Mrs. Ormond assured him that Virginia's sensibility had increased, he was persuaded that she was mistaken, and that his pupil's heart and imagination were yet untouched. The innocent openness with which she expressed her affection for him confirmed him, he said, in his opinion. To do him justice, Clarence had none of the presumption which too often characterizes men who have been successful, as it is called, with the fair sex. His acquaintance with women had increased his persuasion that it is difficult to excite genuine love in the heart; and with respect to himself, he was upon this subject astonishingly incredulous. It was scarcely possible to convince him that he was beloved.

Mrs. Ormond, piqued upon this subject, determined to ascertain more decisively her pupil's sentiments.

"My dear," said she, one day to Virginia, who was feeding her bullfinch, "I do believe you are fonder of that bird than of any thing in the world—fonder of it, I am sure, than of me."

"Oh! you cannot think so," said Virginia, with an affectionate smile.

"Well! fonder than you are of Mr. Hervey, you will allow, at least?"

"No, indeed!" cried she, eagerly: "how can you think me so foolish, so childish, so ungrateful, as to prefer a little worthless bird to him—" (the bullfinch began to sing so loud at this instant, that her enthusiastic speech was stopped). "My pretty bird," said she, as it perched upon her hand, "I love you very much, but if Mr. Hervey were to ask it, to wish it, I would open that window, and let you fly; yes, and bid you fly away far from me for ever. Perhaps he does wish it?—Does he?—Did he tell you so?" cried she, looking earnestly in Mrs. Ormond's face, as she moved towards the window.

Mrs. Ormond put her hand upon the sash, as Virginia was going to throw it up—

"Gently, gently, my love—whither is your imagination carrying you?"

"I thought something by your look," said Virginia, blushing.

"And I thought something, my dear Virginia," said Mrs. Ormond, smiling.

"What did you think?—What could you think?"

"I cannot—I mean, I would rather not at present tell you. But do not look so grave; I will tell you some time or other, if you cannot guess."

Virginia was silent, and stood abashed.

"I am sure, my sweet girl," said Mrs. Ormond, "I do not mean, by any thing I said, to confuse or blame you. It is very natural that you should be grateful to Mr. Hervey, and that you should admire, and, to a certain degree, love him."

Virginia looked up delighted, yet with some hesitation in her manner.

"He is, indeed," said Mrs. Ormond, "one of the first of human beings: such even I have always thought him; and I am sure I like you the better, my dear, for your sensibility," said she, kissing Virginia as she spoke; "only we must take care of it, or this tenderness might go too far."

"How so?" said Virginia, returning her caresses with fondness: "can I love you and Mr. Hervey too much?"

"Not me."

"Nor him, I'm sure—he is so good, so very good! I am afraid that I do not love him enough," said she, sighing. "I love him enough when he is absent, but not when he is present. When he is near I feel a sort of fear mixed with my love. I wish to please him very much, but I should not quite like that he should show his love for me as you do—as you did just now."

"My dear, it would not be proper that he should; you are quite right not to wish it."

"Am I? I was afraid that it was a sign of my not liking him as much as I ought."

"Ah, my poor child! you love him full as much as you ought."

"Do you think so? I am glad of it," said Virginia, with a look of such confiding simplicity, that her friend was touched to the heart.

"I do think so, my love," said Mrs. Ormond; "and I hope I shall never be sorry for it, nor you either. But it is not proper that we should say any more upon this subject now. Where are your drawings? Where is your writing? My dear, we must get forward with these things as fast as we can. That is the way to please Mr. Hervey, I can tell you."

Confirmed by this conversation in her own opinion, Mrs. Ormond was satisfied. From delicacy to her pupil, she did not repeat all that had passed to Mr. Hervey, resolving to wait till the proper moment. "She is too young and too childish for him to think of marrying her yet, for a year or two," thought she; "and it is better to repress her sensibility till her education is more finished; by that time Mr. Hervey will find out his mistake."

In the mean time she could not help thinking that he was blind, for he continued steady in his belief of Virginia's indifference.

To dissipate his own mind, and to give time for the development of hers, he now, according to his resolution, left his pupil to the care of Mrs. Ormond, and mixed as much as possible in gay and fashionable company. It was at this period that he renewed his acquaintance with Lady Delacour, whom he had seen and admired before he went abroad. He found that his gallantry, on the famous day of the battle between the turkeys and pigs, was still remembered with gratitude by her ladyship; she received him with marked courtesy, and he soon became a constant visitor at her house. Her wit entertained, her eloquence charmed him, and he followed, admired, and gallanted her, without scruple, for he considered her merely as a coquette, who preferred the glory of conquest to the security of reputation. With such a woman he thought he could amuse himself without danger, and he every where appeared the foremost in the public train of her ladyship's admirers. He soon discovered, however, that her talents were far superior to what are necessary for playing the part of a fine lady; his visits became more and more agreeable to him, and he was glad to feel, that, by dividing his attention, his passion for Virginia insensibly diminished, or, as he said to himself, became more reasonable. In conversing with Lady Delacour, his faculties were always called into full play; in talking to Virginia, his understanding was passive: he perceived that a large proportion of his intellectual powers, and of his knowledge, was absolutely useless to him in her company; and this did not raise her either in his love or esteem. Her simplicity and naïvete, however, sometimes relieved him, after he had been fatigued by the extravagant gaiety and glare of her ladyship's manners; and he reflected that the coquetry which amused him in an acquaintance would be odious in a wife: the perfect innocence of Virginia promised security to his domestic happiness, and he did not change his views, though he was less eager for the period of their accomplishment. "I cannot expect every thing that is desirable," said he to himself: "a more brilliant character than Virginia's would excite my admiration, but could not command my confidence."

It was whilst his mind was in this situation that he became acquainted with Belinda. At first, the idea of her having been educated by the match-making Mrs. Stanhope prejudiced him against her; but as he had opportunities of observing her conduct, this prepossession was conquered, and when she had secured his esteem, he could no longer resist her power over his heart. In comparison with Belinda, Virginia appeared to him but an insipid, though innocent child: the one he found was his equal, the other his inferior; the one he saw could be a companion, a friend to him for life, the other would merely be his pupil, or his plaything. Belinda had cultivated taste, an active understanding, a knowledge of literature, the power and the habit of conducting herself; Virginia was ignorant and indolent, she had few ideas, and no wish to extend her knowledge; she was so entirely unacquainted with the world, that it was absolutely impossible she could conduct herself with that discretion, which must be the combined result of reasoning and experience. Mr. Hervey had felt gratuitous confidence in Virginia's innocence; but on Belinda's prudence, which he had opportunities of seeing tried, he gradually learned to feel a different and a higher species of reliance, which it is neither in our power to bestow nor to refuse. The virtues of Virginia sprang from sentiment; those of Belinda from reason.

Clarence, whilst he made all these comparisons, became every day more wisely and more fondly attached to Belinda; and at length he became desirous to change the nature of his connexion with Virginia, and to appear to her only in the light of a friend or a benefactor. He thought of giving her a suitable fortune and of leaving her under the care of Mrs. Ormond, till some method of establishing her in the world should occur. Unfortunately, just at the time when Mr. Hervey formed this plan, and before it was communicated to Mrs. Ormond, difficulties arose which prevented him from putting it into execution.

Whilst he had been engaged in the gay world at Lady Delacour's, his pupil had necessarily been left much to the management of Mrs. Ormond. This lady, with the best possible intentions, had not that reach of mind and variety of resource necessary to direct the exquisite sensibility and ardent imagination of Virginia: the solitude in which she lived added to the difficulty of the task. Without companions to interest her social affections, without real objects to occupy her senses and understanding, Virginia's mind was either perfectly indolent, or exalted by romantic views, and visionary ideas of happiness. As she had never seen any thing of society, all her notions were drawn from books; the severe restrictions which her grandmother had early laid upon the choice of these seemed to have awakened her curiosity, and to have increased her appetite for books—it was insatiable. Reading, indeed, was now almost her only pleasure; for Mrs. Ormond's conversation was seldom entertaining, and Virginia had no longer those occupations which filled a portion of her day at the cottage.

Mr. Hervey had cautioned Mrs. Ormond against putting common novels into her hands, but he made no objection to romances: these, he thought, breathed a spirit favourable to female virtue, exalted the respect for chastity, and inspired enthusiastic admiration of honour, generosity, truth, and all the noble qualities which dignify human nature. Virginia devoured these romances with the greatest eagerness; and Mrs. Ormond, who found her a prey to ennui when her fancy was not amused, indulged her taste; yet she strongly suspected that they contributed to increase her passion for the only man who could, in her imagination, represent a hero.

One night Virginia found, in Mrs. Ormond's room, a volume of St. Pierre's Paul and Virginia. She knew that her own name had been taken from this romance; Mr. Hervey had her picture painted in this character; and these circumstances strongly excited her curiosity to read the book. Mrs. Ormond could not refuse to let her have it; for, though it was not an ancient romance, it did not exactly come under the description of a common novel, and Mr. Hervey was not at hand to give his advice. Virginia sat down instantly to her volume, and never stirred from the spot till she had nearly finished it.

"What is it that strikes your fancy so much? What are you considering so deeply, my love?" said Mrs. Ormond, observing, that she seemed lost in thought. "Let us see, my dear," continued she, offering to take the book, which hung from her hand. Virginia started from her reverie, but held the volume fast.—"Will not you let me read along with you?" said Mrs. Ormond. "Won't you let me share your pleasure?"

"It was not pleasure that I felt, I believe," said Virginia. "I would rather you should not see just that particular part that I was reading; and yet, if you desire it," added she, resigning the book reluctantly.

"What can make you so much afraid of me, my sweet girl?"

"I am not afraid of you—but—of myself," said Virginia, sighing.

Mrs. Ormond read the following passage:

"She thought of Paul's friendship, more pure than the waters of the fountain, stronger than the united palms, and sweeter than the perfume of flowers; and these images, in night and in solitude, gave double force to the passion which she nourished in her heart. She suddenly left the dangerous shades, and went to her mother, to seek protection against herself. She wished to reveal her distress to her; she pressed her hands, and the name of Paul was on her lips; but the oppression of her heart took away all utterance, and, laying her head upon her mother's bosom, she only wept."

"And am I not a mother to you, my beloved Virginia?" said Mrs. Ormond. "Though I cannot express my affection in such charming language as this, yet, believe me, no mother was ever fonder of a child."

Virginia threw her arms round Mrs. Ormond, and laid her head upon her friend's bosom, as if she wished to realize the illusion, and to be the Virginia of whom she had been reading.

"I know all you think, and all you feel: I know," whispered Mrs. Ormond, "the name that is on your lips."

"No, indeed, you do not; you cannot," cried Virginia, suddenly raising her head, and looking up in Mrs. Ormond's face, with surprise and timidity: "how could you possibly know all my thoughts and feelings? I never told them to you; for, indeed, I have only confused ideas floating in my imagination from the books I have been reading. I do not distinctly know my own feelings."

"This is all very natural, and a proof of your perfect innocence and simplicity, my child. But why did the passage you were reading just now strike you so much?"

"I was only considering," said Virginia, "whether it was the description of—love."

"And your heart told you that it was?"

"I don't know," said she, sighing. "But of this I am certain, that I had not the name, which you were thinking of, upon my lips."

Ah! thought Mrs. Ormond, she has not forgotten how I checked her sensibility some time ago. Poor girl! she is become afraid of me, and I have taught her to dissemble; but she betrays herself every moment.

"My dear," said Mrs. Ormond, "you need not fear me—I cannot blame you: in your situation, it is impossible that you could help loving Mr. Hervey."

"Is it?"

"Yes; quite impossible. So do not blame yourself for it."

"No, I do not blame myself for that. I only blame myself for not loving him enough, as I told you once before."

"Yes, my dear; and the oftener you tell me so, the more I am convinced of your affection. It is one of the strongest symptoms of love, that we are unconscious of its extent. We fancy that we can never do too much for the beloved object."

"That is exactly what I feel about Mr. Hervey."

"That we can never love him enough."

"Ah! that is precisely what I feel for Mr. Hervey."

"And what you ought—I mean, what it is natural you should feel; and what he will himself, I hope, indeed I dare say, some time or other wish, and be glad that you should feel."

"Some time or other! Does not he wish it now?"

"I—he—my dear, what a question is that? And how shall I answer it? We must judge of what he feels by what he expresses: when he expresses love for you, it will then be the time to show yours for him."

"He has always expressed love for me, I think," said Virginia—"always, till lately," continued she; "but lately he has been away so much, and when he comes home, he does not look so well pleased; so that I was afraid he was angry with me, and that he thought me ungrateful."

"Oh, my love, do not torment yourself with these vain fears! And yet I know that you cannot help it."

"Since you are so kind, so very kind to me," said Virginia, "I will tell you all my fears and doubts. But it is late—there! the clock struck one. I will not keep you up."

"I am not at all sleepy," said the indulgent Mrs. Ormond.

"Nor I," said Virginia,

"Now, then," said Mrs. Ormond, "for these doubts and fears."

"I was afraid that, perhaps, Mr. Hervey would be angry if he knew that I thought of any thing in the world but him."

"Of what else do you think?—Of nothing else from morning till night, that I can see."

"Ah, then you do not see into my mind. In the daytime often think of those heroes, those charming heroes, that I read of in the books you have given me."

"To be sure you do."

"And is not that wrong? Would not Mr. Hervey be displeased if he knew it?"

"Why should he?"

"Because they are not quite like him. I love some of them better than I do him, and he might think that ungrateful."

How naturally love inspires the idea of jealousy, thought Mrs. Ormond. "My dear," said she, "you carry your ideas of delicacy and gratitude to an extreme; but it is very natural you should: however, you need not be afraid; Mr. Hervey cannot be jealous of those charming heroes, that never existed, though they are not quite like him."

"I am very glad that he would not think me ungrateful—but if he knew that I dream of them sometimes?"

"He would think you dreamed, as all people do, of what they think of in the daytime."

"And he would not be angry? I am very glad of it. But I once saw a picture—"

"I know you did—well," said Mrs. Ormond, "and your grandmother was frightened because it was the picture of a man—hey? If she was not your grandmother, I should say that she was a simpleton. I assure you, Mr. Hervey is not like her, if that is what you mean to ask. He would not be angry at your having seen fifty pictures."

"I am glad of it—but I see it very often in my dreams."

"Well, if you had seen more pictures, you would not see this so often. It was the first you ever saw, and very naturally you remember it, Mr. Hervey would not be angry at that," said Mrs. Ormond, laughing.

"But sometimes, in my dreams, it speaks to me."

"And what does it say?"

"The same sort of things that those heroes I read of say to their mistresses."

"And do you never, in your dreams, hear Mr. Hervey say this sort of things?"

"No."

"And do you never see Mr. Hervey in these dreams?"

"Sometimes; but he does not speak to me; he does not look at me with the same sort of tenderness, and he does not throw himself at my feet."

"No; because he has never done all this in reality."

"No; and I wonder how I come to dream of such things."

"So do I; but you have read and thought of them, it is plain. Now go to sleep, there's my good girl; that is the best thing you can do at present—go to sleep."

It was not long after this conversation that Sir Philip Baddely and Mr. Rochfort scaled the garden wall, to obtain a sight of Clarence Hervey's mistress. Virginia was astonished, terrified, and disgusted, by their appearance; they seemed to her a species of animals for which she had no name, and of which she had no prototype in her imagination. That they were men she saw; but they were clearly not Clarence Herveys: they bore still less resemblance to the courteous knights of chivalry. Their language was so different from any of the books she had read, and any of the conversations she had heard, that they were scarcely intelligible. After they had forced themselves into her presence, they did not scruple to address her in the most unceremonious manner. Amongst other rude things, they said, "Damme, my pretty dear, you cannot love the man that keeps you prisoner in this manner, hey? Damme, you'd better come and live with one of us. You can't love this tyrant of a fellow."

"He is not a tyrant—I do love him as much as I detest you," cried Virginia, shrinking from him with looks of horror.

"Damme! good actress! Put her on the stage when he is tired of her. So you won't come with us?—Good bye, till we see you again. You're right, my girl, to be upon your good behaviour; may be you may get him to marry you, child!"

Virginia, upon hearing this speech, turned from the man who insulted her with a degree of haughty indignation, of which her gentle nature had never before appeared capable.

Mrs. Ormond hoped, that after the alarm was over, the circumstance would pass away from her pupil's mind; but on the contrary, it left the most forcible impression. Virginia became silent and melancholy, and whole hours were spent in reverie. Mrs. Ormond imagined, that notwithstanding Virginia's entire ignorance of the world, she had acquired from books sufficient knowledge to be alarmed at the idea of being taken for Clarence Hervey's mistress. She touched upon this subject with much delicacy, and the answers that she received confirmed her opinion. Virginia had been inspired by romances with the most exalted notions of female delicacy and honour! but from her perfect ignorance, these were rather vague ideas than principles of conduct.

"We shall see Mr. Hervey to-morrow; he has written me word that he will come from town, and spend the day with us."

"I shall be ashamed to see him after what has passed," said Virginia.

"You have no cause for shame, my dear; Mr. Hervey will try to discover the persons who insulted you, and he will punish them. They will never return here; you need not fear that. He is willing and able to protect you."

"Yes of that I am sure. But what did that strange man mean, when he said—"

"What, my dear?"

"That, perhaps, Mr. Hervey would marry me."

Virginia pronounced these words with difficulty. Mrs. Ormond was silent, for she was much embarrassed. Virginia having conquered her first difficulty, seemed resolute to obtain an answer.

"You do not speak to me! Will you not tell me, dear Mrs. Ormond," said she, hanging upon her fondly, "what did he mean?"

"What he said, I suppose."

"But he said, that if I behaved well, I might get Mr. Hervey to marry me. What did he mean by that?" said Virginia, in an accent of offended pride.

"He spoke very rudely and improperly; but it is not worth while to think of what he said, or what he meant."

"But, dear Mrs. Ormond, do not go away from me now: I never so much wished to speak to you in my whole life, and you turn away from me."

"Well, my love, well, what would you say?"

"Tell me one thing, only one thing, and you will set my heart at ease. Does Mr. Hervey wish me to be his wife?"

"I cannot tell you that, my dearest Virginia. Time will show us. Perhaps his heart has not yet decided."

"I wish it would decide," said Virginia, sighing deeply; "and I wish that strange man had not told me any thing about the matter; it has made me very unhappy."

She covered her eyes with her hand, but the tears trickled between her fingers, and rolled fast down her arm. Mrs. Ormond, quite overcome by the sight of her distress, was no longer able to keep the secret with which she had been entrusted by Clarence Hervey. And after all, thought she, Virginia will hear it from himself soon. I shall only spare her some unnecessary pain; it is cruel to see her thus, and to keep her in suspense. Besides, her weakness might be her ruin, in his opinion, if it were to extinguish all her energy, and deprive her of the very power of pleasing. How wan she looks, and how heavy are those sleepless eyes! She is not, indeed, in a condition to meet him, when he comes to us to-morrow: if she had some hopes, she would revive and appear with her natural ease and grace.

"My sweet child," said Mrs. Ormond, "I cannot bear to see you so melancholy; consider, Mr. Hervey will be with us to-morrow, and it will give him a great deal of pain to see you so."

"Will it? Then I will try to be very gay."

Mrs. Ormond was so delighted to see Virginia smile, that she could not forbear adding, "The strange man was not wrong in every thing he said; you will, one of these days, be Mr. Hervey's wife."

"That, I am sure," said Virginia, bursting again into tears, "that, I am sure, I do not wish, unless he does."

"He does, he does, my dear—do not let this delicacy of yours, which has been wound up too high, make you miserable. He thought of you, he loved you long and long ago."

"He is very good, too good," said Virginia, sobbing.

"Nay, what is more—for I can keep nothing from you—he has been educating you all this time on purpose for his wife, and he only waits till your education is finished, and till he is sure that you feel no repugnance for him."

"I should be very ungrateful if I felt any repugnance for him," said Virginia; "I feel none."

"Oh, that you need not assure me," said Mrs. Ormond.

"But I do not wish to marry him—I do not wish to marry."

"You are a modest girl to say so; and this modesty will make you ten times more amiable, especially in Mr. Hervey's eyes. Heaven forbid that I should lessen it!"

The next morning Virginia, who always slept in the same room with Mrs. Ormond, wakened her, by crying out in her sleep, with a voice of terror, "Oh, save him!—save Mr. Hervey!—Mr. Hervey!—forgive me! forgive me!"

Mrs. Ormond drew back the curtain, and saw Virginia lying fast asleep; her beautiful face convulsed with agony.

"He's dead!—Mr. Hervey!" cried she, in a voice of exquisite distress: then starting up, and stretching out her arms, she uttered a piercing cry, and awoke.

"My love, you have been dreaming frightfully," said Mrs. Ormond.

"Is it all a dream?" cried Virginia, looking round fearfully.

"All a dream, my dear!" said Mrs. Ormond, taking her hand.

"I am very, very glad of it!—Let me breathe. It was, indeed, a frightful dream!"

"Your hand still trembles," said Mrs. Ormond; "let me put back this hair from your poor face, and you will grow cool, and forget this foolish dream."

"No; I must tell it you. I ought to tell it you. But it was all so confused, I can recollect only some parts of it. First, I remember that I thought I was not myself, but the Virginia that we were reading of the other night; and I was somewhere in the Isle of France. I thought the place was something like the forest where my grandmother's cottage used to be, only there were high mountains and rocks, and cocoa-trees and plantains."

"Such as you saw in the prints of that book?"

"Yes; only beautiful, beautiful beyond description! And it was moonlight, brighter and clearer than any moonlight I ever before had seen; and the air was fresh yet perfumed; and I was seated under the shade of a plane-tree, beside Virginia's fountain."

"Just as you are in your picture?"

"Yes: but Paul was seated beside me."

"Paul!" said Mrs. Ormond, smiling: "that is Mr. Hervey."

"No; not Mr. Hervey's face, though it spoke with his voice—this is what I thought that I must tell you. It was another figure: it seemed a real living person: it knelt at my feet, and spoke to me so kindly, so tenderly; and just as it was going to kiss my hand, Mr. Hervey appeared, and I started terribly, for I was afraid he would be displeased, and that he would think me ungrateful; and he was displeased, and he called me ungrateful Virginia, and frowned, and then I gave him my hand, and then every thing changed, I do not know how suddenly, and I was in a place like the great print of the cathedral, which Mr. Hervey showed me; and there were crowds of people—I was almost stifled. You pulled me on, as I remember; and Mr. Moreton was there, standing upon some steps by what you called the altar; and then we knelt down before him, and Mr. Hervey was putting a ring on my finger; but there came suddenly from the crowd that strange man, who was here the other day, and he dragged me along with him, I don't know how or where, swiftly down precipices, whilst I struggled, and at last fell. Then all changed again, and I was in a magnificent field, covered with cloth of gold, and there were beautiful ladies seated under canopies; and I thought it was a tournament, such as I have read of, only more splendid; and two knights, clad in complete armour, and mounted on fiery steeds, were engaged in single combat; and they fought furiously, and I thought they were fighting for me. One of the knights wore black plumes in his helmet, and the other white; and, as he was passing by me, the vizor of the knight of the white plumes was raised, and I saw it was—"

"Clarence Hervey?" said Mrs. Ormond.

"No; still the same figure that knelt to me; and I wished him to be victorious. And he was victorious. And he unhorsed his adversary, and stood over him with his drawn sword; and then I saw that the knight in the black plumes was Mr. Hervey, and I ran to save him, but I could not. I saw him weltering in his blood, and I heard him say, 'Perfidious, ungrateful Virginia! you are the cause of my death!'—and I screamed, I believe, and that awakened me."

"Well, it is only a dream, my love," said Mrs. Ormond; "Mr. Hervey is safe: get up and dress yourself, and you will soon see him."

"But was it not wrong and ungrateful to wish that the knight in the white plumes should be victorious?"

"Your poor little head is full of nothing but these romances, and love for Mr. Hervey. It is your love for him that makes you fear that he will be jealous. But he is not so simple as you are. He will forgive you for wishing that the knight in the white plumes should be victorious, especially as you did not know that the other knight was Mr. Hervey. Come, my love, dress yourself, and think no more of these foolish dreams, and all will go well."

CHAPTER XXVII — A DISCOVERY

Instead of the open, childish, affectionate familiarity with which Virginia used to meet Clarence Hervey, she now received him with reserved, timid embarrassment. Struck by this change in her manner, and alarmed by the dejection of her spirits, which she vainly strove to conceal, he eagerly inquired, from Mrs. Ormond, into the cause of this alteration.

Mrs. Ormond's answers, and her account of all that had passed during his absence, increased his anxiety. His indignation was roused by the insult which Virginia had been offered by the strangers who had scaled the garden-wall. All his endeavours to discover who they were proved ineffectual; but, lest they should venture to repeat their visit, he removed her from Windsor, and took her directly to Twickenham. Here he stayed with her and Mrs. Ormond some days, to determine, by his own observation, how far the representations that had been made to him were just. Till this period he had been persuaded that Virginia's regard for him was rather that of gratitude than of love; and with this opinion, he thought that he had no reason seriously to reproach himself for the imprudence with which he had betrayed the partiality that he felt for her in the beginning of their acquaintance. He flattered himself that even should she have discerned his intentions, her heart would not repine at any alteration in his sentiments; and if her happiness were uninjured, his reason told him that he was not in honour bound to constancy. The case was now altered. Unwilling as he was to believe, he could no longer doubt. Virginia could neither meet his eyes nor speak to him without a degree of embarrassment which she had not sufficient art to conceal: she trembled whenever he came near her, and if he looked grave, or forbore to take notice of her, she would burst into tears. At other times, contrary to the natural indolence of her character, she would exert herself to please him with surprising energy: she learned every thing that he wished; her capacity seemed suddenly to unfold. For an instant, Clarence flattered himself that both her fits of melancholy and of exertion might arise from a secret desire to see something of that world from which she had been secluded. One day he touched upon this subject, to see what effect it would produce; but, contrary to his expectations, she seemed to have no desire to quit her retirement: she did not wish, she said, for amusements such as he described; she did not wish to go into the world.

It was during the time of his passion for her that Clarence had her picture painted in the character of St. Pierre's Virginia. It happened to be in the room in which they were now conversing, and when she spoke of loving a life of retirement, Clarence accidentally cast his eyes upon the picture, and then upon Virginia. She turned away—sighed deeply; and when, in a tone of kindness, he asked her if she were unhappy, she hid her face in her hands, and made no answer.

Mr. Hervey could not be insensible to her distress or to her delicacy. He saw her bloom fading daily, her spirits depressed, her existence a burden to her, and he feared that his own imprudence had been the cause of all this misery.

"I have taken her out of a situation in which she might have spent her life usefully and happily; I have excited false hopes in her mind, and now she is a wretched and useless being. I have won her affections; her happiness depends totally upon me; and can I forsake her? Mrs. Ormond says, that she is convinced Virginia would not survive the day of my marriage with another. I am not disposed to believe that girls often die or destroy themselves for love; nor am I a coxcomb enough to suppose that love for me must be extraordinarily desperate. But here's a girl, who is of a melancholy temperament, who has a great deal of natural sensibility, whose affections have all been concentrated, who has lived in solitude, whose imagination has dwelt, for a length of time, upon a certain set of ideas, who has but one object of hope; in such a mind, and in such circumstances, passion may rise to a paroxysm of despair."

Pity, generosity, and honour, made him resolve not to abandon this unfortunate girl; though he felt that every time he saw Virginia, his love for Belinda increased. It was this struggle in his mind betwixt love and honour which produced all the apparent inconsistency and irresolution that puzzled Lady Delacour and perplexed Belinda. The lock of beautiful hair, which so unluckily fell at Belinda's feet, was Virginia's; he was going to take it to the painter, who had made the hair in her picture considerably too dark. How this picture got into the exhibition must now be explained.

Whilst Mr. Hervey's mind was in that painful state of doubt which has just been described, a circumstance happened that promised him some relief from his embarrassment. Mr. Moreton, the clergyman who used to read prayers every Sunday for Mrs. Ormond and Virginia, did not come one Sunday at the usual time: the next morning he called on Mr. Hervey, with a face that showed he had something of importance to communicate.

"I have hopes, my dear Clarence," said he, "that I have found out your Virginia's father. Yesterday, a musical friend of mine persuaded me to go with him to hear the singing at the Asylum for children in St. George's Fields. There is a girl there who has indeed a charming voice—but that's not to the present purpose. After church was over, I happened to be one of the last that stayed; for I am too old to love bustling through a crowd. Perhaps, as you are impatient, you think that's nothing to the purpose; and yet it is, as you shall hear. When the congregation had almost left the church, I observed that the children of the Asylum remained in their places, by order of one of the governors; and a middle-aged gentleman went round amongst the elder girls, examined their countenances with care, and inquired with much anxiety their ages, and every particular relative to their parents. The stranger held a miniature picture in his hand, with which he compared each face. I was not near enough to him," continued Mr. Moreton, "to see the miniature distinctly: but from the glimpse I caught of it, I thought that it was like your Virginia, though it seemed to be the portrait of a child but four or five years old. I understand that this gentleman will be at the Asylum again next Sunday; I heard him express a wish to see some of the girls who happened last Sunday to be absent."

"Do you know this gentleman's name, or where he lives?" said Clarence.

"I know nothing of him," replied Mr. Moreton, "except that he seems fond of painting; for he told one of the directors, who was looking at his miniature, that it was remarkably well painted, and that, in his happier days, he had been something of a judge of the art."

Impatient to see the stranger, who, he did not doubt, was Virginia's father, Clarence Hervey went the next Sunday to the Asylum; but no such gentleman appeared, and all that he could learn respecting him was, that he had applied to one of the directors of the institution for leave to see and question the girls, in hopes of finding amongst them his lost daughter; that in the course of the week, he had seen all those who were not at the church the last Sunday. None of the directors knew any thing more concerning him; but the porter remarked, that he came in a very handsome coach, and one of the girls of the Asylum said that he gave her half a guinea, because she was a little like his poor Rachel, who was dead; but that he had added, with a sigh, "This cannot be my daughter, for she is only thirteen, and my girl, if she be now living, must be nearly eighteen."

The age, the name, every circumstance confirmed Mr. Hervey in the belief that this stranger was the father of Virginia, and he was disappointed and provoked by having missed the opportunity of seeing or speaking to him. It occurred to Clarence that the gentleman might probably visit the Foundling Hospital, and thither he immediately went, to make inquiries. He was told that a person, such as he described, had been there about a month before, and had compared the face of the oldest girls with a little picture of a child: that he gave money to several of the girls, but that they did not know his name, or any thing more about him.

Mr. Hervey now inserted proper advertisements in all the papers, but without producing any effect. At last, recollecting what Mr. Moreton told him of the stranger's love of pictures, he determined to put his portrait of Virginia into the exhibition, in hopes that the gentleman might go there and ask some questions about it, which might lead to a discovery. The young artist, who had painted this picture, was under particular obligations to Clarence, and he promised that he would faithfully comply with his request, to be at Somerset-house regularly every morning, as soon as the exhibition opened; that he would stay there till it closed, and watch whether any of the spectators were particularly struck with the portrait of Virginia. If any person should ask questions respecting the picture, he was to let Mr. Hervey know immediately, and to give the inquirer his address.

Now it happened that the very day when Lady Delacour and Belinda were at the exhibition, the painter called Clarence aside, and informed him that a gentleman had just inquired from him very eagerly, whether the picture of Virginia was a portrait. This gentleman proved to be not the stranger who had been at the Asylum, but an eminent jeweller, who told Mr. Hervey that his curiosity about the picture arose merely from its striking likeness to a miniature, which had been lately left at his house to be new set. It belonged to a Mr. Hartley, a gentleman who had made a considerable fortune in the West Indies, but who was prevented from enjoying his affluence by the loss of an only daughter, of whom the miniature was a portrait, taken when she was not more than four or five years old. When Clarence heard all this, he was extremely impatient to know where Mr. Hartley was to be found; but the jeweller could only tell him that the miniature had been called for the preceding day by Mr. Hartley's servant, who said his master was leaving town in a great hurry to go to Portsmouth, to join the West India fleet, which was to sail with the first favourable wind.

Clarence determined immediately to follow him to Portsmouth: he had not a moment to spare, for the wind was actually favourable, and his only chance of seeing Mr. Hartley was by reaching Portsmouth as soon as possible. This was the cause of his taking leave of Belinda in such an abrupt manner: painful indeed were his feelings at that moment, and great the difficulty he felt in parting with her, without giving any explanation of his conduct, which must have appeared to her capricious and mysterious. He was aware that he had explicitly avowed to Lady Delacour his admiration of Miss Portman, and that in a thousand instances he had betrayed his passion. Yet of her love he dared not trust himself to think, whilst his affairs were in this doubtful state. He had, it is true, some faint hopes that a change in Virginia's situation might produce an alteration in her sentiments, and he resolved to decide his own conduct by the manner in which she should behave, if her father should be found, and she should become heiress to a considerable fortune. New views might then open to her imagination: the world, the fashionable world, in all its glory, would be before her; her beauty and fortune would attract a variety of admirers, and Clarence thought that perhaps her partiality for him might become less exclusive, when she had more opportunities of choice. If her love arose merely from circumstances, with circumstances it would change; if it were only a disease of the imagination, induced by her seclusion from society, it might be cured by mixing with the world; and then he should be at liberty to follow the dictates of his own heart, and declare his attachment to Belinda. But if he should find that change of situation made no alteration in Virginia's sentiments, if her happiness should absolutely depend upon the realization of those hopes which he had imprudently excited, he felt that he should be bound to her by all the laws of justice and honour; laws which no passion could tempt him to break. Full of these ideas, he hurried to Portsmouth in pursuit of Virginia's father. The first question he asked, upon his arrival there, may easily be guessed.

"Has the West India fleet sailed?"

"No: it sails to-morrow morning," was the answer.

He hastened instantly to make inquiries for Mr. Hartley. No such person could be found, no such gentleman was to be heard of any where. Hartley, he was sure, was the name which the jeweller mentioned to him, but it was in vain that he repeated it; no Mr. Hartley was to be heard of at Portsmouth, except a pawnbroker. At last, a steward of one of the West Indiamen recollected that a gentleman of that name came over with him in the Effingham, and that he talked of returning in the same vessel to the West Indies, if he should ever leave England again.

"But we have heard nothing of him since, sir," said the steward. "No passage is taken for him with us."

"And my life to a china orange," cried a sailor who was standing by, "he's gone to kingdom come, or more likely to Bedlam, afore this; for he was plaguy crazy in his timbers, and his head wanted righting, I take it, if it was he, Jack, who used to walk the deck, you know, with a bit of a picture in his hand, to which he seemed to be mumbling his prayers from morning to night. There's no use in sounding for him, master; he's down in Davy's locker long ago, or stowed into the tight waistcoat before this time o'day."

Notwithstanding this knowing sailor's opinion, Clarence would not desist from his sounding; because having so lately heard of him at different places, he could not believe that he was gone either into Davy's locker or to Bedlam. He imagined that, by some accident, Mr. Hartley had been detained upon the road to Portsmouth; and in the expectation that he would certainly arrive before the fleet should sail, Clarence waited with tolerable patience. He waited, however, in vain; he saw the Effingham and the whole fleet sail—no Mr. Hartley arrived. As he hailed one of the boats of the Effingham, which was rowing out with some passengers, who had been too late to get on board, his friend the sailor answered, "We've no crazy man here: I told you, master, he'd never go out no more in the Effingham. He's where I said, master, you'll find, or nowhere."

Mr. Hervey remained some days at Portsmouth, after the fleet had sailed, in hopes that he might yet obtain some information; but none could be had; neither could any farther tidings be obtained from the jeweller, who had first mentioned Mr. Hartley. Despairing of success in the object of his journey, he, however, determined to delay his return to town for some time, in hopes that absence might efface the impression which had been made on the heart of Virginia. He made a tour along the picturesque coasts of Dorset and Devonshire, and it was during this excursion that he wrote the letters to Lady Delacour which have so often been mentioned. He endeavoured to dissipate his thoughts by new scenes and employments, but all his ideas involuntarily centred in Belinda. If he saw new characters, he compared them with hers, or considered how far she would approve or condemn them. The books that he read were perused with a constant reference to what she would think or feel; and during his whole journey he never beheld any beautiful prospect, without wishing that it could at the same instant be seen by Belinda. If her name were mentioned but once in his letters, it was because he dared not trust himself to speak of her; she was for ever present to his mind: but while he was writing to Lady Delacour, her idea pressed more strongly upon his heart; he recollected that it was she who first gave him a just insight into her ladyship's real character; he recollected that she had joined with him in the benevolent design of reconciling her to Lord Delacour, and of creating in her mind a taste for domestic happiness. This remembrance operated powerfully to excite him to fresh exertions, and the eloquence which touched Lady Delacour so much in these "edifying" letters, as she called them, was in fact inspired by Belinda.

Whenever he thought distinctly upon his future plans, Virginia's attachment, and the hopes which he had imprudently inspired, appeared insuperable obstacles to his union with Miss Portman; but, in more sanguine moments, he flattered himself with a confused notion that these difficulties would vanish. Great were his surprise and alarm when he received that letter of Lady Delacour's, in which she announced the probability of Belinda's marriage with Mr. Vincent. In consequence of his moving from place to place in the course of his tour, he did not receive this letter till nearly a fortnight after it should have come to his hands. The instant he received it he set out on his way home; he travelled with all that expedition which money can command in England: his first thought and first wish when he arrived in town were to go to Lady Delacour's; but he checked his impatience, and proceeded immediately to Twickenham, to have his fate decided by Virginia. It was with the most painful sensations that he saw her again. The accounts which he received from Mrs. Ormond convinced him that absence had produced none of the effects which he expected on the mind of her pupil. Mrs. Ormond was naturally both of an affectionate disposition and a timid temper; she had become excessively fond of Virginia, and her anxiety was more than in proportion to her love; it sometimes balanced and even overbalanced her regard and respect for Clarence Hervey himself. When he spoke of his attachment to Belinda, and of his doubts respecting Virginia, she could no longer restrain her emotion.

"Oh, indeed, Mr. Hervey," said she, "this is no time for reasoning and doubting. No man in his senses, no man who is not wilfully blind, could doubt her being distractedly fond of you."

"I am sorry for it," said Clarence.

"And why—oh, why, Mr. Hervey? Don't you recollect the time when you were all impatience to call her yours,—when you thought her the most charming creature in the whole world?"

"I had not seen Belinda Portman then."

"And I wish to Heaven you never had seen her! But oh, surely, Mr. Hervey, you will not desert my Virginia!—Must her health, her happiness, her reputation, all be the sacrifice?"

"Reputation! Mrs. Ormond."

"Reputation, Mr. Hervey: you do not know in what a light she is considered here; nor did I till lately. But I tell you her reputation is injured—fatally injured. It is whispered, and more than whispered everywhere, that she is your mistress. A woman came here the other day with the bullfinch, and she looked at me, and spoke in such an extraordinary way, that I was shocked more than I can express. I need not tell you all the particulars; it is enough that I have made inquiries, and am sure, too sure, of what I say, that nothing but your marriage with Virginia can save her reputation; or—"

Mrs. Ormond stopped short, for at this instant Virginia entered the room, walking in her slow manner, as if she were in a deep reverie.

"Since my return," said Clarence, in an embarrassed voice, "I have scarcely heard a syllable from Miss St. Pierre's lips."

"Miss St. Pierre!—He used to call me Virginia," said she, turning to Mrs. Ormond: "he is angry with me—he used to call me Virginia."

"But you were a child then, you know, my love," said Mrs. Ormond.

"And I wish I was still a child," said Virginia, Then, after a long pause, she approached Mr. Hervey with extreme timidity, and, opening a portfolio which lay on the table, she said to him, "If you are at leisure—if I do not interrupt you—would you look at these drawings; though they are not worth your seeing, except as proofs that I can conquer my natural indolence?"

The drawings were views which she had painted from memory, of scenes in the New Forest, near her grandmother's cottage. That cottage was drawn with an exactness that proved how fresh it was in her remembrance. Many recollections rushed forcibly into Clarence Hervey's mind at the sight of this cottage. The charming image of Virginia, as it first struck his fancy,—the smile, the innocent smile, with which she offered him the finest rose in her basket,—the stern voice in which her grandmother spoke to her,—the prophetic fears of her protectress,—the figure of the dying woman,—the solemn promise he made to her,—all recurred, in rapid succession, to his memory.

"You don't seem to like that," said Virginia; and then putting another drawing into his hands, "perhaps this may please you better."

"They are beautiful; they are surprisingly well done!" exclaimed he.

"I knew he would like them! I told you so!" cried Mrs. Ormond, in a triumphant tone.

"You see," said Virginia, "that though you have heard scarcely a syllable from Miss St. Pierre's lips since your return, yet she has not been unmindful of your wishes in your absence. You told her, some time ago, that you wished she would try to improve in drawing. She has done her best. But do not trouble yourself to look at them any longer," said Virginia, taking one of her drawings from his hand; "I merely wanted to show you that, though I have no genius, I have some—"

Her voice faltered so that she could not pronounce the word gratitude.

Mrs. Ormond pronounced it for her; and added, "I can answer for it, that Virginia is not ungrateful."

"Ungrateful!" repeated Clarence; "who ever thought her so? Why did you put these ideas into her mind?"

Virginia, resting her head on Mrs. Ormond's shoulder, wept bitterly.

"You have worked upon her sensibility till you have made her miserable," cried Clarence, angrily. "Virginia, listen to me: look at me," said he, affectionately taking her hand; but she pressed closer to Mrs. Ormond, and would not raise her head. "Do not consider me as your master—your tyrant; do not imagine that I think you ungrateful!"

"Oh, I am—I am—I am ungrateful to you," cried she, sobbing; "but Mrs. Ormond never told me so; do not blame her: she has never worked upon my sensibility. Do you think," said she, looking up, while a transient expression of indignation passed over her countenance, "do you think I cannot feel without having been taught?"

Clarence uttered a deep sigh.

"But if you feel too much, my dearest Virginia,—if you give way to your feelings in this manner," said Mrs. Ormond, "you will make both yourself and Mr. Hervey unhappy."

"Heaven forbid! The first wish of my soul is—" She paused. "I should be the most ungrateful wretch in the world, if I were to make him unhappy."

"But if he sees you miserable, Virginia?"

"Then he shall not see it," said she, wiping the tears from her face.

"To imagine that you were unhappy, and that you concealed it from us, would be still worse," said Clarence.

"But why should you imagine it?" replied Virginia; "you are too good, too kind; but do not fancy that I am not happy: I am sure I ought to be happy."

"Do you regret your cottage?" said Clarence: "these drawings show how well you remember it."

Virginia coloured; and, with some hesitation, answered, "Is it my fault if I cannot forget?"

"You were happier then, Virginia, than you are now, you will confess," said Mrs. Ormond, who was not a woman of refined delicacy, and who thought that the best chance she had of working upon Mr. Hervey's sense of honour was by making it plain to him how much her pupil's affections were engaged.

Virginia made no answer to this question, and her silence touched Clarence more than any thing she could have said. When Mrs. Ormond repeated her question, he relieved the trembling girl by saying, "My dear Mrs. Ormond, confidence must be won, not demanded."

"I have no right to insist upon confessions, I know," said Mrs. Ormond; "but—"

"Confessions! I do not wish to conceal any thing, but I think sincerity is not always in our sex consistent with—I mean—I don't know what I mean, what I say, or what I ought to say," cried Virginia; and she sunk down on a sofa, in extreme confusion.

"Why will you agitate her, Mrs. Ormond, in this manner?" said Mr. Hervey, with an expression of sudden anger. It was succeeded by a look of such tender compassion for Virginia, that Mrs. Ormond rejoiced to have excited his anger; at any price she wished to serve her beloved pupil.

"Do not be in the least apprehensive, my dear Virginia, that we should take ungenerous advantage of the openness and simplicity of your character," said Mr. Hervey.

"Oh, no, no; I cannot, do not apprehend any thing ungenerous from you; you are, you ever have been, my best, my most generous friend! But I fear that I have not the simplicity of character, the openness that you imagine; and yet, I am sure, I wish, from the bottom of my heart—I wish to do right, if I knew how. But there is not one—no, not one—person in the whole world," continued she, her eyes moving from Mrs. Ormond to Mr. Hervey, and from him to Mrs. Ormond again, "not one person in the whole world I dare—I ought—to lay my heart open to. I have, perhaps, said more than is proper already. But this I know," added she, in a firm tone, rising, and addressing herself to Clarence, "you shall never be made unhappy by me. And do not think about my happiness so much," said she, forcing a smile; "I am, I will be, perfectly happy. Only let me always know your wishes, your sentiments, your feelings, and by them I will, as I ought, regulate mine."

"Amiable, charming, generous girl!" cried Clarence.

"Take care," said Mrs. Ormond; "take care, Virginia, lest you promise more than you can perform. Wishes, and feelings, and sentiments, are not to be so easily regulated."

"I did not, I believe, say it was easy; but I hope it is possible," replied Virginia. "I promise nothing but what I am able to perform."

"I doubt it," said Mrs. Ormond, shaking her head. "You are—you will be perfectly happy. Oh, Virginia, my love, do not deceive yourself; do not deceive us so terribly. I am sorry to put you to the blush; but—"

"Not a word more, my dear madam, I beg—I insist," said Mr. Hervey in a commanding tone; but, for the first time in her life, regardless of him, she persisted.

"I only ask you to call to mind, my dearest Virginia," said she, taking her hand, "the morning that you screamed in your sleep, the morning when you told me the frightful dream—were you perfectly happy then?"

"It is easy to force my thoughts from me," said Virginia, withdrawing her hand from Mrs. Ormond; "but it is cruel to do so." And with an air of offended dignity she passed them, and quitted the room.

"I wish to Heaven!" exclaimed Mrs. Ormond, "that Miss Portman was married, and out of the way—I shall never forgive myself! We have used this poor girl cruelly amongst us: she loves you to distraction, and I have encouraged her passion, and I have betrayed her—oh, fool that I was! I told her that she would certainly be your wife."

"You have told her so!—Did I not charge you, Mrs. Ormond—"

"Yes; but I could not help it, when I saw the sweet girl fading away—and, besides, I am sure she thought it, from your manner, long and long before I told it to her. Do you forget how fond of her you were scarce one short year ago? And do you forget how plainly you let her see your passion? Oh, how can you blame her, if she loves you, and if she is unhappy?"

"I blame no one but myself," cried Clarence; "I must abide by the consequences of my own folly. Unhappy!—she shall not be unhappy; she does not deserve to be so."

He walked backward and forward, with hasty steps, for some minutes; then sat down and wrote a letter to Virginia.

When he had finished it, he put it into Mrs. Ormond's hands.

"Read it—seal it—give it to her—and let her answer be sent to town to me, at Dr. X.'s, in Clifford-street."

Mrs. Ormond clasped her hands, in an ecstasy of joy, as she glanced her eye over the letter, for it contained an offer of his hand.

"This is like yourself; like what I always knew you to be, dear Mr. Hervey!" she exclaimed.

But her exclamation was lost upon him. When she looked up, to repeat her praises, she perceived he was gone. After the effort which he had made, he wished for time to tranquillize his mind, before he should again see Virginia. What her answer to this letter would be he could not doubt: his fate was now decided, and he determined immediately to write to Lady Delacour to explain his situation; he felt that he had not sufficient fortitude at this moment to make such an explanation in person. With all the strength of his mind, he endeavoured to exclude Belinda from his thoughts, but curiosity—(for he would suffer himself to call it by no other name)—curiosity to know whether she were actually engaged to Mr. Vincent obtruded itself with such force, that it could not be resisted.

From Dr. X— he thought he could obtain full information, and he hastened immediately to town. When he got to Clifford-street, he found that the doctor was not at home; his servant said, he might probably be met with at Mrs. Margaret Delacour's, as he usually finished his morning rounds at her house. Thither Mr. Hervey immediately went.

The first sound that he heard, as he went up her stairs, was the screaming of a macaw; and the first person he saw, through the open door of the drawing-room, was Helena Delacour. She was standing with her back to him, leaning over the macaw's cage, and he heard her say in a joyful tone, "Yes, though you do scream so frightfully, my pretty macaw, I love you as well as Marriott ever did. When my dear, good Miss Portman, sent this macaw—My dear aunt! here's Mr. Hervey!—you were just wishing to see him."

"Mr. Hervey," said the old lady, with a benevolent smile, "your little friend Helena tells you truth; we were just wishing for you. I am sure it will give you pleasure to hear that I am at last a convert to your opinion of Lady Delacour. She has given up all those that I used to call her rantipole acquaintance. She has reconciled herself to her husband, and to his friends; and Helena is to go home to live with her. Here is a charming note I have just received from her! Dine with me on Thursday next, and you will meet her ladyship, and see a happy family party. You have had some share in the reformation, I know, and that was the reason I wished that you should be with us on Thursday. You see I am not an obstinate old woman, though I was cross the first day I saw you at Lady Anne Percival's. I found I was mistaken in your character, and I am glad of it. But this note of Lady Delacour's seems to have struck you dumb."

There were, indeed, a few words in this note, which deprived him, for some moments, of all power of utterance.

"The report you have heard (unlike most other reports) is perfectly well founded: Mr. Vincent, Belinda's admirer, is here. I will bring him with us on Thursday."

Mr. Hervey was relieved from the necessity of accounting to Mrs. Delacour for his sudden embarrassment, by the entrance of Dr. X— and another gentleman, of whom, in the confusion of his mind, Clarence did not at first take any notice. Dr. X—, with his usual mixture of benevolence and raillery, addressed himself to Clarence, whilst the stranger took out of his pocket some papers, and in a low voice entered earnestly into conversation with Mrs. Delacour.

"Now, tell me, if you can, Clarence," said Dr. X—, "which of your three mistresses you like best? I think I left you some months ago in great doubt upon this subject: are you still in that philosophic state?"

"No," said Clarence; "all doubts are over—I am going to be married."

"Bravo!—But you look as if you were going to be hanged. May I, as it will so soon be in the newspaper, may I ask the name of the fair lady?"

"Virginia St. Pierre. You shall know her history and mine when we are alone," said Mr. Hervey, lowering his voice.

"You need not lower your voice," said Dr. X—, "for Mrs. Delacour is, as you see, so much taken up with her own affairs, that she has no curiosity for those of her neighbours; and Mr. Hartley is as busy as—"

"Mr. who? Mr. Hartley did you say?" interrupted Clarence, eagerly turning his eyes upon the stranger, who was a middle-aged gentleman, exactly answering the description of the person who had been at the Asylum in search of his daughter.

"Mr. Hartley! yes. What astonishes you so much?" said X—, calmly. "He is a West Indian. I met him in Cambridgeshire last summer, at his friend Mr. Horton's; he has been very generous to the poor people who suffered by the fire, and he is now consulting with Mrs. Delacour, who has an estate adjoining to Mr. Horton's, about her tenants, whose houses in the village were burnt. Now I have, in as few words and parentheses as possible, told you all I know of Mr. Hartley's history; but your curiosity still looks voracious."

"I want to know whether he has a miniature?" said Clarence, hastily. "Introduce me to him, for Heaven's sake, directly!"

"Mr. Hartley," cried the doctor, raising his voice, "give me leave to introduce my friend Mr. Hervey to you, and to your miniature picture, if you have one."

Mr. Hartley sighed profoundly as he drew from his bosom a small portrait, which he put into Mr. Hervey's hands, saying, "Alas! sir, you cannot, I fear, give me any tidings of the original; it is the picture of a daughter, whom I have never seen since she was an infant—whom I never shall see again."

Clarence instantly knew it to be Virginia; but as he was upon the point of making some joyful exclamation, he felt Dr. X— touch his shoulder, and looking up at Mr. Hartley, he saw in his countenance such strong workings of passion, that he prudently suppressed his own emotion, and calmly said, "It would be cruel, sir, to give you false hopes."

"It would kill me—it would kill me, sir!—or worse!—worse! a thousand times worse!" cried Mr. Hartley, putting his hand to his forehead. "What," continued he impatiently, "what was the meaning of the look you gave, when you first saw that picture? Speak, if you have any humanity! Did you ever see any one that resembles that picture?"

"I have seen, I think, a picture," said Clarence Hervey, "that has some resemblance to it."

"When? where?—"

"My good sir," said Dr. X—, "let me recommend it to you to consider that there is scarcely any possibility of judging, from the features of children, of what their faces may be when they grow up. Nothing can be more fallacious than these accidental resemblances between the pictures of children and of grown-up people."

Mr. Hartley's countenance fell.

"But," added Clarence Hervey, "you will perhaps, sir, think it worth your while to see the picture of which I speak: you can see it at Mr. F—'s, the painter, in Newman-street; and I will accompany you thither whenever you please."

"This moment, if you would have the goodness: my carriage is at the door; and Mrs. Delacour will be so kind to excuse —"

"Oh, make no apologies to me at such a time as this," said Mrs. Delacour. "Away with you, gentlemen, as soon as you please; upon condition, that if you have any good news to tell, some of you will remember, in the midst of your joy, that such an old woman as Mrs. Margaret Delacour exists, who loves to hear good news of those who deserve it."

"It was so late in the day when they got to Newman-street, that they were obliged to light candles. Trembling with eagerness, Mr. Hartley drew near, while Clarence held the light to the picture.

"It is so like," said he, looking at his miniature, "that I dare not believe my senses. Dr. X—, pray do you look. My head is so dizzy, and my eyes so—What do you think, sir? What do you say, doctor?"

"That the likeness is certainly striking—but this seems to be a fancy piece."

"A fancy piece," repeated Mr. Hartley, with terror: "why then did you bring me here?—A fancy piece!"

"No, sir; it is a portrait," said Clarence; "and if you will be calm, I will tell you more."

"I will be calm—only is she alive?"

"The lady, of whom this is the portrait, is alive," replied Clarence Hervey, who was obliged to exert his utmost command over himself, to maintain that composure which he saw was necessary; "the lady, of whom this is the portrait, is alive, and you shall see her to-morrow."

"Oh, why not now? Cannot I see her now? I must see her to-night—this instant, sir!"

"It is impossible," said Mr. Hervey, "that you should see her this instant, for she is some miles off, at Twickenham."

"It is too late to go thither now; you cannot think of it, Mr. Hartley," continued Dr. X—, in a tone of command, to which he yielded more readily than to reason.

Clarence had the presence of mind to recollect that it would be necessary to prepare poor Virginia for this meeting, and he sent a messenger immediately to request that Mrs. Ormond would communicate the intelligence with all the caution in her power.

The next morning, Mr. Hartley and Mr. Hervey set off together for Twickenham. In their way thither Clarence gradually confirmed Mr. Hartley in the belief that Virginia was his daughter, by relating all the circumstances that he had learned from her grandmother, and from Mrs. Smith, the farmer's wife, with whom she had formerly been acquainted: the name, the age, every particular, as it was disclosed, heightened his security and his joy.

For some time Mr. Hartley's mind was so intent that he could not listen to any thing, but at last Clarence engaged his attention and suspended his anxiety, by giving him a history of his own connexion with Virginia, from the day of his first discovering her in the New Forest, to the letter which he had just written, to offer her his hand. The partiality which it was suspected Virginia felt for him was the only circumstance which he suppressed, because, notwithstanding all Mrs. Ormond had said, and all he had himself heard and seen, his obstinate incredulity required confirmation under her own hand, or positively from her own lips. He still fancied it was possible that change of situation might alter her views and sentiments; and he earnestly entreated that she might be left entirely to her own decision. It was necessary to make this stipulation with her father; for in the excess of his gratitude for the kindness which Clarence had shown to her, he protested that he should look upon her as a monster if she did not love him: he added, that if Mr. Hervey had not a farthing, he should prefer him to every man upon earth; he, however, promised that he would conceal his wishes, and that his daughter should act entirely from the dictates of her own mind. In the fulness of his heart, he told Clarence all those circumstances of his conduct towards Virginia's mother which had filled his soul with remorse. She was scarcely sixteen when he ran away with her from a boarding-school; he was at that time a gay officer, she a sentimental girl, who had been spoiled by early novel-reading. Her father had a small place at court, lived beyond his fortune, educated his daughter, to whom he could give no portion, as if she were to be heiress to a large estate; then died, and left his widow absolutely in penury. This widow was the old lady who lived in the cottage in the New Forest. It was just at the time of her husband's death, and of her own distress, that she heard of the elopement of her daughter from school. Mr. Hartley's parents were so much incensed by the match, that he was prevailed upon to separate from his wife, and to go abroad, to push his fortune in the army. His marriage had been secret: his own friends disavowed it, notwithstanding the repeated, urgent entreaties of his wife and of her mother, who was her only surviving relation. His wife, on her death-bed, wrote to urge him to take charge of his daughter; and, to make the appeal stronger to his feelings, she sent him a picture of his little girl, who was then about four years old. Mr. Hartley, however, was intent upon forming a new connexion with the rich widow of a planter in Jamaica. He married the widow, took possession of her fortune, and all his affections soon were fixed upon a son, for whom he formed, even from the moment of his birth, various schemes of aggrandizement. The boy lived till he was about ten years old, when he caught a fever, which at that time raged in Jamaica, and, after a few days' illness, died. His mother was carried off by the same disease; and Mr. Hartley, left alone in the midst of his wealth, felt how insufficient it was to happiness. Remorse now seized him; he returned to England in search of his deserted daughter. To this neglected child he now looked forward for the peace and happiness of the remainder of his life. Disappointment in all his inquiries for some months preyed upon his spirits to such a degree, that his intellects were at times disordered; this derangement was the cause of his not sooner recovering his child. He was in confinement during the time that Clarence Hervey's advertisements were inserted in the papers; and his illness was also the cause of his not going to Portsmouth, and sailing in the Effingham, as he had originally intended. The history of his connexion with Mr. Horton would be uninteresting to the reader; it is enough to say, that he was prevailed upon, by that gentleman, to spend some time in the country with him, for the recovery of his health; and it was there that he became acquainted with Dr. X—, who introduced him, as we have seen, to Mrs. Margaret Delacour, at whose house he met Clarence Hervey. This is the most succinct account that we can give of him and his affairs. His own account was ten times as long; but we spare our readers his incoherences and reflections, because, perhaps, they are in a hurry to get to Twickenham, and to hear of his meeting with Virginia.

Mrs. Ormond found it no easy task to prepare Virginia for the sight of Mr. Hartley. Virginia had scarcely ever spoken of her father; but the remembrance of things which she had heard of him from her grandmother was fresh in her mind; she had often pictured him in her fancy, and she had secretly nourished the hope that she should not for ever be a deserted child. Mrs. Ormond had observed, that in those romances, of which she was so fond, every thing that related to children who were deserted by their parents affected her strongly.

The belief in what the French call la force du sang was suited to her affectionate temper and ardent imagination, and it had taken full possession of her mind. The eloquence of romance persuaded her that she should not only discover but love her father with intuitive filial piety, and she longed to experience those yearnings of affection of which she had read so much.

The first moment that Mrs. Ormond began to speak of Mr. Clarence Hervey's hopes of discovering her father, she was transported with joy.

"My father!—How delightful that word father sounds!—My father?—May I say my father?—And will he own me, and will he love me, and will he give me his blessing, and will he fold me in his arms, and call me his daughter, his dear daughter?—Oh, how I shall love him! I will make it the whole business of my life to please him!"

"The whole business?" said Mrs. Ormond, smiling.

"Not the whole," said Virginia; "I hope my father will like Mr. Hervey. Did not you say that he is rich? I wish that my father may be very rich."

"That is the last wish that I should have expected to hear from you, my Virginia."

"But do you not know why I wish it?—that I may show my gratitude to Mr. Hervey."

"My dear child," said Mrs. Ormond, "these are most generous sentiments, and worthy of you; but do not let your imagination run away with you at this rate—Mr. Hervey is rich enough."

"I wish he were poor," said Virginia, "that I might make him rich."

"He would not love you the better, my dear," said Mrs. Ormond, "if you had the wealth of the Indies. Perhaps your father may not be rich; therefore do not set your heart upon this idea."

Virginia sighed: fear succeeded to hope, and her imagination immediately reversed the bright picture that it had drawn.

"But I am afraid," said she, "that this gentleman is not my father—how disappointed I shall be! I wish you had never told me all this, my dear Mrs. Ormond."

"I would not have told it to you, if Mr. Hervey had not desired that I should; and you maybe sure he would not have desired it, unless he had good reason to believe that you would not be disappointed."

"But he is not sure—he does not say he is quite sure. And, even if I were quite certain of his being my father, how can I be certain that he will not disown me—he, who has deserted me so long? My grandmother, I remember, often used to say that he had no natural affection."

"Your grandmother was mistaken, then; for he has been searching for his child all over England, Mr. Hervey says; and he has almost lost his senses with grief and with remorse!"

"Remorse!"

"Yes, remorse, for having so long deserted you: he fears that you will hate him."

"Hate him!—is it possible to hate a father?" said Virginia.

"He dreads that you should never forgive him."

"Forgive him!—I have read of parents forgiving their children, but I never remember to have read of a daughter forgiving her father. Forgive! you should not have used that word. I cannot forgive my father: but I can love him, and I will make him quite forget all his sorrows—I mean, all his sorrows about me."

After this conversation Virginia spent her time in imagining what sort of person her father would be; whether he was like Mr. Hervey; what words he would say; where he would sit; whether he would sit beside her; and, above all, whether he would give her his blessing.

"I am afraid," said she, "of liking my father better than any body else."

"No danger of that, my dear," said Mrs. Ormond, smiling.

"I am glad of it, for it would be very wrong and ungrateful to like any thing in this world so well as Mr. Hervey."

The carriage now came to the door: Mrs. Ormond instantly ran to the window, but Virginia had not power to move—her heart beat violently.

"Is he come?" said she.

"Yes, he is getting out of the carriage this moment!"

Virginia stood with her eyes eagerly fixed upon the door: "Hark!" said she, laying her hand upon Mrs. Ormond's arm, to prevent her from moving: "Hush! that we may hear his voice."

She was breathless—no voice was to be heard: "They are not coming," said she, turning as pale as death. An instant afterwards her colour returned—she heard the steps of two people coming up the stairs.

"His step!—Do you hear it?—Is it my father?"

Virginia's imagination was worked to the highest pitch; she could scarcely sustain herself: Mrs. Ormond supported her. At this instant her father appeared.

"My child!—the image of her mother!" exclaimed he, stopping short: he sunk upon a chair.

"My father!" cried Virginia, springing forward, and throwing herself at his feet.

"The voice of her mother!" said Mr. Hartley. "My daughter!—My long lost child!"

He tried to raise her, but could not; her arms were clasped round his knee, her face rested upon it, and when he stooped to kiss her cheek, he found it cold—she had fainted.

When she came to her senses, and found herself in her father's arms, she could scarcely believe that it was not a dream.

"Your blessing!—give me your blessing, and then I shall know that you are indeed my father!" cried Virginia, kneeling to him, and looking up with an enthusiastic expression of filial piety in her countenance.

"God bless you, my sweet child!" said he, laying his hand upon her; "and God forgive your father!"

"My grandmother died without giving me her blessing," said Virginia; "but now I have been blessed by my father! Happy, happy moment!—O that she could look down from heaven, and see us at this instant!"

Virginia was so much astonished and overpowered by this sudden discovery of a parent, and by the novelty of his first caresses, that after the first violent effervescence of her sensibility was over, she might, to an indifferent spectator, have appeared stupid and insensible. Mrs. Ormond, though far from an indifferent spectator, was by no means a penetrating judge of the human heart: she seldom saw more than the external symptoms of feeling, and she was apt to be rather impatient with her friends if theirs did not accord with her own.

"Virginia, my dear," said she, in rather a reproachful tone, "Mr. Hervey, you see, has left the room, on purpose to leave you at full liberty to talk to your father; and I am going—but you are so silent!"

"I have so much to say, and my heart is so full!" said Virginia.

"Yes, I know you told me of a thousand things that you had to say to your father, before you saw him."

"But now I see him, I have forgotten them all. I can think of nothing but of him."

"Of him and Mr. Hervey," said Mrs. Ormond.

"I was not thinking of Mr. Hervey at that moment," said Virginia, blushing.

"Well, my love, I will leave you to think and talk of what you please," said Mrs. Ormond, smiling significantly as she left the room.

Mr. Hartley folded his daughter in his arms with the fondest expressions of parental affection, and he was upon the point of telling her how much he approved of the choice of her heart; but he recollected his promise, and he determined to sound her inclinations farther, before he even mentioned the name of Clarence Hervey.

He began by painting the pleasures of the world, that world from which she had hitherto been secluded.

She heard him with simple indifference: not even her curiosity was excited.

He observed, that though she had no curiosity to see, it was natural that she must have some pleasure in the thoughts of being seen.

"What pleasure?" said Virginia.

"The pleasure of being admired and loved: beauty and grace such as yours, my child, cannot be seen without commanding admiration and love."

"I do not want to be admired," replied Virginia, "and I want to be loved by those only whom I love."

"My dearest daughter, you shall be entirely your own mistress; I will never interfere, either directly or indirectly, in the disposal of your heart."

At these last words, Virginia, who had listened to all the rest unmoved, took her father's hand, and kissed it repeatedly.

"Now that I have found you, my darling child, let me at least make you happy, if I can—it is the only atonement in my power; it will be the only solace of my declining years. All that wealth can bestow—"

"Wealth!" interrupted Virginia: "then you have wealth?"

"Yes, my child—may it make you happy! that is all the enjoyment I expect from it: it shall all be yours."

"And may I do what I please with it?—Oh, then it will indeed make me happy. I will give it all, all to Mr. Hervey. How delightful to have something to give to Mr. Hervey!"

"And had you never any thing to give to Mr. Hervey till now?"

"Never! never! he has given me every thing. Now—oh, joyful day!—I can prove to him that Virginia is not ungrateful!"

"Dear, generous girl," said her father, wiping the tears from his eyes, "what a daughter have I found! But tell me, my child," continued he, smiling, "do you think Mr. Hervey will be content if you give him only your fortune? Do you think that he would accept the fortune without the heart? Nay, do not turn away that dear blushing face from me; remember it is your father who speaks to you. Mr. Hervey will not take your fortune without yourself, I am afraid: what shall we do? Must I refuse him your hand?"

"Refuse him! do you think that I could refuse him any thing, who has given me every thing?—I should be a monster indeed! There is no sacrifice I would not make, no exertion of which I am not capable, for Mr. Hervey's sake. But, my dear father," said she, changing her tone, "he never asked for my hand till yesterday."

But he had won your heart long ago, I see, thought her father.

"I have written an answer to his letter; will you look at it, and tell me if you approve of it?"

"I do approve of it, my darling child: I will not read it—I know what it must be: he has a right to the preference he has so nobly earned."

"Oh, he has—he has, indeed!" cried Virginia, with an expression of strong feeling; "and now is the time to show him that I am not ungrateful."

"How I love you for this, my child!" cried her father, fondly embracing her. "This is exactly what I wished, though I did not dare to say so till I was sure of your sentiments. Mr. Hervey charged me to leave you entirely to yourself; he thought that your new situation might perhaps produce some change in your sentiments: I see he was mistaken; and I am heartily glad of it. But you are going to say something, my dear; do not let me interrupt you."

"I was only going to beg that you would give this letter, my dear father, to Mr. Hervey. It is an answer to one which he wrote to me when I was poor"—and deserted, she was near saying, but she stopped herself.

"I wish," continued she, "Mr. Hervey should know that my sentiments are precisely the same now that they have always been. Tell him," added she, proudly, "that he did me injustice by imagining that my sentiments could alter with my situation. He little knows Virginia." Clarence at this moment entered the room, and Mr. Hartley eagerly led his daughter to meet him.

"Take her hand," cried he; "you have her heart—you deserve it; and she has just been very angry with me for doubting. But read her letter,—that will speak better for her, and more to your satisfaction, no doubt, than I can."

Virginia hastily put the letter into Mr. Hervey's hand, and, breaking from her father, retired to her own apartment.

With all the trepidation of a person who feels that the happiness of his life is to be decided in a few moments, Clarence tore open Virginia's letter, and, conscious that he was not able to command his emotion, he withdrew from her father's inquiring eyes. Mr. Hartley, however, saw nothing in this agitation but what he thought natural to a lover, and he was delighted to perceive that his daughter had inspired so strong a passion.

Virginia's letter contained but these few lines:

"Most happy shall I be if the whole of my future life can prove to you how deeply I feel your goodness.

"VIRGINIA ST. PIERRE."

[End of C. Hervey's packet.]

An acceptance so direct left Clarence no alternative: his fate was decided. He determined immediately to force himself to see Belinda and Mr. Vincent; for he fancied that his mind would be more at ease when he had convinced himself by ocular demonstration that she was absolutely engaged to another; that, consequently, even if he were free, he could have no chance of gaining her affections. There are moments when we desire the conviction which at another time would overwhelm us with despair: it was in this temper that Mr. Hervey paid his visit to Lady Delacour; but we have seen that he was unable to support for many minutes that philosophic composure to which, at his first entrance into the room, he had worked up his mind. The tranquillity which he had expected would be the consequence of this visit, he was farther than ever from obtaining. The extravagant joy with which Lady Delacour received him, and an indescribable something in her manner when she looked from him to Belinda, and from Belinda to Mr. Vincent, persuaded him her ladyship wished that he were in Mr. Vincent's place. The idea was so delightful, that his soul was entranced, and for a few minutes Virginia, and every thing that related to her, vanished from his remembrance. It was whilst he was in this state that Lady Delacour (as the reader may recollect) invited him into her lord's dressing-room, to tell her the contents of the packet, which had not then reached her hands. The request suddenly recalled him to his senses, but he felt that he was not at this moment able to trust himself to her ladyship's penetration; he therefore referred her to his letter for that explanation which he dreaded to make in person, and he escaped from Belinda's presence, resolving never more to expose himself to such danger.

What effect his packet produced on Lady Delacour's mind and on Belinda's, we shall not at present stop to inquire; but having brought up Clarence Hervey's affairs to the present day, we shall continue his history.

CHAPTER XXVIII — E O

Though Clarence Hervey was not much disposed to see either Virginia or her father whilst he was in the state of perturbation into which he had been thrown by his interview with Belinda, yet he did not delay to send his servant home with a note to Mrs. Ormond, to say that he would meet Mr. Hartley, whenever he pleased, at his lawyer's, to make whatever arrangements might be necessary for proper settlements.

As he saw no possibility of receding with honour, he, with becoming resolution, desired to urge things forward as fast as possible, and to strengthen in his mind the sense of the necessity of the sacrifice that he was bound to make. His passions were naturally impetuous, but he had by persevering efforts brought them under the subjection of his reason. His power over himself was now to be put to a severe trial.

As he was going to town, he met Lord Delacour, who was riding in the park: he was extremely intent upon his own thoughts, and was anxious to pass unnoticed. In former times this would have been the most feasible thing imaginable, for Lord Delacour used to detest the sight of Clarence Hervey, whom he considered as the successor of Colonel Lawless in his lady's favour; but his opinion and his feelings had been entirely changed by the perusal of those letters, which were perfumed with ottar of roses: even this perfume had, from that association, become agreeable to him. He now accosted Clarence with a warmth and cordiality in his manner that at any other moment must have pleased as much as it surprised him; but Clarence was not in a humour to enter into conversation.

"You seem to be in haste, Mr. Hervey," said his lordship, observing his impatience; "but, as I know your good-nature, I shall make no scruple to detain you a quarter of an hour."

As he spoke he turned his horse, and rode with Clarence, who looked as if he wished that his lordship had been more scrupulous, and that he had not such a reputation for good-nature.

"You will not refuse me this quarter of an hour, I am sure," continued Lord Delacour, "when you hear that, by favouring me with your attention, you may perhaps materially serve an old, or rather a young, friend of yours, and one whom I once fancied was a particular favourite—I mean, Miss Belinda Portman."

At the name of Belinda Portman, Clarence Hervey became all attention: he assured his lordship that he was in no haste; and all his difficulty now was to moderate the eagerness of his curiosity.

"We can take a turn or two in the park, as well as any where," said his lordship: "nobody will overhear us, and the sooner you know what I have to say the better."

"Certainly," said Clarence.

The most malevolent person upon earth could not have tired poor Clarence's patience more than good-natured Lord Delacour contrived to do, with the best intentions possible, by his habitual circumlocution.

He descanted at length upon the difficulties, as the world goes, of meeting with a confidential friend, whom it is prudent to trust in any affair that demands delicacy, honour, and address. Men of talents were often, he observed, devoid of integrity, and men of integrity devoid of talents. When he had obtained Hervey's assent to this proposition, he next paid him sundry handsome, but long-winded compliments: then he complimented himself for having just thought of Mr. Hervey as the fittest person he could apply to: then he congratulated himself upon his good luck in meeting with the very man he was just thinking of. At last, after Clarence had returned thanks for all his kindness, and had given assent to all his lordship's truisms, the substance of the business came out.

Lord Delacour informed Mr. Hervey, "that he had been lately commissioned, by Lady Delacour, to discover what attractions drew a Mr. Vincent so constantly to Mrs. Luttridge's—"

Here he was going to explain who Mr. Vincent was; but Clarence assured him that he knew perfectly well that he had been a ward of Mr. Percival's, that he was a West Indian of large fortune, &c.

"And a lover of Miss Portman's—that is the most material part of the story to me," continued Lord Delacour; "for otherwise, you know, Mr. Vincent would be no more to me than any other gentleman. But in that point of view—I mean as a lover of Belinda Portman, and I may say, not quite unlikely to be her husband—he is highly interesting to my Lady Delacour, and to me, and to you, as Miss Portman's well-wisher, doubtless."

"Doubtless!" was all Mr. Hervey could reply.

"Now, you must know," continued his lordship, "that Lady Delacour has, for a woman, an uncommon share of penetration, and can put things together in a wonderful way: in short, it has come to her (my Lady Delacour's) knowledge, that before Miss Portman was at Oakly-park last summer, and after she left it this autumn, Mr. Vincent was a constant visitor at Mrs. Luttridge's, whilst at Harrowgate, and used to play high (though unknown to the Percivals, of course) at billiards with Mr. Luttridge—a man, I confess, I disliked always, even when I carried the election for them. But no matter: it is not from enmity I speak now. But it is very well known that Luttridge has but a small fortune, and yet lives as if he had a large one; and all the young men who like high play are sure to be well received at his house. Now, I hope Mr. Vincent is not well received on that footing.

"Since my Lady Delacour and I have been such good friends," continued his lordship, "I have dropped all connexion with the Luttridges; so cannot go there myself: moreover, I do not wish to be tempted to lose any more thousands to the lady. But you never play, and you are not likely to be tempted to it now; so you will oblige me and Lady Delacour if you will go to Luttridge's to-night: she is always charmed to see you, and you will easily discover how the land lies. Mr. Vincent is certainly a very agreeable, open-hearted young man; but, if he game, God forbid that Miss Portman should ever be his wife!"

"God forbid!" said Clarence Hervey.

"The man," resumed Lord Delacour, "must, in my opinion, be very superior indeed who is deserving of Belinda Portman. Oh, Mr. Hervey, you do not—you cannot know her merit, as I do. It is one thing, sir, to see a fine girl in a ball-room, and another—quite another—to live in the house with her for months, and to see her, as I have seen Belinda Portman, in every-day life, as one may call it. Then it is one can judge of the real temper, manners, and character; and never woman had so sweet a temper, such charming manners, such a fair, open, generous, decided yet gentle character, as this Miss Portman."

"Your lordship speaks con amore," said Clarence.

"I speak, Mr. Hervey, from the bottom of my soul," cried Lord Delacour, pulling in his horse, and stopping short. "I should be an unfeeling, ungrateful brute, if I were not sensible of the obligations—yes, the obligations—which my Lady Delacour and I have received from Belinda Portman. Why, sir, she has been the peacemaker between us—but we will not talk of that now. Let us think of her affairs. If Mr. Vincent once gets into Mrs. Luttridge's cursed set, there's no knowing where it will end. I speak from my own experience, for I really never was fond of high play; and yet, when I got into that set, I could not withstand it. I lost by hundreds and thousands; and so will he, before he is aware of it, no doubt. Mrs. Luttridge will look upon him as her dupe, and make him such. I always—but this is between ourselves—suspected that I did not lose my last thousand to her fairly. Now, Hervey, you know the whole, do try and save Mr. Vincent, for Belinda Portman's sake."

Clarence Hervey shook hands with Lord Delacour, with a sentiment of real gratitude and affection; and assured him that his confidence was not misplaced. His lordship little suspected that he had been soliciting him to save his rival. Clarence's love was not of that selfish sort which the moment that it is deprived of hope sinks into indifference, or is converted into hatred. Belinda could not be his; but, in the midst of the bitterest regret, he was supported by the consciousness of his own honour and generosity: he felt a noble species of delight in the prospect of promoting the happiness of the woman upon whom his fondest affections had been fixed; and he rejoiced to feel that he had sufficient magnanimity to save a rival from ruin. He was even determined to make that rival his friend, notwithstanding the prepossession which, he clearly perceived, Mr. Vincent felt against him.

"His jealousy will be extinguished the moment he knows my real situation," said Clarence to himself. "He will be convinced that I have a soul incapable of envy; and, if he suspect my love for Belinda, he will respect the strength of mind with which I can command my passions. I take it for granted that Mr. Vincent must possess a heart and understanding such as I should desire in a friend, or he could never be—what he is to Belinda."

Full of these generous sentiments, Clarence waited with impatience for the hour when he might present himself at Mrs. Luttridge's. He went there so early in the evening, that he found the drawing-room quite empty; the company, who had been invited to dine, had not yet left the dining-room, and the servants had but just set the card-tables and lighted the candles. Mr. Hervey desired that nobody should be disturbed by his coming so early; and, fortunately, Mrs. Luttridge was detained some minutes by Lady Newland's lingering glass of Madeira. In the mean time, Clarence executed his design. From his former observations, and from the hints that Lord Delacour had let fall, he suspected that there was sometimes in this house not only high play, but foul play: he recollected that once, when he played there at billiards, he had perceived that the table was not perfectly horizontal; and it occurred to him, that perhaps the E O table might be so contrived as to put the fortunes of all who played at it in the power of the proprietor. Clarence had sufficient ingenuity to invent the method by which this might be done; and he had the infallible means in his possession of detecting the fraud. The E O table was in an apartment adjoining to the drawing-room: he found his way to it; and he discovered, beyond a possibility of doubt, that it was constructed for the purposes of fraud. His first impulse was to tell this immediately to Mr.

Vincent, to put him on his guard; but, upon reflection, he determined to keep his discovery to himself, till he was satisfied whether that gentleman had or had not any passion for play.

"If he have," thought Clarence, "it is of the utmost consequence to Miss Portman that he should early in life receive a shock that may leave an indelible impression upon his mind. To save him a few hours of remorse, I will not give up the power of doing him the most essential service. I will let him go on—if he be so inclined—to the very verge of ruin and despair: I will let him feel all the horrors of a gamester's fate, before I tell him that I have the means to save him. Mrs. Luttridge must, when I call upon her, refund whatever he may lose: she will not brave public shame—she cannot stand a public prosecution."

Scarcely had Clarence arranged his scheme, when he heard the voices of the ladies, who were coming up stairs.

Mrs. Luttridge made her appearance, accompanied by a very pretty, modish, affected young lady, Miss Annabella Luttridge, her niece. Her little coquettish airs were lost upon Clarence Hervey, whose eye was intently fixed upon the door, watching for the entrance of Mr. Vincent. He was one of the dinner party, and he came up soon after the ladies. He seemed prepared for the sight of Mr. Hervey, to whom he bowed with a cold, haughty air; and then addressed himself to Miss Annabella Luttridge, who showed the most obvious desire to attract his attention.

From all that passed this evening, Mr. Hervey was led to suspect, notwithstanding the reasons which made it apparently improbable, that the fair Annabella was the secret cause of Mr. Vincent's frequent visits at her aunt's. It was natural that Clarence should be disposed to this opinion, from the circumstances of his own situation. During three hours that he stayed at Mrs. Luttridge's, Mr. Vincent never joined any of the parties at play; but, just as he was going away, he heard some one say—"How comes it, Vincent, that you've been idle all night?" This question revived Mr. Hervey's suspicions; and, uncertain what report he should make to Lord Delacour, he resolved to defer making any, till he had farther opportunities of judging.

When Mr. Hervey asked himself how it was possible that the pupil of Mr. Percival could become a gamester, he forgot that Mr. Vincent had not been educated by his guardian; that he had lived in the West Indies till he was eighteen; and that he had only been under the care of Mr. Percival for a few years, after his habits and character were in a great measure formed. The taste for gambling he had acquired whilst he was a child; but, as it was then confined to trifles, it had been passed over, as a thing of no consequence, a boyish folly, that would never grow up with him: his father used to see him, day after day, playing with eagerness at games of chance, with his negroes, or with the sons of neighbouring planters; yet he was never alarmed: he was too intent upon making a fortune for his family to consider how they would spend it; and he did not foresee that this boyish fault might be the means of his son's losing, in a few hours, the wealth which he had been many years amassing. When young Vincent came over to England, Mr. Percival had not immediate opportunities of discovering this particular foible in his ward; but he perceived that in his mind there was that presumptuous belief in his special good fortune which naturally leads to the love of gambling. Instead of lecturing him, his guardian appealed to his understanding, and took opportunities of showing him the ruinous effects of high play in real life. Young Vincent was touched, and, as he thought, convinced; but his emotion was stronger than his conviction— his feelings were always more powerful than his reason. His detestation of the selfish character of a gamester was felt and expressed with enthusiasm and eloquence; and his indignation rose afterwards at the slightest hint that he might ever in future be tempted to become what he abhorred. Unfortunately he disdained prudence, as the factitious virtue of inferior minds: he thought that the feelings of a man of honour were to be his guide in the first and last appeal; and for his conduct through life, as a man and as a gentleman, he proudly professed to trust to the sublime instinct of a good heart. His guardian's doubts of the infallibility and even of the existence of this moral instinct wounded Mr. Vincent's pride instead of alarming his understanding; and he was rather eager than averse to expose himself to the danger, that he might prove his superiority to the temptation. How different are the feelings in different situations! Yet often as this has been repeated, how difficult it is to impress the truth upon inexperienced, sanguine minds!—Whilst young Vincent was immediately under his guardian's eye at Oakly-park, his safety from vice appeared to him inglorious; he was impatient to sally forth into the world, confident rather of his innate than acquired virtue.

When he first became acquainted with Mrs. Luttridge at Harrowgate, he knew that she was a professed gambler, and he despised the character; yet without reflecting on the danger, or perhaps for the pleasure of convincing Mr. Percival that he was superior to it, he continued his visits. For some time he was a passive spectator. Billiards, however, was a game of address, not chance; there was a billiard-table at Oakly-park, as well as at Mr. Luttridge's, and he had played with his guardian. Why, then, should he not play with Mr. Luttridge? He did play: his skill was admired; he betted, and his bets were successful: but he did not call this gaming, for the bets were not to any great amount, and it was only playing at billiards. Mr. Percival was delayed in town some weeks longer than usual, and he knew nothing of the manner in which his young friend spent his time. As soon as Mr. Vincent heard of his arrival at Oakly-park, he left half finished his game at billiards; and, fortunately for him, the charms of Belinda made him forget for some months that such a thing as a billiard-table existed. All that had happened at Mr. Luttridge's passed from his mind as a dream; and whilst his heart was agitated by his new passion, he could scarcely believe that he had ever been interested by any other feelings. He was surprised when he accidentally recollected the eagerness with which he used to amuse himself in Mr. Luttridge's company; but he was certain that all this was passed for ever; and precisely because he was under the dominion of one strong passion, he thought he could never be under the dominion of another. Thus persisting in his disdain of reason as a moral guide, Mr. Vincent thought, acted, and suffered as a man of feeling. Scarcely had Belinda left Oakly-park for one week when the ennui consequent to violent passion became insupportable; and to console himself for her absence he flew to the billiard-table. Emotion of some kind or other was become necessary to him; he said that not to feel was not to live; and soon the suspense, the anxiety, the hopes, the fears, the perpetual vicissitudes of a gamester's life, seemed to him almost as delightful as those of a lover's. Deceived by these appearances, Mrs. Luttridge thought that his affection for Belinda either was or might be conquered, and her hopes of obtaining his fortune for her niece Annabella revived. As Mr. Vincent could not endure Mrs. Freke, she abstained, at her friend's particular desire, from appearing at her house whilst he was there, and Mrs. Luttridge interested him much in her own favour, by representing her indignation at Harriot's conduct to be such that it had occasioned a total breach in their friendship. Mrs. Freke's sudden departure from Harrowgate confirmed the probability of this quarrel; yet these two ladies were secretly leagued together in a design of breaking off Mr. Vincent's match with Belinda, against whom Mrs. Freke had vowed revenge. The anonymous letter, which she hoped would work her purpose, produced, however, an effect totally unexpected upon his generous mind: he did not guess the writer; but his indignation against such base accusations burst forth with a violence that astounded Mrs. Luttridge. His love for Belinda appeared ten times more enthusiastic than before—the moment she was accused, he felt himself her defender, as well as her lover. He was dispossessed of the evil spirit of gambling as if by a miracle; and the billiard-table, and Mrs. Luttridge, and Miss Annabella, vanished from his view. He breathed nothing but love; he would ask no permission, he would wait for none from Belinda: he declared that instant he would set out in search of her, and he would tear that infamous letter to atoms in her presence; he would show her how impossible suspicion was to his nature. The first violence of the hurricane Mrs. Luttridge could not stand, and thought not of opposing; but whilst his horses and curricle were getting ready, she took such an affectionate leave of his dog Juba, and she protested so much that she and Annabella should not know how to live without poor Juba, that Mr. Vincent, who was excessively fond of his dog, could not help sympathizing in their sorrow: reasoning just as well as they wished, he extended his belief in their affection for this animal to friendship, if not love, for his master. He could not grant Mrs. Luttridge's earnest supplication to leave the dog behind him under her protection; but he promised—and laid his hand upon his heart when he promised—that Juba should wait upon Mrs. Luttridge as soon as she went to town. This appointment being made, Miss Annabella permitted herself to be somewhat consoled. It would be injustice to omit that she did all that could be done by a cambric handkerchief to evince delicate sensibility in this parting scene. Mrs. Luttridge also deserves her share of praise for the manner in which she reproved her niece for giving way to her feelings, and for the address with which she wished to Heaven that poor Annabella had the calm philosophic temper of which Miss Portman was, she understood, a most uncommon example.

As Mr. Vincent drove toward London he reflected upon these last words; and he could not help thinking that if Belinda had more faults she would be more amiable.

These thoughts were, however, driven from his mind, and scarcely left a trace behind them, when he once more saw and conversed with her. The dignity, sincerity, and kindness which she showed the evening that he put the anonymous letter into her hands charmed and touched him, and his real feelings and his enthusiasm conspired to make him believe that his whole happiness depended on her smiles. The confession which she made to him of her former attachment to Clarence Hervey, as it raised in Vincent's mind strong emotions of jealousy, increased his passion as much as it piqued his pride; and she appeared in a new and highly interesting light when he discovered that the coldness of manner which he had attributed to want of sensibility arose probably from its excess—that her heart should have been preoccupied was more tolerable to him than the belief of her settled indifference. He was so intent upon these delightful varieties in his love for Belinda that it was not till he had received a reproachful note from Mrs. Luttridge, to remind him of his promised visit with Juba, that he could prevail upon himself to leave Twickenham, even for a few hours. Lady Delacour's hatred or fear of Juba, which he accidentally mentioned to Miss Annabella, appeared to her and to her aunt "the most extraordinary thing upon earth;" and when it was contrasted with their excessive fondness, it seemed to him indeed unaccountable. From pure consideration for her ladyship's nerves, Mrs. Luttridge petitioned Vincent to leave the dog with her, that Helena might not be in such imminent danger from "the animal's monstrous jaws." The petition was granted; and as the petitioners foresaw, Juba became to them a most useful auxiliary. Juba's master called daily to see him, and sometimes when he came in the morning Mrs. Luttridge was not at home, so that his visits were repeated in the evening; and the evening in London is what in other places is called the night. Mrs. Luttridge's nights could not be passed without deep play. The sight of the E O table at first shocked Mr. Vincent: he thought of Mr. Percival, and he turned away from it; but to his active social disposition it was extremely irksome to stand idle and uninterested where all were busy and eager in one common pursuit; to his generous temper it seemed ungentlemanlike to stand by the silent censor of the rest of the company; and when he considered of how little importance a few hundreds or even thousands could be to a man of his large fortune, he could not help feeling that it was sordid, selfish, avaricious, to dread their possible loss; and thus social spirit, courage, generosity, all conspired to carry our man of feeling to the gaming-table. Once there, his ruin was inevitable. Mrs. Luttridge, whilst she held his doom in her power, hesitated only whether it would be more her interest to marry him to her niece, or to content herself with his fortune. His passion for Belinda, which she saw had been by some means or other increased, in spite of the anonymous letter, gave her little hopes of Annabella's succeeding, even with the assistance of Juba and delicate sensibility. So the aunt, careless of her niece's disappointment, determined that Mr. Vincent should be her victim; and sensible that she must not give him time for reflection, she hurried him on, till, in the course of a few evenings spent at the E O table, he lost not only thousands, but tens of thousands. One lucky night, she assured him, would set all to rights; the run could not always be against him, and fortune must change in his favour, if he tried her with sufficient perseverance.

The horror, the agony of mind, which he endured at this sudden ruin which seemed impending over him—the recollection of Belinda, of Mr. Percival, almost drove him to distraction. He retreated from the E O table one night, swearing that he never would hazard another guinea. But his ruin was not yet complete—he had thousands yet to lose, and Mrs. Luttridge would not thus relinquish her prey. She persuaded him to try his fortune once more. She now suffered him to regain courage, by winning back some of his own money. His mind was relieved from the sense of immediate danger; he rejoiced to be saved from the humiliation of confessing his losses to Mr. Percival and Belinda. The next day he saw her with unusual pleasure, and this was the very morning Clarence Hervey paid his visit. The imprudence of Lady Delacour, joined perhaps to his own consciousness that he had a secret fault, which ought to lower him in the esteem of his mistress, made him misinterpret every thing that passed—his jealousy was excited in the most sudden and violent manner. He flew from Lady Delacour's to Mrs. Luttridge's—he was soothed and flattered by the apparent kindness with which he was received by Annabella and her aunt; but after dinner, when one of the servants whispered to Mrs. Luttridge, who sat next to him, that Mr. Clarence Hervey was above stairs, he gave such a start, that the fair Annabella's lap did not escape a part of the bumper of wine which he was going to drink to her health. In the confusion and apologies which this accident occasioned, Mrs. Luttridge had time to consider what might be the cause of the start, and she combined her suspicions so quickly and judiciously that she guessed the truth—that he feared to be seen at the E O table by a person who might find it for his interest to tell the truth to Belinda Portman. "Mr. Vincent," said she, in a low voice, "I have such a terrible headache, that I am fit for nothing—I am not up to E O to-night, so you must wait for your revenge till to-morrow."

Mr. Vincent was heartily glad to be relieved from his engagement, and he endeavoured to escape Clarence's suspicions, by devoting his whole time this evening to Annabella, not in the least apprehensive that Mr. Hervey would return the next night. Mr. Vincent was at the E O table at the usual hour, for he was excessively anxious to regain what he had lost, not so much for the sake of the money, which he could afford to lose, but lest the defalcation in his fortune should lead Mr. Percival to the knowledge of the means which had occasioned it. He could not endure, after his high vaunts, to see himself humbled by his rash confidence in himself, and he secretly vowed, that if he could but reinstate himself, by one night's good luck, he would for ever quit the society of gamblers. A few months before this time, he would have scorned the idea of concealing any part of his conduct, any one of his actions, from his best friend, Mr. Percival; but his pride now reconciled him to the meanness of concealment; and here, the acuteness of his feelings was to his own mind an excuse for dissimulation: so fallacious is moral instinct, unenlightened or uncontrolled by reason and religion.

Mr. Vincent was disappointed in his hopes of regaining what he had lost. This was not the fortunate night, which Mrs. Luttridge's prognostics had vainly taught him to expect: he played on, however, with all the impetuosity of his natural temper; his judgment forsook him; he scarcely knew what he said or did; and, in the course of a few hours, he was worked up to such a pitch of insanity, that in one desperate moment he betted nearly all that he was worth in the world—and lost! He stood like one stupified: the hum of voices scarcely reached his ear—he saw figures moving before him; but he did not distinguish who or what they were.

Supper was announced, and the room emptied fast, whilst he remained motionless leaning on the E O table. He was roused by Mrs. Luttridge saying, as she passed, "Don't you sup to-night, Mr. Hervey?"— Vincent looked up, and saw Clarence Hervey opposite to him. His countenance instantly changed, and the lightning of anger flashed through the gloom of despair: he uttered not a syllable; but his looks said, "How is this, sir? Here again to-night to watch me?—to enjoy my ruin?—to be ready to carry the first news of it to Belinda?"

At this last thought, Vincent struck his closed hand with violence against his forehead; and rushing by Mr. Hervey, who in vain attempted to speak to him, he pressed into the midst of the crowd on the stairs, and let himself be carried along with them into the supper-room. At supper he took his usual seat between Mrs. Luttridge and the fair Annabella; and, as if determined to brave the observing eyes of Clarence Hervey, who was at the same table, he affected extravagant gaiety; he ate, drank, talked, and laughed, more than any of the company. Toward the end of the supper, his dog, who was an inmate at Mrs. Luttridge's, licked his hand to put him in mind that he had given him nothing to eat.

"Drink, Juba!—drink, and never have done, boy!" cried Vincent, holding a bumper of wine to the dog's mouth; "he's the only dog I ever saw taste wine." Then snatching up some of the flowers, which ornamented the table, he swore that Juba should henceforward be called Anacreon, and that he deserved to be crowned with roses by the hand of beauty. The fair Annabella instantly took a hothouse rose from her bosom, and assisted in making the garland, with which she crowned the new Anacreon. Insensible to his honours, the dog, who was extremely hungry, turned suddenly to Mrs. Luttridge, by whom he had, till this night, regularly been fed with the choicest morsels, and lifting up his huge paw, laid it, as he had been wont to do, upon her arm. She shook it off: he, knowing nothing of the change in his master's affairs, laid the paw again upon her arm; and with that familiarity to which he had long been encouraged, raised his head almost close to the lady's cheek.

"Down, Juba!—down, sir, down!" cried Mrs. Luttridge, in a sharp voice.

"Down, Juba!—down, sir!" repeated Mr. Vincent, in a tone of bitter feeling, all his assumed gaiety forsaking him at this instant: "Down, Juba!—down, sir, down!" as low as your master, thought he; and pushing back his chair, he rose from table, and precipitately left the room.

Little notice was taken of his retreat; the chairs closed in; and the gap which his vacant place left was visible but for a moment: the company were as gay as before; the fair Annabella smiled with a grace as attractive; and Mrs. Luttridge exulted in the success of her schemes—whilst her victim was in the agonies of despair.

Clarence Hervey, who had watched every change of Vincent's countenance, saw the agony of soul with which he rose from the table, and quitted the room: he suspected his purpose, and followed him immediately; but Mr. Vincent had got out of the house before he could overtake him; which way he was gone no one could tell, for no one had seen him; the only information he could gain was, that he might possibly be heard of at Nerot's Hotel, or at Governor Montford's, in Portland-place. The hotel was but a few yards from Mrs. Luttridge's. Clarence went there directly. He asked for Mr. Vincent. One of the waiters said, that he was not yet come in; but another called out, "Mr. Vincent, sir, did you say? I have just shown him up to his room."

"Which is the room?—I must see him instantly," cried Hervey.

"Not to-night—you can't see him now, sir. Mr. Vincent won't let you in, I can assure you, sir. I went up myself three minutes ago, with some letters, that came whilst he was away, but he would not let me in. I heard him double-lock the door, and he swore terribly. I can't go up again at this time o'night—for my life I dare not, sir."

"Where is his own man?—Has Mr. Vincent any servant here?—Mr. Vincent's man!" cried Clarence; "let me see him!"

"You can't, sir. Mr. Vincent has just sent his black, the only servant he has here, out on some message. Indeed, sir, there's no use in going up," continued the waiter, as Clarence sprang up two or three stairs at once: "Mr. Vincent has desired nobody may disturb him. I give you my word, sir, he'll be very angry; and, besides, 'twould be to no purpose, for he'll not unlock the door."

"Is there but one door to the room?" said Mr. Hervey; and, as he asked the question, he pulled a guinea out of his pocket, and touched the waiter's hand with it.

"Oh, now I recollect—yes, sir, there's a private door through a closet: may be that mayn't be fastened."

Clarence put the guinea into the waiter's hand, who instantly showed him the way up the back staircase to the door that opened into Mr. Vincent's bed-chamber.

"Leave me now," whispered he, "and make no noise."

The man withdrew; and as Mr. Hervey went close to the concealed door, to try if it was fastened, he distinctly heard a pistol cocked. The door was not fastened: he pushed it softly open, and saw the unfortunate man upon his knees, the pistol in his hand, his eyes looking up to heaven. Clarence was in one moment behind him; and, seizing hold of the pistol, he snatched it from Vincent's grasp with so much calm presence of mind and dexterity, that, although the pistol was cocked, it did not go off.

"Mr. Hervey!" exclaimed Vincent, starting up. Astonishment overpowered all other sensations. But the next instant recovering the power of speech, "Is this the conduct of a gentleman, Mr. Hervey—of a man of honour," cried he, "thus to intrude upon my privacy; to be a spy upon my actions; to triumph in my ruin; to witness my despair; to rob me of the only—"

He looked wildly at the pistol which Clarence held in his hand; then snatching up another, which lay upon the table, he continued, "You are my enemy—I know it; you are my rival; I know it; Belinda loves you! Nay, affect not to start—this is no time for dissimulation—Belinda loves you—you know it: for her sake, for your own, put me out of the world—put me out of torture. It shall not be called murder: it shall be called a duel. You have been a spy upon my actions—I demand satisfaction. If you have one spark of honour or of courage within you, Mr. Hervey, show it now—fight me, sir, openly as man to man, rival to rival, enemy to enemy—fire."

"If you fire upon me, you will repent it," replied Clarence calmly; "for I am not your enemy—I am not your rival."

"You are," interrupted Vincent, raising his voice to the highest pitch of indignation: "you are my rival, though you dare not avow it! The denial is base, false, unmanly. Oh, Belinda, is this the being you prefer to me? Gamester—wretch, as I am, my soul never stooped to falsehood! Treachery I abhor; courage, honour, and a heart worthy of Belinda, I possess. I beseech you, sir," continued he, addressing himself, in a tremulous tone of contempt, to Mr. Hervey, "I beseech you, sir, to leave me to my own feelings—and to myself."

"You are not yourself at this moment, and I cannot leave you to such mistaken feelings," replied Hervey: "command yourself for a moment, and hear me; use your reason, and you will soon be convinced that I am your friend."

"My friend!"

"Your friend. For what purpose did I come here? to snatch this pistol from your hand? If it were my interest, my wish, that you were out of the world, why did I prevent you from destroying yourself? Do you think that the action of an enemy? Use your reason."

"I cannot," said Vincent, striking his forehead; "I know not what to think—I am not master of myself. I conjure you, sir, for your own sake, to leave me."

"For my own sake!" repeated Hervey, disdainfully: "I am not thinking of myself; nor can any thing you have said provoke me from my purpose. My purpose is to save you from ruin, for the sake of a woman, whom, though I am no longer your rival, I have loved longer, if not better, than you have."

There was something so open in Hervey's countenance, such a strong expression of truth in his manner, that it could not be resisted, and Vincent, in an altered voice, exclaimed, "You acknowledge that you have loved Belinda—and could you cease to love her? Impossible!—And, loving her, must you not detest me?"

"No," said Clarence, holding out his hand to him; "I wish to be your friend. I have not the baseness to wish to deprive others of happiness because I cannot enjoy it myself. In one word, to put you at ease with me for ever, I have no pretensions, I can have none, to Miss Portman. I am engaged to another woman—in a few days you will hear of my marriage."

Mr. Vincent threw the pistol from him, and gave his hand to Hervey.

"Pardon what I said to you just now," cried he; "I knew not what I said—I spoke in the agony of despair: your purpose is most generous—but it is in vain—you come too late—I am ruined, past all hope."

He folded his arms, and his eyes reverted involuntarily to his pistols.

"The misery that you have this night experienced," said Mr. Hervey, "was necessary to the security of your future happiness."

"Happiness!" repeated Vincent; "happiness—there is no happiness left for me. My doom is fixed—fixed by my own folly—my own rash, headstrong folly. Madman that I was, what could tempt me to the gaming-table? Oh! if I could recall but a few days, a few hours of my existence! But remorse is vain—prudence comes too late. Do you know," said he, fixing his eyes upon Hervey, "do you know that I am a beggar? that I have not a farthing left upon earth? Go to Belinda; tell her so: tell her, that if she had ever the slightest regard for me, I deserve it no longer. Tell her to forget, despise, detest me. Give her joy that she has escaped having a gamester for a husband."

"I will," said Clarence, "I will, if you please, tell her what I believe to be true, that the agony you have felt this night, the dear-bought experience you have had, will be for ever a warning."

"A warning!" interrupted Vincent: "Oh, that it could yet be useful to me!—But I tell you it comes too late—nothing can save me."

"I can," said Mr. Hervey. "Swear to me, for Belinda's sake—solemnly swear to me, that you will never more trust your happiness and hers to the hazard of a die—swear that you will never more, directly or indirectly, play at any game of chance, and I will restore to you the fortune that you have lost."

Mr. Vincent stood as if suspended between ecstasy and despair: he dared not trust his senses: with a fervent and solemn adjuration he made the vow that was required of him; and Clarence then revealed to him the secret of the E O table.

"When Mrs. Luttridge knows that I have it in my power to expose her to public shame, she will instantly refund all that she has iniquitously won from you. Even among gamblers she would be blasted for ever by this discovery: she knows it, and if she dared to brave public opinion, we have then a sure resource in the law—prosecute her. The laws of honour, as well as the laws of the land, will support the prosecution. But she will never let the affair go into a court of justice. I will see her early, as early as I can to-morrow, and put you out of suspense."

"Most generous of human beings!" exclaimed Vincent; "I cannot express to you what I feel; but your own heart, your own approbation—"

"Farewell, good night," interrupted Clarence; "I see that I have made a friend—I was determined that Belinda's husband should be my friend—I have succeeded beyond my hopes. And now I will intrude no longer," said he, as he closed the door after him. His sensations at this instant were more delightful even than those of the man he had relieved from the depth of despair. How wisely has Providence made the benevolent and generous passions the most pleasurable!

CHAPTER XXIX — A JEW

In the silence of the night, when the hurry of action was over, and the enthusiasm of generosity began to subside, the words, which had escaped from Mr. Vincent in the paroxysm of despair and rage—the words, "Belinda loves you"—recurred to Clarence Hervey; and it required all his power over himself to banish the sound from his ear, and the idea from his mind. He endeavoured to persuade himself that these words were dictated merely by sudden jealousy, and that there could be no real foundation for the assertion: perhaps this belief was a necessary support to his integrity. He reflected, that, at all events, his engagement with Virginia could not be violated; his proffered services to Mr. Vincent could not be withdrawn: he was firm and consistent. Before two o'clock the next day, Vincent received from Clarence this short note:

"Enclosed is Mrs. Luttridge's acknowledgment, that she has no claims upon you, in consequence of what passed last night. I said nothing about the money she had previously won, as I understand you have paid it.

"The lady fell into fits, but it would not do. The husband attempted to bully me; I told him I should be at his service, after he had made the whole affair public, by calling you out.

"I would have seen you myself this morning, but that I am engaged with lawyers and marriage settlements.

"Yours sincerely,

"CLARENCE HERVEY."

Overjoyed at the sight of Mrs. Luttridge's acknowledgment, Vincent repeated his vow never more to hazard himself in her dangerous society. He was impatient to see Belinda; and, full of generous and grateful sentiments, in his first moment of joy, he determined to conceal nothing from her; to make at once the confession of his own imprudence and the eulogium of Clarence Hervey's generosity. He was just setting out for Twickenham, when he was sent for by his uncle, Governor Montford, who had business to settle with him, relative to his West India estates. He spent the remainder of the morning with his uncle; and there he received a charming letter from Belinda—that letter which she had written and sent whilst Lady Delacour was reading Clarence Hervey's packet. It would have cured Vincent of jealousy, even if he had not, in the interim, seen Mr. Hervey, and learnt from him the news of his approaching marriage. Miss Portman, at the conclusion of her letter, informed him that Lady Delacour purposed being in Berkeley-square the next day; that they were to spend a week in town, on account of Mrs. Margaret Delacour, who had promised her ladyship a visit; and to go to Twickenham would be a formidable journey to an infirm old lady, who seldom stirred out of her house.

Whatever displeasure Lady Delacour felt towards her friend Belinda, on account of her coldness to Mr. Hervey, and her steadiness to Mr. Vincent, had by this time subsided. Angry people, who express their passion, as it has been justly said, always speak worse than they think. This was usually the case with her ladyship.

The morning after they arrived in town, she came into Belinda's room, with an air of more than usual sprightliness and satisfaction. "Great news!—Great news!—Extraordinary news!—But it is very imprudent to excite your expectations, my dear Belinda. Pray, did you hear a wonderful noise in the square a little while ago?"

"Yes, I thought I heard a great bustle; but Marriott appeased my curiosity, by saying that it was only a battle between two dogs."

"It is well if this battle between two dogs do not end in a duel between two men," said Lady Delacour.

"This prospect of mischief seems to have put your ladyship in wonderfully good spirits," said Belinda, smiling.

"But what do you think I have heard of Mr. Vincent?" continued Lady Delacour: "that Miss Annabella Luttridge is dying for love of him—or of his fortune. Knowing, as I do, the vanity of mankind, I suppose that your Mr. Vincent, all perfect as he is, was flattered by the little coquette; and perhaps he condescends to repay her in the same coin. I take it for granted—for I always fill up the gaps in a story my own way—I take it for granted that Mr. Vincent got into some entanglement with her, and that this has been the cause of the quarrel with the aunt. That there has been a quarrel is certain, for your friend Juba told Marriott so. His massa swore that he would never go to Mrs. Luttridge's again; and this morning he took the decisive measure of sending to request that his dog might be returned. Juba went for his namesake. Miss Annabella Luttridge was the person who delivered up the dog; and she desired the black to tell his master, with her compliments, that Juba's collar was rather too tight; and she begged that he would not fail to take it off as soon as he could. Perhaps, my dear, you are as simple as the poor negro, and suspect no finesse in this message. Miss Luttridge, aware that the faithful fellow was too much in your interests to be either persuaded or bribed to carry a billet-doux from any other lady to his master, did not dare to trust him upon this occasion; but she had the art to make him carry her letter without his knowing it. Colin maillard, vulgarly called blind man's buff, was, some time ago, a favourite play amongst the Parisian ladies: now hide and seek will be brought into fashion, I suppose, by the fair Annabella. Judge of her talents for the game by this instance:—she hid her billet-doux within the lining of Juba's collar. The dog, unconscious of his dignity as an ambassador, or rather as a chargé d'affaires, set out on his way home. As he was crossing Berkeley-square he was met by Sir Philip Baddely and his dog. The baronet's insolent favourite bit the black's heels. Juba, the dog, resented the injury immediately, and a furious combat ensued. In the height of the battle Juba's collar fell off. Sir Philip Baddely espied the paper that was sewed to the lining, and seized upon it immediately: the negro caught hold of it at the same instant: the baronet swore; the black struggled: the baronet knocked him down. The great dog left his canine antagonist that moment, flew at your baronet, and would have eaten him up at three mouthfuls, if Sir Philip had not made good his retreat to Dangerfield's circulating library. The negro's head was terribly cut by the sharp point of a stone, and his ankle was sprained; but, as he has just told me, he did not feel this till afterward. He started up, and pursued his master's enemy. Sir Philip was actually reading Miss Luttridge's billet-doux aloud when the black entered the library. He reclaimed his master's property with great intrepidity; and a gentleman who was present took his part immediately.

"In the mean time, Lord Delacour, who had been looking at the battle from our breakfast-room window, determined to go over to Dangerfield's, to see what was the matter, and how all this would end. He entered the library just as the gentleman who had volunteered in favour of poor Juba was disputing with Sir Philip. The bleeding negro told my lord, in as plain words as he could, the cause of the dispute; and Lord Delacour, who, to do him justice, is a man of honour, joined instantly in his defence. The baronet thought proper at length to submit; and he left the field of battle, without having any thing to say for himself but—'Damme!—very extraordinary, damme!'—or words to that effect.

"Now, Lord Delacour, besides being a man of honour, is also a man of humanity. I know that I cannot oblige you more, my dear Belinda, than by seasoning my discourse with a little conjugal flattery. My lord was concerned to see the poor black writhing in pain; and with the assistance of the gentleman who had joined in his defence, he brought Juba across the square to our house. Guess for what:—to try upon the strained ankle an infallible quack balsam recommended to him by the Dowager Lady Boucher. I was in the hall when they brought the poor fellow in: Marriott was called. 'Mrs. Marriott,' cried my lord, 'pray let us have Lady Boucher's infallible balsam—this instant!' Had you but seen the eagerness of face, or heard the emphasis, with which he said 'infallible balsam'—you must let me laugh at the recollection. One human smile must pass, and be forgiven."

"The smile may be the more readily forgiven," said Belinda, "since I am sure you are conscious that it reflected almost as much upon yourself as upon Lord Delacour."

"Why, yes; belief in a quack doctor is full as bad as belief in a quack balsam, I allow. Your observation is so malicious, because so just, that to punish you for it, I will not tell you the remainder of my story for a week to come; and I assure you that the best part of it I have left untold. To return to our friend Mr. Vincent:—could you but know what reasons I have, at this instant, for wishing him in Jamaica, you would acknowledge that I am truly candid in confessing that I believe my suspicions about E O were unfounded; and I am truly generous in admitting that you are right to treat him with justice."

This last enigmatical sentence Belinda could not prevail upon Lady Delacour to explain.

In the evening Mr. Vincent made his appearance. Lady Delacour immediately attacked him with raillery, on the subject of the fair Annabella. He was rejoiced to perceive that her suspicions took this turn, and that nothing relative to the transaction in which Clarence Hervey had been engaged had transpired. Vincent wavered in his resolution to confess the truth to Belinda. Though he had determined upon this in the first moment of joyful enthusiasm, yet the delay of four-and-twenty hours had made a material change in his feelings; his most virtuous resolves were always rather the effect of sudden impulse than of steady principle. But when the tide of passion had swept away the landmarks, he had no method of ascertaining the boundaries of right and wrong. Upon the present occasion his love for Belinda confounded all his moral calculations: one moment, his feelings as a man of honour forbade him to condescend to the meanness of dissimulation; but the next instant his feelings as a lover prevailed; and he satisfied his conscience by the idea that, as his vow must preclude all danger of his return to the gaming-table in future, it would only be creating an unnecessary alarm in Belinda's mind to speak to her of his past imprudence. His generosity at first revolted from the thought of suppressing those praises of Clarence Hervey, which had been so well deserved; but his jealousy returned, to combat his first virtuous impulse. He considered that his own inferiority must by comparison appear more striking to his mistress; and he sophistically persuaded himself that it would be for her happiness to conceal the merits of a rival, to whom she could never be united. In this vacillating state of mind he continued during the greatest part of the evening. About half an hour before he took his leave, Lady Delacour was called out of the room by Mrs. Marriott. Left alone with Belinda, his embarrassment increased, and the unsuspecting kindness of her manner was to him the most bitter reproach. He stood in silent agony whilst in a playful tone she smiled and said,

"Where are your thoughts, Mr. Vincent? If I were of a jealous temper, I should say with the fair Annabella—"

"You would say wrong, then," replied Mr. Vincent, in a constrained voice. He was upon the point of telling the truth; but to gain a reprieve of a few minutes, he entered into a defence of his conduct towards Miss Luttridge.

The sudden return of Lady Delacour relieved him from his embarrassment, and they conversed only on general subjects during the remainder of the evening; and he at last departed, secretly rejoicing that he was, as he fancied, under the necessity of postponing his explanation; he even thought of suppressing the history of his transaction with Mrs. Luttridge. He knew that his secret was safe with Clarence Hervey: Mrs. Luttridge would be silent for her own sake; and neither Lady Delacour nor Belinda had any connexion with her society.

A few days afterward, Mr. Vincent went to Gray, the jeweller, for some trinkets which he had bespoken. Lord Delacour was there, speaking about the diamond ring, which Gray had promised to dispose of for him. Whilst his lordship and Mr. Vincent were busy about their own affairs, Sir Philip Baddely and Mr.

Rochfort came into the shop. Sir Philip and Mr. Vincent had never before met. Lord Delacour, to prevent him from getting into a quarrel about a lady who was so little worth fighting for as Miss Annabella Luttridge, had positively refused to tell Mr. Vincent what he knew of the affair, or to let him know the name of the gentleman who was concerned in it.

The shopman addressed Mr. Vincent by his name, and immediately Sir Philip whispered to Rochfort, that Mr. Vincent was "the master of the black." Vincent, who unluckily overheard him, instantly asked Lord Delacour if that was the gentleman who had behaved so ill to his servant? Lord Delacour told him that it was now of no consequence to inquire. "If," said his lordship, "either of these gentlemen choose to accost you, I shall think you do rightly to retort; but for Heaven's sake do not begin the attack!"

Vincent's impetuosity was not to be restrained; he demanded from Sir Philip, whether he was the person who had beaten his servant? Sir Philip readily obliged him with an answer in the affirmative; and the consequence was the loss of a finger to the baronet, and a wound in the side to Mr. Vincent, which, though it did not endanger his life, yet confined him to his room for several days. The impatience of his mind increased his fever, and retarded his recovery.

When Belinda's first alarm for Mr. Vincent's safety was over, she anxiously questioned Lord Delacour as to the particulars of all that had passed between Mr. Vincent and Sir Philip, that she might judge of the manner in which her lover had conducted himself. Lord Delacour, who was a man of strict truth, was compelled to confess that Mr. Vincent had shown more spirit than temper, and more courage than prudence. Lady Delacour rejoiced to perceive that this account made Belinda uncommonly serious.

Mr. Vincent now thought himself sufficiently recovered to leave his room; his physicians, indeed, would have kept him prisoner a few days longer, but he was too impatient of restraint to listen to their counsels.

"Juba, tell the doctor, when he comes, that you could not keep me at home; and that is all that is necessary to be said."

He had now summoned courage to acknowledge to Belinda all that had happened, and was proceeding, with difficulty, down stairs, when he was suddenly struck by the sound of a voice which he little expected at this moment; a voice he had formerly been accustomed to hear with pleasure, but now it smote him to the heart:—it was the voice of Mr. Percival. For the first time in his life, he wished to deny himself to his friend. The recollection of the E O table, of Mrs. Luttridge, of Mr. Percival as his guardian, and of all the advice he had heard from him as his friend, rushed upon his mind at this instant; conscious and ashamed, he shrunk back, precipitately returned to his own room, and threw himself into a chair, breathless with agitation. He listened, expecting to hear Mr. Percival coming up stairs, and endeavoured to compose himself, that he might not betray, by his own agitation, all that he wished most anxiously to conceal. After waiting for some time, he rang the bell, to make inquiries. The waiter told him that a Mr. Percival had asked for him; but, having been told by his black that he was just gone out, the gentleman being, as he said, much hurried, had left a note; for an answer to which he would call at eight o'clock in the evening. Vincent was glad of this short reprieve. "Alas!" thought he, "how changed am I, when I fear to meet my best friend! To what has this one fatal propensity reduced me!"

He was little aware of the new difficulties that awaited him.

Mr. Percival's note was as follows:—

"My dear friend!

"Am not I a happy man, to find a friend in my ci-devant ward? But I have no time for sentiment; nor does it become the character, in which I am now writing to you—that of a DUN. You are so rich, and so prudent, that the word in capital letters cannot frighten you. Lady Anne's cousin, poor Mr. Carysfort, is dead. I am guardian to his boys; they are but ill provided for. I have fortunately obtained a partnership in a good house for the second son. Ten thousand pounds are wanting to establish him—we cannot raise the money amongst us, without dunning poor Mr. Vincent. Enclosed is your bond for the purchase-money of the little estate you bought from me last summer. I know that you have double the sum we want in ready money—so I make no ceremony. Let me have the ten thousand this evening, if you can, as I wish to leave town as soon as possible.

"Yours most sincerely,

"HENRY PERCIVAL."

Now Mr. Vincent had lost, and had actually paid to Mrs. Luttridge, the ready money which had been destined to discharge his debt to Mr. Percival: he expected fresh remittances from the West Indies in the course of a few weeks; but, in the mean time, he must raise this money immediately: this he could only do by having recourse to Jews—a desperate expedient. The Jew, to whom he applied, no sooner discovered that Mr. Vincent was under a necessity of having this sum before eight o'clock in the evening than he became exorbitant in his demands; and the more impatient this unfortunate young man became, the more difficulties he raised. At last, a bargain was concluded between them, in which Vincent knew that he was grossly imposed upon; but to this he submitted, for he had no alternative. The Jew promised to bring him ten thousand pounds at five o'clock in the evening, but it was half after seven before he made his appearance; and then he was so dilatory and circumspect, in reading over and signing the bonds, and in completing the formalities of the transaction, that before the money was actually in Vincent's possession, one of the waiters of the hotel knocked at the door to let him know that Mr. Percival was coming up stairs. Vincent hurried the Jew into an adjoining apartment, and bid him wait there, till he should come to finish the business. Though totally unsuspicious, Mr. Percival could not help being struck with the perturbation in which he found his young friend. Vincent immediately began to talk of the duel, and his friend was led to conclude that his anxiety arose from this affair. He endeavoured to put him at ease by changing the conversation. He spoke of the business which brought him to town, and of the young man whom he was going to place with a banker. "I hope," said he, observing that Vincent grew more embarrassed, "that my dunning you for this money is not really inconvenient."

"Not in the least—not in the least. I have the money ready—in a few moments—if you'll be so good as to wait here—I have the money ready in the next room."

At this instant a loud noise was heard—the raised voices of two people quarrelling. It was Juba, the black, and Solomon, the Jew. Mr. Vincent had sent Juba out of the way, on some errand, whilst he had been transacting his affairs with the Jew; but the black, having executed the commission on which he had been sent, returned, and went into his master's bedchamber, to read at his leisure a letter which he had just received from his wife. He did not at first see the Jew, and he was spelling out the words of his wife's letter.

"My dear Juba,

"I take this op-por-tu—" —nity he would have said; but the Jew, who had held his breath in to avoid discovery, till he could hold it no longer, now drew it so loud, that Juba started, looked round, and saw the feet of a man, which appeared beneath the bottom of the window curtain. Where fears of supernatural appearances were out of the question, our negro was a man of courage; he had no doubt that the man who was concealed behind the curtain was a robber, but the idea of a robber did not unnerve him like that of an Obeah woman. With presence of mind worthy of a greater danger, Juba took down his master's pistol, which hung over the chimney-piece, and marching deliberately up to the enemy, he seized the Jew by the throat, exclaiming—

"You rob my massa?—You dead man, if you rob my massa."

Terrified at the sight of the pistol, the Jew instantly explained who he was, and producing his large purse, assured Juba that he was come to lend money, and not to take it from his master; but this appeared highly improbable to Juba, who believed his master to be the richest man in the world; besides, the Jew's language was scarcely intelligible to him, and he saw secret terror in Solomon's countenance. Solomon had an antipathy to the sight of a black, and he shrunk from the negro with strong signs of aversion. Juba would not relinquish his hold; each went on talking in his own angry gibberish as loud as he could, till at last the negro fairly dragged the Jew into the presence of his master and Mr. Percival.

It is impossible to describe Mr. Vincent's confusion, or Mr. Percival's astonishment. The Jew's explanation was perfectly intelligible to him; he saw at once all the truth. Vincent, overwhelmed with shame, stood the picture of despair, incapable of uttering a single syllable.

"There is no necessity to borrow this money on my account," said Mr. Percival, calmly; "and if there were, we could probably have it on more reasonable terms than this gentleman proposes."

"I care not on what terms I have it—I care not what becomes of me—I am undone!" cried Vincent.

Mr. Percival coolly dismissed the Jew, made a sign to Juba to leave the room, and then, addressing himself to Vincent, said, "I can borrow the money that I want elsewhere. Fear no reproaches from me—I foresaw all this—you have lost this sum at play: it is well that it was not your whole fortune. I have only one question to ask you, on which depends my esteem—have you informed Miss Portman of this affair?"

"I have not yet told her, but I was actually half down stairs in my way to tell her."

"Then, Mr. Vincent, you are still my friend. I know the difficulty of such an avowal—but it is necessary."

"Cannot you, dear Mr. Percival, save me the intolerable shame of confessing my own folly? Spare me this mortification! Be yourself the bearer of this intelligence, and the mediator in my favour."

"I will with pleasure," said Mr. Percival; "I will go this instant: but I cannot say that I have any hope of persuading Belinda to believe in your being irrevocably reclaimed from the charms of play."

"Indeed, my excellent friend, she may rely upon me: I feel such horror at the past, such heartfelt resolution against all future temptation, that you may pledge yourself for my total reformation."

Mr. Percival promised that he would exert all his influence, except by pledging his own honour; to this he could not consent. "If I have any good news for you, I will return as soon as possible; but I will not be the bearer of any painful intelligence," said he; and he departed, leaving Mr. Vincent in a state of anxiety, which, to his temper, was a punishment sufficient for almost any imprudence he could have committed.

Mr. Percival returned no more that night. The next morning Mr. Vincent received the following letter from Belinda. He guessed his fate: he had scarcely power to read the words.

"I promised you that, whenever my own mind should be decided, I would not hold yours in suspense; yet at this moment I find it difficult to keep my word.

"Instead of lamenting, as you have often done, that my esteem for your many excellent qualities never rose beyond the bounds of friendship, we have now reason to rejoice at this, since it will save us much useless pain. It spares me the difficulty of conquering a passion that might be fatal to my happiness; and it will diminish the regret which you may feel at our separation. I am now obliged to say, that circumstances have made me certain we could not add to our mutual felicity by any nearer connexion.

"The hope of enjoying domestic happiness with a person whose manners, temper, and tastes suited my own, inclined me to listen to your addresses. But this happiness I could never enjoy with one who has any propensity to the love of play.

"For my own sake, as well as for yours, I rejoice that your fortune has not been materially injured; as this relieves me from the fear that my present conduct should be imputed to interested motives. Indeed, such is the generosity of your own temper, that in any situation I should scarcely have reason to apprehend from you such a suspicion.

"The absolute impossibility of my forming at present a connexion with another, will prevent you from imagining that I am secretly influenced by sentiments different from those which I avow; nor can any weak doubts on this subject expose me to my own reproaches.

"You perceive, sir, that I am not willing utterly to lose your esteem, even when I renounce, in the most unequivocal manner, all claim upon your affections. If any thing should appear to you harsh in this letter, I beg you to impute it to the real cause—my desire to spare you all painful suspense, by convincing you at once that my determination is irrevocable. With sincere wishes for your happiness, I bid you farewell.

"BELINDA PORTMAN."

A few hours after Mr. Vincent had read this letter he threw himself into a post-chaise, and set out for Germany. He saw that all hopes of being united to Belinda were over, and he hurried as far from her as possible. Her letter rather soothed than irritated his temper; her praises of his generosity were highly gratifying, and they had so powerful an effect upon his mind, that he was determined to prove that they were deserved. His conscience reproached him with not having made sufficiently honourable mention of Clarence Hervey's conduct, on the night when he was on the point of destroying himself. Before he left London he wrote a full account of this whole transaction, to be given to Miss Portman after his departure.

Belinda was deeply touched by this proof of his generosity. His letter—his farewell letter—she could not read without great emotion. It was written with true feeling, but in a manly style, without one word of vain lamentation.

"What a pity," thought Belinda, "that with so many good and great qualities, I should be forced to bid him adieu for ever!"

Though she strongly felt the pain of this separation, yet she could not recede from her decision: nothing could tempt her to connect herself with a man who had the fatal taste for play. Even Mr. Percival, much as he loved his ward, much as he wished for his union with Belinda, dared not pledge his honour for Mr. Vincent on this point.

Lady Anne Percival, in a very kind and sensible letter, expressed the highest approbation of Belinda's conduct; and the most sincere hope that Belinda would still continue to think of her with affection and esteem, though she had been so rash in her advice, and though her friendship had been apparently so selfish.

CHAPTER XXX — NEWS

"Do not expect that I should pretend to be sorry for Mr. Vincent," said Lady Delacour. "Let him be as generous and as penitent as he pleases, I am heartily glad that he is on his way to Germany. I dare say he will find in the upper or lower circles of the empire some heroine in the Kotzebue taste, who will alternately make him miserable till he is happy, and happy till he is miserable. He is one of those men who require great emotions: fine lovers these make for stage effect—but the worst husbands in the world!

"I hope, Belinda, you give me credit, for having judged better of Mr. Vincent than Lady Anne Percival did?"

"For having judged worse of him, you mean? Lady Anne always judges as well as possible of every body."

"I will allow you to play upon words in a friend's defence, but do not be alarmed for the reputation of Lady Anne's judgment. If it will be any satisfaction to you, I can with thorough sincerity assure you that I never liked her so well in my life as since I have detected her in a mistake. It saves her, in my imagination, from the odium of being a perfect character."

"And there was something so handsome in her manner of writing to me, when she found out her error," said Belinda.

"Very true, and my friend Mr. Percival behaved handsomely. Where friendships clash, it is not every man who has clearness of head sufficient to know his duty to his neighbour. Mr. Percival said no more than just the thing he ought, for his ward. You have reason to be obliged to him: and as we are returning thanks to all persons concerned in our deliverance from this imminent danger, Juba, the dog, and Juba, the black, and Solomon, the Jew, ought to come in for their share; for without that wrestling match of theirs, the truth might never have been dragged to light, and Mr. Vincent would have been in due course of time your lord and master. But the danger is over; you need not look so terrified: do not be like the man who dropped down dead with terror, when he was shown by daylight the broken bridge which he had galloped over in the dark."

Lady Delacour was in such high spirits that, without regard to connexion, she ran on from one subject to another.

"You have proved to me, my dear," said she, "that you are not a girl to marry, because the day was fixed, or because things had gone so far. I give you infinite credit for your civil courage, as Dr. X— calls it: military courage, as he said to me yesterday—military courage, that seeks the bubble reputation even in the cannon's mouth, may be had for sixpence a day. But civil courage, such as enabled the Princess Parizade, in the Arabian Tales, to go straight up the hill to her object, though the magical multitude of advising and abusive voices continually called to her to turn back, is one of the rarest qualities in man or woman, and not to be had for love, money, or admiration."

"You place admiration not only above money, but above love, in your climax, I perceive," said Belinda, smiling.

"I will give you leave to be as philosophically sarcastic as you please, my dear, if you will only smile, and if you will not look as pale as Seneca's Paulina, whose story we heard—from whom?"

"From Mr. Hervey, I believe."

"His name was ready upon your lips; I hope he was not far from your thoughts?"

"No one could be farther from my thoughts," said Belinda.

"Well, very likely—I believe it, because you say it; and because it is impossible."

"Rally me as much as you please, my dear Lady Delacour, I assure you that I speak the simple truth."

"I cannot suspect you of affectation, my dear. Therefore honestly tell me, if Clarence Hervey were at your feet this instant, would you spurn him from you?"

"Spurn him! no—I would neither spurn him, nor motion him from me; but without using any of the terms in the heroine's dictionary—"

"You would refuse him?" interrupted Lady Delacour, with a look of indignation—"you would refuse him?"

"I did not say so, I believe."

"You would accept him?"

"I did not say so, I am sure."

"Oh, you would tell him that you were not accustomed to him?"

"Not exactly in those words, perhaps."

"Well, we shall not quarrel about words," said Lady Delacour; "I only beg you to remember your own principles; and if ever you are put to the trial, be consistent. The first thing in a philosopher is to be consistent."

"Fortunately, for the credit of my philosophy, there is no immediate danger of its being put to the test."

"Unfortunately, you surely mean; unless you are afraid that it might not stand the test. But I was going, when I spoke of consistency, to remind you that all your own and Mr. Percival's arguments about first loves may now, with equal propriety, be turned against you."

"How against me?"

"They are evidently as applicable to second as to first loves, I think."

"Perhaps they are," said Belinda; "but I really and truly am not inclined to think of love at present; particularly as there is no necessity that I should."

Belinda took up a book, and Lady Delacour for one half hour abstained from any farther raillery. But longer than half an hour she could not be silent on the subject uppermost in her thoughts.

"If Clarence Hervey," cried she, "were not the most honourable of blockheads, he might be the most happy of men. This Virginia!—oh, how I hate her!—I am sure poor Clarence cannot love her."

"Because you hate her—or because you hate her without having ever seen her?" said Belinda.

"Oh, I know what she must be," replied Lady Delacour: "a soft, sighing, dying damsel, who puts bullfinches into her bosom. Smile, smile, my dear; you cannot help it; in spite of all your generosity, I know you must think as I do, and wish as I do, that she were at the bottom of the Black Sea this instant."

Lady Delacour stood for some minutes musing, and then exclaimed, "I will move heaven and earth to break off this absurd match."

"Good Heavens! my dear Lady Delacour, what do you mean?"

"Mean! my dear—I mean what I say, which very few people do: no wonder I should surprise you."

"I conjure you," cried Belinda, "if you have the least regard for my honour and happiness—"

"I have not the least, but the greatest; and depend upon it, my dear, I will do nothing that shall injure that dignity of mind and delicacy of character, which I admire and love, as much as Clarence Hervey did, and does. Trust to me: not Lady Anne Percival herself can be more delicate in her notions of propriety than I am for my friends, and, since my reformation, I hope I may add, for myself. Fear nothing." As she finished these words, she rang for her carriage. "I don't ask you to go out with me, my dear Belinda; I give you leave to sit in this armchair till I come back again, with your feet upon the fender, a book in your hand, and this little table beside you, like Lady S.'s picture of Comfort."

Lady Delacour spent the rest of the morning abroad; and when she returned home, she gave no account of what she had been doing, or of what or whom she had seen. This was so unusual, that Belinda could not avoid taking notice of it. Notwithstanding her ladyship's eulogium upon her own delicate sense of propriety, Miss Portman could not confide, with perfect resignation, in her prudence.

"Your ladyship reproached me once," said she, in a playful tone, "for my provoking want of curiosity: you have completely cured me of this defect, for never was woman more curious than I am, at this instant, to know the secret scheme that you have in agitation."

"Have patience a little longer, and the mystery will be unravelled. In the mean time, trust that every thing I do is for the best. However, as you have behaved pretty well, I will give you one leading hint, when you have explained to me what you meant by saying that your heart is not at present inclined to love. Pray, have you quarrelled with love for ever?"

"No; but I can exist without it."

"Have you a heart?"

"I hope so."

"And it can exist without love? I now understand what was once said to me by a foolish lordling:—' Of what use is the sun to the dial?'"

Company came in, and relieved Belinda from any further raillery. Lady Boucher and Mrs. Margaret Delacour were, amongst a large party, to dine at Lady Delacour's. At dinner, the dowager seized the first auspicious moment of silence to announce a piece of intelligence, which she flattered herself would fix the eyes of all the world upon her.

"So Mr. Clarence Hervey is married at last!"

"Married!" cried Lady Delacour: she had sufficient presence of mind not to look directly at Belinda; but she fixed the dowager's eyes, by repeating, "Married! Are you sure of it?"

"Positive—positive! He was privately married yesterday at his aunt, Lady Almeria's apartments, at Windsor, to Miss Hartley. I told you it was to be, and now it is over; and a very extraordinary match Mr. Hervey has made of it, after all. Think of his going at last, and marrying a girl who has been his mistress for years! Nobody will visit her, to be sure. Lady Almeria is excessively distressed; she did all she could to prevail on her brother, the bishop, to marry his nephew, but he very properly refused, giving it as a reason, that the girl's character was too well known."

"I thought the bishop was at Spa," interposed a gentleman, whilst the dowager drew breath.

"O dear, no, sir; you have been misinformed," resumed she. "The bishop has been returned from Spa this great while, and he has refused to see his nephew, to my certain knowledge. After all, I cannot but pity poor Clarence for being driven into this match. Mr. Hartley has a prodigious fine fortune, to be sure, and he hurried things forward at an amazing rate, to patch up his daughter's reputation. He said, as I am credibly informed, yesterday morning, that if Clarence did not marry the girl before night, he would carry her and her fortune off the next day to the West Indies. Now the fortune was certainly an object."

"My dear Lady Boucher," interrupted Lord Delacour, "you must be misinformed in that particular: fortune is no object to Clarence Hervey; he is too generous a fellow to marry for fortune. What do you think—what do you say, Lady Delacour?"

"I say, and think, and feel, as you do, my lord," said Lady Delacour.

"You say, and think, and feel the same as my lord.—Very extraordinary indeed!" said the dowager. "Then if it were not for the sake of the fortune, pray why did Mr. Hervey marry at all? Can any body guess?"

"I should guess because he was in love," said Lord Delacour "for I remember that was the reason I married myself."

"My dear good lord—but when I tell you the girl had been his mistress, till he was tired of her—"

"My Lady Boucher," said Mrs. Margaret Delacour, who had hitherto listened in silence, "my Lady Boucher, you have been misinformed; Miss Hartley never was Clarence Hervey's mistress."

"I'm mighty glad you think so, Mrs. Delacour; but I assure you nobody else is so charitable. Those who live in the world hear a great deal more than those who live out of the world. I can promise you, nobody will visit the bride, and that is the thing by which we are to judge."

Then the dowager and the rest of the company continued to descant upon the folly of the match. Those who wished to pay their court to Lady Delacour were the loudest in their astonishment at his throwing himself away in this manner. Her ladyship smiled, and kept them in play by her address, on purpose to withdraw all eyes from Miss Portman, whilst, from time to time, she stole a glance at Belinda, to observe how she was affected by what passed: she was provoked by Belinda's self-possession. At last, when it had been settled that all the Herveys were odd, but that this match of Clarence's was the oddest of all the odd things that any of the family had done for many generations, Mrs. Delacour calmly said, "Are you sure, Lady Boucher, that Mr. Hervey is married?"

"Positive! as I said before, positive! Madam, my woman had it from Lady Newland's Swiss, who had it from Lady Singleton's Frenchwoman, who had it from Longueville, the hairdresser, who had it from Lady Almeria's own woman, who was present at the ceremony, and must know if any body does."

"The report has come to us zigzag as quick as lightning, yet it does not flash conviction upon me," said Lady Delacour.

"Nor upon me," said Mrs. Delacour, "for this simple reason. I have seen Miss Hartley within these two hours, and I had it from herself that she is not married."

"Not married!" cried the dowager with terror.

"I rather think not; she is now with her father, at my house at dinner, I believe, and Clarence Hervey is at Lady Almeria's, at Windsor: her ladyship is confined by a fit of the gout, and sent for her nephew yesterday. If people who live out of the world hear less, they sometimes hear more correctly than those who live in it."

"Pray when does Mr. Hervey return from Windsor?" said the incorrigible dowager.

"To-morrow, madam," said Mrs. Delacour. "As your ladyship is going to several parties this evening, I think it but charitable to set you right in these particulars, and I hope you will be so charitable as to contradict the report of Miss Hartley's having been Clarence's mistress."

"Why, as to that, if the young lady is not married, we must presume there are good reasons for it," said the dowager. "Pray, on which side was the match broken off?"

"On neither side," answered Mrs. Delacour.

"The thing goes on then; and what day is the marriage to take place?" said Lady Boucher.

"On Monday—or Tuesday—or Wednesday—or Thursday—or Friday—or Saturday—or Sunday, I believe," replied Mrs. Delacour, who had the prudent art of giving answers effectually baffling to the curiosity of gossips.

The dowager consoled herself in her utmost need with a full plate of brandy peaches, and spoke not a word more during the second course. When the ladies retired after the dessert, she again commenced hostilities: she dared not come to open war with Mrs. Delacour; but in a bye-battle, in a corner, she carried every thing before her; and she triumphantly whispered, "We shall see, ma'am, that it will turn out, as I told you, that Miss Rachel, or Virginia, or whatever he pleases to call her, has been what I said; and, as I said, nobody will visit her, not a soul: fifty people I can count who have declared to me they've made up their minds; and my own's made up, I candidly confess; and Lady Delacour, I am sure by her silence and looks, is of my way of thinking, and has no opinion of the young lady: as to Miss Portman, she is, poor thing, of course, so wrapped up in her own affairs, no wonder she says nothing. That was a sad business of Mr. Vincent's! I am surprised to see her look even so well as she does after it. Mr. Percival, I am told," said the well-informed dowager, lowering her voice so much that the lovers of scandal were obliged to close their heads round her—"Mr. Percival, I am informed, refused his consent to his ward (who is not of age) on account of an anonymous letter, and it is supposed Mr. Vincent desired it for an excuse to get off handsomely. Fighting that duel about her with Sir Philip Baddely settled his love—so he is gone to Germany, and she is left to wear the willow, which, you see, becomes her as well as everything else. Did she eat any dinner, ma'am? you sat next her."

"Yes; more than I did, I am sure."

"Very extraordinary! Then perhaps Sir Philip Baddely's on again—Lord bless me, what a match would that be for her! Why, Mrs. Stanhope might then, indeed, deserve to be called the match-maker general. The seventh of her nieces this. But look, there's Mrs. Delacour leading Miss Portman off into the trictrac cabinet, with a face full of business—her hand in hers—Lord, I did not know they were on that footing! I wonder what's going forward. Suppose old Hartley was to propose for Miss Portman—there would be a dénouement! and cut his daughter off with a shilling! Nothing's impossible, you know. Did he ever see Miss Portman? I must go and find out, positively."

In the mean time, Mrs. Delacour, unconscious of the curiosity she had excited, was speaking to Belinda in the trictrac cabinet.

"My dear Miss Portman," said she, "you have a great deal of good-nature, else I should not venture to apply to you on the present occasion. Will you oblige me, and serve a friend of mine—a gentleman who, as I once imagined, was an admirer of yours?"

"I will do any thing in my power to oblige any friend of yours, madam," said Belinda; "but of whom are you speaking?"

"Of Mr. Hervey, my dear young lady."

"Tell me how I can serve him as a friend," said Belinda, colouring deeply.

"That you shall know immediately," said Mrs. Delacour, rummaging and rustling for a considerable time amongst a heap of letters, which she had pulled out of the largest pockets that ever woman wore, even in the last century.

"Oh, here it is," continued she, opening and looking into them. "May I trouble you just to look over this letter? It is from poor Mr. Hartley; he is, as you will see, excessively fond of his daughter, whom he has so fortunately discovered after his long search: he is dreadfully nervous, and has been terribly annoyed by these idle gossiping stories. You find, by what Lady Boucher said at dinner, that they have settled it amongst them that Virginia is not a fit person to be visited; that she has been Clarence's mistress instead of his pupil. Mr. Hartley, you see by this letter, is almost out of his senses with the apprehension that his daughter's reputation is ruined. I sent my carriage to Twickenham, the moment I received this letter, for the poor girl and her gouvernante. They came to me this morning; but what can I do? I am only one old woman against a confederacy of veteran gossips; but if I could gain you and Lady Delacour for my allies, I should fear no adversaries. Virginia is to stay with me for some days; and Lady Delacour, I see, has a great mind to come to see her; but she does not like to come without you, and she says that she does not like to ask you to accompany her. I don't understand her delicacy about the matter—I have none; believing, as I do, that there is no foundation whatever for these malicious reports, which, entre nous, originated, I fancy, with Mrs. Marriott. Now, will you oblige me? If you and Lady Delacour will come and see Virginia to-morrow, all the world would follow your example the next day. It's often cowardice that makes people ill-natured: have you the courage, my good Miss Portman, to be the first to do a benevolent action? I do assure you," continued Mrs. Delacour with great earnestness, "I do assure you I would as soon put my hand into that fire, this moment, as ask you to do any thing that I thought improper. But forgive me for pressing this point; I am anxious to have your suffrage in her favour: Miss Belinda Portman's character for prudence and propriety stands so high, and is fixed so firmly, that she may venture to let us cling to it; and I am as well convinced of the poor girl's innocence as I am of yours; and when you see her, you will be of my opinion."

"I assure you, Mrs. Delacour," said Belinda, "that you have wasted a great deal of eloquence upon this occasion, for—"

"I am sorry for it," interrupted Mrs. Delacour, rising from her seat, with a look of some displeasure. "I meant not to distress or offend you, Miss Portman, by my eloquence: I am only concerned that I should have so far mistaken your character as to expose myself to this refusal."

"I have given no refusal," said Belinda, mildly: "you did not let me finish my sentence."

"I beg pardon; that is a foolish old trick of mine."

"Mrs. Delacour, I was going to say, has wasted a great deal of eloquence: for I am entirely of her opinion, and I shall, with the greatest readiness, comply with her request."

"You are a charming, generous girl, and I am a passionate old fool—thank you a thousand times."

"You are not at all obliged to me," said Belinda. "When I first heard this story, I believed it, as Lady Boucher now does—but I have had reason to alter my opinion, and perhaps the same means of information would have changed hers; once convinced, it is impossible to relapse into suspicion."

"Impossible to you: the most truly virtuous women are always the least suspicious and uncharitable in their opinion of their own sex. Lady Anne Percival inspired me with this belief, and Miss Portman confirms it. I admire your courage in daring to come forward in the defence of innocence. I am very rude, alas! for praising you so much."

"I have not a right to your admiration," said Belinda; "for I must honestly confess to you that I should not have this courage if there were any danger in the case. I do not think that in doubtful cases it is the business of a young woman to hazard her own reputation by an attempt to preserve another's: I do not imagine, at least, that I am of sufficient consequence in the world for this purpose; therefore I should never attempt it. It is the duty of such women as Mrs. Delacour, whose reputation is beyond the power of scandal, to come forward in the defence of injured innocence; but this would not be courage in Belinda Portman, it would be presumption and temerity."

"Well, if you will not let me admire your courage, or your generosity, or your prudence," said Mrs. Delacour laughing, "you must positively let me admire you altogether, and love you too, for I cannot help it. Farewell."

After the company was gone, Lady Delacour was much surprised by the earnestness with which Belinda pressed the request that they might the next morning pay a visit to Virginia.

"My dear," said Lady Delacour, "to tell you the truth, I am full of curiosity, and excessively anxious to go. I hesitated merely on your account: I fancied that you would not like the visit, and that if I went without you, it might be taken notice of; but I am delighted to find that you will come with me: I can only say that you have more generosity than I should have in the same situation."

The next morning they went together to Mrs. Delacour's. In their way thither, Belinda, to divert her own thoughts, and to rouse Lady Delacour from the profound and unnatural silence into which she had fallen, petitioned her to finish the history of Sir Philip Baddely, the dog, Miss Annabella Luttridge, and her billet-doux.

"For some of my high crimes and misdemeanours, you vowed that you would not tell me the remainder of the story till the whole week had elapsed; now will you satisfy my curiosity? You recollect that you left off just where you said that you were come to the best part of the story."

"Was I? did I?—Very true, we shall have time enough to finish it by-and-by, my dear," said Lady Delacour; "at present my poor head is running upon something else, and I have left off being an accomplished actress, or I could talk of one subject and think of another as well as the best of you.—Stop the carriage, my dear; I am afraid they have forgot my orders."

"Did you carry what I desired this morning to Mrs. Delacour?" said her ladyship to one of the footmen.

"I did, my lady."

"And did you say from me, that it was not to be opened till I came?'

"Yes, my lady."

"Where did you leave it?"

"In Mrs. Delacour's dressing-room, my lady:—she desired me to take it up there, and she locked the door, and said no one should go in till you came."

"Very well—go on. Belinda, my dear, I hope that I have worked up your curiosity to the highest pitch."

CHAPTER XXXI — THE DENOUEMENT

Curiosity was not, at this instant, the strongest passion in Belinda's mind. When the carriage stopped at Mrs. Delacour's door, her heart almost ceased to beat; but she summoned resolution to go through, with firmness and dignity, the task she had undertaken.

Clarence Hervey was not in the room when they entered, nor was Virginia: Mrs. Ormond said that she had been extremely feverish during the night, and that she had advised her not to get up till late in the day. But Mrs. Delacour immediately went for her, and in a few minutes she made her appearance.

Belinda and Lady Delacour exchanged a glance of surprise and admiration. There was a grace and simplicity in her manner, joined to an air of naïveté, that made an irresistible impression in her favour. Lady Delacour, however, after the first surprise was over, seemed to relapse into her former opinion; and the piercing looks which her ladyship from time to time cast upon Virginia as she spoke, produced their effect. She was abashed and silent. Belinda endeavoured to engage her in conversation, and to her she talked with ease and even with freedom. Virginia examined Miss Portman's countenance with a species of artless curiosity and interest, that was not restrained by factitious politeness. This examination was not peculiarly agreeable to Belinda, yet it was made with so much apparent simplicity, that she could not be displeased.

On the first pause in the conversation, Mrs. Delacour said, "Pray, my dear Lady Delacour, what is this wonderful present that you sent to me this morning, which you desired that no one should see till you came?"

"I cannot satisfy your curiosity yet," replied Lady Delacour. "I must wait till Clarence Hervey comes, for the present is intended for him."

An air of solemn mystery in her ladyship's manner, as she pronounced these words, excited general attention. There was a dead silence, which lasted several minutes: some feeble attempts were then made by each of the company to start a fresh subject of conversation; but it would not do—all relapsed into the silence of expectation. At last Clarence Hervey arrived. Belinda rejoiced that the universal curiosity which Lady Delacour had inspired prevented any one's observing the sudden change in Mr. Hervey's countenance when he beheld her.

"A pretty set of curious children you are!" cried Lady Delacour, laughing. "Do you know, Clarence, that they are all dying with impatience to see un gage d'amitié that I have brought for you; and the reason that they are so curious is simply because I had the address to say, in a solemn voice, 'I cannot satisfy your curiosity till Clarence Hervey arrives.' Now follow me, my friends; and if you be disappointed, lay the blame, not on me, but on your own imaginations."

She led the way to Mrs. Delacour's dressing-room, and all the company followed.

"Now, what do you expect to see?" said she, putting the key into the door.

After waiting some moments for a reply, but in vain, she threw open the door, and they saw, hung before the wall opposite to them, a green curtain.

"I thought, my dear Clarence," resumed Lady Delacour, "that no present could be more agreeable to you than a companion for your Virginia. Does this figure," continued she, drawing back the curtain, "does this figure give you the idea of Paul?"

"Paul!" said Clarence; "it is a naval officer in full uniform: what can your ladyship mean?"

"Virginia perhaps will know what I mean, if you will only stand out of her way, and let her see the picture."

At these words Clarence made way for Virginia: she turned her eyes upon the picture, uttered a piercing shriek, and fell senseless upon the floor.

"Take it coolly," said Lady Delacour, "and she will come to her senses presently. Young ladies must shriek and faint upon certain occasions; but men (looking at Clarence Hervey) need not always be dupes. This is only a scene; consider it as such, and admire the actress as I do."

"Actress! Oh, she is no actress!" cried Mrs. Ormond.

Clarence Hervey raised her from the ground, and Belinda sprinkled water over her face.

"She's dead!—she's dead! Oh, my sweet child! she's dead!" exclaimed Mrs. Ormond, trembling so violently, that she could not sustain Virginia.

"She is no actress, indeed," said Clarence Hervey: "her pulse is gone!"

Lady Delacour looked at Virginia's pale lips, touched her cold hands, and with a look of horror cried out, "Good Heavens! what have I done? What shall we do with her?"

"Give her air—give her air, air, air!" cried Belinda.

"You keep the air from her, Mrs. Ormond," said Mrs. Delacour. "Let us leave her to Miss Portman; she has more presence of mind than any of us." And as she spoke she forced Mrs. Ormond away with her out of the room.

"If Mr. Hartley should come, keep him with you, Mrs. Delacour," said Clarence Hervey. "Is her pulse quite gone?"

"No; it beats stronger and stronger," said Belinda.

"Her colour is returning," said Lady Delacour. "There! raise her a little, dear Belinda; she is coming to herself."

"Had not you better draw the curtain again before that picture," said Miss Portman, "lest she should see it the moment she opens her eyes?"

Virginia came slowly to her recollection, saw Lady Delacour drawing the curtain before the picture, then fixed her eyes upon Clarence Hervey, without uttering a word.

"Are you better now?" said he, in a gentle tone.

"Oh, do not speak—do not look so kindly!" cried Virginia. "I am well—quite well—better than I deserve to be;" and she pressed Belinda's hand, as if to thank her for assisting and supporting her.

"We may safely leave her now," whispered Belinda to Lady Delacour; "we are strangers, and our presence only distresses her."

They withdrew. But the moment Virginia found herself alone with Mr. Hervey, she was seized with a universal tremor; she tried to speak, but could not articulate. At last she burst into a flood of tears; and when this had in some measure relieved her, she threw herself upon her knees, and clasping her hands, exclaimed, as she looked up to heaven—

"Oh, if I knew what I ought to do!—if I knew what I ought to say!"

"Shall I tell you, Virginia? And will you believe me?"

"Yes, yes, yes!"

"You ought to say—the truth, whatever it may be."

"But you will think me the most ungrateful of human beings?"

"How often must I assure you, Virginia, that I make no claim upon your gratitude? Speak to me—I conjure you, as you value your happiness and mine—speak to me without disguise! What is all this mystery? Why should you fear to let me know what passes in your heart? Why did you shriek at the sight of that picture?"

"Oh, forgive me! forgive me!" cried Virginia: she would have sunk at his feet, if he had not prevented her.

"I will—I can forgive any thing but deceit. Do not look at me with so much terror, Virginia—I have not deserved it: my wish is to make you happy. I would sacrifice even my own happiness to secure yours; but do not mislead me, or you ruin us both. Cannot you give me a distinct answer to this simple question—Why did you shriek at the sight of that picture?"

"Because—but you will call me 'perfidious, ungrateful Virginia!'—because I have seen that figure—he has knelt to me—he has kissed my hand—and I—"

Clarence Hervey withdrew his arms, which had supported her, and placing her upon a sofa, left her, whilst he walked up and down the room for some minutes in silence.

"And why, Virginia," said he, stopping short, "was it necessary to conceal all this from me? Why was it necessary to persuade me that I was beloved? Why was it necessary that my happiness should be the sacrifice?"

"It shall not!—it shall not! Your happiness shall not be the sacrifice. Heaven is my witness, that there is no sacrifice I would not make for you. Forgive me that shriek! I could not help fainting, indeed! But I will be yours—I ought to be yours; and I am not perfidious—I am not ungrateful: do not look upon me as you did in my dream!"

"Do not talk to me of dreams, my dear Virginia; this is no time for trifling; I ask no sacrifice from you—I ask nothing but truth."

"Truth! Mrs. Ormond knows all the truth: I have concealed nothing from her."

"But she has concealed every thing from me," cried Clarence; and, with a sudden impulse of indignation, he was going to summon her, but when his hand was upon the lock of the door he paused, returned to Virginia, and said, "Let me hear the truth from your lips: it is all I shall ever ask from you. How—when—where did you see this man?"

"What man?" said Virginia, looking up, with the simple expression of innocence in her countenance.

Clarence pointed to the picture.

"At the village in the New Forest, at Mrs. Smith's house," said Virginia, "one evening when I walked with her from my grandmother's cottage."

"And your grandmother knew of this?"

"Yes," said Virginia, blushing, "and she was very much displeased."

"And Mrs. Ormond knew of this?" pursued Clarence.

"Yes; but she told me that you would not be displeased at it."

Mr. Hervey made another hasty step toward the door, but restraining his impetuous temper, he again stopped, and leaning ever the back of a chair, opposite to Virginia, waited in silence for her to proceed. He waited in vain.

"I do not mean to distress you, Miss Hartley," said he.

She burst into tears. "I knew, I knew," cried she, "that you would be displeased; I told Mrs. Ormond so. I knew you would never forgive me."

"In that you were mistaken," said Clarence, mildly; "I forgive you without difficulty, as I hope you may forgive yourself: nor can it be my wish to extort from you any mortifying confessions. But, perhaps, it may yet be in my power to serve you, if you will trust to me. I will myself speak to your father. I will do every thing to secure to you the object of your affections, if you will, in this last moment of our connexion, treat me with sincerity, and suffer me to be your friend."

Virginia sobbed so violently for some time, that she could not speak: at last she said, "You are—you are the most generous of men! You have always been my best friend! I am the most ungrateful of human beings! But I am sure I never wished, I never intended, to deceive you. Mrs. Ormond told me—"

"Do not speak of her at present, or perhaps I may lose my temper," interrupted Clarence in an altered voice: "only tell me—I conjure you, tell me—in one word, who is this man and where is he to be found?"

"I do not know. I do not understand you," said Virginia.

"You do not know! You will not trust me. Then I must leave you to—to Mr. Hartley."

"Do not leave me—oh, do not leave me in anger!" cried Virginia, clinging to him. "Not trust you!—I!—not trust you! Oh, what can you mean? I have no confessions to make! Mrs. Ormond knows every thought of my mind, and so shall you, if you will only hear me. I do not know who this man is, I assure you; nor where he is to be found."

"And yet you love him? Can you love a man whom you do not know, Virginia?"

"I only love his figure, I believe," said Virginia.

"His figure!"

"Indeed I am quite bewildered," said Virginia, looking round wildly; "I know not what I feel."

"If you permitted this man to kneel to you, to kiss your hand, surely you must know that you love him, Virginia?"

"But that was only in a dream; and Mrs. Ormond said—"

"Only a dream! But you met him at Mrs. Smith's, in the New Forest?"

"That was only a picture."

"Only a picture!—but you have seen the original?"

"Never—never in my life; and I wish to Heaven I had never, never seen the fatal picture! the image haunts me day and night. When I read of heroes in the day, that figure rises to my view, instead of yours. When I go to sleep at night, I see it, instead of yours, in my dreams; it speaks to me, it kneels to me. I long ago told Mrs. Ormond this, but she laughed at me. I told her of that frightful dream. I saw you weltering in your blood; I tried to save you, but could not. I heard you say, 'Perfidious, ungrateful Virginia! you are the cause of my death!' Oh, it was the most dreadful night I ever passed! Still this figure, this picture, was before me; and he was the knight of the white plumes; and it was he who stabbed you; but when I wished him to be victorious, I did not know that he was fighting against you. So Mrs. Ormond told me that I need not blame myself; and she said that you were not so foolish as to be jealous of a picture; but I knew you would be displeased—I knew you would think me ungrateful—I knew you would never forgive me."

Whilst Virginia rapidly uttered all this, Clarence marked the wild animation of her eyes, the sudden changes of her countenance; he recollected her father's insanity; every feeling of his mind gave way to terror and pity; he approached her with all the calmness that he could assume, took both her hands, and holding them in his, said, in a soothing voice—

"My dear Virginia, you are not ungrateful. I do not think you so. I am not displeased with you. You have done nothing to displease me. Compose yourself, dear Virginia."

"I am quite composed, now you again call me dear Virginia. Only I am afraid, as I always told Mrs. Ormond, that I do not love you enough; but she said that I did, and that my fear was the strongest proof of my affection."

Virginia now spoke in so consistent a manner that Clarence could not doubt that she was in the clear possession of her understanding. She repeated to him all that she had said to Mrs. Ormond; and he began to hope that, without any intention to deceive, Mrs. Ormond's ignorance of the human heart led her into a belief that Virginia was in love with him; whilst, in fact, her imagination, exalted by solitude and romance, embodied and became enamoured of a phantom.

"I always told Mrs. Ormond that she was mistaken," said Clarence. "I never believed that you loved me, Virginia, till—(he paused and carefully examined her countenance)—till you yourself gave me reason to think so. Was it only a principle of gratitude, then, that dictated your answer to my letter?"

She looked irresolute: and at last, in a low voice, said, "If I could see, if I could speak to Mrs. Ormond—"

"She cannot tell what are the secret feelings of your heart, Virginia. Consult no Mrs. Ormond. Consult no human creature but yourself."

"But Mrs. Ormond told me that you loved me, and that you had educated me to be your wife."

Mr. Hervey made an involuntary exclamation against Mrs. Ormond's folly.

"How, then, can you be happy," continued Virginia, "if I am so ungrateful as to say I do not love you? That I do not love you!—Oh! that I cannot say; for I do love you better than any one living except my father, and with the same sort of affection that I feel for him. You ask me to tell you the secret feelings of my heart: the only secret feeling of which I am conscious is—a wish not to marry, unless I could see in reality such a person as—But that I knew was only a picture, a dream; and I thought that I ought at least to sacrifice my foolish imaginations to you, who have done so much for me. I knew that it would be the height of ingratitude to refuse you; and besides, my father told me that you would not accept of my fortune without my hand, so I consented to marry you: forgive me, if these were wrong motives—I thought them right. Only tell me what I can do to make you happy, as I am sure I wish to do; to that wish I would sacrifice every other feeling."

"Sacrifice nothing, dear Virginia. We may both be happy without making any sacrifice of our feelings," cried Clarence. And, transported at regaining his own freedom, Virginia's simplicity never appeared to him so charming as at this moment. "Dearest Virginia, forgive me for suspecting you for one instant of any thing unhandsome. Mrs. Ormond, with the very best intentions possible, has led us both to the brink of misery. But I find you such as I always thought you, ingenuous, affectionate, innocent."

"And you are not angry with me?" interrupted Virginia, with joyful eagerness; "and you will not think me ungrateful? And you will not be unhappy? And Mrs. Ormond was mistaken? And you do not wish that I should love you, that I should be your wife, I mean? Oh, don't deceive me, for I cannot help believing whatever you say."

Clarence Hervey, to give her a convincing proof that Mrs. Ormond had misled her as to his sentiments, immediately avowed his passion for Belinda.

"You have relieved me from all doubt, all fear, all anxiety," said Virginia, with the sweetest expression of innocent affection in her countenance. "May you be as happy as you deserve to be! May Belinda—is not that her name?—May Belinda—"

At this moment Lady Delacour half opened the door, exclaiming—"Human patience can wait no longer!"

"Will you trust me to explain for you, dear Virginia?" said Clarence.

"Most willingly," said Virginia, retiring as Lady Delacour advanced. "Pray leave me here alone, whilst you, who are used to talk before strangers, speak for me."

"Dare you venture, Clarence," said her ladyship, as she closed the door, "to leave her alone with that picture? You are no lover, if you be not jealous."

"I am not jealous," said Clarence, "yet I am a lover—a passionate lover."

"A passionate lover!" cried Lady Delacour, stopping short as they were crossing the antechamber:— "then I have done nothing but mischief. In love with Virginia? I will not—cannot believe it."

"In love with Belinda!—Cannot you, will not you believe it?"

"My dear Clarence, I never doubted it for an instant. But are you at liberty to own it to any body but me?"

"I am at liberty to declare it to all the world."

"You transport me with joy! I will not keep you from her a second. But stay—I am sorry to tell you, that, as she informed me this morning, her heart is not at present inclined to love. And here is Mrs. Margaret Delacour, poor wretch, in this room, dying with curiosity. Curiosity is as ardent as love, and has as good a claim to compassion."

As he entered the room, where there were only Mrs. Margaret Delacour and Belinda, Clarence Hervey's first glance, rapid as it was, explained his heart.

Belinda put her arm within Lady Delacour's, trembling so that she could scarcely stand. Lady Delacour pressed her hand, and was perfectly silent.

"And what is Miss Portman to believe," cried Mrs. Margaret Delacour, "when she has seen you on the very eve of marriage with another lady?"

"The strongest merit I can plead with such a woman as Miss Portman is, that I was ready to sacrifice my own happiness to a sense of duty. Now that I am at liberty—"

"Now that you are at liberty," interrupted Lady Delacour, "you are in a vast hurry to offer your whole soul to a lady, who has for months seen all your merits with perfect insensibility, and who has been, notwithstanding all my operations, stone blind to your love."

"The struggles of my passion cannot totally have escaped Belinda's penetration," said Clarence; "but I like her a thousand times the better for not having trusted merely to appearances. That love is most to be valued which cannot be easily won. In my opinion there is a prodigious difference between a warm imagination and a warm heart."

"Well," said Lady Delacour, "we have all of us seen Pamela maritata—let us now see Belinda in love, if that be possible. If! forgive me this last stroke, my dear—in spite of all my raillery, I do believe that the prudent Belinda is more capable of feeling real permanent passion than any of the dear sentimental young ladies, whose motto is

'All for love, or the world well lost.'"

"That is just my opinion," said Mrs. Margaret Delacour.

"But pray, what is become of Mr. Hartley?" looking round: "I do not see him."

"No: for I have hid him," said Lady Delacour: "he shall be forthcoming presently."

"Dear Mr. Clarence Hervey, what have you done with my Virginia?" said Mrs. Ormond, coming into the room.

"Dear Mrs. Ormond, what have you done with her?" replied Clarence. "By your mistaken kindness, by insisting upon doing us both good against our wills, you were very near making us both miserable for life. But I blame nobody; I have no right to blame any one so much as myself. All this has arisen from my own presumption and imprudence. Nothing could be more absurd than my scheme of educating a woman in solitude to make her fit for society. I might have foreseen what must happen, that Virginia would consider me as her tutor, her father, not as her lover, or her husband; that with the most affectionate of hearts, she could for me feel nothing but gratitude."

"Nothing but gratitude!" repeated Mrs. Ormond, with a degree of amazement in her countenance, which made every body present smile: "I am sure I thought she was dying for love of you."

"My dear Belinda," whispered Lady Delacour, "if I might judge of the colour of this cheek, which has been for some moments permanent crimson, I should guess that you were beginning to find out of what use the sun is to the dial."

"You will not let me hear what Mr. Hervey is saying," replied Belinda; "I am very curious."

"Curiosity is a stronger passion than love, as I told him just now," said Lady Delacour.

In spite of all his explanations, Mrs. Ormond could not be made to comprehend Virginia's feelings. She continually repeated, "But it is impossible for Virginia, or for any body, to be in love with a picture."

"It is not said that she is in love with a picture," replied Mrs. Delacour, "though even for that I could find you a precedent."

"My Lady Delacour," said Mrs. Ormond, "will you explain to us how that picture came into your possession, and how it came here, and, in short, all that is to be known about it?"

"Ay, explain! explain! my dear Lady Delacour," cried Mrs. Delacour: "I am afraid I am grown almost as curious as my Lady Boucher. Explain! explain!"

"Most willingly," said Lady Delacour. "To Marriott's ruling passion for birds you are all of you indebted for this discovery. Some time ago, whilst we were at Twickenham, as Marriott was waiting at a stationer's, to bid her last adieus to a bullfinch, a gentleman came into the shop where she and Bobby (as she calls this bird) were coquetting, and the gentleman was struck even more than Marriott with the bullfinch. He went almost distracted on hearing a particular tune, which this bird sang. I suspected, from the symptoms, that the gentleman must be, or must have been, in love with the bullfinch's mistress. Now the bullfinch was traced home to the ci-devant Virginia St. Pierre, the present Miss Hartley. I had my reasons for being curious about her loves and lovers, and as soon as I learned the story from Marriott, I determined, if possible, to find out who this stranger, with the strange passion for bullfinches, might be. I questioned and cross-questioned all those people at the stationer's who were present when he fell into ecstasies; and, from the shopman, who had been bribed to secrecy, I learned that our gentleman returned to the stationer's the day after he met Marriott, and watched till he obtained a sight of Virginia, as she came to her window. Now it was believed by the girl of this shop, who had lived for some time with Mrs. Ormond—Forgive me, Mr. Hervey, for what I am going to say— forgive me, Mrs. Ormond—scandal, like death, is common to all—It was believed that Virginia was Mr. Hervey's mistress. My stranger no sooner learned this than he swore that he would think of her no more; and after bestowing a variety of seamen's' execrations upon the villain who had seduced this heavenly creature, he departed from Twickenham, and was no more seen or heard of. My inquiries after him were indefatigable, but for some time unsuccessful: and so they might have continued, and we might have been all making one another unhappy at this moment, if it had not been for Mr. Vincent's great dog Juba—Miss Annabella Luttridge's billet-doux—Sir Philip Baddely's insolence—my Lord Delacour's belief in a quack balsam—and Captain Sunderland's humanity."

"Captain Sunderland! who is Captain Sunderland? we never heard of him before," cried Mrs. Ormond.

"You shall hear of him just as I did, if you please," said Lady Delacour, "and if Belinda will submit to hear me tell the same story twice."

Here her ladyship repeated the history of the battle of the dogs; and of Sir Philip Baddely's knocking down Juba, the man, for struggling in defence of Juba, the dog.

"Now the gentleman who assisted my Lord Delacour in bringing the disabled negro across the square to our house, was Captain Sunderland. My lord summoned Marriott to produce Lady Boucher's infallible balsam, that it might be tried upon Juba's sprained ankle. Whilst my lord was intent upon the balsam, Marriott was intent upon Captain Sunderland. She recollected that she had met him somewhere before, and the moment he spoke, she knew him to be the gentleman who had fallen into ecstasies in the shop at Twickenham, about the bullfinch. Marriott hastened to me with the news; I hastened to my lord, made him introduce Captain Sunderland to me, and I never rested till he had told me all that I wanted to know. Some years ago, just before he went to sea, he paid a visit to his mother, who then lodged with a widow Smith, in the New Forest. Whilst he was there, he heard of the young beauty who lived in the Forest, with a grandmother, who was not a little particular; and who would not permit any body to see her.

"My captain's curiosity was excited; one day, unseen by the duenna, he obtained a distinct view of Virginia, watering her roses and tending her bees. Struck with her uncommon beauty, he approached carefully to the thicket in which the cottage was enclosed, and found a lair, where he concealed himself, day after day, and contemplated at leisure the budding charms of the fair wood-nymph. In short, he became so enamoured, that he was determined to gain admittance at the cottage, and declare his passion: but to his honour be it told, that when the history of the poor girl's mother, and the situation and fears of the old lady, who was her only friend, were known to him, in consideration of the extreme youth of the ward, and the extreme age of her guardian, he determined to defer his addresses till his return from the West Indies, whither he was shortly to sail, and where he had hopes of making a fortune, that might put him in a situation to render the object of his affections independent. He left a bullfinch with Mrs. Smith, who gave it to Virginia, without telling to whom it had belonged, lest her grandmother might be displeased.

"I really thought that all this showed too nice a moral sense for a young dashing lieutenant in the navy, and I was persuaded that my gentleman was only keeping his mistress's secret like a man of honour. With this belief, I regretted that Clarence Hervey should throw himself away upon a girl who was unworthy of him."

"I hope," interrupted Clarence, "you are perfectly convinced of your mistake."

"Perfectly! perfectly!—I am convinced that Virginia is only half mad. But let me go on with my story. I was determined to discover whether she had any remains of affection for this captain. It was in vain he assured me that she had never seen him. I prevailed upon him to let me go on my own way. I inquired whether he had ever had his picture drawn. Yes, he had for his mother, just when he first went out to sea. It had been left at the widow Smith's. I begged him to procure it for me. He told me it was impossible. I told him I trampled on impossibilities. In short, he got the picture for me, as you see. 'Now,' thought I, 'if he speaks the truth, Virginia will see this picture without emotion, and it will only seem to be a present for Clarence. But if she had ever seen him before, or had any secret to conceal, she will betray herself on the sudden appearance of this picture.' Things have turned out contrary to all my expectations, and yet better.—And now, Clarence, I must beg you will prevail on Miss Hartley to appear; I can go on no farther without her."

Lady Delacour took Virginia by the hand, the moment she entered the room.

"Will you trust yourself with me, Miss Hartley?" said she. "I have made you faint once to-day by the sight of a picture; will you promise me not to faint again, when I produce the original?"

"The original!" said Virginia. "I will trust myself with you, for I am sure you cannot mean to laugh at me, though, perhaps, I deserve to be laughed at."

Lady Delacour threw open the door of another apartment. Mr. Hartley appeared, and with him Captain Sunderland.

"My dear daughter," said Mr. Hartley, "give me leave to introduce to you a friend, to whom I owe more obligations than to any man living, except to Mr. Hervey. This gentleman was stationed some years ago at Jamaica, and in a rebellion of the negroes on my plantation he saved my life. Fortune has accidentally thrown my benefactor in my way. To show my sense of my obligations is out of my power."

Virginia's surprise was extreme; her vivid dreams, the fond wishes of her waking fancy, were at once accomplished. For the first moment she gazed as on an animated picture, and all the ideas of love and romance associated with this image rushed upon her mind.

But when the realities by which he was surrounded dispelled the illusion, she suddenly withdrew her eyes, and blushed deeply, with such timid and graceful modesty as charmed every body present.

Captain Sunderland pressed forward; but was stopped by Lady Delacour.

"Avaunt, thou real lover!" cried she: "none but the shadow of a man can hope to approach the visionary maid. In vain has Marraton forced his way through the bushes and briars, in vain has he braved the apparition of the lion; there is yet a phantom barrier apparently impassable between him and his Yaratilda, for he is in the world of shadows. Now, mark me, Marraton: hurry not this delicate spirit, or perchance you frighten and lose her for ever; but have patience, and gradually and gracefully she will venture into your world of realities—only give her time."

"Time! O yes, give me time," cried Virginia, shrinking back.

"My dear Miss Hartley," continued Lady Delacour, "in plain prose, to prevent all difficulties and embarrassments, I must inform you, that Captain Sunderland will not insist upon prompt payment of your father's debt of gratitude: he has but one quarter of an hour to spend with us—he is actually under sailing orders; so that you will have time to compose your mind before his return. Clarence, I advise you to accompany Captain Sunderland on this cruise; don't you, Belinda?

"And now, my good friends," continued Lady Delacour, "shall I finish the novel for you?"

"If your ladyship pleases; nobody can do it better," said Clarence Hervey.

"But I hope you will remember, dear Lady Delacour," said Belinda, "that there is nothing in which novelists are so apt to err as in hurrying things toward the conclusion: in not allowing time enough for that change of feeling, which change of situation cannot instantly produce."

"That's right, my dear Belinda; true to your principles to the last gasp. Fear nothing—you shall have time enough to become accustomed to Clarence. Would you choose that I should draw out the story to five volumes more? With your advice and assistance, I can with the greatest ease, my dear. A declaration of love, you know, is only the beginning of things; there may be blushes, and sighs, and doubts, and fears, and misunderstandings, and jealousies without end or common sense, to fill up the necessary space, and to gain the necessary time; but if I might conclude the business in two lines, I should say,

'Ye gods, annihilate both space and time,
And make four lovers happy.'"

"Oh, that would be cutting matters too short," said Mrs. Margaret Delacour. "I am of the old school; and though I could dispense with the description of Miss Harriot Byron's worked chairs and fine china, yet I own I like to hear something of the preparation for a marriage, as well as of the mere wedding. I like to hear how people become happy in a rational manner, better than to be told in the huddled style of an old fairy tale—and so they were all married, and they lived very happily all the rest of their days."

"We are not in much danger of hearing such an account of modern marriages," said Lady Delacour. "But how shall I please you all?—Some people cry, 'Tell me every thing;' others say, that,

'Le secret d'ennuyer est celui de tout dire.'"

"Something must be left to the imagination. Positively I will not describe wedding-dresses, or a procession to church. I have no objection to saying that the happy couples were united by the worthy Mr. Moreton; that Mr. Percival gave Belinda away; and that immediately after the ceremony, he took the whole party down with him to Oakly-park. Will this do?—Or, we may conclude, if you like it better, with a characteristic letter of congratulation from Mrs. Stanhope to her dearest niece, Belinda, acknowledging that she was wrong to quarrel with her for refusing Sir Philip Baddely, and giving her infinite credit for that admirable management of Clarence Hervey, which she hopes will continue through life."

"Well, I have no objection to ending with a letter," said Mrs. Delacour; "for last speeches are always tiresome."

"Yes," said her ladyship; "it is so difficult, as the Critic says, to get lovers off upon their knees. Now I think of it, let me place you all in proper attitudes for stage effect. What signifies being happy, unless we appear so?—Captain Sunderland—kneeling with Virginia, if you please, sir, at her father's feet: you in the act of giving them your blessing, Mr. Hartley. Mrs. Ormond clasps her hands with joy—nothing can be better than that, madam—I give you infinite credit for the attitude. Clarence, you have a right to Belinda's hand, and may kiss it too: nay, Miss Portman, it is the rule of the stage. Now, where's my Lord Delacour? he should be embracing me, to show that we are reconciled. Ha! here he comes—Enter Lord Delacour, with little Helena in his hand—very well! a good start of surprise, my love—stand still, pray; you cannot be better than you are: Helena, my love, do not let go your father's hand. There! quite pretty and natural! Now, Lady Delacour, to show that she is reformed, comes forward to address the audience with a moral—a moral! Yes,

"Our tale contains a moral; and, no doubt,
You all have wit enough to find it out.'"

Maria Edgeworth – A Short Biography

Maria Edgeworth was born at Black Bourton, Oxfordshire on January 1st 1768, the second child of Richard Lovell Edgeworth and Anna Maria Edgeworth (née Elers).

Her early years were with her mother's family in England. Sadly, her mother died when Maria was only five. When her father married his second wife, Honora Sneyd, in 1773, the family went to live at his estate, Edgeworthstown, in County Longford, Ireland.

Maria was later sent to Mrs. Lattafière's school in Derby after Honora fell ill in 1775. There she studied dancing, French and other subjects. After Honora died in 1780 Maria's father married Honora's sister, Elizabeth, causing much social disapproved.

Maria transferred to Mrs. Devis's school in Upper Wimpole Street, London. Her father began to focus more attention on Maria in 1781 when she nearly lost her sight to an eye infection.

She returned home to Ireland at 14, and took charge of her younger siblings. She herself was home-tutored by her father in Irish economics and politics, science, literature and law. Despite her youth literature was in her blood.

She became her father's assistant in managing the Edgeworthstown estate, which had become run-down during the family's absence. Maria would now live and write there for the rest of her life.

With her father she began a lifelong academic collaboration. She meticulously detailed daily Irish life; a valuable lodestone of references for later use in her novels. Maria mixed with the Anglo-Irish gentry, and her aunt, Margaret Ruxton of Blackcastle, supplied her with the novels of Anne Radcliffe and William Godwin and encouraged her ambition to write.

Edgeworth's first published work in 1795 was 'Letters for Literary Ladies'. That same year 'An Essay on the Noble Science of Self-Justification', written for a female audience, states that the fair sex is endowed with an art of self-justification and women should use their gifts to continually challenge the force and power of men, especially their husbands, with wit and intelligence.

In 1796 her first children's book, 'The Parent's Assistant', which included the much loved short story 'The Purple Jar' was published.

In 1798 her father married for the fourth and last time, this time to Frances Beaufort. Frances was a year younger than Maria and they quickly became close.

'Practical Education' (1798) is a progressive work on education that combines the ideas of Locke and Rousseau with scientific inquiry. Edgeworth believed that "learning should be a positive experience and that the discipline of education is more important during the formative years than the acquisition of knowledge." The ultimate goal of Edgeworth's system was to create an independent thinker who understands the consequences of his or her actions.

Her first novel, 'Castle Rackrent' (1800) was published anonymously without her father's knowledge. It was an immediate success and firmly established Maria's appeal to the public.

'Belinda' (1801), was her first full-length novel. It dealt with love, courtship, and marriage, and she examined these as conflicts within her "own personality and environment; conflicts between reason and feeling, restraint and individual freedom, and society and free spirit." Startingly, 'Belinda' also included a depiction of interracial marriage between an African servant and an English farm-girl. Later editions of the novel, in line with unforgiving times, removed these sections.

Frances also pushed the family to travel more first London (1800), the Midlands (1802) and later the continent; first to Brussels and then to France. They met all the notables, with Maria even receiving a proposal of marriage from a Swedish courtier.

'Tales of Fashionable Life' (1809 and 1812) is a 2-series collection of short stories that often had its focus on the life of women. The second series was so successful that she was now the most commercially successful novelist of her age and ranked alongside her contemporaries Jane Austen and Sir Walter Scott.

On a visit to London in 1813, she met many notables including Lord Byron. She entered into a long correspondence with Sir Walter Scott after the publication of 'Waverley' in 1814, in which he acknowledged her influence, and they formed a lasting friendship. She visited him in Scotland at Abbotsford House in 1823 and the following year he visited Edgeworthstown.

After debating the issue with the economist David Ricardo, Maria came to believe that better management and the further use of science in agriculture would raise food production and help to lower prices. They were both in favour of Catholic Emancipation, enfranchisement for Catholics without property restrictions, agricultural reform and increased educational opportunities for women.

She worked particularly hard to improve the living standards of the poor in Edgeworthstown and to provide schools for the local children whatever their denomination.

After her father's death in 1817 she edited his memoirs, and extended them with her biographical addenda. Her father had married 4 times and sired 22 children. At the height of her creative endeavours, Maria had written, "Seriously it was to please my Father I first exerted myself to write, to please him I continued."

Maria worked for the relief of the famine-stricken Irish peasants during the Irish Potato Famine. She wrote 'Orlandino' and gave the proceeds to the Relieve Fund. However, during the famine her 'business head' insisted that only those tenants who had paid their full rent would receive any relief. She also punished any tenants who voted against her Tory preferences.

'Helen' (1834) is Maria Edgeworth's final novel, the only one she wrote after her father's death. Here the focus was on characters and situation and not moral lessons.

William Rowan Hamilton was elected president of the Royal Irish Academy and Maria's advice was constantly sought especially regarding literature in Ireland. She suggested that women should be allowed to participate in Academy events. Hamilton made Maria an honorary member in 1837.

After a visit to see her relations Maria was struck with severe chest pains and died suddenly of a heart attack in Edgeworthstown on 22nd May 1849. She was 81.

Maria Edgeworth is buried in the family tomb at St. John's Church, Edgeworthstown, Longford, Ireland.

Maria Edgeworth – A Concise Bibliography

Letters for Literary Ladies (1795) Second Edition (1798)
An Essay on the Noble Science of Self-Justification (1795)
The Parent's Assistant (1796)
Practical Education (1798) (2 Vols; collaborated with her father and step-mother)
Castle Rackrent (1800) Novel
Early Lessons (1801)
Moral Tales (1801)
Belinda (1801) Novel
The Mental Thermometer (1801)
Essay on Irish Bulls (1802)
Popular Tales (1804)
The Modern Griselda (1804)
Moral Tales for Young People (1805) (6 Vols)
Leonora (1806)
Essays in Professional Education (1809)
Tales of Fashionable Life (1809)
Ennui (1809) Novel
The Absentee (1812) Novel
Patronage (1814) Novel
Harrington (1817) Novel
Ormond (1817) Novel
Comic Dramas (1817)
Memoirs of Richard Lovell Edgeworth (1820) Editor
Rosamond: A Sequel to Early Lessons (1821)
Frank: A Sequel to Frank in Early Lessons (1822)
Tomorrow (1823) Novel
Helen (1834) novel
Orlandino (1848) Temperance novel